Saving and Investment ir Century

"An impressive, and convincing theoretical dive into the fundamentals behind secular stagnation, with very strong implications for actual debt policy. Public debt may be needed to improve welfare."

—Olivier Blanchard
Senior Fellow at the Peterson Institute
for International Economics and Professor of Economics Emeritus
at Massachusetts Institute of Technology (MIT).
Chief Economist
at the International Monetary Fund
from 2008 to 2015

"Saving and Investment in the Twenty-First Century gives a wholly new perspective on macroeconomics. With the low interest rates associated with the modern abundance of capital, constraints on fiscal policy can be greatly relaxed. As just one implication, Weizsäcker and Krämer describe a simple, practical solution to the underemployment that has plagued Southern Europe for more than a decade. But that application of their New Macroeconomics is just the tip of an iceberg: of the penumbra of possibilities for a much better world."

—George Akerlof
Nobel Laureate in Economics, 2001.
Professor at the McCourt School of Public Policy
at Georgetown University
and Professor of Economics Emeritus
at the University of California, Berkeley

"We live in a world where there is abundant saving, and outstanding investment opportunities. Yet we have been unable to transform investment opportunities into investment demand on a sufficient scale to match planned saving. The result has been very low, or negative, real interest rates and 'secular stagnation'. This remarkable book shows, using serious economic theory and careful empirical work, how this has come about. It also helps us see a way forward led by investment demand. We must invest strongly to overcome the immense risk of climate change, and to find new and much more attractive, resilient, and sustainable forms of growth and development. In doing so, the world as a whole can foster investment in developing countries, with potential high returns and great benefits to all. This is a profound and original contribution that can help us to understand and act on the great issues of our times."

—Nicholas Stern
Grantham Research Institute on Climate Change
and the Environment at the London School of Economics.
Author of the Stern Review Report
on the Economics of Climate Change.
Chief Economist at the World Bank
from 2000 to 2003

Carl Christian von Weizsäcker ·
Hagen M. Krämer

Saving and Investment in the Twenty-First Century

The Great Divergence

 Springer

Authors
Carl Christian von Weizsäcker
Max Planck Institute for Research
on Collective Goods
Bonn, Germany

Hagen M. Krämer
Karlsruhe University of Applied Sciences
Karlsruhe, Germany

Translated by
John D. Rosenthal

ISBN 978-3-030-75033-6   ISBN 978-3-030-75031-2   (eBook)
https://doi.org/10.1007/978-3-030-75031-2

This Springer imprint is published by the registered company Springer Nature Switzerland AG
The registered company address is: Gewerbestrasse 11, 6330 Cham, Switzerland

Preface

During the World Financial Crisis of 2008–2009, Carl Christian von Weizsäcker developed the idea that good old capital theory could be an appropriate reference point for an understanding of what was going on in the world. He had been a member of the Cambridge USA camp in the well-known Cambridge-Cambridge controversy of the sixties and seventies of the twentieth century. The leading figures of that camp were Paul Samuelson and Robert Solow, who also were the academic teachers that had the greatest influence on Carl Christian von Weizsäcker. However, even before his stay at MIT, Friedrich Lutz of the University of Zurich made him aware of Eugen von Böhm-Bawerk as the Austrian founder of capital theory. Carl Christian von Weizsäcker learned about the fundamental importance of John Maynard Keynes at the University of Basel from Gottfried Bombach and then, of course, from Samuelson and Solow and, later on, from Joan Robinson and Nicolas Kaldor. Combining Böhm-Bawerk and Keynes, using modern mathematical techniques, seemed to him a good approach for understanding the world economy of 2008–2009.

The central idea of this book is a generalization of Böhm-Bawerk's period of production T to the supply side of the capital market, where the "waiting period" Z plays a role that is symmetrical to T on the demand side. In a steady-state equilibrium with full employment, Z and T have to match. And if this cannot be accomplished by a feasible non-negative real rate of interest, public debt has to help out, so that the supply of capital can be lowered to $Z - D = T$, with D being the "public debt period."

$D > 0$ turns out to be necessary, because in the twenty-first century we live in a world of capital affluence. Gone is capital scarcity, which was Böhm-Bawerk's explanation of a positive real rate of interest. It is no longer the case for the world economy that even more roundaboutness of production raises labor productivity. Technical progress and thereby obsolescence set a limit to the fruits of the roundaboutness of production. Technical and medical progress, on the other hand, bring about a secular growth of the waiting period Z. Hence, we are confronted by the "Great Divergence" on the capital market between private supply Z and private demand T.

In a first publication in 2010 and several later publications (mainly in German), Carl Christian von Weizsäcker explained his theory. As time went on, without the real rate of interest rising again from its level near zero, the idea of deepening the empirical basis for the theory became more and more attractive. Carl Christian von Weizsäcker invited Hagen M. Krämer, an economist from the Keynesian school, to join in this work, in particular on the empirical issues. Using the capital-theoretic approach, most of the key empirical variables are stock variables: like the real capital stock, like land values, like public debt. Thanks to certain innovations in national accounting, it was possible to make empirical estimates of these stock variables. This allowed us to obtain an empirical picture for the group of OECD member states plus the Peoples Republic of China.

We published our book in German in the summer of 2019. The present English Edition contains additional empirical material, which became available during 2020. We also inserted a section on COVID-19 in relation to capital theory: Even in a steady state after "corona," T will be lower than before due to greater digitalization.

In parallel to the work on this topic, Carl Christian von Weizsäcker organized a German language e-mail discussion group on macroeconomic topics. We want to thank the active participants in these sometimes quite lively discussions. We want especially to thank Martin Hellwig, Hans-Werner Sinn and Jakob von Weizsäcker, and then in alphabetical order: Rudi Bachmann, Ingo Barens, Gerald Braunberger, Friedrich Breyer, Markus Brunnermeier, Michael Burda, Christoph Engel, Gabriel Felbermayr, Lars Feld, Joachim Fels, Nicola Fuchs-Schündeln, Clemens Fuest, Heike Göbel, Daniel Gros, Martin Höpner, Matthias Hoffmann, Carl-Ludwig Holtfrerich, Stefan Homburg, Otmar Issing, Wolfgang Kuhle, Heinz D. Kurz, Stephan Luck, Gernot Müller, Karl-Heinz Paqué, Albrecht Ritschl, Fritz Scharpf, Paul Schemp, Ekkehart Schlicht, Johannes Schmidt, Gunther Schnabl, Isabel Schnabel, Moritz Schularick, Hermann Simon, Wolfgang Streeck, Jens Südekum, Ulrich van Suntum, Harald Uhlig and Thomas von Ungern-Sternberg.

In preparing the book and especially the empirical material, we were supported by Christina Anselmann, Andreas Drexler, Ludwig Eckmann, Sven Schnellbacher and Johannes Schmidt, all of whom are or were members of the staff of the Karlsruhe University of Applied Sciences. Many thanks for their assistance.

Bonn, Germany   Carl Christian von Weizsäcker
Karlsruhe, Germany   Hagen M. Krämer
February 2021

Contents

About the Authors

Photo Edgar Schoepal

Carl Christian von Weizsäcker received his Ph.D. in 1961 from the University of Basel for a dissertation in which he showed that the optimal rate of interest is equal to the growth rate. Edmund Phelps published the same result also in 1961 and called it the "Golden Rule of Accumulation." Following research visits at MIT and the University of Cambridge, he became full professor of economics in Heidelberg at the age of 27. From 1968 to 1970, he taught as a full professor at the Economics Department of MIT. His students included Robert Merton, Robert Shiller and Stanley Fischer. During these years, he co-authored papers with Paul Samuelson and Robert Solow in the field of capital theory and macroeconomics. Later, Carl Christian von Weizsäcker turned to microeconomic topics: in particular, topics in industrial economics, the economics of telecommunications and energy economics. He developed a theory of adaptive preferences that can serve as a basis for welfare economics beyond the *homo economicus*. He taught at the universities of Bielefeld, Bonn, Bern and Cologne. Since his retirement from teaching, he has been working at the Max Planck Institute for Research on Public Goods, Bonn (Germany).

In 1977, he was elected to the Board of Academic Advisors of the German Minister for Economic Affairs, of which he is still a member today. From 1986 to 1998, he was a member of Germany's Monopolies Commission, and from 1989 to 1998, he was its chair. Since the outbreak of the financial crisis in 2008, he has principally focused on macroeconomics and capital theory. The present book developed out of his research in these areas.

Carl Christian von Weizsäcker is a Fellow of the Econometric Society, holds an honorary doctorate from the University of Freiburg and is a member of the American Academy of Arts and Sciences, the North Rhine-Westphalian Academy of Sciences and Germany's National Academy of Science and Engineering.

Photo Uwe Krebs

Hagen M. Krämer is Professor of Economics at the Department of Management Sciences and Engineering of the Karlsruhe University of Applied Sciences in Germany. He studied economics at the University of Bremen and the New School for Social Research (New York). After completing a first degree in economics, he worked for five years as a research assistant at the IKSF, an economics research institute at the University of Bremen, where he received his doctorate in 1995 for a dissertation on income distribution and technical progress. He then worked for six years as an economist at a leading German automotive company in Stuttgart and Berlin.

Hagen M. Krämer has been a visiting scholar or visiting professor at several institutes and universities, including The German Institute for Economic Research (DIW-Berlin), the Macroeconomic Policy Institute (IMK-Düsseldorf), the Fraunhofer Institute for Systems and Innovation Research (ISI-Karlsruhe), the University of Graz (Austria) and the New School for Social Research (New York).

He is a founding member of the German Keynes Society, a member of the Council of the European Society for the History of Economic Thought, of the Scottish Economic Society and of the German Association for Political Economy. He serves as an elected member of both the Committee for the History of Economic Thought and the Committee for Economic Policy of the German Economic Association, the *Verein für Socialpolitik*. His preferred areas of research are income distribution, macroeconomics, the economics of the service sector and the history of economic thought.

Symbols

a	Length of working life in savings triangle
b	Length of retirement period in savings triangle
c	Consumption per "worker"
e	Inheritance in years of consumption
$f(k)$	Solow production function: output per "worker"
g	Nominal or real annual rate of growth
h	Rate of time preference (Irving Fisher)
k	Capital intensity in Solow production function
$l = L/\omega$	"Reliability period"
ln	Natural logarithm
m	Proportionality parameter in balanced account agreement
p	Price of a TRILL
q	Rental income per "worker"
r	Nominal or real risk-free rate of interest
v	Value of capital per "worker"
$\hat{v}$	Private wealth per "worker"
$\hat{v}(t)$	Individual wealth as a function of age in savings triangle
$\bar{v}$	Average individual wealth in savings triangle
w	"Net net" output per "worker" = "wage"; if $\beta_1 = 0$: = marginal product of "other" inputs, if $\beta_1 \neq 0$: = marginal product of "other" inputs, but not "wage"
w	Exchange rate dollar/rupee (in Chap. 12)
$\hat{w}$	$= w[1 - (r - g)D]$= "net net" output minus primary fiscal surplus
x	$= w - q =$ "net net" output per worker minus rental income per worker
y	Net output per worker
$r = \frac{s}{c+v}$	$r=$ profit rate, $s = $ *surplus value*, $c = $ *constant capital*, $v = $ *variable capital* (in Sect. 4.1.3 on Marx)
A	$= \frac{\bar{R}}{r+\alpha-g} = $ Wealth as capitalized rent of a plot of land
C	Consumption in the economy as a whole
D	Net public debt period = Net public debt per "worker" divided by "net net income" w
$\dot{D}$	Derivative of D with respect to calendar time t

$\tilde{D}$	Explicit net and implicit public debt
E	Time endpoint of a transitional deviation from steady state
EX	Exports
GW	Government wealth
I	Investment
$\tilde{I}$	Investment per "worker" in steady state
IM	Imports
K_H, K_F, K_G, K_P	Real capital of households K_H, of firms K_F, of government K_G, of private sector K_P
$L = l\omega$	Wealth per "net net income" w from future rental income
L_H, L_F, L_G, L_P	Land owned by private households L_H, by firms L_F, by the government L_G, by the private sector L_P
N	Number of TRILLS owned by investor
NW	(National) net wealth
PW	Private wealth
Q	Tobin's Q
R	Rental income from a piece of land
$\bar{R}$	Value of R at time zero (= the present)
S	Saving
T	Period of production
$\tilde{T}$	Net taxes
U	Lifetime utility of the representative consumer
V	Excess value of corporate sector
X	National trade balance as share of annual consumption
Y	National income
Z	"Waiting period"
α	Risk premium (same dimension as r and g)
β_1	Bias parameter of rate of interest r in the production system
β_2	Bias parameter of the rate of interest r in the consumption system
γ	Coefficient of intertemporal substitution (CIS) in the consumption system
δ	Shrinkage rate of a TRILL ("radioactive decay") (in Chap. 6)
δ	Value-added share of the digital sector in the economy (in Chap. 8)
ε	A variable that is a dimensionless real number
η	Consumption-labor pattern of the representative consumer; $\eta(r; U)$ = pattern corresponding to a given interest rate r and a given lifetime utility U
$Eta\,(U)$	Set of all consumption-labor patterns that generate lifetime utility U
θ	Production technique; $\theta(r)$= production technique that is applied in a steady state at rate of interest r
$Theta$	The set of steady-state production techniques that are used at some rate of interest r

λ	First constant of integration of Solow production function
μ	Second constant of integration of Solow production function
ρ	Natural rate of interest = value of r at $D = 0$
φ	Steady-state marginal productivity of capital
ψ	Coefficient of intertemporal substitution (CIS) in the production system
ω	Rental share in "net net income" $\omega = q/w$
Ω	Proportional welfare loss when r deviates from its optimal value g, evaluated by second-degree Taylor approximation

List of Figures

List of Tables

Introduction: Private Wealth and Public Debt

1

*Was ist das Schwerste von allem? Was dir das Leichteste dünket
Mit den Augen zu sehen, was vor den Augen dir liegt*
J. W. Goethe, Zahme Xenien

*The difficulty lies, not in the new ideas, but in escaping from the
old ones, which ramify, for those brought up as most of us have
been, into every corner of our minds*
J. M. Keynes, Preface to The General Theory; last sentence

Abstract

In the economic area comprising the OECD countries plus China, almost half of private wealth consists of net public debt. Private wealth is nearly twice the size of private real assets. Due to the continuing rise in life expectancy, the share of public debt in private wealth is growing. As long as public debt does not become too great, real interest rates can be low, but positive in the twenty-first century. The main reason for this is private retirement planning in light of high life expectancy. Investment cannot keep up with increasing private saving. In the twenty-first century, public debt is a macroeconomic steering instrument. Fiscal policy uses it to ensure that a positive, but low real interest rate level continues to prevail.

1.1   Overture

People are getting older and older. But the opposite is true for machines: They are being replaced faster and faster. The capital market reacts with interest rates that are falling lower and lower.

Carl Christian von Weizsäcker's nephew Jakob von Weizsäcker, who is likewise an economist, composed the following haiku on the subject:

Humans live longer
Machines retire faster
Capital abounds

This book is about these findings and their consequences for economic policy. We have assembled and analyzed empirical data that has been obtained by others: Above all, by public agencies. The nation states belonging to the OECD represent the geographical scope of our investigation. We have also grouped China together with them. For the purpose of our calculations, we can, as a first approximation, take the balance of the capital flows between this area and the rest of the world and set this balance to zero. Further details are provided in Sect. 3.11. Hence, for the OECD plus China region, the following equation must roughly hold:

$$S = I$$
"Saving = Investment"

The savings that are accumulated over time correspond to the growth in total wealth in this area. The accumulated net investment represents the area's stock of real capital. The value of land has to be added to the latter, such that real assets are comprised of real capital and land.

We divide this area theoretically into a private and a public sector. Private wealth is comprised, then, of the real assets in private hands plus the balance of claims and liabilities vis-à-vis the state.

Figure 1.1 shows our estimate of the current composition of the private wealth of the population in the OECD plus China region.

Nearly half of private wealth (or, to be more precise, 7/15 of the latter) consists of the balance of claims vis-à-vis the state. 5/15 or one-third of total private wealth is real capital and 3/15 or one-fifth is the value of land.

This is a rough estimate. But we do not need a more precise measurement. Consider that even the owner of an owner-occupied, single-family house or a condominium unit does not know the exact market value of his or her property. What is of significance for us is the following finding:

Private wealth is nearly twice private real assets. Almost half of private wealth consists of net public debt.

Fig. 1.1 Three forms of private wealth and their relative shares. *Source* Authors' own presentation

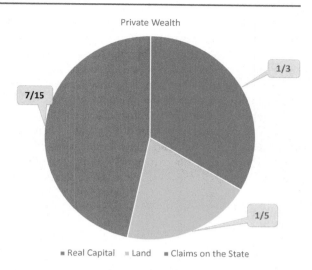

Private Wealth

7/15

1/3

1/5

■ Real Capital   ■ Land   ■ Claims on the State

Our estimate refers to the present. Nonetheless, we also assert that there is a trend: *The relative share of net claims of the private sector on the state is undergoing a secular increase.* It was smaller in the past. And in the future, it will be larger than it is today. Hence, supposing we have somewhat overestimated the share of net claims of the private sector on the state as concerns the present, then the composition of private wealth depicted in the graph will hold at some point in the 2020s or 2030s.

The first part of this book is devoted to demonstrating the thesis that we have just formulated. This part is theoretically and empirically oriented. The second part of the book deals with economic policy. What are the consequences that follow for government action from the findings of the first part? The following main topics are covered: 1. the relative size of the public sector and the requirement of price stability. 2. reforming the rules of international trade. 3. Europe, the euro and the problem of German demographics. 4. Friedrich List and developing countries. In a concluding chapter, we will address how the required reforms can be implemented in an intelligent way.

1.2   The Welfare State and the Concept of Private Wealth

Both the public debate on government debt and the discussion among economists focus on the *explicit* debt presented in the official statistics. But this only represents the lesser part of the totality of the state's obligations vis-à-vis its citizens. The explicit public debt is just the tip of the iceberg. The *implicit* public debt is much larger than the explicit. It consists in particular, but not only, of the retirement benefits accorded to citizens in the context of social security and the retirement benefits accorded to public sector employees and civil servants. If the state were, like private businesses, an institution that has to prepare a balance sheet, then this implicit public debt would be explicit. A private business forms provisions for promised retirement benefits on the liabilities side of its balance sheet. Because the state is not required to prepare a balance sheet, the capital equivalent of these future obligations is not entered into the books as an explicit obligation.

Nonetheless, for citizens, the claim to these future retirement benefits and pensions is undoubtedly a form of wealth. Their life-planning and, in particular, their present consumption behavior are geared toward these expected future payments. On average, the voluntary savings of eligible citizens in all the OECD countries would be far from adequate for them to be able to consume in their old age as they are accustomed. Citizens with claims to retirement benefits that will later be paid by the state behave as if these claims were part of their wealth.

Hence, from an economic point of view, these claims must also be regarded as wealth. But the rules of balance sheet accounting demand then that the party required to make the payment also enters the present value of these future retirement benefits in the balance sheet as a liability. Anything else would be sophistry.

Since 1980, the jurisprudence of Germany's constitutional court, the *Bundesverfassungsgericht*, has persistently recognized that claims to retirement benefits deriving from the public retirement plan enjoy the protection of property guaranteed by Article 14 of Germany's constitution or "Basic Law." Hence, they are also wealth from this constitutional point of view (BVerfGE 53, 257). In the cited ruling, moreover, the *Bundesverfassungsgericht* also emphasizes the way in which the claim to retirement benefits contributes to the beneficiary's freedom, just as other forms of property procure freedom for the owner.

1.3   The Ambiguous Image of Public Debt

"Public debt is a burden for future generations." This is the negative view of the phenomenon of public debt. "Thanks to public debt, the private wealth of the individual citizen is on average twice average private real assets." This is the positive view of public debt.

The phenomenon of ambiguous images is well known. An example is provided in Fig. 1.2. Is this the head of a duck or the head of a rabbit?

Public debt is similarly confounding for citizens. Should they have pity on the next generations of their children and grandchildren? Or should they be happy that the state owes them and their neighbors—and later also their children and grandchildren—so much?

The economist has a clear answer here: "It depends!" There is an indicator available for which of the two views is the correct one. This indicator is the equilibrium, inflation-adjusted and risk-free rate of interest corresponding to full employment. It is also known as the real rate of interest.

Fig. 1.2   Ambiguous image: duck or rabbit? *Source* Jastrow (1899)

The higher the real rate of interest, the more justified is the pessimistic point of view. The greater the interest that the state has to pay on its debt, the greater the burden that this interest represents for future generations. When the interest rate is very low, the optimistic view of public debt is the correct one. The interest rate is the price signal that tells economic policy how to deal with public debt.

This idea will be a recurrent theme throughout the entire analysis that we develop in this book. The factors that influence this equilibrium rate of interest will be a particular focus.

1.4   The Secular Growth of Prosperity

Those who are living in desperate poverty will behave, whether they like it or not, in the way that Jesus described in the Sermon on the Mount: "Behold the fowls of the air: for they sow not, neither do they reap, nor gather into barns; yet your heavenly Father feedeth them. Are ye not much better than they?" At the subsistence minimum, we think, above all, of the *here and now*. We are not able to make provision for the distant future by amassing wealth.

In the "modern" period, i.e., in the last two and a half centuries, prosperity has considerably increased. And with it, so too has average life expectancy. And so too the "third stage of life," in which people continue to consume, but no longer work for money. The welfare state, which exists in all OECD countries, creates a powerful system of provision for old age and free access to healthcare services that prolong life. Modern, democratic, market-based society enables virtually everyone to make provision for their own futures over decades. And by way of its laws, the state obligates its citizens to make such provision. The state thus mandates that practically all of its citizens must dispose of considerable wealth corresponding to their high life expectancy.

Beyond this observation, it is also clear that the trend of growing prosperity will continue. No matter how we measure economic growth or how we should measure it (cf. Harberger 1998 or, for example, Meadows et al. 1972), it is indisputable that life expectancy will continue to rise in the future. As consequence, the third stage of life will likewise continue to get longer. Therefore, the wealth amassed for retirement will also constantly continue to grow in comparison to current consumption per year.

This can also be expressed as follows: The saving rate (voluntary and mandatory combined) of persons in the active work force will continue to rise as life expectancy rises. And life expectancy is not only rising in the OECD countries. It is rising in poorer countries even faster than in rich countries. The global south is catching up. Hence, we can also expect there to be rising saving rates in the developing countries in the future.

In the global history of modernity, human behavior exhibits something like a Law of Increasing Future-Directedness. For the details, see Chap. 3 titled "Wealth and Desired Wealth".

1.5   The Limits of Complexity: The Capital Coefficient Has Remained Constant for the Last One Hundred Years

Kaldor's famous stylized facts (Kaldor 1961) include the finding that the capital coefficient or capital–output ratio, as he puts it, has no upward trend. This finding still remains valid today. The capital coefficient is the ratio between the value of real capital stock and annual value output. Leaving aside cyclical fluctuations, it undergoes virtually no change at all. This provides an interesting contrast to the previously discussed secular increase in the private wealth amassed for the purpose of retirement planning. How can this difference be explained?

The explanation is the institution of money: Money is the great simplifier. As aspiring economists already learn in the first semester of studies, money allows the transaction costs of exchange to be reduced by orders of magnitude. It is precisely this simplifier that makes the great complexity of modern economic life manageable. Böhm-Bawerk's principle of the "greater productivity of more roundabout production" could only be truly exploited in the modern period, because it was only thanks to money that the division of labor could be fully developed. The division of labor is, however, the main source of prosperity—at any rate, according to Adam Smith (Smith 1776; Böhm-Bawerk 1891 [1889]).

But the future-directedness of savers and the future-directedness of investors run along entirely different lines. If a currency with stable purchasing power is given, savers can at least—if they so desire—avoid risks to the value of their financial assets. They can even eliminate certain life-risks that go beyond these risks to the value of their assets. They can, for instance, take out a policy with an insurance company that assures them a life annuity. And social security even provides such insurance for practically everyone. As the need for safeguarding one's future increases, the risks incurred by individual savers need not increase as well. Thus, under certain institutional conditions, the constantly increasing need for future-directedness can be made manageable. What is crucial in this connection is that savers do not have to decide today *which* goods they will purchase with their savings in the future. In a market economy, the goods required for satisfying your needs are practically always available, so long as you are willing to pay the market price for them. General purchasing power in the form of money and financial assets has a considerable option value, precisely because you do not have to determine in advance which goods you will buy later. You can save to buy goods later that do not even exist yet today.

Matters look entirely different in the case of investors. Investment in real capital is always by its very nature tied to value risks. As an investor, you invest in a *concrete* object, not in *abstract* purchasing power, as savers do. The concrete objects of investment are deprived of the option value of money. The value risk may be greater or smaller. It is not without interest that the example chosen by Adam Smith to illustrate the functioning of the "invisible hand" concerns precisely this difference in risk. "As every individual, therefore, endeavours as much as he can both to employ his capital in the support of domestic industry, and so to direct the industry that its produce may be of the greatest value; every individual necessarily labours to render the annual revenue of the society as great as he can. He generally, indeed, neither intends to promote the public interest, nor knows how much he is promoting it. *By preferring the support of domestic to that of foreign industry, he intends only his own security;* and by directing that industry in such a manner as its produce may be of the greatest value, he intends only his own gain, and he is in this, as in many other cases, led by an invisible hand to promote an end which was no part of his intention" (Smith 1776, Iv.ii.9; authors' emphasis).

You have always to take care of a piece of real capital in a specific way. Its profitability crucially depends on the owner attending to the building, the fleet of vehicles, the machines and the inventories and attempting to ward off dangers. There is, so to say, a constant struggle against decay, against the Second Law of Thermodynamics: the law of increasing disorder. But even an investment object that is well looked-after is not immune to changes in its environment or changes in the market.

Not even diversification can eliminate such risks. Entrepreneurs have to attend to *their* business. If they were involved in many businesses, in order to spread out their risk, then considerable principal-agent problems would arise, entailing further risks and costs in turn. Experience teaches that focusing on your own business generates better results than dividing yourself up among numerous engagements.

A decisive point for our analysis is that the risks of real capital ownership increase with increasing future-directedness. Even if a building or a production facility is well maintained, its value is exposed to less risk, the faster it is recouped. This gives rise to all sorts of rules of thumb in economic practice. Many investments are only made if the expected payback period does not exceed a generally established threshold. Other proposed investments have to generate an expected return that is well above the financing costs.

But the requirement of high returns means that the future-directedness of investors is limited, even when there are very low, risk-free real interest rates. It is only when there are very negative real interest rates—or, in other words, when there is considerable inflation—that the calculation of risk is reversed, inasmuch as the desire to preserve value triggers a "flight to tangible assets." But from the point of view of the economy, this "flight" is unproductive, since the marginal yield of such investments is typically negative.

In a dynamic, growth-oriented economy, there is no guarantee that the return on investment for the investor will correspond to the overall return for the economy as a whole. Nonetheless, there is also a sound economic reason why it would not make sense for the capital coefficient always to continue to rise. The keyword is "complexity."

The capital coefficient has the dimension of "time." As shown in Weizsäcker (2021), it roughly corresponds to the average period of production, a concept developed by Böhm-Bawerk. The latter represents the average time lag between labor inputs and the availability of the consumer goods to which, by way of roundabout production, these labor inputs ultimately give rise. Roundaboutness of production signifies the "complexity" of the social production process as a whole. The greater the time lag between labor and the availability of consumer goods—the longer, in other words, the average period of production—the more complicated is the social production process as a whole. But complexity is tied to complexity costs. Many of these complexity costs can be placed under the rubric of the "transaction costs" that have become a focus of interest in economic theory thanks to Coase's work (Coase 1937, 1960).

Hence, the basic principle of the greater productivity of more roundabout production must be weighed against the added costs of increased complexity. The difference between increased productivity and complexity costs can be expected to reach a maximum value with a certain period of production. At this point, it is not economically rational to extend the period of production beyond this maximum. We discuss this question in greater detail in Chap. 4 on real capital.

1.6 Digitalization

The public, politicians and academic specialists have made questions concerning digitalization a focus of their interest. Despite intensive debate, it is difficult to predict the social path that digitalization will take. The only point on which everyone agrees is that artificial intelligence and other variants of digitalization will fundamentally change society and especially the economic spheres of society. Many expect accelerated technical "progress" as a result. We place "progress" in quotes, because some people do not regard this transformation as progress.

But, regardless of whether one wants to speak of digitalization as progress or not, an acceleration of technical change undoubtedly signifies faster obsolescence of the different forms taken by real capital. If, however, real capital is replaced more quickly due to faster obsolescence, then the apparatus of production is able to tie up less economic value as measured against its annual productive output. This suggests that digitalization contributes to a fall in the capital coefficient, rather than to its increase.

Economic policy has, in any case, to be prepared for the possibility that the capital requirements of the production sector will decline relative to the total product.

1.7 The Consequence: Low Interest Rates, Today and Tomorrow

If, with rising life expectancy and rising prosperity, people want to increase their wealth faster than their annual consumption; if, however, on the other hand, the system of production balks at increased complexity and increased roundaboutness of production; then capital supply puts more and more pressure on prices. Over-supply makes prices fall. The price of capital, however, is the interest rate. If there were not a countervailing force, it would have to become negative under conditions of full employment. This countervailing force is the state: more precisely, public action to offset the growing capital supply. The state has to develop a *negative capital supply* by increasing public debt just enough so that, despite the private savings glut, full employment is preserved at a non-negative real rate of interest.

Public debt is thus the macroeconomic steering instrument with whose help interest rates are prevented from becoming negative.

This is easier said than done. For, even if one has a positive view of public debt, the latter is not so easy to manage in both political and economic terms. In the past, public debt has been abused again and again.

The positive view of the ambiguous image of public debt depends on interest rates remaining low. Excessive public debt can be recognized by rising interest rates, by threats to price stability, by the government ultimately resorting to emergency measures, like price controls, that suspend the mechanism of market regulation via prices. The state and hence policymakers are thus themselves responsible for ensuring that the condition for a positive view of public debt is preserved in the form of low interest rates. In Chap. 13, the concluding chapter of our book, we will return to this political task.

1.8 "Secular Stagnation"

Since 2010, Carl Christian von Weizsäcker has been defending the thesis that there is a structural oversupply of private savings (Weizsäcker 2010; Weizsäcker 2014). This thesis has often been described as a variant of the "secular stagnation" thesis.

The term was coined by Alvin Hansen in 1939 (Hansen 1939). Hansen explained what he called "secular stagnation" by other causes than we do in this book, however. Since Larry Summers' intervention in 2013 (Summers 2013), "secular stagnation" is again being discussed internationally by economists: for example, in a recent article by Rachel and Summers (Rachel and Summers 2019), which contains a detailed econometric analysis of the evolution of the "neutral" interest rate. The connection between low interest rates and public debt is also the subject of Olivier Blanchard's 2019 Presidential Address to the American Economic Association (Blanchard 2019). In Chap. 7, we deal with both the original and the more recent discussion of secular stagnation in detail.

The phenomenon described in our book is compatible with the findings described by Summers, Rachel, Blanchard and others. But the term "secular stagnation" is misleading. For the oversupply of private savings can be seen as the result of gratifying progress in prosperity and life expectancy. And, so long as the "private savings glut" is offset by net public debt in a way that is reasonable and not excessive, it by no means has to lead to stagnation. In a certain way, we thus come closer to realizing a capitalist variant of the Communist utopia formulated by Marx and Engels in 1846 (Marx and Engels 1970 [1846]). A more precise analysis is provided in our "utopian" Chap. 12.

1.9 "Dynamic Inefficiency" and the Concern for Future Generations

As stated above, it is crucial for the positive view of public debt that the state can take on debt at low interest rates. As Blanchard has noted for recent decades in the USA, the real yield on public debt has, far more often than not, been lower than the growth rate (Blanchard 2019). Hence, this low interest rate is not a brand-new phenomenon. Now, at the same time, we have to bear in mind that during this period, the USA, also far more often than not, imported on balance considerably more capital than it exported. But this reflects the fact that the effective, risk-free real yields in the rest of the world have also been low. For this is the only way to explain the massive net inflow of capital into the USA.

If the risk-adjusted real interest rate is for the most part lower than the system's growth rate, then there is good reason to conclude that a condition of "dynamic inefficiency" exists: The economy in question could consume more today without having to forego future consumption. This could only be otherwise if the state is able to take on debt at a risk-free interest rate that is lower than the marginal productivity of capital. We will return to this last point in Sect. 2.10. For the purpose of the following argument, we assume that the yield on the public debt of countries like Germany and the USA represents a correct price signal for the marginal productivity of capital (In Sect. 2.2, we show that this is not an arbitrary assumption. See also Weizsäcker 2021, Chap. 2, Sect. 12).

Moreover, if the real rate of interest is so low that dynamic inefficiency exists, then it can no longer be said that public debt is a burden for future generations. For the consequence of current and future foregoing of this public debt would be that there is insufficient demand for savings at the given interest rate. This would have as consequence in turn that the interest rate would have to fall even further and possibly become negative. This would certainly not help future generations. On the contrary, the resulting disadvantages for the current generation would in all likelihood affect the children as well. There would be fewer consumer goods to distribute both today and in the future.

The precise investigation of questions of intergenerational distribution requires a steady-state analysis, such as that carried out by Carl Christian von Weizsäcker in Weizsäcker (2021). This analysis confirms the conclusion that we just drew: At low, real equilibrium rates of interest, public debt is *not* a burden for future generations.

1.10   A Brief Overview of the Following Chapters

In the next chapter, Chap. 2, we introduce the concept of the "natural" rate of interest. We define it as the hypothetical real rate at full employment corresponding to zero net public debt. Within the framework of a steady-state analysis, we then discuss the implications of public debt for prosperity. This chapter is an abridged version of Weizsäcker (2021).

Chapter 3 is about people's desired wealth. It deals with the thesis, for which there is strong empirical support, that with rising prosperity and hence rising life expectancy, desired wealth rises faster than current consumption.

There then follow three chapters on the three different forms of private wealth that we distinguish: 1. real capital, 2. land and 3. net claims on the state. In each of Chaps. 4, 5 and 6, there is a theoretical part and an empirical part on the respective form of wealth. The analysis always concerns the OECD plus China region.

Chapter 7 provides a flow-variable-based analysis of the Great Divergence between saving and investment from a Keynesian perspective.

Chapter 8 concludes the theoretical–empirical part of our book.

The second, economic policy part begins in Chap. 9 with pleas for an adequate volume of welfare-state benefits and for price stability as prerequisites of a stable, liberal-democratic economic and social order.

Chapter 10 is about the effects of a low interest rate world on international trade. We show here why and how the WTO has to be supplemented by a macroeconomic component. This entails, in particular, greater efforts—including efforts involving fiscal policy—to achieve balanced current accounts.

Chapter 11 applies the suggestions in Chap. 10 to the European Union and, in particular, the eurozone. Here too, in the interest of stabilizing the euro and promoting full employment, there has to be agreement on national fiscal policies that aim at achieving balanced current accounts.

Chapter 12 is a "utopian" proposal for improving the situation in developing countries. It is based on the idea that these countries could take the Chinese "economic miracle" as model—and that the OECD countries could encourage this approach by providing favorable conditions for imports from the developing countries. In order to preserve full employment in the OECD countries, fiscal policy, involving a deliberate increase in net public debt, should be employed to promote prosperity and to stem migratory movements from the developing countries. This sort of win-win cooperation between rich countries and developing countries is possible thanks to the structural surplus of private savings in the OECD countries.

In Chapter 13, we conclude the book with some provisional reflections on how an astute policy of the required net borrowing can be implemented in the OECD plus China region without being abused for populist purposes.

References

Blanchard, Olivier. 2019. Public Debt and Low Interest Rates, AEA Presidential Lecture 2019. *American Economic Review* 109 (4): 1197–1229.

Böhm-Bawerk, Eugen Ritter von. 1891 [1889]. *The Positive Theory of Capital*, trans. William Smart. London and New York: Macmillan.

Bundesverfassungsgericht, BVerfGE 53, 257.

Coase, Ronald H. 1937. The Nature of the Firm. *Economica* 4 (16): 386–405.

Coase, Ronald H. 1960. The Problem of Social Cost. *Journal of Law and Economics* 3: 1–44.

Hansen, Alvin H. 1939. Economic Progress and Declining Population Growth. *American Economic Review* 29 (1): 1–15.

Harberger, Arnold C. 1998. A Vision of the Growth Process. *American Economic Review* 88 (1): 1–32.

Jastrow, Joseph. 1899. The Mind's Eye. *Popular Science Monthly* 54: 299–312.

Kaldor, Nicholas. 1961. Capital Accumulation and Economic Growth. In *The Theory of Capital*, ed. F.A. Lutz and D. C. Hague, 177–222. London: St. Martin's Press.

Marx, Karl and Friedrich Engels. 1970 [1846]. *The German Ideology*, ed. C. J. Arthur. New York: International.

Meadows, Dennis L., Donella H. Meadows, Jørgen Randers, William W. Behrens III. 1972. *The Limits to Growth. A Report for the Club of Rome's Project on the Predicament of Mankind.* New York (NY): Universe Books.

Rachel, Lukasz und Lawrence H. Summers. 2019. On Falling Neutral Real Rates, Fiscal Policy, and the Risk of Secular Stagnation. *Brookings Papers on Economic Activity* March 4: 1–66.

Smith, Adam. 1776. *An Inquiry into the Nature and Causes of the Wealth of Nations*. London: W. Strahan and T. Cadell.

Summers, Lawrence H. 2013. *Speech at IMF Fourteenth Annual Research Conference in Honor of Stanley Fischer.* 8 November 2013. Washington (D.C.): International Monetary Fund.

Weizsäcker, Carl Christian von. 2010. Das Janusgesicht der Staatsschulden. *Frankfurter Allgemeine Zeitung.* 4 June 2010: 12 (published in the appendix to this book as "The Two Faces of Public Debt").

Weizsäcker, Carl Christian von. 2014. Public Debt and Price Stability. *German Economic Review* 15 (1): 42–61.

Weizsäcker, Carl Christian von. 2021. Capital Theory of the Steady State—Or: T + L = Z–D. https://www.coll.mpg.de/Weizsaecker/CapitalTheory2021 and https://www.springer.com/9783658273620.

Part I
Theory and Empirical Evidence

The Natural Rate of Interest and the Optimal Rate of Interest in the Steady State

2

Abstract

The "natural rate of interest" is the hypothetical, risk-free real rate of interest that would obtain in a closed economy, if net public debt were zero. It is considerably less than the optimal steady-state rate of interest, which is equal to the system's growth rate. This holds for a very general "meta-model." The fundamental equation of capital theory holds on the optimal steady-state path: $T = Z - D$, where T is the overall economic period of production, Z is the representative private "waiting period" of consumers and D is the public debt ratio. Prosperity is at least 30% lower at the natural rate of interest than at the optimal rate.

2.1 Definition of the Natural Rate of Interest

The term "natural rate of interest" goes back to Knut Wicksell (Wicksell [1898]). In his important book *Interest and Prices*, Wicksell identified the function that a central bank is supposed to fulfill by way of its interest rate policy. He compared the interest rate set or at least influenced by the central bank to the "natural rate of interest." The latter is the interest rate that the central bank should strive to achieve, since at it there is a threat neither of inflation nor of deflation. If the central bank sets the interest rate below the natural rate, there is a threat of inflation. If it sets the interest rate above the natural rate, there is a threat of deflation. The natural rate of interest is thus also the dividing line between those interest rates at which a self-reinforcing process of inflation is set into motion and those rates at which a self-reinforcing process of deflation is to be expected.

A different problem is the focus of our analysis. The short-term macroeconomic management of the economy using the central bank's monetary policy is not our primary concern. Our concern is rather the question of whether public debt is required in the 21st century, if we want to combine price stability and full

© The Author(s) 2021
C. C. von Weizsäcker and H. M. Krämer, *Saving and Investment in the Twenty-First Century*, https://doi.org/10.1007/978-3-030-75031-2_2

employment. Hence, for analytical purposes, we are interested in the question of how high the real full employment interest rate would be, if there were no public debt. This is the interest rate that we call the "natural rate."

We are thus posing the same question that Eugen von Böhm-Bawerk already raised in the second volume of his *Capital and Interest: The Positive Theory of Capital* (Böhm-Bawerk [1889]). His answer was that this natural rate of interest is positive. And we suspect that his answer was empirically correct for his time. Although there was also a great deal of public debt back then, he was not principally interested in explaining the current level of the interest rate. He wanted to explain the phenomenon of interest as such. For this purpose, it was necessary to exclude the state as a participant in the capital market. Just as, at around the same time, Léon Walras and, later, his followers, all the way up to Arrow and Debreu, analyzed general equilibrium and its Pareto optimality using a model without government influence on markets, in the same way, Böhm-Bawerk wanted to explain interest as part of a general equilibrium in which the state plays no role. What was important for him was understanding *interest as a scarcity price* (for scarce capital). His book was thus the response of "bourgeois economics" to the exploitation theory of profit that Karl Marx had developed in the first volume of *Capital* (Marx 1976 [1867]).

We will come back to Marx and Böhm-Bawerk in the first part of Chap. 4 on real capital. In particular, we will closely examine Böhm-Bawerk's "law of the greater productivity of more roundabout production." For Böhm-Bawerk, this law was one of the three reasons why the real rate of interest is positive in a stationary general equilibrium.

Böhm-Bawerk's model was a model of a stationary closed economy. Generalizing Böhm-Bawerk, we nowadays argue within the framework of a model of a closed economy that is growing at a constant rate.

> **Definition** For us, the natural rate of interest is the risk-free, real rate of interest that is compatible with full employment in a closed economy without public debt that is growing at a constant rate.

The natural rate of interest defined in this way is the *reference point* from which we consider the current global economic landscape. The latter, of course, includes a high level of net public debt. We can presume that the real full-employment equilibrium rate of interest is higher with this public debt than the "natural rate" as we have defined it. Following more recent terminology (cf., for example, Rachel and Summers 2019), what Wicksell meant by the "natural" rate of interest, we call rather the *neutral rate*. We will come back to the neutral rate in Sect. 7.6.

2.2 Profit, Risk, Interest and Overall Economic Returns

The lending business is sometimes not without risk for the lender. Hence, professional providers of loans—like, for example, banks—will demand a premium on the interest rate, which, from the point of view of the lender, represents adequate compensation for the risk assumed. The "spread" that a country like Italy has to pay on the capital market as compared to German government bonds is an example of this risk-based premium, which is thus also described as a risk premium. Interest rates that are high because the capital market assesses the borrower's risk of nonpayment as high are obviously not a good indicator of the internal rate of return of the financed investment project for the economy as a whole. This applies for private and public borrowers alike. If we want to use interest rates to draw conclusions about the marginal social productivity of investments, then we have to use interest rates that have been cleansed of this risk premium.

Banks and other businesses that are routinely involved in making loans devote considerable resources—in particular, human resources—to selecting those borrowers who are "creditworthy" or, in other words, with whom the lender can expect to do "good business." If competition between lenders functions properly, then ideally it should bring interest margins down to the point at which the risk premium of the bank for the last successful loan-seeker is just sufficient to cover the risk assumed in providing the loan. The expenses incurred by the bank in selecting "creditworthy" borrowers must, however, be taken into account in this calculation. We can thus propose the following formula as an equilibrium condition for a competitive credit market: "Interest margin = pro-rata selection expenses + provisions for default in the case of the last successful loan-seeker." Thus, the bank does not earn anything more on the last successful loan-seeker.

In practice, this purely formal presentation is rendered more complicated by, among other things, the fact that the default risks of individual borrowers are positively correlated for reasons relating both to the overall economic climate and to industry-specific risks. As consequence, lenders often work with consolidated risk assessments and consolidated provisions for default. Some part of the selection expenses, moreover, cannot be assigned to individual loan applications either. The loan officers have to acquire know-how and experience. Research has to be done on industry-wide developments or political developments. Hence, consolidated values are also used to a considerable extent in the calculation of selection expenses. This use of consolidated values also means that price differentiation (in this case, interest margin differentiation) between individual borrowers is not perfect. As a result, the "price" (in this case, the interest margin) is, as it were, above the "marginal cost" for the lender of dealing with the individual borrower, but, on the other hand, "fixed costs" of lending are also created, which must, so to say, be "passed on" to all borrowers if the bank does not want to incur losses.

The lending business of banks can be best represented using the model of monopolistic competition or, alternatively, using a model of heterogeneous oligopolistic competition. In the case of monopolistic competition, suppliers do not generate any profits beyond a risk premium for the capital employed. For, ultimately, there are not any significant barriers to entry for the lending business. In modern financial markets, there is an interbank money market, which always allows solvent banks to obtain the resources required for extending loans. Profits that are above-average as compared to other industries are thus eliminated by the competition of both new market entrants and the expanded business of banks that were already present in the market. On average, the marginal borrower thus gives rise to additional costs for the lending bank that, including appropriate (and possibly consolidated) risk provisions, exactly correspond to the interest margin.

Of course, this statement is only valid "on average," since, depending on the current economic climate, there are times when banks can extend more loans than usual without a proportionate increase in short-term expenditure—and there are times when lending is less than usual, such that it is not possible fully to cover the costs that, in the short term, are to be regarded as fixed.

This on-average statement about the marginal borrower means that the overall economic return on the investment that he or she makes with the loan is not greater than the risk-free market rate of interest. This can be seen most clearly in the case of the government bonds of countries that are regarded as absolutely no-risk borrowers. For, so long as the circulation of the tradable debt of this borrower ensures sufficient liquidity, the opportunity costs of the bank in using money to extend loans are derived from the use of this money to buy government bonds. The lender calculates an expected return on the investment for the marginal borrower that is based on the interest that the borrower has to pay to the bank. If the return expected by the lender were greater than this interest, then the borrower would not in fact be the marginal borrower, but rather an inframarginal borrower. The interest margin that the marginal borrower has to pay corresponds to the costs to which he or she gives rise, on average, for the bank. If we subtract these costs—which are also costs for the economy as a whole—from the expected profit of the borrower, then what remains is an expected overall economic return that is exactly equal to the risk-free interest rate.

What applies for the private borrower, also applies for the public borrower from whom the capital market demands a risk premium. If government bonds are traded with a yield that is greater than the yield of the most secure government debt, then the same causes determine the lender's costs as in the case of the bank loan discussed previously. The yield of the bond of a private issuer reflects the average risk assessment of its current and potential creditors. If there were a large number of potential buyers who do not see any risk in the bond, then it would be traded with a yield corresponding to the risk-free interest rate. If the bond is seen as a risk by the investors, then, at the margin, these investors are indifferent between a small increase in the holdings of this bond in their portfolios and additional holdings of risk-free bonds. For the economy as a whole, this means that the ex-ante value of a small additional investment with the one borrower is equal to the ex-ante value of a small additional investment with the other borrower. It is thus clear that despite the higher yield (due to the risk premium) of the bond of the private borrower, the additional investment of the latter is not ex-ante worth more for the economy as a whole than that of the risk-free borrower.

This conclusion is not invalidated by the liquidity argument. The difference in yield between private bonds and government bonds that are regarded as absolutely risk-free is sometimes also explained by the different liquidity of the securities in question. However correct this explanation is, it is important to understand that this liquidity premium is a special case of a risk premium. But the risk now lies not with the borrower, but rather with the lender, whose own future liquidity requirements cannot be foreseen with certainty. Hence, the lender demands compensation in the form of additional yield for an investment that is relatively illiquid.

The profit of the "Schumpeterian" innovative entrepreneur (Schumpeter 1934 [1911]) is an example of what is known as entrepreneurial profit in economic theory. We all know how essential innovations are for economic progress. But every innovation is tied to risks, and the profit or loss resulting from it cannot be exactly estimated in advance. Innovations have usually to be financed with equity. If we follow the Schumpeterian theory, according to which the activity of risk-taking innovators is the basis of economic progress, then attempted innovations create, on average, a social return that is greater than their costs. As a rule, this social return on innovation is not entirely eliminated by competition, since innovations give rise, on average, to positive externalities. But successful innovations usually attract imitators, such that in the long run, albeit with a certain delay, the entrepreneurial profits of innovation can be eliminated by competition. The fact that there are such innovations with their associated positive externalities does not, however, contradict our conclusion that the risk-free interest rate is the correct price signal for the marginal return on investment for the economy as a whole. We have to distinguish between the economically useful willingness of entrepreneurs to take risks and the marginal return on the capital involved. As concerns the latter, there is no systematic reason why lower interest rates should lead to more Schumpeterian innovation.

There is no consensus among economists on this point. Lower interest rates may well facilitate the financing of new projects. But, on the other hand, very low interest rates can, on the view of some economists, contribute to preserving "zombie firms," which tie up resources—especially human resources—in activities that are scarcely productive for the economy as a whole, thus making it more difficult for Schumpeterian entrepreneurs to carry out their innovative experiments. Similarly, the incentive to undertake productive changes may diminish, if a kind of "zombie full employment" is preserved by way of low interest rates. The Japan specialist Gunther Schnabl is an eloquent proponent of this last thesis (cf. Schnabl 2019).

We will refrain from taking sides in this debate here. Our view is thus that when comparing steady states, the interest rate level is neutral with respect to the intensity of Schumpeterian innovation. This is, however, an agnostic position with regard to the question. We thus stand by the conclusion that the risk-free interest rate on public debt is the correct price signal for the intertemporal trade-off between consumption at different points in time. In Sect. 2.10, we will consider the case when the risk-free interest rate on public debt does not correspond to the intertemporal trade-off between consumption at different points in time.

2.3   Capital-Theoretical Foundations

We will now work with the following assumption, which is grounded in capital theory.

Assumption 1 A. In a closed economy, there is exactly one natural rate of interest. B. A risk-free, steady-state interest rate above the natural rate is connected to positive net public debt. A risk-free, steady-state interest rate below the natural rate is connected to negative net public debt.

In Carl Christian von Weizsäcker's "Capital Theory of the Steady State", this premise is derived from certain price-theoretical assumptions: in particular, from the Law of Demand (Weizsäcker 2021; cf. Theorem 4). But here we can already refer to the following intuition: In a growing closed economy, we expect there to be a lower equilibrium rate of interest at a higher saving rate. A higher steady-state public debt ratio in a growing economy means that public debt is rising in absolute terms and that thus, with given private saving behavior, the saving rate is lower than it would be without this higher steady-state public debt. We therefore expect a higher risk-free equilibrium rate of interest.

2.4   The Generalized Golden Rule of Accumulation

The macroeconomic production function of the Solow Model is often used in the macroeconomic literature. Solow first presented his model in 1956 and then provided an empirical supplement to it in 1957 (Solow 1956, 1957). Within the framework of this model, in 1961, Phelps and von Weizsäcker, independently from one another, developed a theory of the optimal steady-state rate of interest, which became known under the name coined by Phelps: the "Golden Rule of Accumulation" (Phelps 1961; von Weizsäcker 1961 and 1962). It turns out that the theoretical derivation of the natural rate of interest becomes much clearer and more accessible, once it is understood that the well-known "Golden Rule of Accumulation" can be generalized far beyond the Solow Model. This generalized Golden Rule of Accumulation produces a reference point in the form of an interest rate $r = g$, where g is the growth rate of the system. We can then compare the natural rate of interest ρ with this reference point. This gives rise to insights that are useful for further empirical analysis.

Before beginning with the formal analysis, a word about our chosen unit of measurement. The flow variables employed, like total product or total wage payments, and the stock variables, like real capital, are conceived as *nominal values*. Thus, for example, the total net national product as measured in euros per year, is divided by the number of labor years performed annually, to yield annual net output per labor year y. Or the real capital stock of the economy, as measured in euros, is divided by the number of labor years performed annually to yield the capital stock per labor year, v. Needless to say, we are ultimately interested in inflation-adjusted "real" quantities. Nonetheless, we are conscious of the fact that no unambiguous answer can be given to the question of how great real growth is on the long-term average. In the real world, the basket of goods consumed is constantly changing: not only proportionally, but also due to differing growth rates of its components, as well as the addition of new components or the complete disappearance of old ones. The resulting lack of clarity in measuring real growth over longer periods of time is well known to statisticians under the heading of the "index number problem." If we work with nominal quantities, however, we can circumvent these hazards within the framework of a steady-state analysis, by assuming that the nominal total product grows at a given rate g per year that remains constant over time. It is possible that structural change lies behind this nominal growth rate. But we have no need to take this structural change into consideration in this chapter. We can, of course, choose the growth rate g in such a way that it corresponds to a constant price level in the short term. It would then represent a good short-term to medium-term approximation of the real growth rate.

The interest rate r with which we will be working in the following analysis is likewise the nominal rate of interest. If, however, the growth rate of the system is chosen in such a way that the price level remains constant in the short term, then r is also the real rate of interest.

We now begin the formal analysis. We divide up the net product y per labor unit (= a full labor year) as follows

$$y = w(r; \theta) + rv(r; \theta)$$

Here, v is the value of the real capital employed per worker (= per labor year), r is the risk-free rate of interest at which the government is able to borrow, and θ is the name of the production technique employed. We assume that θ is a function of r. We now introduce the following *naming convention*: $\theta(r) = r$. The variable $w(r; \theta)$ is the "remainder" of the total product per labor year that is left over once we have subtracted the risk-free interest on the capital employed $rv(r; \theta)$. The letter "w" reminds us that ever since Böhm-Bawerk, and all the way up to the Cambridge versus Cambridge capital theory controversy of the 1960s and 1970s, this quantity has been identified in capital-theoretical models with a worker's yearly wage. But for us, w represents far more than the wage. Thus, for example, it also includes risk premiums on the capital employed. Hence, w should not be used for the purpose of distributional analyses.

Nonetheless, the variable *w* is "more fundamental" than the variable *y*. With a given real allocation and a given price level, nominal net output is dependent upon the rate of inflation. This phenomenon is well-known in macroeconomics. The same thing does not apply for the variable *w*, however, because the nominal interest rate moves in lockstep with the inflation rate. Hence, we also call *w* the "net-net product" per labor year.

We use *Theta* to designate the set of production techniques that are employed at some given rate of interest in the steady state. We can thus write the following formula

$$Theta = \{\theta : \exists r \, st \, \theta = \theta(r) \equiv r\}.$$

The economic meaning of this definition of the set *Theta* is that we are limiting the comparison among production techniques to those techniques that will be used in a steady state. We are thus not looking for a production technique that is Pareto-optimal. The set *Theta* can contain many inefficiencies. The following assumption is thus not to be confused with the assumption of Pareto optimality. We will call it the Assumption of Steady-State Efficiency.

Assumption 2 Steady-State Efficiency 1: For every rate of interest *r* and all $\theta \in Theta$, $w(r; \theta(r)) \geq w(r; \theta)$ holds.

This means that *the risk-free rate of interest is a correct price signal* for the choice of the "right" production technique as a function of the interest rate, so long as this only concerns production techniques that are used at some steady-state rate *r*. The production technique will be chosen from the set *Theta* of techniques θ which have the property that there exists a rate of interest *r*, so that θ maximizes the surplus *w* of the total product over the interest on the capital employed. It should be noted that an even stronger assumption was customary in the capital-theoretical literature.

Here, we will also briefly discuss this Assumption 2 as it relates to the literature on the theory of public debt. Pierre Yared has provided an overview of this literature in Yared (2019). The issue that he addresses is whether one of the different theoretical approaches can explain the secular growth of the public debt ratio. He divides the theoretical approaches into two groups: 1. *optimal government debt policy*, 2. *political economy forces behind rising government debt*. He is not convinced by explanations drawing on optimal government debt policy: According to Yared, neither tax smoothing nor safe asset provision nor the elimination of dynamic inefficiency can explain the secular trend of the public debt ratio. In connection with the approach of this book, we are particularly interested in his rejection of the argument that debt could serve to eliminate dynamic inefficiency. Yared does not regard there as being any dynamic inefficiency in reality: "However, there is no evidence of capital overaccumulation in the United States or advanced economies in the post World War II period (Abel, Mankiw, Summers and Zeckhauser 1989)." In a footnote, he adds: "Geerolf (2018) reaches the same result when applying the methodology of Abel, Mankiw, Summers, and Zeckhauser (1989) to more recent US data. Using a different methodology and data, however, this work finds less-strong evidence in favor of dynamic efficiency." But if we read Geerolf's paper (Geerolf 2018), its main finding is clearly that if the data is correctly interpreted, then dynamic inefficiency is present at least in two countries (Japan and South Korea), and that dynamic inefficiency cannot be ruled out in any OECD member state. The main reason for the discrepancy between this finding and earlier findings is the prior overestimation of the marginal productivity of capital, since returns were included in the rate of return on capital that in fact have nothing to do with the marginal productivity of capital. According to Geerolf, recently released OECD data allows these apparent rates of return on capital to be distinguished from the "real" rates. Our argument in Section 2.2 above is thus given empirical support, as is our Assumption 2 on Steady-State Efficiency. From the latter, we will derive below the conclusion that the risk-free rate of interest r is a correct price signal for the marginal productivity of capital in the steady-state context.

In conjunction with the naming convention $\theta(r) = r$, it follows from the Steady-State Efficiency Assumption that for the partial derivative of $\theta(r) = r$ with respect to θ, at $\theta = r$,

$$\frac{\partial w(r; \theta)}{\partial \theta} = 0 \, for \, \theta = r$$

holds.

Weizsäcker 2021, Chap. 2, Sect. 12 is a an extensive discussion of the basic assumption of the present chapter that the risk-free real rate of interest is a price signal for the steady state marginal productivity of capital.

Besides the division of the net product that we have introduced here, there is also the conventional division into consumption and investment

$$y = c + \tilde{I}$$

In this equation, c is consumption per labor year and $\tilde{I}$ represents net investment per labor year. We now introduce a further assumption:

Assumption 3 The ratio between consumption per labor year, c, and the value of capital goods per labor year, v, remains constant over time for a given rate of interest.

For reasons that will become clear later on, we depart from the usual definition of the capital coefficient and define the capital coefficient rather as the ratio v/c, whereby we always understand consumption c here as steady-state consumption per labor year. Using this definition, we can also express Assumption 3 as follows:

Assumption 3 (alternative formulation): For a given interest rate, the capital coefficient remains constant over time.

We will later examine the case in which Assumption 3 does not hold, but rather the capital coefficient exhibits a trend at a given rate of interest.

Let g designate the steady-state growth rate of the closed economy in question. Given Assumption 3, net investment per labor year in the steady state is then equal to $gv(r; \theta)$. We thus have:

$$y = c + gv(r; \theta)$$

In Weizsäcker (2021), Carl Christian von Weizsäcker shows why c is only dependent on θ, but not on r. Ultimately, this is due to the fact that in working with nominal values, we are free to define the price level of the different steady-state paths.

We thus get the equation

$$c(\theta) + gv(r;\theta) = w(r;\theta) + rv(r;\theta)$$

We partially differentiate this equation with respect to θ

$$\frac{dc}{d\theta} + g\frac{\partial v}{\partial \theta} = \frac{\partial w}{\partial \theta} + r\frac{\partial v}{\partial \theta}$$

At $\theta = r$, we previously derived

$$\frac{\partial w(r; \theta)}{\partial \theta} = 0$$

Hence, at $\theta = r$, the following holds

$$\frac{dc}{d\theta} + g\frac{\partial v}{\partial \theta} = r\frac{\partial v}{\partial \theta}$$

Let φ be the "marginal productivity of capital": i.e., the change in total product resulting from a marginal change in θ divided by the marginal change in the value of capital, with prices being held constant or, in other words, with r held constant. Hence, so long as $\partial v/\partial \theta \neq 0$, then

$$\varphi = \frac{dc/d\theta + g\,\partial v/\partial \theta}{\partial v/\partial \theta} = \frac{r\partial v/\partial \theta}{\partial v/\partial \theta} = r$$

If r is a correct price signal, then it is also a correct price signal for the marginal productivity of capital.

If there is a $\theta*$ in *Theta* that leads to a level of consumption per labor year that is at least as high as the consumption per labor year of all other $\theta \in$ *Theta*, then the partial derivative of c with respect to θ must be equal to zero at $\theta*$: i.e.,

$$\frac{dc}{d\theta} = 0$$

at $\theta = \theta*$.

Moreover, on the assumption of steady-state efficiency, for every r and the associated $\theta(r) = r$, the equation

$$\frac{\partial w}{\partial \theta} = 0$$

holds.

Hence, for $\theta*$, this gives the equation

$$0 + g\frac{\partial v}{\partial \theta} = 0 + r\frac{\partial v}{\partial \theta} = 0 + \theta*\frac{\partial v}{\partial \theta}$$

So long as capital value changes with marginal changes in production technique, i.e., so long as

$$\frac{\partial v}{\partial \theta} \neq 0$$

it follows from the above equation that

$$\theta* = g$$

This is the Golden Rule of Accumulation. It thus holds far more generally than just in the Solow Growth Model in which it has been traditionally derived. The famous Golden Rule in the Solow Model is just a special case of this far more general Golden Rule.

The Golden Rule of Capital Accumulation holds whenever steady-state efficiency holds, the capital coefficient is constant over time in the steady state, and a marginal change in the production technique within the set Theta entails a change in the capital tied up in the production technique.

In Sect. 2.10, we will discuss the case when steady-state efficiency does not hold. For this case, we can derive a modified Golden Rule of Accumulation, which we will also use further on in the book.

2.5 The Public Debt Ratio and the Period of Production

We now turn to the question of the effect of net public debt in the steady state. We first introduce the variable $\hat{w}$. Mathematically, it is defined as follows:

$$\hat{w}(r; \theta; D) = w(r; \theta)(1 - (r - g)D)$$

Here, D is the steady-state public debt ratio. It is defined as the ratio of net public debt per labor year to the variable w. The expression rwD thus represents the government's interest expenditure per labor year. The expression gwD represents net borrowing per labor year, inasmuch as D remains constant over time. The difference between these two variables is the fiscal "primary surplus" per labor year corresponding to a constant debt ratio D. If we consider that this primary surplus is generated by a tax on private households, then the economic interpretation of $\hat{w}$ is clear: It is the "remaining" income w per labor year minus the government's tax-financed primary surplus. The remaining taxes and charges paid to the government are then exactly equal to remaining government expenditure, such that the private sector in this respect transfers exactly as much to the government as it receives from the government in payments.

We now consider a general equilibrium corresponding to zero public debt: i.e., with $D = 0$. The rate of interest associated with this equilibrium is what we have defined as the natural rate. We will designate this interest rate by the Greek letter "rho," written ρ. We can now observe the following:

As a rule, $\hat{w}(r; \theta(r); D)$ is different from $w(r; \theta(r))$. At $r = g$ and at $r = \rho$, however, the primary surplus disappears, and therefore

$$\hat{w}(\rho; \theta(\rho); 0) = w(\rho; \theta(\rho)) \text{ and } \hat{w}(g; \theta^*; D) = w(g; \theta^*)$$

holds.

It will be useful now to consider the partial derivative of w with respect to the steady-state rate of interest in somewhat greater detail. Purely formally, we first write

$$\frac{\partial w}{\partial r} = -Tw \text{ or equivalently} \frac{\partial w / \partial r}{w} = -T$$

A dimensional analysis of the variables involved shows that the variable T has the dimension of *time*. We can as a rule assume that the "remaining" income decreases in the steady state, if the risk-free interest rate r increases. Hence, T is a

positive length of time. What is the economic meaning of T? For the usual
capital-theoretical models, we can show that T represents the current average period
of production, which in Böhm-Bawerk determines capital requirements per worker
and which he used to formulate his "law of the greater productivity of more
roundabout production." The period of production is the average time lag between
employed labor hours and the point in time when the consumer goods produced
with them become available. For the expression T that we have introduced here to
have this economic meaning, the labor inputs have to be weighed by their present
values when calculating the average of this time lag. The average period of production defined in this way goes back to Hicks's *Value and Capital* (Hicks 1939).

Capital theorists traditionally only worked with *labor* as the original factor of
production. The roots of this approach are to be found in the efforts of "bourgeois"
economics to respond to Karl Marx's labor theory of value. It was only Samuelson's integration of Ricardian land rent into capital theory (Samuelson 1959a, b)
that changed things somewhat. But even the famous Cambridge versus Cambridge
capital debate was conducted without the factor of land. If we include scarce land in
the capital-theoretical calculation, then the above-defined temporal expression T has
a different meaning than it does in Böhm-Bawerk. In Chap. 5 on *land* as a component of wealth, we will explicitly separate the period of production as such and a
temporal expression for the capital value of future land rents. But here we combine
both temporal expressions in the variable T. We, nonetheless, call T the "period of
production" in our verbal argument.

In the spirit of Böhm-Bawerk, we will now make a connection between the
capital requirements of the production process and the average period of production. From the equation

$$c(\theta) + gv(r; \theta) = w(r; \theta) + rv(r; \theta)$$

we can, for the case $r \neq g$, derive an equation for the capital requirements

$$v(r; \theta) = \frac{c(\theta) - w(r; \theta)}{r - g}$$

By L'Hôpital's rule, at $r = g$, we obtain the equation

$$v(g; \theta(g)) = \frac{-\partial w/\partial r}{1} = wT = cT$$

If $r = g$, then the capital required per labor year is equal to the product of the
"annual wage" times the period of production or the product of consumption per
labor year times the period of production. Böhm-Bawerk's intuition is thus justified
precisely when the interest rate has the value at which steady-state consumption
reaches its maximum. We call

$$v(g; \theta(g)) = wT = cT$$

the "Böhm-Bawerk equation." To the best of our knowledge, it was first derived in the context of a capital-theoretical model in von Weizsäcker (1971).

2.6 Private Wealth *T* + *D*

Here again our definitional equation for $\hat{w}$.

$$\hat{w}(r; \theta; D) = w(r; \theta)(1 - (r - g)D)$$

Assumption 1 essentially means that $D(r)(r - \rho) > 0$, so long as $r \neq \rho$.

We observe that for each r in the middle range between ρ and g, the inequality $\hat{w}$ $(r; \theta(r); D) > w(r; \theta(r))$ holds, while outside the interval between ρ and g, on the contrary, $\hat{w}(r; \theta(r); D) < w(r; \theta(r))$ holds. This conclusion holds for both $\rho < g$ and $\rho > g$. If $\rho = g$, then the middle range drops out, but the inequality $D(r)(r - \rho) > 0$ still holds, so long as $r \neq \rho$.

Now, let $\hat{v}$ be the wealth of private households per labor year. In what follows, we assume that all real capital is privately owned. In the steady state, an equation must hold for households that runs parallel to the equation that was already specified above for the production sector

$$\hat{c} + g\hat{v}(r; \theta(r)) = \hat{w}(r; \theta(r); D(r)) + r\hat{v}(r; \theta(r))$$

Here, $\hat{c}$ is consumption per labor year, which has, of course, to be equal to the volume of consumer goods produced by the production sector per labor year. The left hand side divides household income per labor year into consumption and savings. The right hand side divides household income per labor year into risk-free interest on assets and other income. For $r \neq g$, we obtain the following equation for private wealth

$$\hat{v}(r; \theta(r)) = \frac{c(\theta(r)) - \hat{w}(r; \theta(r))}{r - g} = v(r; \theta(r)) + wD(r)$$

Accordingly, for $r = g$, we calculate

$$\hat{v}(g; \theta^*) = w(g; \theta^*)(T(g) + D(g)) = c(\theta^*)(T(g) + D(g))$$

Private wealth is greater than national wealth, if net public debt is positive. It is less than national wealth, if net public debt is negative.

2.7 The Golden Rule for the Lifetime Utility of the Representative Household

Analogously to the period of production T on the production side, we can introduce a waiting period Z on the household side. It indicates the average time lag, expressed in present values, between performed labor and the consumption expenditure financed by it. The waiting period can also be negative: for example, if, in order to consume today, someone takes out a loan, which he or she will repay later from labor income. The normal case, however, is a positive Z. The situation of the household's wealth is tightly connected to the waiting period Z. We examine this matter in detail in Chap. 3 on desired wealth.

What interests us here is the waiting period in the steady state, since it is related to the Golden Rule of Accumulation. In parallel to the Phelps-Weizsäcker theorem on maximum steady-state consumption, there is also a theorem, which goes back to Samuelson (1958), on the optimal interest rate for the utility-maximizing distribution of consumption over the lifetime of the private household.

Like Samuelson did, we will use the idea of the representative household. Just as, for purposes of simplification, we did not distinguish between land rent and labor income in our discussion of the "period of production," so too in dealing with the waiting period, we will discuss the case in which no wealth is left as inheritance to the next generation. We go into the topic of inheritance in detail in Chap. 3 on desired wealth.

The Samuelson theorem on the optimal steady-state life plan for work and consumption can be formulated as follows. If, in a model with overlapping generations, we compare different steady states with different interest rates, we can ask how great, depending on the interest rate, average consumption per labor year must be, in order to obtain a specified level of lifetime utility U. As Samuelson shows using a simple example in his famous 1958 "overlapping generations" article, the required steady-state consumption per labor year for a specified level of utility is at a minimum when the interest rate is equal to the growth rate. We can derive this result in generalized form by making Assumption 4 of Steady-State Efficiency 2.

First, let us introduce a definition. Let $Eta(U)$ be the set of all work-consumption patterns η of the representative household that generate a lifetime utility level of U. Let $\overline{w}(\eta; r)$ be the level of the "remaining income" that at a risk-free interest rate r is just sufficient to finance the work and consumption pattern η. As above in the case of θ, let $\eta(r) = r$ be the name of the work-consumption pattern that is realized in the steady state at an interest rate r and at "remaining income" $\hat{w} = \mathrm{w}(r; \theta(r))$ $(1 - (r - g)D(r))$. We now consider the lifetime utility level $U(\eta(r))$.

Assumption 4 Steady-State Efficiency 2: For all $\eta \in Eta(U)(\eta(r))$, $\hat{w}(\eta; r) \geq \underset{\mathrm{w}}{\overline{}}(r; \eta(r))$ holds.

The economic meaning of this assumption is that the representative household maximizes its lifetime utility within the framework of the intertemporal budget that is given by r and $\hat{w}(r)$.

We now consider the consumption per labor year that results from a hypothetical steady state in which the interest rate $r = g$ and the work-consumption pattern $\eta \in Eta(U(\eta(g))$ is realized. Here, $\overline{w}(\eta; g) = \overline{c}(\eta)$ holds, whereby $\overline{c}(\eta)$ is the consumption per labor year corresponding to the work-consumption pattern η in the steady state. Hence, on account of Steady-State Efficiency 2, the following holds:

$$\overline{c}(\eta) = \overline{w}(\eta; g) \geq \hat{w}(g; \eta(g)) = w(g; \theta^*) = c(\theta^*)$$

In conjunction with the Golden Rule of Accumulation, this inequality shows that the steady-state lifetime utility of the representative household is maximized at an interest rate of $r = g$. We have thus derived:

> **The Golden Rule for the Lifetime Utility of the Representative Household**
> In comparing different steady states, the lifetime utility of the representative household is maximized when the equilibrium rate of interest is equal to the growth rate: r = g.

On this proposition see also Weizsäcker (2021, Chap. 2, Sect. 2).

As already mentioned above, this Golden Rule for Lifetime Utility was already demonstrated by Samuelson in 1958 for a special case. In the model he used at the time, the production process did not need any capital. Thus, Samuelson left other economists the opportunity to discover the Phelps-Weizsäcker Golden Rule of Accumulation.

2.8   At the Optimum, the Overall Economic Period of Production = The Overall Economic Waiting Period

We now return to the waiting period Z. For every given work-consumption pattern η, it can be shown that:

$$\frac{\partial \overline{w}(\eta; r)}{\partial r} = -Z(\eta; r)\overline{w}(\eta; r)$$

Let us introduce the *indirect* lifetime utility function $U(r; \hat{w})$. From the above equation,

$$\frac{\partial U}{\partial r} = \frac{\partial U}{\partial w} Z\hat{w}$$

follows for its partial derivatives.

For, of course, lifetime utility does not change, if a marginal increase in the interest rate is accompanied by a reduction in the wage, which just makes it possible to finance the hitherto existing work-consumption pattern.

Moreover, we can grasp lifetime utility as a function of the respective steady-state rate of interest. This results in

$$\frac{dU}{dr} = \frac{\partial U}{\partial r} + \frac{\partial U}{\partial \hat{w}}\frac{d\hat{w}}{dr} = \frac{\partial U}{\partial r} + \frac{\partial U}{\partial \hat{w}}\left\{-Tw(1 - (r - g)D) - wD - w(r - g)\frac{dD}{dr}\right\}$$

Since steady-state utility is maximized at $r = g$, it follows that at $r = g$,

$$\frac{\partial U}{\partial r} + \frac{\partial U}{\partial \hat{w}}\{-w(T + D)\} = 0$$

holds.

From this equation and the above equation

$$\frac{\partial U}{\partial r} = \frac{\partial U}{\partial w} Z\hat{w}$$

for $r = g$, we deduce the equation (remembering $\hat{w} = w$ at $r = g$)

$$T(g) + D(g) = Z(g)$$

This can be expressed as follows: The sum of the private waiting period Z and the public waiting period $-D$ is, so to say, the "waiting period" *of the economy as a whole* or the overall economic waiting period. In the steady-state optimum, the overall economic waiting period $Z - D$ is thus equal to the overall economic period of production T. Steady-state lifetime utility is thus maximized when the overall economic waiting period is equal to the overall economic period of production. We call the related equation

$$T = Z - D$$

the *Fundamental Equation of Steady-State Capital Theory.*

We established that the inequality $D(r)(r - \rho) > 0$ holds for every rate of interest other than the natural rate ρ. In conjunction with the equation that we just derived for $r = g$, this shows us that the natural rate of interest is smaller than g precisely when, at a rate of interest $r = g$, the private waiting period is greater than the period of production.

2.9   Deviations from the Steady State: The Interest Rate as Price Signal and the Risk Premium

We are not analyzing the properties of steady states because we believe that the latter correspond to reality. Steady states are not a matter of art for art's sake. In the natural sciences as well, hypothetical steady states are studied, in order to understand the mechanics of a system in motion. As Keynes wrote in *The General Theory*, on his view, "the system…whilst it is subject to severe fluctuations…it is not violently unstable" (Keynes 1936, p. 249). The overwhelming majority of economists are of the opinion that it makes sense to study hypothetical steady states, in order to understand the dynamics of the economy as a whole. It is not our intention here to undertake any comprehensive dynamic analysis, which nowadays is sometimes done using highly complex macro models. Our purpose is merely to introduce certain concepts from stochastic dynamics that we also want to use for steady-state analysis. For the properties of a social steady state are, of course, also influenced by the fact that there can be deviations from this steady state. If, for instance, we consider a condition of balance of power between rival nations, such "peaceful co-existence" will normally be a condition of armed peace. The nations involved will devote a considerable part of their national product to armaments expenditures, even though the armaments are not currently being used.

We are especially interested in two things that are only to be encountered outside of the steady state: 1. The exact significance of the internal rate of return on a current foregoing of consumption—to which we already referred above; and 2. the fact that saving and investment activities are always associated with risk.

In his book *Capital Theory and the Rate of Return*, the founder of the neoclassical theory of growth, Robert Solow, described how models can be developed in which the prevailing interest rate is a price signal for the ratio of a current foregoing of consumption to additional future consumption that is made possible by it (Solow 1964). We assume, for example, that the economy is in a steady state corresponding to a given rate of interest r. Now, we modulate the consumption path of the economy by a small (marginal) change $\varepsilon \Delta c(t)$, such that, at the beginning, $\Delta c(0) < 0$ (= current foregoing of consumption), later, however, it is positive for a while, in order then, starting at some finite point in time $E > 0$, to be zero again. Let us use r^* to designate the internal rate of return of this small deviation from the steady state consumption path. Hence, this is the rate for which the following equation holds:

$$\int_0^E e^{-r^* t} \varepsilon \, \Delta c(t) dt = 0$$

As long as the steady-state rate of interest r is an unbiased price signal for the internal rate of return r^*, the inequality $r^* \leq r$ holds. We can, moreover, construct a corresponding deviation path for every ε—and then grasp r^* as a function of ε:

that is, $r^*(\varepsilon)$. If the rate of interest r is an unbiased price signal, then r^* reaches its maximum at $\varepsilon = 0$ and

$$r^*(0) = r$$

holds.

It should be explicitly noted that this equation also holds if $r < g$: that is, if "dynamic inefficiency" is present. The reason is that in this thought experiment, we return to the steady-state path with its associated capital endowment at a finite point in time E. Dynamic inefficiency stems, after all, from the fact that at $r < g$, one can forego the steady-state growth of the capital endowment and, from then on, always work with a lesser capital stock than on the steady-state path. In the Solow-Tobin-Weizsäcker-Yaari paper from 1966, the authors showed that the interest rate as price signal is also unbiased in a standard "vintage" model (Solow et al. 1966).

Assumption 2 only relates to the comparison of production techniques that are employed in some steady state (the set *Theta*). It can be shown that if the interest rate is also a correct price signal outside of steady states, then Assumption 2 also holds. The converse is not the case.

The steady state that we have presented thus far does not have any risk component. But in every economy, there is also, of course, macroeconomically relevant risk. Since public debt is the focus of our book, our analysis has also to include the risk borne by owners of government bonds and other government liabilities. We will go into some of the various forms of government liabilities, in particular, in Chap. 6: the chapter dealing with public debt.

In Germany or in the USA, there are government bonds that are regarded on the capital market as having a default risk of zero. They can thus serve as a "benchmark," in order to calculate a risk premium on the government bonds of other countries. The risk premium is, for instance, the additional return on a bond as compared to the return on German government bonds. In this book, we will use the Greek letter "alpha"—α—to designate this risk premium. Such a risk premium also exists in the case of real assets: like real capital and land. For these risk premiums, we also use the symbol α.

2.10   What if the Interest Rate Represents a Biased Price Signal?

The Golden Rule of Accumulation and the Golden Rule for Lifetime Utility were derived above on the assumption of the steady-state efficiency of both the production system (Assumption 2) and the domain of consumption (Assumption 4). The rate of interest at which the optimality condition $r = g$ holds is, then, the risk-free rate of interest at which the government can borrow. In this section, we replace these two assumptions by a more general framework, such that the assumptions that we have hitherto made are merely special cases. In this more general framework, the Golden Rules of accumulation and of lifetime utility no longer hold in their previous form. The new "Golden Rule" is somewhat more complicated than the prior ones. Nonetheless, the variable r retains its prior meaning: It is still the risk-free rate of interest at which the government can borrow.

One motivation for this generalization is the criticism of the monetary policy of the ECB that is often heard in Germany. The ECB is often accused of distorting the interest rate downwards by way of an expansionary monetary policy. Thus, the market rates are alleged to be lower than the interest rate corresponding to full-employment equilibrium in the real economy. Another way of formulating this is that due to ECB policy, the interest rate has fallen to a level that is lower than the internal rate of return on currently foregoing consumption in favor of increased future consumption. In the spirit of this critical motivation, the reader may conceive the bias parameter β_1 to be introduced momentarily as positive. Nonetheless, the formal apparatus we are introducing also works with negative bias parameters. We are carrying out this analysis, because it shows that our approach does not depend on the assumption that the rate of interest r is a correct price signal in both the production sector and the consumption sector.

We now introduce a bias parameter β_1 for the production sector. In order to use it rationally for modeling purposes, we first need, in purely formal terms, to redefine our variable w. We define it as follows:

$$w(r; \theta) = y - (r + \beta_1)v(r; \theta)$$

The variable w is thus the surplus of the total product per labor year above $(r + \beta_1)$-times the capital employed. The expression $(r + \beta_1)$ is the internal rate of return on a deviation from the steady state by way of a small (infinitesimal) current foregoing of consumption in favor of additional future consumption, like we presented in the last section. Without a price signal bias, this internal rate of return would be exactly equal to r. The bias parameter is thus the exact difference between what the interest rate should be signaling and its actual value.

To the extent that there is no bias ($\beta_1 = 0$), w also stands for the flow of all other income: i.e., all income apart from risk-free capital income. If β_1 is positive, then the risk-free capital income per unit of capital is less than the internal rate of return on a current marginal foregoing of consumption. Accordingly, at macroeconomically constant returns to scale, the income of all factors of production apart from capital is greater than the combined "marginal product" of all factors of production apart from capital. Conversely, if β_1 is negative, at macroeconomically constant returns to scale, the income of all factors of production apart from capital is less than the combined "marginal product" of all factors of production apart from capital. At macroeconomically constant returns to scale, the modified expression w $(r; \theta) = y - (r + \beta_1)v(r; \theta)$ represents the combined "marginal product" of all factors of production apart from capital.

Using this generalized definition of the surplus w, we now introduce the following assumption, which gives expression to the price-signal bias of the interest rate:

> **Assumption 2-Beta** For every rate of interest r and all $\theta \in Theta$, $w(r; \theta(r + \beta_1)) \geq w(r; \theta)$ holds.

This assumption means that the price signal r is biased precisely in the sense that the "marginal productivity of capital" is β_1 greater than the interest rate r. If $\beta_1 = 2\%$ per year, then an interest rate of 0%, for example, signals that a production technique is being used that would correspond to an interest rate of 2% per year without bias.

If φ is the marginal product of capital and we give the production technique $\theta(\varphi)$ the name φ, then the equation

$$\frac{\partial w(r; \theta(r + \beta_1))}{\partial \theta} = 0$$

follows from our Assumption 2-Beta.

Let us again consider the equation

$$c(\theta) + gv(r; \theta) = w(r; \theta) + (r + \beta_1)v(r; \theta)$$

By way of partial differentiation with respect to θ, we have then in general

$$\frac{dc}{d\theta} + g\frac{\partial v(r; \theta)}{\partial \theta} = \frac{\partial w}{\partial \theta} + (r + \beta_1)\frac{\partial v(r; \theta)}{\partial \theta}$$

From this, we can calculate, in an analogous manner to our procedure in Sect. 2.4, that the marginal productivity of capital is given by the equation

$$\varphi = r + \beta_1$$

Let θ^* be the steady state production technique from the set *Theta* that maximizes consumption per labor year in the steady state. Let there be only one such θ^*. It is only here, then, that we obtain the result

$$\frac{dc}{d\theta} = 0.$$

Moreover, due to Assumption 2-Beta, at $\theta = (r + \beta_1)$, the partial derivative is

$$\frac{\partial w}{\partial \theta} = 0.$$

Thus, for $\theta = (r + \beta_1)$, we obtain the equation

$$\frac{dc}{d\theta} + g\frac{\partial v(r;\theta)}{\partial \theta} = 0 + (r+\beta_1)\frac{\partial v(r;\theta)}{\partial \theta}$$

We assume that

$$\frac{\partial v(r;\theta)}{\partial \theta} \neq 0.$$

For $r + \beta_1 = g$, this gives

$$\frac{dc}{d\theta} = 0.$$

And for every value $r + \beta_1 \neq g$,

$$\frac{dc}{d\theta} \neq 0$$

holds.

The optimal steady-state rate of interest for the maximization of steady-state consumption per labor year is thus given by the equation

$$r = g - \beta_1.$$

For this optimum, moreover, we can note that

$$w = c(\theta^*) + gv(g-\beta_1;\theta^*) - gv(g-\beta_1;\theta^*) = c(\theta^*)$$

Thus, in the steady state optimum, the combined "marginal product" of all factors of production apart from capital is equal to consumption in the economy as whole—so long as there are macroeconomically constant returns to scale.

If we are interested in the maximization of the lifetime utility U of the representative household, then we also have to take into account the interest rate as a price signal in the consumption sector. In Sect. 4.1.5 of Chap. 4 on real capital, we propose the introduction of a coefficient of intertemporal substitution. The latter can be defined for both the production sector and the consumption sector. We call it ψ for the production sector and γ for the consumption sector. Drawing on Weizsäcker (2021), we show in Sect. 4.1.6 that the percentage loss in welfare Ω brought about by a deviation of the empirical interest rate from its lifetime utility-maximizing value g can be roughly calculated using the formula

$$\Omega = (\psi T^2 + \gamma Z^2)(r-g)^2/2.$$

This formula holds, if the rate of interest is a correct price signal in both the production sector and the consumption sector, since in that case, the optimal rate of interest is the same in both sectors: namely, g.

In Weizsäcker (2021), we demonstrate an approximation formula for the optimal compromise between the sector-optimal rate of interest $r = g - \beta_1$ in the production sector and the sector-optimal rate of interest $r = g$ in the consumption sector. It is assumed here that the interest rate represents a correct price signal for intertemporal consumption decisions.

We can arrive at a good approximation of the optimal compromise $r*$ between the rate of interest $r = g - \beta_1$ and the rate of interest $r = g$ by using the following formula

$$r^* = \frac{\psi T^2}{\psi T^2 + \gamma Z^2}(g - \beta_1) + \frac{\gamma Z^2}{\psi T^2 + \gamma Z^2}g.$$

$r*$ is thus a weighted average of $g - \beta_1$ and g, whereby the weights correspond to the percentage contributions of the respective sectors to the overall percentage loss Ω that results, provided the sectoral rates are correct price signals on both sides, when the rate of interest r deviates from its optimal value g.

On our empirical estimate, the "waiting period" Z is at least double the period of production T. Moreover, the coefficient of intertemporal substitution γ is at least equal to ψ. Since T and Z enter into the weighting formula for $r*$ with their squares, the weight of g, even at $\psi = \gamma$ and a value of $Z = 2T$, would be approximately four times greater than the weight of $g - \beta_1$. Hence, the optimal compromise rate of interest $r*$ is considerably closer to g than to $g - \beta_1$. At $\psi = \gamma$ and $Z = 2T$, we get the equation

$$r^* = \frac{1}{5}(g - \beta_1) + \frac{4}{5}g.$$

2.11   Calibrating Welfare Losses for $r \neq g$: An Example

In Chap. 3, Sect. 3.9 of Weizsäcker (2021) we have given a calibration of the steady state loss in welfare that would occur if one pursued a policy of zero public debt. The maximum welfare is achieved at a rate of interest equal to the rate of growth, as we have shown above. Using the approximation formula for welfare loss

$$\Omega = (\psi T^2 + \gamma Z^2)(r - g)^2/2$$

and using the empirical results later to be described in the present volume (Chaps. 4, 5, and 6), we have developed methods to obtain estimates of the parameters of this equation. We assume the natural rate of interest to be $\rho = -2\%$ per year. This is not really an estimate, because we believe that it is impossible to know how far into the negative the natural rate will plunge. Saving and investment behavior changes completely once people are faced with substantial inflation and still a zero nominal rate of interest. Thus ρ may in fact be far below -2% per year.

At a steady-state rate of growth of 3% per year for the OECD + China region, we then can work with a difference between g and ρ of 5% per year. Using our empirical work, we have the following values at $r = g$: 10 years for the waiting period and 4 years for the period of production. Using the Solow production function and the fact that the capital-output ratio does not exhibit any trend over more than a century leads us to the conclusion that ψ has a value of approximately 1. The established empirical work on intertemporal substitution in the consumption sector allows us to derive the inequality $\gamma \geq \psi$. To be on the safe side, we assume $\gamma = \psi = 1$. In that case, the value of Ω would be 29%.

If we assume $\gamma = 1.5$ instead, we obtain a value $\Omega = 41.5\%$.

This estimate of the percentage welfare loss at an annual real rate of interest of -2% ignores the additional problem that it would then be much more difficult to obtain and maintain full employment: The central bank cannot overcome the Keynesian liquidity trap.

2.12 Conclusion

In this chapter, we have shown that by using a steady-state analysis, we can work out connections between saving and investment that can help us to understand secular trends in the natural rate of interest. We have tried here to get by with just a few assumptions representing sufficient conditions for the derived "Golden Rules." It has proven to be fruitful to relate private saving to the "waiting period" Z and to relate investment to Böhm-Bawerk's period of production as modernized by Hicks or T. We have just given an example of what occurs if we deviate from the assumption that the risk-free interest rate r is a correct price signal for intertemporal production decisions (investment decisions). We will discuss further deviations from the assumptions of the steady-state model in subsequent chapters. For the purpose of understanding public debt, it is interesting to note that the steady-state optimum ($r = g$) entails the equality of the overall economic waiting period $Z - D$ and the overall economic period of production T. Generalizing findings of Diamond (1965), we can say that public debt serves here to bring about this equality. The following is also of interest: Since the natural rate of interest ρ is nowadays far lower than the growth rate, Samuelson's Golden Rule is far more important in quantitative terms than the Phelps-Weizsäcker Golden Rule. It is a mistake that Samuelson's Golden Rule is hardly taken into account in contemporary economic theory.

References

Abel, Andrew B., N. Gregory Mankiw, Lawrence Summers and Richard Zeckhauser.1989. Assessing Dynamic Efficiency: Theory and Evidence. *Review of Economic Studies* 56 (1): 1-19.
Böhm-Bawerk, Eugen Ritter von. 1891 [1889]. *The Positive Theory of Capital*, trans. William Smart. London and New York: Macmillan.
Diamond, Peter A. 1965. National Debt in a Neoclassical Growth Model. *American Economic Review* 55 (5): 1126-1150.
Geerolf, Francois. 2018. *Reassessing Dynamic Efficiency*. Manuscript UCLA.
Hicks, John R. 1939. *Value and Capital*. Oxford: Clarendon Press.

Keynes, John Maynard. 1936. *The General Theory of Employment, Interest and Money*. London: Macmillan.

Marx, Karl. 1976 [1867]. *Capital: A Critique of Political Economy*, vol. 1, trans. Ben Fowkes. London: Penguin/New Left Books.

Phelps, Edmund S. 1961. The Golden Rule of Capital Accumulation. *American Economic Review* 51 (4): 638-643.

Rachel, Lukasz and Lawrence H. Summers. 2019. On Falling Neutral Real Rates, Fiscal Policy, and the Risk of Secular Stagnation. *Brookings Papers on Economic Activity* March 4: 1-66.

Samuelson, Paul A. 1958. An Exact Consumption-Loan Model of Interest with or without the Social Contrivance of Money. *Journal of Political Economy* 66 (6): 467-482.

Samuelson, Paul A. 1959a. A Modern Treatment of the Ricardian Economy I: The Pricing of Goods and of Labor and Land Services. *Quarterly Journal of Economics* 73 (1): 1-35.

Samuelson, Paul A. 1959b. A Modern Treatment of the Ricardian Economy II: Capital and Interest Aspects of the Pricing Process. *Quarterly Journal of Economics* 73 (2): 217-231.

Schnabl, Gunther. 2019. Central Banking and Crisis Management from the Perspective of Austrian Business Cycle Theory. In *The Oxford Handbook of the Economics of Central Banking 2019*, eds. David G. Mayes, Pierre L. Siklos and Jan-Egbert Sturm, 551-584. Oxford: Oxford University Press.

Schumpeter, Joseph. A. 1934 [1911]. *The Theory of Economic Development*, trans. Redvers Opie. Cambridge, MA: Harvard University Press.

Solow, Robert M. 1956. A Contribution to the Theory of Economic Growth. *Quarterly Journal of Economics* 70 (1): 65-94.

Solow, Robert M. 1957. Technical Change and the Aggregate Production Function. *Review of Economics and Statistics* 39 (3): 312-320.

Solow, Robert M. 1963. *Capital Theory and the Rate of Return*. De Vries Lectures. Amsterdam: North-Holland.

Solow, Robert M., James Tobin, Carl Christian von Weizsäcker und Menahem Yaari. 1966. Neoclassical Growth with Fixed Factor Proportions. *Review of Economic Studies* XXXIII (2): 79–115.

Weizsäcker, Carl Christian von. 1961. *Wachstum, Zins und optimale Investitionsquote*. Dissertation, Universität Basel. Published as: Weizsäcker, Carl Christian von. 1962. *Wachstum, Zins und optimale Investitionsquote*. Tübingen: Mohr-Siebeck.

Weizsäcker, Carl Christian von. 1971. *Steady State Capital Theory*. Heidelberg: Springer.

Weizsäcker, Carl Christian von. 2021. *Capital Theory of the Steady State – Or: T+L = Z–D*. https://www.coll.mpg.de/Weizsaecker/CapitalTheory2021 and https://www.springer.com/9783658273620.

Wicksell, Knut. 1936 [1898]. *Interest and Prices: A Study of the Causes Regulating the Value of Money*, trans. R. F. Kahn. London: Macmillan.

Yared, Pierre. 2019. Rising Government Debt: Causes and Solutions for a Decades Old Trend. *Journal of Economic Perspectives* 33 (2): 115-140.

Wealth and Desired Wealth

3

Abstract

With increasing general prosperity, desired wealth increases faster than current consumption. There is thus a secular tendency for the "waiting period" Z to grow. This is already the case for demographic reasons that hold for the global population as a whole. The proportion of the global population living in absolute poverty is rapidly declining. A monetary system offering stable purchasing power represents an important contribution of society to facilitating adequate private provision for the future. The "savings triangle" is a highly simplified, but neat representation of these interrelationships. It offers a good approximation of the facts.

3.1 The Concept of Desired Wealth

Other things being equal, most people prefer more wealth to less wealth. But when we speak of "desired wealth," we mean something else. Let us assume that individual A has a given intertemporal budget for consumption purposes at his or her disposal and that this budget consists of initial wealth and expected labor income. Let us assume, furthermore, that the individual is confronted by certain returns on invested wealth. This individual decides then on a given *work and consumption plan η*. We also speak here of a *life plan*. We can now ask: How does the wealth of this individual evolve in connection with the life plan η that he or she has chosen? The values that are thus derived for the individual's wealth are what we call the "desired wealth."

The concept of desired wealth thus always involves the individual's awareness that there is a trade-off between consumption at different points in time. If you want to consume more today, then this comes at the cost of future consumption or at the

© The Author(s) 2021
C. C. von Weizsäcker and H. M. Krämer, *Saving and Investment in the Twenty-First Century*, https://doi.org/10.1007/978-3-030-75031-2_3

cost of future leisure. This understanding of desired wealth corresponds to the usual neoclassical explanatory scheme for consumption and saving behavior.

For a closed economy, we can state the following: Desired wealth has always to be distinguished from actual private wealth; but in full-employment equilibrium, it must be the case that aggregate desired private wealth and aggregate actual private wealth are equal. This statement corresponds to the more common formulation that in macroeconomic, full-employment equilibrium, "voluntary" or "planned" investment must be equal to "voluntary" or "planned" saving in the economy as a whole. It is not, however, identical to the latter, since, on the one hand, we are speaking of desired *private* wealth and actual *private* wealth, but, on the other, of *overall* investment and saving.

The reason why we speak of desired wealth, instead of saving, and of actual wealth, instead of investment, is connected to our approach. We primarily consider steady states, in order to make use of the clarity of the steady state's intertemporal relationships. In addition, we distinguish between the private sector and the state. If the state is a net borrower, the wealth of private persons is greater than national wealth. In this case, the desired wealth of private persons can also exceed national wealth.

The main thesis of this book is that a free economic and social order can only be stabilized in the twenty-first century if private persons are accorded their desired level of wealth under conditions of price stability—and that this is not possible without considerable net public debt.

The derivation of this main thesis only succeeds if we work with the stock variables "wealth" and "desired wealth," from which the flow variables "saving" and "investment" are then derived.

3.2 Demographics: The Example of the Savings Triangle

A simple example for deriving desired wealth is the "savings triangle." Although we are aware that the assumptions for deriving the savings triangle involve an extreme simplification of people's actual arrangements for their futures, we develop this example, because it makes the influence that demographic conditions have on desired wealth particularly clear. Moreover, it has the additional benefit of fitting the facts of a country like Germany quite well (see Sect. 3.3).

Let us consider an individual who expects to live $a + b$ years as an adult. Here, a is the length of time in which the individual earns money by working. The length of time b is the subsequent period of retirement. In order to be able to finance consumption during retirement, the individual has to amass savings during the length of time a: i.e., to accumulate wealth. In order to simplify the presentation, let us assume that, firstly, the annual labor income remains constant (equals $\hat{w}$), that, secondly, the individual wants to distribute consumption equally over his or her entire lifetime (consumption per year $= \hat{c}$), and that, thirdly, the rate of interest is zero. We should note, however, that the same result is obtained, if labor income and consumption increase at the rate g per year and the rate of interest is $r = g$.

It is evident that

$$\hat{c} = \frac{a}{a+b}\hat{w}$$

then applies.

During the length of time until a, the individual annually saves the amount

$$\hat{s} = \frac{b}{a+b}\hat{w} = \frac{b}{a}\hat{c}.$$

For $0 \leq t \leq a$, this gives an evolution of wealth

$$\hat{v}(t) = \frac{bt}{a}\hat{c}$$

and for $a \leq t \leq a + b$,

$$\hat{v}(t) = (b + a - t)\hat{c}.$$

Averaged over the whole adult life of the individual, we obtain "average wealth" $\bar{v}$

$$\bar{v} = \frac{a}{a+b}\frac{b}{a}\frac{a}{2}\hat{c} + \frac{b}{a+b}\frac{b}{2}\hat{c} = \frac{b}{2}\hat{c}.$$

The ratio between intertemporal average wealth $\bar{v}$ and annual consumption $\hat{c}$ is thereby given through half of the retirement period. This is, however, precisely the waiting period $Z = b/2$. The waiting period is the average time lag between labor income and consumption expenditure. The temporal "center of gravity" of labor income is at $a/2$. The temporal "center of gravity" of consumption expenditure is at $(a + b)/2$. The average time lag between income and expenditure is thus

$$\frac{a+b}{2} - \frac{a}{2} = \frac{b}{2}.$$

If, for a population in a steady state, we now consider this steady-state economy as a whole with overlapping generations that are all of this same sort, then the per capita wealth of the population is equal to the above-calculated current average wealth of an individual during his or her lifetime. This is a simple example of the result derived in Chap. 2: At a rate of interest $r = g$, per capita wealth is equal to the waiting period Z times consumption per capita (Fig. 3.1).

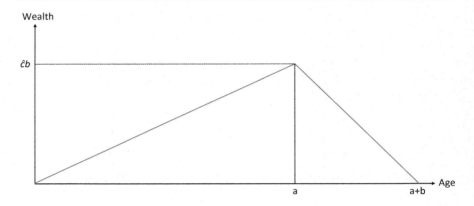

Fig. 3.1 The savings triangle. *Source* Author's own presentation

The wealth of the individual age cohorts or the evolution of the wealth of an individual person during his or her different stages of life can also be graphically represented. This brings us to the savings triangle.

It is clear that the average height of the red line between 0 and $a + b$ is equal to $\hat{c}b/2$.

3.3   The Savings Triangle Closely Fits the Saving Rate of the Members of the German Social Security System

Although this model is a gross simplification of reality, consider the following facts as regards Germany.

We can assume that the average length of time that compulsory participants in the social security system remain in the active labor force is not more than 40 years. So, to be on the safe side, let us here postulate 40 years. The average length of time that social security beneficiaries are paid retirement benefits is today around 20 years and the tendency is rising. As a rule of thumb, we can thus say that for this group of people, the ratio b/a is around ½. In our simple model, this gives a value $b/(a + b) = 1/3$ for the saving rate during an employee's active working life.

It is interesting to note that this value roughly corresponds to the actual value for Germany. The conventionally measured saving rate of employees enrolled in Germany's social security system is just under ten percent. This is "voluntary" saving. The employee and employer contributions to what is known as the Statutory Retirement Insurance—in other words, the public retirement plan—have to be added to the latter. These contributions currently represent between 18 and 19% of the gross wage. A not inconsiderable part of contributions to the Statutory Health Insurance—viz., Germany's public health care plan—must also be included as de facto saving. As is well known, the public health insurance providers generate a high contribution surplus among active employees, which serves to compensate for the contribution deficit among retirees. This contribution surplus in the Statutory Health Insurance can be seen as analogous to old-age provisions in private health insurance, which likewise have to be interpreted as a form of saving on the part of the insured. For the details, see Sect. 6.2. Finally, public nursing care insurance is also to a very large extent to be regarded as a form of saving, since the contributions of younger people to nursing care insurance far exceed the contemporaneous claims made on it within the age cohort. Details on this matter are likewise to be found in Sect. 6.2.

If we add together these items, we get a saving rate of at least one-third. Here, we have to put the following in the denominator: gross wage income minus income tax and minus the employee contribution to the Statutory Health Insurance and plus the employer contribution to the Statutory Retirement Insurance. This is the "real" net wage income of the employee. Income tax is obviously not part of it. But the contribution to the Statutory Health Insurance is also a "tax," since its amount has nothing to do with a premium calculated using actuarial methods. Along with the employer's contribution to the Statutory Health Insurance, it is, for all intents and purposes, a second income tax. On the other hand, the employer contribution to the retirement plan is a (tax-free) form of saving for the employee, which, in accordance with Germany's retirement benefits formula, results in greater benefits. Depending on the level of the (average) income tax rate, this corrected net wage payment is higher or lower than the gross wage. The overall deviation from the gross wage for all employees is, on average, relatively small.

3.4 The Law of Increasing Relative Desired Wealth

Formulated very generally, we can put forward the following empirically robust proposition:

> The Law of Increasing Relative Desired Wealth: With increasing general prosperity, desired wealth increases faster than current consumption.

We can, in particular, make the following three observations: 1. In every national economy, in a given year, the conventionally measured saving rate of individual households rises with annual household income (cross-sectional analysis). 2. With rising average prosperity over time and, consequently, rising life expectancy, the time during which retirement benefits are drawn rises considerably faster than the duration of an employee's active working life. In the language of the above example: b/a rises with increasing national wealth and rising life expectancy. For most OECD countries, the ratio b/a is today about twice what it was a half century ago (trend analysis). 3. As concerns conventionally measured wealth, the share that is left as inheritance also rises with rising prosperity.

In the following sections, we will discuss the second point (demographics) and the third point (inheritance). The cross-sectional import of the first point is obvious.

3.5 Demographics: The Third Stage of Life Is Increasing Around the World

Provision for retirement age is greatly increasing. In Germany, for instance, life expectancy has risen by around 10 years in the last half century. Parallel to this rise, the length of time during which retirees draw benefits from the Statutory Retirement Insurance has likewise risen by around 10 years. This is to say that the b in our simple example has doubled, whereas the a has remained more-or-less constant.

We can expect a further increase in life expectancy in the future: both around the world and in the OECD plus China region. Figure 3.2 is taken from the latest world population forecast of the United Nations. If we can assume, in keeping with the trends observed up to now, that by the end of the twenty-first century, many of what are today developing countries will also figure among the "rich" countries, then the UN forecast of continued growth in life expectancy suggests that the third stage of life b will also continue to increase on average worldwide. If we assume, on the "model" of Germany in the last half century, that one hundred percent of the further rise in life expectancy will be used for extending the third stage of life, then life-stage b will grow by around 12 years by 2100 on the global average.

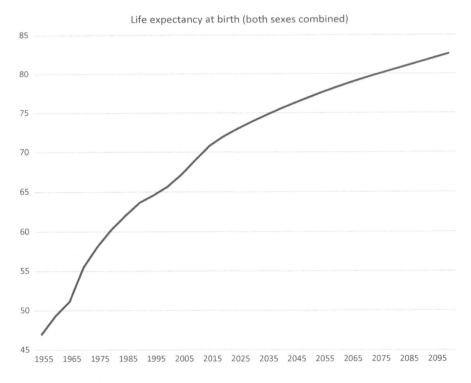

Fig. 3.2 Life expectancy of the world population. *Source* United Nations DESA/Population Division, World Population Prospects 2017

Of course, it is possible to have doubts about whether the "use" of rising life expectancy will entirely consist of extending the third life-stage. In Germany and many other OECD member states, there are often calls for people to work longer, in order to avoid overburdening the welfare state. This is a reasonable demand, but up to now an unpopular one. For this reason alone, an increase in the length of active working life in parallel to the rise in life expectancy is not to be expected. On average, the value of b will rise globally.

The answer to the question of how much b will rise depends in large measure on the further evolution of the institutional conditions. But the latter are subject to the vagaries of politics. In order to provide recommendations to policymakers in this regard, it is interesting for economists to engage in a thought experiment. We should ask the following question: On average, when do people want to retire, if, firstly, the social security system gives them the freedom to decide the point in time when they retire and if, secondly, it offers them retirement benefits that have been correctly calculated using actuarial methods as a function of their contributions. We are not able to answer this question here. Theoretical and empirical research on the issue would thus be useful.

We want merely to call attention to one point that affects all countries. It can be formulated as a question: How, on average, is the "*disutility of labor*" evolving in the population? There are prominent economists, like, for instance, Edmund Phelps, who complain that economic growth is lower today than it was in the past (Phelps 2013). Phelps explains this by massively increased "corporatism." Nonetheless, we have to ask whether we have a correct measure of economic growth. Or could it be that our measure leaves out or only partially includes an important characteristic of social progress: namely, the "quality" of jobs?

Decades ago already, Robert Solow observed, "You can see the computer age everywhere but in the productivity statistics" (Solow 1987). In light of the current, virtually universal debate on digitalization, this quote is more relevant than ever. Does the progress obtained by humanity from the trend toward digitalization lie, above all, in the fact that the average "disutility of labor" has decreased and will continue to decrease? According to the neoclassical calculation, voluntary work for pay will continue up to the point at which an additional hour of paid labor brings about a negative marginal utility whose amount is equal to the additional marginal utility of consumption from the wage for this labor. This negative marginal utility is described as the "marginal disutility of labor."

Now, we can observe that there is a secular tendency for the share of paid labor-time in people's lifetimes to decrease. This fact alone suggests that the overall disutility of labor is considerably lower today than it was in the past. But indicators like work-related accidents and illnesses also suggest that the disutility of labor has become less significant. Therefore, it may be that nowadays a larger part of the annual growth in welfare is yielded in the form of a reduction in the disutility of labor. This could mean that, taking into account this effect, growth in rich countries has not decreased, but merely changed its form. The measured decline in growth could be based then on an error in the definition of what is to be understood by "growth."

We bring up this question in connection with our main thesis, because the secular decrease in the disutility of labor could also lead to people persistently wanting indeed to work until a more advanced age. This would have a dampening effect on the further growth of b.

Economists who are worried about the stability of public finances propose that the statutory retirement age should be raised in proportion to the rise in the life expectancy of social security beneficiaries, such that the coefficient b/a remains constant. If this recommendation were to be put into practice, the saving rate of employees in our savings triangle example would remain constant at $b/(a + b)$. The contributions of employers and employees to the retirement plan would not have to rise in relation to the net wage defined above. Nonetheless, even in this case, rising life expectancy means that the ratio of retirement-related desired wealth to current consumption will continue to rise in parallel to the rise in life expectancy. This ratio is, after all, given by the value $b/2$. In other words, even if the rate at which employees save for retirement purposes remains constant, with the greater length of active working life (i.e., in our savings triangle model, with rising a), the ratio between average wealth during a lifetime and current consumption rises.

The thesis of rising desired wealth for retirement purposes in relation to current consumption is thus secure, even if the call for not reducing the share of active working life in total adult life should prevail.

> The rising life expectancy of the global population is thus the robust demographic cause for the increase in desired wealth for retirement purposes in relation to current consumption.

Here, we should mention an idea that often gets expressed, but that involves a structural error. The rising coefficient between "elderly" and "active" is frequently attributed to the gradual passage of "baby boomers" into retirement. On this account, the age coefficient will later fall again when a balanced age structure is restored. With a given average life expectancy, this analysis is correct. In the meanwhile, however, life expectancy is continuing to rise. Therefore, we cannot realistically expect a return to the status quo ante of the elderly/active coefficient. The three dominant factors influencing this coefficient are life expectancy, the average retirement age and the growth rate of the population. We will come back to this last factor in Chap. 12.

3.6 The Inheritance of Wealth

Continuing our simple example on retirement planning, we can connect the motive of transmitting an inheritance and desired wealth. We again assume a steady-state economy and consider an individual who expects to earn money by working a years and to be a retiree for b years. He or she tries to distribute consumption equally over the lifetime $a + b$. As before, the annual wage $\hat{w}$ is constant and the rate of interest is zero. In contrast to the previous example, this individual can expect an inheritance corresponding to e years of consumption. The individual wants, however, to leave the same amount to his or her heirs.

Thus, consumption per year remains at the same level as without any inheritance motive. The average wealth is, however, simply increased by the amount of the inheritance, i.e.,

$$\overline{v} = \frac{b}{2}\hat{c} + e\hat{c} = \left(\frac{b}{2} + e\right)\hat{c}.$$

It is again the case that the calculation remains valid, if annual income and annual consumption grow at the rate g, the rate of interest is $r = g$, and the planned inheritance likewise grows proportionally with annual consumption. Here too, we can speak of a "waiting period" $Z = b/2 + e$. In this respect, we can theoretically apply the "First In—First Out" principle to the individual's wealth: Current consumption expenditure is always financed by the financial resources that have been available the longest. Thus, the consumption expenditure of individual A in the first e years is assigned to the labor performed by the testator, whereas, on the other hand, the first e years of the consumption of the heir of individual A are assigned to the labor income of individual A. The temporal "center of gravity" of the labor performed by individual A is thereby $a/2$, as before, whereas the temporal "center of gravity" of the consumption expenditure assigned to the related labor income is now $(a + b)/2 + e$, since it is now a matter of consumption expenditure between time e and time $a + b + e$. The difference between these two centers of gravity is thus $Z = b/2 + e$.

More generally speaking, the motive of leaving wealth to one's heirs is part of the future-directedness of human action. Our theory is thus a version of the hypothesis of an increasing future-directedness of human action as prosperity increases. We will come back to this hypothesis momentarily.

Before we do, however, we would like, in connection with the inheritance motive for desired wealth, to point to the *interdependence between the inheritance motive and the motive of risk planning*. In our simple example, we assumed that individual A can foretell the moment of his or her death. Needless to say, this is unrealistic. In modern society, there is, however, the institution of life insurance and, more specifically, the availability of life annuities serving as a kind of "longevity insurance." The annuity paid by the life insurance company treats the purchasers of such insurance, with regard to their annual consumption for their age, as if the time of their death corresponds to the average for their age cohort. The insurance provider is able to do this by internalizing the balancing of risk among them. The conclusion of a life annuity contract is, however, tied to considerable "transaction costs" for the purchaser. The insurance provider can only continue to exist, if, from the premiums paid in, it is able to obtain a considerable actuarial surplus over the annuities paid out. This surplus is needed to cover the provider's administrative and acquisition costs. As consequence, the premiums that have to be paid are considerably greater than the expected value of the annuities. There is thus a strong incentive to do without this type of risk protection: all the more so inasmuch as there is another form of protection against the risk of longevity, which we will discuss now.

It has always been the case—and hence was already the case even before there were life insurance companies—that an individual A who wanted to leave an inheritance to his or her descendants could make the potential heir into an implicit or explicit life annuity insurer. When individual A creates a risk cushion, he or she does not pay too dearly, since, to the extent that it is not used, the wealth thus amassed can be bequeathed as an inheritance. The use of the inheritance mitigates the testator's own sacrifice in foregoing consumption to build up a cushion against the risk of longevity. The longevity risk is borne by the heir.

In the social strata in which the inheritance of wealth is customary, there has thus existed for ages an implicit intra-family, but intergenerational longevity insurance in the form of an implicit life annuity for the testator.

3.7 With Increasing Prosperity, the Future-Directedness of Human Action Increases

We now return to the *thesis of the increasing future-directedness of human action as prosperity increases.* This thesis has strong anthropological support. In the animal kingdom, there is an instinctually anchored, limited future-directedness. The drives or instincts—like hunger and thirst, like the sex drive, like nest-building or, in other words, the rearing of immediate descendants—fulfill the function of preserving the species. Thanks to its cognitive abilities and the ability to pursue more distant goals that is based on the latter, as well as thanks to its differentiated language-based ability to cooperate, Homo sapiens has far greater possibilities for acting in a future-directed way. Unlike animals, Homo sapiens can elaborate means in the present that enable it, beyond its instinctual life, to pursue aims in the distant future.

Thousands of years ago, the first "Great Transformation" from the Stone Age hunter-gatherer society to agrarian society took place. In the latter, available land was used far more productively than before. This was accompanied by a further reinforcement of human future-directedness. New forms of social coexistence came into being. In particular, the common lands that were intensively used in agriculture were transformed into objects with strictly limited possibilities of access: the "property rights" of the Property Rights School. Their main function consisted in the fact that with this altered legal structure, far greater agricultural output could be achieved, which, however, for the most part required a longer period of "waiting." The natural processes of maturation of crops and domesticated animals were used to obtain high net yields. But this maturation required time. Furthermore, one had to adjust to the seasons, since the yields were largely obtained in a different season than the need for them as food. It was thus necessary to maintain considerable stocks—and to take measures to ensure that they did not spoil too soon. In addition, agricultural equipment, pack and draft animals, and often also buildings were needed, in order productively to cultivate the land. Hence, in comparison to the earlier society of hunters and gatherers, there was an increase in the average time lag between the expenditure of labor and the use of the agricultural products generated by it.

But an additional consequence of this first "Great Transformation" was that the massive rise in agricultural output was accompanied by rapid population growth. Hence, the standard of living rose far less than agricultural output. Considerably more people now had to be fed per cultivated unit of land. In retrospect, the economic anthropologist Marshall Sahlins thus calls the society of hunters and gatherers the "original affluent society," in which the burden of labor was significantly lower than in the subsequent agrarian society (Sahlins). At the same time, the new institutions led to a vertical stratification of many societies. There was increasingly now a difference between rich and poor, between landowners and those who worked the land, between nobles, bourgeois and slaves. The ruling upper stratum developed a system of domination whose stabilization required long-term thinking and action. The rule of some over others—often also in ideologically distorted form—was legitimated by, among other things, the idea that the ruling class was able to think and act in the long term, whereas the subjects and, above all, the slaves could not. The predominant religion in each society likewise served to stabilize the vertical status quo. The articles of faith suggested by it made this-worldly action susceptible to punishment by way of other-worldly sanctions: hence, sanctions in a distant future.

Up until industrialization, the standard of living of the vast majority of people remained close to the subsistence minimum. A monetary and credit system had, however, already emerged in classical antiquity. This system made it possible to amass wealth without having to acquire tangible assets to the same extent in the form of means of production. The difference between "saving" and "investment" thus became relevant. For many people, this facilitated an economic orientation toward the future.

Along with the Industrial Revolution or, as Karl Polanyi called it, the "Great Transformation," "modernity" developed (Polanyi 1944). The latter is characterized by a constantly increasing division of labor. Here, it is worth citing the—as it were —"prophetic" opening sentence of *The Wealth of Nations*: "The greatest improvement in the productive powers of labour, and the greater part of the skill, dexterity, and judgement with which it is anywhere directed, or applied, seem to have been the effects of the division of labour" (Smith 1776, I.i.1). Karl Marx would later describe this process of gradual differentiation of human production activities as the "socialization of labor" (Marx and Engels 1967 [1848]; Marx 1976 [1867]).

Max Weber was also fascinated by this historical process of modernity. He subsumed it under the law of increasing societal rationalization. His thesis of religiously motivated "inner-worldly asceticism" as the basis of the capitalist economic system captures both aspects: the increasing rationality and the increasing future-directedness of social—and especially, economic—action. Growing calculability goes together with increasing future-directedness, which is manifest in the dynamic of the capitalist saving and investment process (Weber 1992 [1904–05]).

In Marx, we find the exhortation: "Accumulate, accumulate! That is Moses and the prophets!" (Marx 1976 [1867], p. 742). In *Capital*, he justifies this motto of the capitalist class as an inescapable norm, which is imposed on the individual capitalist by competition on the market. The idea of—to use the modern expression—increasing returns to scale already lies behind Marx's argument. As a structural feature of modernity, economic competition (or competition per se: also in intellectual life, in school, in politics, in the most intimate parts of the private sphere) compels individuals to adopt an orientation toward the future when the absence of such an orientation would lead to their downfall.

3.8 Overcoming Poverty Leads to Increasing Future-Directedness

There is a powerful obstacle to the future-directedness of individual action that is commonly designated by the term "poverty." For future-directed action only makes sense if you can expect also to live to experience the future in question. If an individual A does not save, this is not necessarily an indication of unwillingness to make provision for the future. Effective provision for the future is determined by two factors: firstly, the desire to make provision for the future and, secondly, the real possibilities of doing so. An aspect of such real possibilities is that you are very likely also to live to experience this future. To make arrangements for a future that you are highly likely never to experience is not rational. Hence, failing to make such arrangements is not in and of itself an indication that the desire to make provision for the future is lacking.

It thus also becomes clear, however, that we cannot expect an individual A who is barely surviving on the subsistence minimum to "set aside" much for the future. It is not rational to make provision for the future, if by making such provision, you put your present at risk. We do not want to go into detail about this here, but we recommend reading the book *Poor Economics* by Banerjee and Duflo (2011).

We can thus formulate the following "on average" statement: As concerns low incomes, effective provision for the future increases as prosperity increases. One reason for this is that with rising income, provision for the future is less and less detrimental to the likelihood of living to experience the future in question.

A second reason is that with rising prosperity, there is an increasing "return" on currently foregoing consumption to provide for one's future. For greater prosperity makes possible better knowledge of the possibilities of providing for one's future.

Furthermore, there are economies of scale in the use of this knowledge. This especially applies to investment of savings.

If we can assume that absolute poverty is an obstacle to saving, then a dramatically rapid fall in the proportion of the global population living in absolute poverty must represent a powerful impetus to increased saving. The classic example for this is China. In 1980 (as a legacy of Mao Zedong's "Cultural Revolution"), three-quarters of China's population was still living in absolute poverty. Nowadays, absolute poverty is practically unknown among the Han Chinese. Of course, this does not completely explain the high average saving of the Chinese population. The fact that a highly unequal distribution of income has come into being in the course of China's tumultuous economic growth has also contributed to the high saving rate.

In the language of conventional demand theory, demand for current consumer goods has an income elasticity of less than one and demand for goods to be consumed in the future has an income elasticity of greater than one.

3.9 The Separation of Saving and Investment Results in Greater Provision for the Future

Given the desire to make provision for the future, effective provision for the future increases with increasing possibilities for making such provision. The separation between saving and investment is highly significant here. The individual A can save without having to invest. He or she can make provision for the future without taking entrepreneurial risks. If society, moreover, offers a currency with stable purchasing power to individual A, then the cognitive demands of rationally planning for the future are not too great. Thus, we derive the following proposition:

> A monetary system offering stable purchasing power represents an important contribution of society to a high degree of individual provision for the future.

Conversely, the financial system frees investors from the limit of only being able to invest at the level of their own savings. Investors can borrow—and they can provide shares of their business to third parties who make financial resources available to them. On both sides—provision for the future through saving and provision for the future through investment—provision for the future is promoted by money with stable purchasing power.

3.10　The Measure *Z* of Relative Effective Provision for the Future

On the ancillary condition of full employment and with a given level of public debt, a balance between wealth and desired wealth is brought about via the level of the interest rate. As usually maintained in economics and as also shown in Chapter 2 on the natural rate of interest, we expect that in a steady state, amassed wealth will be less with a higher interest rate, but desired wealth will be greater. Without public debt, it is via the natural rate of interest that aggregate wealth and aggregate desired wealth are made to match.

The waiting period Z that we have defined provides a measure of relative desired wealth. If the risk-free rate of interest r is equal to the growth rate g, then Z also indicates the ratio between desired wealth and current consumption. Our theory thus amounts to the thesis that with tendentially rising average prosperity, Z also has the tendency to rise.

In Chap. 2, we showed that the equation $Z - D = T$ holds for a steady-state equilibrium with a risk-free rate of interest $r = g$. The optimal rate of interest leads the overall economic period of production and the overall economic waiting period to be the same size.

> It is the "optimal" public debt level D that has to ensure that aggregate desired wealth $Z - D$ and aggregate wealth T balance out.

In the following chapters, we will discuss the three components of private wealth in a closed economy that we have defined. These three components are: firstly, the real capital required for the production process; secondly, the value of land in the economy in question; and, thirdly, the net claims of the private sector on the state.

Why these three components of private wealth? To begin with, let us reiterate two presuppositions. We are considering a very large economic area: the OECD countries plus China. We can show that the net asset position of this area vis-à-vis the rest of the world is small. We will thus not be committing any major error, if we regard this area as a closed economy with respect to net asset positions. Secondly, we are interested in distinguishing between the private sector and the state, since we are primarily concerned with the role of public debt in economic policy. Hence, we need to regard the net claims of the private sector on the state as a category of wealth. The distinction between real capital and land is based on the fact that price formation is very different for these two categories. Real capital derives its value principally from its historical acquisition costs or, respectively, its replacement costs, which under competitive conditions are very closely related to the production costs of the investment goods industry. Depreciation is also based on the empirical values for the useful life of investment goods.

Land prices have an entirely different origin. They correspond to the capitalized present value of future land rents. They are thus dependent, firstly, on the level of these future land rents, but then also upon the interest rates with which the present values are calculated.

We do not consider one economically important form of wealth: namely, human capital. The reason for this is that, apart from a few exceptions, it is not available to third parties as a capital investment object. Within the family, there are wealth transfers—in particular, from parents to children—that promote the formation of human capital. But we forego any attempt to quantify human capital, since the latter is not directly relevant to the capital market.

The private sector includes both households and firms. In the consolidated balance sheet for the private sector, we assign the wealth of firms to the shareholders in proportion to their shares.

3.11 The Assumption of a Closed Economy for the OECD Plus China Economic Area

When we say in this book that the group of countries comprising the OECD members and China represent a closed economy, what we mean is that the exports of the OECD plus China region to the rest of the world are more or less the same size as the imports of the OECD and China area from the rest of the world. Put differently, we start from the assumption that the OECD plus China region has sustainably and on average approximately balanced trade or a balanced current account vis-à-vis the rest of the world. In this case, the OECD plus China region would also have a balanced capital account vis-à-vis the rest of the world. For the reasons already laid out above, we are less interested in flow variables than in stock variables. In an economic area with a balanced current and capital account, the stock of foreign claims is at the same level as the stock of foreign liabilities. In the long term, the OECD plus China region would thus have a net foreign asset position of zero. This assumption is relevant in our present context, because in this case, the level of wealth desired by the citizens of the OECD plus China region can only be achieved within this economic area itself. In what follows, we show why the assumption of a zero net foreign asset position of the OECD plus China region is roughly correct.

As we define it, the OECD plus China region is comprised of 35 countries altogether: including 34 OECD countries and the People's Republic of China.[1] In order to check whether the OECD and China group of countries has balanced trade vis-à-vis the rest of the world, we need, as a first step, to determine the bilateral trade relations of the 35 countries among themselves and of each of them with the rest of the world. For this purpose, we can use data on the global trade in goods and

---

[1]We include all the countries that had joined the OECD by 2015 among the OECD countries. Hence, neither Latvia (accession: 2016) nor Lithuania (accession: 2018) are included in our group of countries.

services of these countries that is provided by the OECD in one of its databases (OECD 2017).[2] The individual country data is then aggregated, in order to be able to derive the trade relations of the OECD plus China group with the rest of the world.[3]

The result of these calculations is represented in Fig. 3.3, which shows the balance of trade of the OECD plus China region with the rest of the world between 1995 and 2011.[4] The balance of trade for each year is given as a percentage of the entire gross domestic product of the region. At the start of the period under consideration, this economic region had a slightly positive balance of trade with the rest of the world of, on average, about 0.5% of gross domestic product. At the end of the 1990s, the balance of trade of the OECD plus China region then became negative. Between 2000 and 2008, the balance oscillated between around − 0.4% and − 0.8% of gross domestic product. During the 2009 global economic crisis, the balance of trade of the region improved for a short time. In 2010, however, it again went into the minuses.

In the period from 1995 to 2011 under consideration here, the negative balance of trade of the OECD plus China region with the rest of the world was, on average, 0.24% of the gross domestic product of this economic area.

Due to the incompleteness of the data, it is not possible to undertake a similar analysis of the net foreign asset position of the OECD plus China region vis-à-vis the rest of the world, using a procedure analogous to that used in the calculation of the balance of trade. The International Monetary Fund (IMF 2017) makes available data on the net foreign asset position of each member country; the data is not broken down by individual target countries or countries of origin, however, but only given in the aggregate for each country vis-à-vis all other countries. Hence, it is not possible to purge the net holdings in other OECD countries and China from the overall net foreign asset position of each country, so as to be able to determine just the net foreign asset position of the OECD plus China area countries vis-à-vis the rest of the world. In what follows, we can thus only present the aggregate *Net International Investment Position* (NIIP) of all countries of the OECD plus China region with respect to all other countries.

Analyzing the result obtained using this data, we find that the group consisting of the OECD countries and China had a fluctuating and—apart from two years representing exceptions—consistently negative balance of its aggregate net foreign asset position from 1991 to 2016 (cf. Figure 3.4). Most recently (in 2016), this

---

[2]It would have made sense to carry out an investigation on the basis of current account balances. But the data needed to be able to analyze all the reciprocal current account relationships among countries and between them and the rest of the world is not available for all the countries of the OECD plus China region.

[3]The reliability of the results was also tested using World Bank (2017) data.

[4]We are entirely aware of the limitations of the data on global trade and capital interrelations. For example, from the data of the OECD, IMF, etc., it is possible to calculate a global current account balance that was continuously negative between 1980 and 2005 and has been positive since then (approximately − 0.8% or, respectively, + 0.8% of global GDP). Since the earth does not trade with other planets, this is evidently based on data collection problems—above all, concerning capital flows.

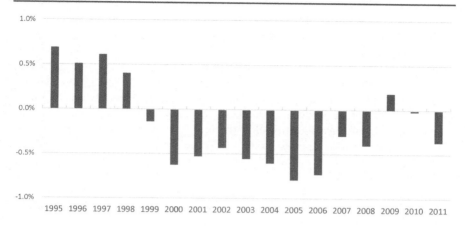

Fig. 3.3 Balance of trade of the OECD plus China area with the rest of the world in percent of gross domestic product. *Source* OECD (2017); Author's own calculations

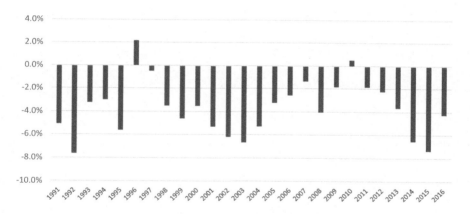

Fig. 3.4 Common net international investment position (NIIP) of the countries of the OECD plus China area toward the rest of the world. *Source* IMF (2017); Author's own calculations

balance amounted to around − 2.3 trillion US dollars, corresponding to 4% of the gross domestic product of the region or the total product of about two weeks.

From 1991 to 2016, the aggregate net foreign asset position of the countries of the OECD plus China region vis-à-vis the rest of the world was, on average, around − 4.8% of the gross domestic product of this economic area.

The analysis of the trade data and the data on net foreign asset positions makes clear that, although not completely closed, the OECD plus China region can certainly be regarded as a nearly closed economic area. In the period from 1995 to 2011, the balance of trade of the OECD plus China economic region vis-à-vis the rest of the world was -0.24% of gross domestic product. Even if we only consider the period after 2000, when the balance of trade became negative, the result is merely a slightly negative balance of, on average, -0.4% of gross domestic product. The net foreign asset position of the OECD plus China region is also fairly balanced, being on the order of approximately -4 to -6% of gross domestic product over the last two decades. Although the available data only allows for an approximate judgment, we can, nonetheless, conclude even from analysis of the data on net foreign asset position that the OECD plus China economic area is relatively closed vis-à-vis the rest of the world. Hence, it will be legitimate to treat the OECD plus China region as a closed economy in the further course of the present book.

The cited statistics thus clearly show that the rest of the world does not represent an "outlet" for possible surplus savings of the OECD plus China economic area.

3.12 The Gist

In this chapter, we have discussed desired wealth. The main hypothesis is:

> The Law of Increasing Relative Desired Wealth: The greater the average prosperity of a country, the greater is the ratio between desired wealth and annual consumption of goods.

We have derived this law from the *thesis of the increasing effective future-directedness of human action as prosperity increases.*

References

Banerjee, Abhijit und Esther Duflo. 2011. *Poor Economics: A Radical Rethinking of the Way to Fight Global Poverty.* New York (NY): Public Affairs.
IMF. 2017 *Coordinated Direct Investment Survey (CDIS).* https://data.imf.org/CDIS. Accessed: 1 December 2017.
Marx, Karl and Friedrich Engels. 1967 [1848]. *The Communist Manifesto,* trans. Samuel Moore. London: Penguin.
Marx, Karl. 1976 [1867]. *Capital: A Critique of Political Economy,* vol. 1, trans. Ben Fowkes. London: Penguin/New Left Books.
OECD. 2017. *Trade in Value Added (TiVA) Database.* https://stats.oecd.org/index. aspx?DatasetCode =TIVA_2016_C1. Accessed: 1 December 2017.
Phelps, Edmund. 2013. *Mass Flourishing: How Grass Roots Innovation Created Jobs, Challenge and Change.* Princeton (NJ): Princeton University Press.
Query ID=`Q1' Text=`Unable to parse this reference. Kindly do manual structure' Polanyi, Karl. 1944. *The Great Transformation.* New York (NY): Farrar and Rinehart.
Sahlins, Marshall. 1968. Notes on the Original Affluent Society. In *Man the Hunter,* eds. Richard B. Lee und Irene DeVore, 85–89. New York (NY): Aldine.

Smith, Adam. 1776. *An Inquiry into the Nature and Causes of the Wealth of Nations*. London: W. Strahan and T. Cadell.

Solow, Robert M. 1987. We'd Better Watch Out. Book Review of Stephen S. Cohen and John Zysman, *Manufacturing Matters* (New York: Basic Books). *New York Times Book Review*, July 12, 1987: 36.

United Nations. 2017. *United Nations, Department of Economic and Social Affairs, Population Division, World Population Prospects: The 2017 Revision, Key Findings and Advanced Tables*. ESA/P/WP/248. New York (NY): United Nations.

Weber, Max. 1992 [1904–05]. *The Protestant Ethic and the Spirit of Capitalism*, trans. Talcott Parsons. London: Routledge.

World Bank. 2017. *World Integrated Trade Solution (WITS) Database*. https://wits.worldbank.org/faqs.html. Accessed: 1 December 2017.

Real Capital

4

Abstract

Preshaped by the influence of Marx, Böhm-Bawerk and modern neoclassical economics, the general opinion is that the marginal product of capital must always be positive. With the help of the "period of production" T, we define a coefficient of intertemporal substitution ψ that is always non-negative. It can also be used when the real interest rate is negative. With the help of the concept of the "waiting period" Z, we can also define an always non-negative coefficient of intertemporal substitution γ for the household side. The "loss formula" for deviations of the rate of interest from the growth rate is one application of ψ and γ. $\Omega = (\psi T^2 + \gamma Z^2)(r - g)^2/2$ provides a good approximation of the relative loss Ω. Overcomplexity of the system of production leads to negative marginal returns on capital. It can be empirically presumed that the OECD plus China region is on the cusp of overcomplexity. The hypothetical natural rate of interest in the eurozone is well into the minuses. To determine the value of the real capital of the private sector in the OECD plus China region, we use a framework of data taken from the World Inequality Database (WID.world). We have supplemented the data available there with data from other sources and adapted it to our theoretical objectives. According to our estimates, private wealth in the form of real capital in the OECD plus China region comes to approximately four times total annual consumption.

4.1 Real Capital: Theoretical Foundations

4.1.1 The Point of Differentiating Between Real Capital and Land

Real capital consists of produced goods that are used in turn for the production of other goods: this in contrast to produced goods that are consumed by households and the public sector. We call the value of the latter "total annual consumption."

© The Author(s) 2021
C. C. von Weizsäcker and H. M. Krämer, *Saving and Investment in the Twenty-First Century*, https://doi.org/10.1007/978-3-030-75031-2_4

Land also enters into the production process as a factor of production. But as opposed to real capital, although land is worked, it is not produced. Hence, the value of land cannot be derived from any sort of production costs. By contrast, the value of goods comprising real capital is largely based on their production costs.

The value of the economy's total stock of real capital goods is *not identical*, however, to its production costs. Capital goods are physically altered by their use in the production process. The notion of "depreciation for wear and tear" is thus regularly employed in assessing the value of a company's assets. But capital goods can also lose value by being replaced one day by more efficient capital goods or, in other words, by being rendered obsolete. The economically useful life of goods is usually shorter than their potential physical life. Finally, changes in value can also be the result of changed market conditions or simply of changes in a company's business outlook.

Maintenance costs, like repairs, can be added to the production costs. They increase the value of the goods in question or prevent them from losing value as a result of diminishing functionality. Nonetheless, maintenance costs are largely entered under running costs. Thus, company management can simulate profit by forgoing maintenance measures and suggesting to the outside world that the goods, nonetheless, have not lost any functionality.

As shown in practice, when ownership of a company changes hands, the price paid almost never corresponds to the reported equity on the transfer date. The economic literature speaks of "Tobin's Q" almost never reaching exactly the value of 1. Tobin's Q specifies the ratio of the market value of the firm to the value of equity reported in its balance sheet (Tobin and Brainard 1977). In the case of publicly traded company shares, Tobin's Q can be determined, in effect, on a quarterly basis as a function of the stock market valuation of the company.

For the purposes of our book, the market value of firms is decisive. We want, after all, to establish how much wealth citizens have. In full-employment equilibrium, their wealth has to be equal to the desired wealth discussed in Chap. 3.

One of the reasons why the market valuation of a company deviates from its reported equity is the following. There are expenditures that are elicited by revenues in the same year. And there are expenditures that can only be justified by revenues in subsequent years. In practice, however, it is often impossible to distinguish between these two categories of expenditure in such a way that differences of opinion cannot arise about which are which. If this difficulty did not exist, then it would be possible to treat expenditures relating to revenues in later years as "investment," to which, then, there would also correspond related depreciation in later years. Because business operations are not so simple, however, it is also possible for companies to manipulate how they report expenditures and revenues. In order to eliminate this threat of manipulation, accounting rules have to be formulated in such a way as easily to allow for intersubjective verification. The consequence, however, is that expenditures that are directed toward a future beyond the current calendar year are often not entered in a way reflecting this—namely as investment—but rather as having an immediate negative impact on earnings. The capital market, however, always reserves the right to make its own judgment about the "true" value of a publicly traded company.

When it does so, a company is often assessed as being far more valuable than its reported equity suggests. But it is also not unusual to come across the opposite case. For the assets side of a company's balance sheet often includes purchases whose depreciation has been underestimated and hence whose reported value is far greater than the value that they still have on the view of the capital market.

As discussed in detail in Sect. 4.2, we use a database that has been elaborated by qualified economists, in which the value of real capital is determined according to the principle of market valuation. A Tobin's Q that is not equal to one is thus already taken into account here. This is why, in this chapter, we combine reported equity and a Tobin's Q different from 1.

In Chap. 5, we cover land as factor of production (Sect. 5.1) and as form of wealth (Sect. 5.2).

4.1.2 The Capital-Output Ratio Does Not Exhibit Any Trend

In 1961, Nicholas Kaldor already observed that the capital-output ratio does not exhibit any trend over time (Kaldor 1961). This observation was later extended by other authors to their respective presents. Figure 4.1 can serve as an example.

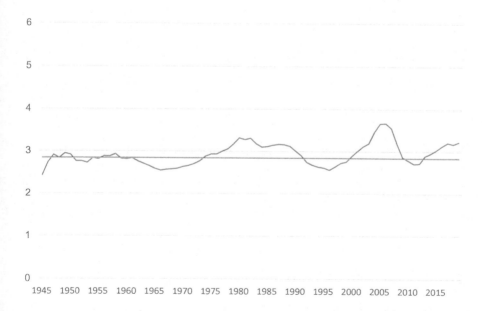

Fig. 4.1 Capital Coefficient USA, 1945–2019. *Source* Integrated Macroeconomic Accounts for the United States, https://www.federalreserve.gov/apps/fof/FOFTables.aspx, accessed: 19 January 2021; Authors' own calculations

It shows that the capital-output ratio has been nearly constant in the USA since the end of the Second World War. Similar results could be shown for most other countries. A similar picture is obtained, if real capital stock is compared to annual consumption, as in our analysis. For the ratio of GDP to consumption has hardly changed for decades. Our putting current consumption in the denominator has to do with the steady-state analysis that we have presented in Chap. 2 and in Weizsäcker (2021). Consumption is, after all, the ultimate purpose of production. Hence, it makes sense to compare the intermediate products, in the form of real capital, to this ultimate purpose of production.

The fact that the capital-output ratio, or what we will call the capital coefficient, is historically constant contrasts with the substantial increase in the ratio between private wealth and current consumption. We speak here of the *wealth coefficient*. Up to now, no comprehensive empirical presentation of private wealth has been available for the OECD countries. Our book provides a first look at the current relationship between private wealth and current consumption for the OECD plus China region (Sects. 4.2, 5.2, 6.2 and Chap. 8).

What is still missing, however, is a presentation of the historical evolution of this wealth coefficient. There have indeed been recent studies on the evolution of private wealth, but private wealth is defined differently in them than in our book: Implicit public debt vis-à-vis a country's citizens—which is highly significant in quantitative terms—is, namely, missing from these time series. On our view, this implicit public debt has to be counted as an additional element of private wealth. In particular, Piketty (2014) and Jordà et al. (2019) should be mentioned here. Both studies show considerable secular growth in the ratio between this more narrowly defined private wealth and national product or income. This secular growth would probably be even more pronounced, if our broader concept of wealth were used. For the implicit public debt that we take into account is based on the welfare state. But in all OECD countries, the welfare state has undergone massive expansion in recent decades—driven to a not inconsiderable extent by the secular increase in life expectancy—and in China too, it has started to grow.

Nonetheless, the consequences for economic policy of this growing discrepancy between capital coefficient and wealth coefficient have not yet been thought through. Intellectual obstacles that can be traced back to venerable traditions play a role here. The next three sections are devoted to such prefabricated thinking. What is at issue is, above all, that the possibility of a long-term, massively negative real interest rate and the dangers to which it gives rise are alien to such traditional economic thinking.

4.1.3   Prefabricated Thought 1: Marx

Still today, our thinking is guided by books and articles from long ago. In the context of interest to us here, we are referring, in particular, to Karl Marx, Eugen von Böhm-Bawerk and the Solow model's CES production function. These antecedents make it hard for us to accept the possibility of a negative natural rate of interest. In what follows, we will show why.

Firstly, on Karl Marx: Thinkers who are close to Marx, both within theoretical economics and outside of the latter, adopt Marx's idea of the "internal contradictions" of the capitalist economic system. The "Law of the Tendential Fall in the Rate of Profit" is an essential component of Marx's thought in this connection. In Marx, this law is derived from the thesis of a constantly increasing "organic composition of capital," which is associated with the creation of relative surplus-value. The unfolding of capital in historical time already contains the seeds of its collapse, because it is more and more difficult for capital to find profitable investment outlets. Later, Rosa Luxemburg and other members of the Marxian school developed the theory of imperialism from Marx's finding in this regard (Luxemburg 1913). They argued that imperialism serves temporarily to delay the valorization problems of capital by providing preferential sales opportunities for domestic capital in the colonies. The theory was also used to explain the World War among the capitalist nation states.

In this context, it is worth re-reading the Marxian theory of the creation of relative surplus-value. The pertinent chapters in the first volume of *Capital* bear repeated reading, even if we do not adopt the theory that goes with them. For they describe the broad outlines of the historical development of economic modernity with a sure brushstroke—although only, of course, up to roughly the end of the nineteenth century (a third edition having been published shortly after Marx's death in 1883). (Cf., in particular, Chap. 15 of *Capital*, vol. I, titled "Machinery and Large-Scale Industry".)

Marx derives the "Law of the Tendential Fall in the Rate of Profit" in the third volume of *Capital* (Cf. also Marx's letter to Engels of 30 April 1868). The profit rate r is defined or rather explained by Marx as follows:

$$r = \frac{s}{c+v}.$$

Here, s is the surplus-value appropriated by capital, v is the variable capital employed and c is the constant capital employed. The ratio s/v is the "degree of exploitation." It specifies the ratio in which the value created by labor is divided into wages (v) and profit or surplus-value (s). The variable capital v is thus the wage due, but not yet paid to, the worker. Marx is thinking here—in a way that is realistic for his time—that workers work for the whole week, but only receive their wage at the end of it. During the week, workers thus advance capitalists, on average, half their weekly wage. Hence, v is half the weekly wage. It also follows that the rate of profit calculated in this way represents the rate of profit for half a week.

The constant capital employed, c, is embodied in the means of production: i.e., in raw materials and equipment or, in other words, precisely in what we today call real capital. "Past labor" is embodied in the constant capital.

Marx calls the ratio between the total capital employed and the variable capital the "organic composition of capital." The rate of profit can thus be understood as

$$\text{rate of profit} = \frac{s}{c+v} = \frac{\frac{s}{v}}{\frac{c+v}{v}} = \frac{\text{degree of exploitation}}{\text{organic composition}}.$$

The creation of *relative* surplus-value by capital takes place on the level of the individual business by moving from the previous methods of production to new methods, which increase the productivity of labor. This allows capitalists to increase their surplus-value by decreasing the share of wages in the value created during a working day of a given length: in other words, by raising the degree of exploitation. But inasmuch as competing capitalists do the same thing, the surplus-value falls again, such that the rate of profit returns to its previous level.

Nonetheless, at the same time, the move to new methods of production is associated with an increase in the organic composition of capital. Marx describes this relationship in Chap. 25 of *Capital*, vol. I, titled "The General Law of Capitalist Accumulation." In its second section—titled "A Relative Diminution of the Variable Part of Capital Occurs in the Course of the Further Progress of Accumulation and of the Concentration Accompanying It"—Marx writes: "Apart from natural conditions, such as the fertility of the soil, etc., and apart from the skill of independent and isolated producers (shown rather qualitatively in the high standard of their products than quantitatively in their mass), the level of the social productivity of labour is expressed in the relative extent of the means of production that one worker, during a given time, with the same degree of intensity of labour-power, turns into products. The mass of means of production with which he functions in this way increases with the productivity of his labour. But whether condition or consequence, the growing extent of the means of production, as compared with the labour-power incorporated into them, is an expression of the growing productivity of labour. The increase of the latter appears, therefore, in the diminution of the mass of labour in proportion to the mass of means of production moved by it, or in the diminution of the subjective factor of the labour process as compared with the objective factor. This change in the technical composition of capital, this growth in the mass of the means of production, as compared with the mass of the labour-power that vivifies them, is reflected in its value-composition by the increase of the constant constituent of capital at the expense of its variable constituent (Marx 1976 [1867], p. 773).

Nonetheless, Marx is aware of the fact that the mass represented by the constant capital (measured in kilos perhaps?) increases faster than the constant capital, *c*, as measured in labor-value. Thus, shortly further on in the same chapter, he writes: "However, this diminution in the variable part of capital as compared with the constant part, or, in other words, this change in the composition of the value of the capital, provides only an approximate indication of the change in the composition of its material constituents. The value of the capital employed today in spinning is ⅞ constant and ⅛ variable, while at the beginning of the eighteenth century it was ½ constant and ½ variable. Yet, in contrast to this, the mass of raw material, instruments of labour, etc. that a certain quantity of spinning labour consumes productively today is many hundred times greater than at the beginning of the eighteenth century. The reason is simple: with the increasing productivity of labour, the mass of the means of production consumed by labour increases, but their value in comparison with their mass diminishes. Their value therefore rises absolutely, but not in proportion to the increase in their mass" (Marx 1976 [1867], p. 774).

Marx's "Law of the Tendential Fall in the Rate of Profit" depends on the growing organic composition of capital. This law is of fundamental importance in the Marxist tradition, since it manifests the internal contradictions of the capitalist system and is thus also indispensable for the prophecy of the system's collapse. This is why it has never been called into question in Marxism.

What is of interest for us is that Marxism—translated into the categories of modern macroeconomics—thus assumes a law of a tendentially increasing capital-output ratio. For, along with the rise in the organic composition of capital, the ratio between the stock of real capital c and the resulting periodic value output $v + s$ also rises.

It is not necessary for us to discuss the well-known "transformation problem" in the present context: namely, the problem of the transformation of (labor-)values into prices of production. One of us analyzed this aspect in a paper decades ago (Weizsäcker 1977). Interestingly, the simplification undertaken by Marx in this connection, inasmuch as he expresses the rate of profit in labor values rather than competitive prices, amounts to a linearization of a curved relationship between rate of profit and real capital; this simplification is identical to the simplification undertaken by Böhm-Bawerk in his *Capital and Interest*—which we will discuss below—inasmuch as he works with simple interest rather than compound interest, as, strictly speaking, he should. As a by-product, we find that the Marxian "organic composition of capital" is *identical* to Böhm-Bawerk's average period of production. For, on closer inspection, the "organic composition of capital" is a quantity with the dimension of "time." This is only obscured by the fact that the time unit in which Marx defines the rate of profit is a highly unconventional one: namely the average time "advanced" by the worker to the capitalist. If wages are paid at the end of the week, this average time advanced is three days. When calculating the annual rate of profit, the variable capital is thus negligibly small in comparison to the constant capital. The rate of profit is then the inverse of the (constant) capital employed divided by the annual profit. But the latter expression is an amount of time that is commensurable with Böhm-Bawerk's period of production. Now, if Marx calculates using labor-values instead of prices of production and Böhm-Bawerk calculates using simple instead of compound interest, then it becomes clear that the coefficient composed of constant capital and annual value output is equal to the period of production.

It is thus virtually dogma in the politically highly influential Marxian school that the ratio between the stock variable "real capital" and the flow variable "value output" tends constantly to increase. Returning to Marx, however, we find that while he recognizes the difference between the physical composition of "past labor" and its "value" c, he does not draw the consequence of going on to verify whether —despite the noted constant decrease in the coefficient composed of the value of the means of production divided by their quantity—this value has a tendency to increase in relation to variable capital. Such verification is omitted. As we now know, had it been undertaken, it would have shown that the "organic composition of capital" has not increased.

4.1.4   Prefabricated Thought 2: Böhm-Bawerk

Efforts to explain the phenomenon of interest in neoclassical theory began with Eugen von Böhm-Bawerk. Even if he was criticized often and ingenuously, the influence of his work on the theory of interest was ultimately greater than that of any other neoclassical economist. It was only the modern neoclassical economics of the period since the Second World War that broke away from Böhm-Bawerk, in order, in general equilibrium theory and modern macroeconomics, to work with models that distanced themselves from his ideas. In the 1930s, there was still intensive discussion of the period of production, in which authors like Boulding, Marschak, Hayek, Oskar Morgenstern, Machlup, Gaitskell, Keynes, Knight, Kaldor, Oskar Lange, Ludwig von Mises, Harrod, Eucken and Hicks took part. (Cf. Lutz 1967, p. 56 and p. 96.)

After the Second World War, the Solow production function replaced the heavily debated period of production as a practical tool for empirical analysis within the framework of macroeconomic models. Only Böhm-Bawerk's "second reason" was retained: namely, in the form of the "time preference" that goes back to Irving Fisher.

Böhm-Bawerk adduced three reasons why the natural rate of interest is positive. The first reason is "the different circumstances of want and provision in present and future": namely, the need intertemporally to shift the means of providing for want (purchasing power). According to Böhm-Bawerk, thanks to the possibility of maintaining stocks, which costs little in the case of money, shifting to a future point in time is unproblematic, whereas shifting from the future to the present or from a distant future to a nearer future is either impossible or indeed costly. This asymmetry in the possibilities of intertemporal shifting of the means of providing for want leads, on his account, to a "lesser value being attached to future goods as compared to presently available goods." This "first reason" was already the target of harsh criticism during Böhm-Bawerk's lifetime—and, in our opinion, justifiably so. For maintaining a stock of physical goods is associated with considerable costs and risks. And even under conditions of price stability in the economy as a whole, maintaining a stock in the form of money presupposes that either a borrower is available who, for reasons other than the "first reason," is willing to assume this position of borrower or that enough money is available in the form of central bank money to satisfy this need for maintaining a stock. The latter, however, by no means goes without saying. If, for reasons that we have presented in Chap. 3 on desired wealth, the desire to shift resources into the future is very great, money with stable purchasing power can at most ensure that the real rate of interest does not fall below zero. The "first reason" cannot serve to explain a positive natural rate.

The "second reason" for the lesser value attached to future goods is the "undervaluation of future needs as compared to current ones." Irving Fisher introduced the expression "time preference" for this phenomenon, which plays a significant role in his theory of interest. In modern presentations, it is mostly depicted as follows. We presuppose that the individual in question maximizes a utility integral that looks like this:

$$\int_0^{t_0} e^{-ht} u_t(c(t)) dt; \quad h > 0; \quad t_0 > 0$$

Here, $c(t)$ is the consumption flow, h stands for the rate of "time preference" and u_t represents the period utility function at time t.

Other things being equal, the equilibrium rate of interest will undoubtedly be higher in a macroeconomic model, if the rate of time preference h is higher. But on its own, a positive h will not be sufficient to raise the equilibrium rate of interest to a positive level. It is easy to construct counterexamples here.

The "third reason" given by Böhm-Bawerk to explain a positive rate of interest is the "greater productivity of more roundabout production." This greater productivity is the real core of the "temporal" theory of capital, which is often also referred to as "Austrian" capital theory. In Chap. 2 on the natural rate of interest, we carried out an "Austrian" analysis: The natural rate of interest ρ is lower than the rate of growth g precisely when, at $r = g$, the private waiting period Z is greater than the period of production T.

For Böhm-Bawerk, the measure of the roundaboutness of production in the economy is the average period of production. On his account, labor productivity rises with a longer period of production. Furthermore, the capital requirements of the economy are, for him, the product of total annual wages and the period of production. In Böhm-Bawerk, the rate of interest is the price signal for the extent of the raised productivity as measured by a marginal increase in the period of production. In other words, for him, the rate of interest r equals the marginal yield in labor productivity of the period of production divided by labor productivity. If the (real) rate of interest is 5% per year, then a one-year increase in the period of production leads to a 5% increase in labor productivity.

The idea that the amount of real capital corresponds to the extent of the roundaboutness of production has become deeply embedded in the intuition of economists. And with it, so too has the notion that more roundaboutness of production leads to a rise in labor productivity. This intuition has also been taken over by modern macroeconomics: namely in the idea that equipping jobs with more real capital leads to increased labor productivity. It is treated as self-evident that labor productivity is a monotonically increasing function of capital intensity.

Böhm-Bawerk predicted that the average period of production would become longer and longer in the twentieth century, due to the greater productivity of more roundabout production and due to increasing prosperity. He thus essentially adopted the same position as the Marxian school. Both schools, the "bourgeois" or "neoclassical" and the Marxian, were long in agreement that the capital-output ratio would continue to rise. But they were wrong. One of the most well-known "Kaldor facts" is that the capital-output ratio does not exhibit any secular upwards trend.

4.1.5   Prefabricated Thought 3: The CES Production Function

After the Second World War, Böhm-Bawerk's concept of the period of production was set aside and replaced by the Solow production function. The latter involves a symmetrical treatment of the factors of production "labor" and "capital" in the macroeconomic production function. This approach even survived the Cambridge versus Cambridge capital controversy—despite harsh criticism on the part of the theorists from Cambridge in the UK. The fact that empirical work in macroeconomics is greatly facilitated by working with the Solow production function is certainly one reason why. For information on labor inputs and real capital inputs is abundantly available. Solow's pioneering 1957 study, which gave rise to the flourishing field of growth accounting, already made use of the long time series for labor and real capital inputs that were available for the USA. (And Solow himself, who both knew the capital-theoretical literature well and made important contributions to it, always stressed that the Solow production function is to be understood as an approximation, which, depending on the context, either successfully adds to our knowledge or is misleading.)

The symmetrical treatment of labor and capital in the macroeconomic production function also allows for an empirically relevant approach to the topic of substitution. The notion of elasticity of substitution between two factors of production has been known since the 1930s. The notion was already developed by Hicks in 1932 in his *Theory of Wages*, where it was applied to the factors "labor and capital." Building on Hicks's work, Arrow, Chenery, Minhas and Solow introduced the CES production function into the literature in 1961. The latter is defined by the property that the elasticity of substitution between the two factors is the same for every combination of factors. By virtue of the assumption that it is a constant, the value of the elasticity of substitution, which is a local property of the production function, becomes a global property of the production function.

This, however, makes empirical work on macroeconomic models considerably easier. Since the latter are usually supposed to describe economic growth, researchers have to cope with drastic changes in the ratio in which capital and labor are employed. In order, for instance, to make predictions, researchers have to deal with the consequences of future capital intensities that are far removed from those observed in the past. It is helpful here to assume the elasticity of substitution that has been econometrically estimated using historical values as a constant, in order thus to be able also to model the behavior of the production function at future capital intensities.

But it is a property of the CES production function that the marginal products of both factors remain positive, regardless of the factor ratio at which the marginal products are being evaluated. It is thus ruled out in advance that the factor "capital" could also have a negative marginal product. The CES production function thus rules out the main thesis of this book by assumption.

We can, of course, work with forms of the Solow production function in which a negative marginal product of capital is possible. But then we lose the property of a constant elasticity of substitution between labor and capital.

Let us sum up the three Sects. 4.1.3–4.1.5. Hitherto, models have predominated in macroeconomics whose simplifying strategies imply that there can never be a negative natural rate of interest. Both Marx and Böhm-Bawerk believed that there would be an increasing capital-output ratio in the future. In Marx, this is the tendentially rising organic composition of capital, from which he derives the tendential fall of the profit rate. Böhm-Bawerk predicted that there would be increasing roundaboutness of production in the twentieth century. Both of them assumed, however, that this rising capital-output ratio would be associated with a rate of profit or, respectively, a rate of interest that remains positive. And modern, neoclassical macroeconomics and growth theory does not hesitate to work with the CES production function, which excludes a negative marginal product of capital from the outset. Our thesis of a negative natural rate of interest has thus to struggle against a prevailing intuition, according to which, at full employment, the equilibrium rate of interest cannot be negative.

4.1.6   The Coefficient of Intertemporal Substitution

It is worthwhile to look for another instrument for measuring the phenomenon of substitution at the macroeconomic level. To this end, it is useful to reconsider the temporal theory of capital, which was founded by Böhm-Bawerk with his notion of the "roundaboutness of production" and which we already touched upon in Chap. 2 on the natural rate of interest. We found there that Böhm-Bawerk's idea of an equality between capital requirements per worker, on the one hand, and the product of the period of production and annual wages, on the other, comes true precisely in that steady state in which the risk-free interest rate equals the growth rate. But this means that this equation holds precisely when the prosperity-maximizing rate of interest has been realized. Moreover, the period of production T for the economy as a whole is then equal to the waiting period $Z - D$ for the economy as a whole. The assumptions that we have to make to obtain this result are, in principle, largely independent of the specific growth model. *This means, however, that it is a fundamental finding.* In particular, it does not depend on the restrictive assumptions of the Solow model. The Solow model is here merely a special case of a far more general result. Hence, we call the equation

$$T = Z - D$$

the *Fundamental Equation of Steady-State Capital Theory*.

We thus propose replacing the traditional elasticity of substitution between labor and capital by a *coefficient of intertemporal substitution*. The latter indicates the influence of the interest rate level on the steady-state period of production.

In the chapter on the natural rate of interest, we discussed the period of production *T*. If we compare different steady states, then *T* varies with the rate of interest. In general, we can write: $T = T(r; \theta)$. For *T* was defined as

$$T = -\frac{\partial w(r; \theta)/\partial r}{w(r; \theta)} = -\frac{\partial \ln w(r; \theta)}{\partial r}.$$

As already mentioned, it was Hicks who, in 1939 in *Value and Capital*, recognized that (as against Böhm-Bawerk's procedure) the period of production should be calculated using present values, in order to arrive at useful results. But this means that the period of production is not only dependent on the physical structure of the production apparatus, but also on the rate of interest used to calculate the present values of wages for labor inputs and the present values of consumer good outputs.

We can now form the partial derivative of *T* with respect to θ, remembering that, thanks to our naming convention, $\theta(r) = r$ holds. This partial derivative looks, then, as follows, whereby we calculate the derivative at $\theta = \theta(r) = r$:

$$\frac{\partial T(r; \theta)}{\partial \theta} = -\frac{\partial^2 \ln w(r; \theta)}{\partial r \partial \theta}.$$

The partial derivative of the period of production with respect to the production technique $\theta(r)$ induced by the rate of interest is thus the negative value of the mixed second partial derivative of the natural logarithm of the wage with respect to the rate of interest and with respect to the production technique. Now, in "Capital Theory of the Steady State" (Weizsäcker 2021) we show that

$$\frac{\partial T(r; \theta)}{\partial \theta}$$

is negative (Theorem 7A). The economic intuition corresponding to this mathematical result is not difficult to grasp. Let us imagine a completely vertically integrated *virtual firm*, whose only input is "labor" and whose only output is a basket of consumer goods. The period of production specifies the average time lag between the consumer goods that become available later and the wages that are due earlier. A higher rate of interest means that the relative prices of future goods become lower and of past goods become higher. Hence, the average wage must fall. This is expressed by the equation

$$T = -\frac{\partial w(r; \theta)/\partial r}{w(r; \theta)} = -\frac{\partial \ln w(r; \theta)}{\partial r}$$

The virtual firm responds to the change in relative prices by economizing on the inputs whose prices have increased the most: namely the labor inputs that are furthest in the past. It modifies its output by reducing the consumer good output that is furthest in the future, since this is the output whose prices have fallen the most, in favor of additional production of output in the near future. Both changes—on the input side and on the output side—bring about a shortening of the period of production. We can now conceive of the economy growing in the steady state as a collection of overlapping, completely vertically integrated, virtual firms. It can thus be shown that the inequality

$$\frac{\partial T(r;\theta)}{\partial \theta} = -\frac{\partial^2 \ln w(r;\theta)}{\partial r \partial \theta} \leq 0$$

also holds for the economy as a whole.

Analogously to the traditional elasticity of substitution, we want to define a measure of substitution that is dimensionless and hence is not dependent on the chosen unit of measurement. In this case, it is

$$\psi = \frac{\partial(1/T)}{\partial \theta}.$$

Since the rate of interest r and hence also $\theta(r) = r$ have the dimension "1/the unit of time," they have the same dimension as the expression $1/T$. Hence, the derivative of the latter expression with respect to the former is dimensionless. Moreover, this derivative is naturally positive, since T becomes smaller with an increasing θ. At the limit, when there is no substitution at all, ψ is equal to zero.

This procedure would only run into difficulties, if the period of production were not continuously, i.e., at every relevant rate of interest, positive. However, we can rule out this possibility as "pathological," since it would mean that the economy is producing without capital. But we must not rule out the possibility of the rate of interest r becoming negative. And this is significant for our approach.

We call the theorem showing that ψ is always non-negative the *Law of Intertemporal Substitution*: The change of production technique induced by a rise in the rate of interest replaces earlier than average inputs by later than average inputs; and it replaces later than average outputs by earlier than average outputs. It thus corresponds to a pattern of intertemporal substitution: a pattern that exhibits a definite direction of substitution. It can be regarded as analogous to well-known substitution effects where the good that has become more expensive is replaced as input by the good that has become cheaper—and where the good that has become cheaper is replaced as output by the good that has become more expensive.

We can also consider the waiting period Z on the household side in an analogous fashion to the production side. Here too, there is an analogous Law of Intertemporal Substitution. As already discussed in Chap. 2 on the natural rate of interest, we can assign a work-consumption pattern $\eta(r)$ of the representative consumer to each steady state. Using an appropriate naming convention, we can write $\eta(r) = r$.

We define $\bar{w}$ $(\eta;\ r)$ as the "wage" that is required to finance a given work-consumption pattern at a given rate of interest r. As shown in Weizsäcker (2021), the equation

$$\frac{\partial \bar{w}}{\partial r} = -Z(r;\eta)\bar{w}(\eta;r);$$

holds; such that

$$\frac{\partial \ln(\bar{w}(\eta;r))}{\partial r} = -Z(r;\eta).$$

From this, at $\eta = \eta(r)$, we derive

$$\frac{\partial Z}{\partial \eta} = -\frac{\partial^2 \ln(\bar{w}(\eta;r))}{\partial r \partial \eta}.$$

We show that this expression for the partial derivative of Z with respect to the work-consumption pattern is always positive (Theorem 7B). The work-consumption pattern responds to a rise in the interest rate by the household moving its labor supply forward in time and, conversely, postponing its consumption. This too is a variant of the well-known neoclassical substitution theorem: Supply falls and demand rises for what becomes cheaper; and supply rises and demand falls for what becomes more expensive. Accordingly, we can define a coefficient of intertemporal substitution γ on the household side. Let it be

$$\gamma = -\frac{\partial(1/Z)}{\partial \eta}.$$

This coefficient is non-negative, since $\partial Z/\partial \eta$ is non-negative.

4.1.7 An Application of the Coefficient of Intertemporal Substitution

In Weizsäcker (2021), we show an application of both coefficients of intertemporal substitution. In many respects, our *meta-model* is far more general than the models that are typically developed in macroeconomics, capital theory and growth theory. It owes its usefulness to the restriction to a steady-state perspective. For the purpose of addressing the main question of our book—namely that of the natural rate of interest—this restriction to steady states is entirely appropriate. The assumptions made amount to the claim that the steady-state rate of interest is a correct price signal for intertemporal allocation. If the steady-state rate is a correct price signal, then the Golden Rule of Accumulation holds. Its validity is thus not dependent on more specific assumptions that are made in each model.

But the more specific assumptions made in each model do, of course, have an influence on the extent to which the standard of living declines with respect to the optimum, when the rate of interest is not equal to the rate of growth.

Nonetheless, on the basis of the meta-model, we can already derive a second-degree Taylor approximation for the relative loss of wealth. With the help of the notion of a steady-state standard of living, we will here provide an abridged presentation of the result that is mathematically derived in Weizsäcker (2021). We speak here of the "standard of living" of a representative household and not of its real consumption, since, by the Samuelson Theorem (Samuelson 1958), what is important is not only the amount of consumption per labor year, but also the intertemporal distribution of the latter. By the generalized Phelps-Weizsäcker Theorem, real steady-state consumption is lower at $r \neq g$ than at $r = g$. By the generalized Samuelson Theorem, at the same steady-state consumption per labor year, lifetime utility U is lower at $r \neq g$ than at $r = g$. We can now derive an approximation formula for the relative loss in the standard of living as a second-degree Taylor approximation. We call this percentage loss in standard of living Ω. The following, then, holds:

$$\Omega \approx \left(\psi T^2 + \gamma Z^2\right)(r - g)^2/2$$

whereby the symbol "$\approx$" indicates that we are dealing here with a second-degree Taylor approximation.

The "error" that we commit using this Taylor approximation is, of course, dependent on the properties of the specific model we use to calculate the exact loss in standard of living. At realistic values for T and Z, it turns out, in the case of the Solow Model and a lifetime utility model with realistic values for intertemporal substitution, that the deviations of the Taylor approximation of the meta-model from the real values for Ω are small as long as we are working with deviations of the annual rate of interest from the rate of growth of up to five percentage points. It is evident that the meta-model is very well-suited for calculating the loss in standard of living as long as we work with small, but still perceptible, deviations of the rate of interest from its optimal value.

In Weizsäcker (2021), we assessed the approximation formula

$$\Omega \approx \left(\psi T^2 + \gamma Z^2\right)(r - g)^2/2$$

using a numerical example. At the values $\psi = 1$, $\gamma = 3$, $T = 4$ years, $Z = 10$ years, $g = 3\%$ per year, and $r = -2\%$ per year, there is a resulting decline in prosperity of more than 40% as compared to prosperity under the Golden Rule $r = g$. If we assume a natural rate of interest of -2% per year, then, by comparison, a public-debt-free steady state exhibits this decline in prosperity. A public debt period of $D = Z - T - L = 4$ years corresponds to $r = g$. L is here the capitalized value of land rents, as expressed in annual consumption units. Cf. the following Chap. 5.

In Chap. 6 on public debt, we show that the estimates of $T = 4$ years and $Z = 10$ years roughly reflect the current reality in the OECD plus China region.

4.1.8 A Model with Constant Intertemporal Substitution

In this context, it makes sense to ask what consequences it would have, if we assumed that the coefficient of intertemporal substitution ψ is constant. In Weizsäcker (2021), we calculate the formula in the case of the Solow production function. For a constant ψ and on the assumption of constant returns to scale, we get the following result. Let $f(k)$ be value output per labor year as a function of capital intensity. We make the following standard assumptions:

$$f = f(k) \geq 0; f'(k) \geq 0 \text{ for } 0 \leq k \leq \bar{k}; f''(k) < 0; \ k \geq 0$$

The value $\bar{k}$ maximizes the value output per labor year. $\bar{k}$ can be either finite or infinite. For every production function of this sort, we can calculate the "local" coefficient of intertemporal substitution ψ for every positive k. If we assume now that ψ is a positive constant, we can explicitly calculate the associated production function by way of double integration of an ordinary second order differential equation. For $\psi > 1$, the following holds:

$$f(k) = \lambda k^{\frac{1}{\psi}} - \mu k, \lambda > 0, \mu \geq 0.$$

For $\psi < 1$, we obtain

$$f(k) = \bar{\bar{\mu}} k - \bar{\lambda} k^{\frac{1}{\psi}}, \bar{\bar{\mu}} > 0, \bar{\lambda} > 0.$$

For $\psi = 1$, we get

$$f(k) = \frac{k}{T} \left\{ \ln \bar{k} - \ln k + 1 \right\} = \frac{k}{T} \left(1 + \ln \frac{\bar{k}}{k} \right).$$

To the extent that when $\psi > 1$, the value μ is strictly positive, then in all three cases, we get the result that labor productivity f reaches its maximum at a finite value $\bar{k}$ for capital intensity and falls again beyond this value, with k continuing to increase. The case in which $\psi > 1$ with $\mu = 0$ is that of the well-known Cobb-Douglas production function. If at $\psi > 1$, the constant of integration μ is strictly positive, then we can interpret $f(k)$ as a Cobb-Douglas function for gross output from which a value for depreciation proportionate to the capital stock is subtracted annually.

Empirically, there are good reasons to assume that ψ is not far from unity, to the extent that we are satisfied with the approximation that the Solow production function represents. These reasons are laid out in Weizsäcker (2021). Hence, the case where $\psi = 1$ merits our particular attention. If we differentiate this production function with respect to k and interpret this derivative as an interest rate, we get the equation

$$r = f'(k) = \frac{1}{T} \ln \frac{\overline{k}}{k}.$$

The marginal productivity of capital is inversely proportional to the logarithm of the capital intensity. If the latter is greater than $\overline{k}$, then the marginal productivity is negative. The "wage" per labor year, w, is

$$w = f(k) - kr(k) = \frac{k}{T}.$$

It is proportional to the capital intensity. The factor of proportionality is the inverse of the period of production T, which is constant in this case, since at $\psi = 1$, the substitution effect of the change in the interest rate and the weighting effect of the change in interest rate cancel one another out when calculating present values. This wage function can be expressed as follows: The "wage" that is generated within the period of production is equal to the capital employed along with the worker.

4.1.9 And What, then, of the "Greater Productivity of More Roundabout Production"?

We now return to the subject of the "greater productivity of more roundabout production". The kernel of truth in Böhm-Bawerk's theory was that the capital requirements of a production technique are explained by the fact that the original means, i.e., the labor input, has to be available earlier than the ultimate purpose of all production: namely consumption. The analogy of a lake makes this especially clear for a stationary economy without interest. In a stationary state, the volume of water in the lake is equal to the product of the inflowing quantity of water per hour (= the outflowing quantity of water in the hour) times the average amount of time the water molecules remain in the lake. In a system of production, this average amount of time corresponds to the period of production T. The hourly inflow of water corresponds, for example, to the annual flow of value in the form of labor years times annual wage. The water outflow corresponds to the value of annual consumption.

The same result can be achieved for a growing system. If we assume that the parts of the total mass increase annually on their own (i.e., without inflow) at the percentage rate r and if we assume, furthermore, that the inflow quantity (like the outflow quantity) also increases each year at the percentage rate g, then the ratio between volume and inflow remains constant precisely when $r = g$. And then it again holds that the volume equals the inflow quantity times the amount of time the water molecules remain in the lake. The same holds for a system of production that is growing in a steady state with a rate of interest that equals the growth rate.

Böhm-Bawerk takes the period of production T to be the measure of the average roundaboutness of production in the economy as a whole, which, precisely on the condition that $r = g$, is also equal to the capital coefficient (capital divided by annual consumption = capital divided by "total annual wages"). The claim that a higher capital coefficient also leads to greater consumption per labor year follows from the stipulated "greater productivity of more roundabout production."

Since thinking within Böhm-Bawerk's model is a form of thinking in stationary systems, Böhm-Bawerk was still not able to grasp the theory of a steadily growing system of production. Already in Böhm-Bawerk's lifetime, Josef Schumpeter attempted, in his *Theory of Economic Development* (Schumpeter 1934 [1911]), to break free from thinking in stationary systems. At the start, however, his theory of entrepreneurial activity—to which he later gave then name "creative destruction" and which, over the years, has become, in effect, the standard theory—suffered from a misinterpretation of what Böhm-Bawerk had achieved using his model of a stationary equilibrium. Schumpeter's claim that a stationary equilibrium is always distinguished by an interest rate of zero could not stand up to the incisive criticism of a Böhm-Bawerk (Böhm-Bawerk 1913).

It was only modern, neoclassical growth theory—and, in particular, the Golden Rule of Accumulation—that demonstrated that the maximization of prosperity is not tied to the greatest possible capital stock. But it thereby became clear to all economists that it does not make sense to increase the roundaboutness of production as much as possible. The optimal degree of roundaboutness of production was at most that corresponding to a situation in which the rate of interest is equal to the rate of growth. And, thanks in large measure to the influence of the Solow production function, there was no one anymore who did not recognize that there could be a problem of excessive accumulation of capital. An early proponent of the thesis of overinvestment was Horvat (1958).

Surprisingly, however, apart from a few exceptions (like precisely Horvath, for example), the universal validity of Böhm-Bawerk's idea of the greater productivity of more roundabout production was not called into question. It was recognized that the marginal productivity of capital can be less than a positive growth rate, but not that it could become negative.

4.1.10   Roundaboutness of Production, Division of Labor and Complexity

If we recall the thoroughly familiar concept of *complexity*, however, the idea that there could be a limit to the increased productivity of more roundabout production seems almost obvious. Living from hand to mouth is a simple life. We imagine the life of hunters and gatherers in the Stone Age as having been such a simple life (cf. Sahlins 1968). The transition to a sedentary agrarian society, which we already discussed in Chap. 3, was connected to considerably more roundaboutness of production and hence also to greater capital intensity. But it thus also involved greater complexity. As the Property Rights School has taught us, in order to be able to cope with this increased complexity, private property in land, and in the structures built on it, was introduced. Private property means precisely a significant *reduction of complexity*, since it eliminated a considerable part of the interference between the different members of society. Too many cooks spoil the pot. Private property functions as a wide-reaching principle of non-interference. In this way, the results of production spanning long periods of time could be internalized. The incentive to engage in production processes spanning long periods of time on account of their roundaboutness was thus greatly increased. For productive complexity to become feasible, a system of institutions has to prevail in society that allows us to take advantage of opportunities for reducing complexity.

It is conceivable, however, that too much complexity comes into being in the end. In the social sciences and social philosophy, liberal thinkers (in the sense of classical liberalism) often employ the notion of "overregulation." It was Adam Smith who established economics as an academic discipline. From an administrative point of view, his plea for free trade—also and especially, free international trade—was a condemnation of the authorities' creation of artificial complexity by way of governmental prohibitions and requirements. We mention this merely as an example of the possibility of unproductive overcomplexity.

The idea of the division of labor is highly instructive in this connection. As is well known, Adam Smith's *The Wealth of Nations* begins with the sentence: "The greatest improvement in the productive powers of labour, and the greater part of the skill, dexterity, and judgement with which it is anywhere directed, or applied, seem to have been the effects of the division of labour" (Smith 1776, I.i.1). This sentence captures the decisive role of the division of labor in modernity. The division of labor makes it possible to exploit a large store of useful knowledge. This knowledge grows over time, since, in a constant process of trial and error, a further refinement of the division of labor, and hence a further accumulation of knowledge, always proves on average to represent progress. But it is important that this is a process of trial and error (in the Popperian sense), which also includes precisely numerous wrong turns. Thus, the scourge of overspecialization arises again and again.

An increase in the division of labor or specialization is an increase in complexity. There is no doubt about the usefulness of this complexity. But when there is a problem of excessive specialization, of excessive division of labor, then there can also be a problem of excessive complexity.

We can distinguish between horizontal and vertical division of labor. The horizontal division of labor is manifest, for example, in the wide variety of goods that people consume nearly simultaneously parallel to one other. Or in the variety of professions. The vertical division of labor concerns the fact that labor is, on average, employed before its ultimate use, in the form of consumer goods, falls due. The vertical division of labor is thus closely tied to the capital requirements of the system of production.

The mere fact that there can be excessive specialization or an excessive division of labor already makes it plausible that there can be an excessive vertical division of labor and hence an excessive capital stock—and this even when we are dealing with a stationary system of production or at least one that is not growing.

We can present this idea in somewhat greater detail. Division of labor or specialization provides us with well-known advantages: in particular, because it makes it possible massively to increase the stock of knowledge that is useful for the system of production. This knowledge includes the "tacit knowledge" to which Michael Polanyi has referred. The division of labor or specialization distributes the overall process of production among many different people. This gives rise to transaction costs in Coase's (1937, 1960) sense. The optimal degree of division of labor is reached at the point at which the additional knowledge obtained thanks to a further refinement of the division of labor is exactly offset by the additional transaction costs it creates, such that, as a result, this additional division of labor is not worthwhile.

We now apply this general idea to the vertical division of labor. Let us first consider a strictly stationary economy. Its rate of growth g is zero. The generalized Golden Rule of Accumulation tells us that the standard of living of the population reaches its maximum when the marginal productivity of an additional extension of the period of production (which, according to Böhm-Bawerk, can be read off from the real rate of interest) is zero. A longer period of production means a greater vertical division of labor: People involved in the production of today's consumer goods are more widely distributed across the axis of time; hence, at a given length of the active working life of the individual, there must also be more of them. If we keep this in mind, then the transaction costs of the vertical division of labor must rise. It is thus to be expected that the net yield of an extension of the period of production falls to zero at some finite value and beyond this point becomes negative.

To express this idea in terms of the history of economic doctrines: We bring together Adam Smith ("division of labor") with Ronald Coase ("transaction costs") and combine this team with the Austrian team of Carl Menger ("lower and higher order goods") and Eugen von Böhm-Bawerk ("roundaboutness of production" and/or "period of production"), in order thus to derive the conclusion that the prosperity-maximizing period of production, and hence the prosperity-maximizing capital coefficient, is finite in a stationary economy. There is a limit to the law of the "greater productivity of more roundabout production."

The same idea can also be expressed more in terms of "business economics." Every firm and all business operations are persistently confronted by the question of outsourcing. The business obtains some intermediate products from external suppliers and thus reduces the complexity of its own production process. But apart from this advantage, there is also the disadvantage that additional transaction costs are incurred. This was the main idea of Coase's study on "The Nature of the Firm." Typically, the business purchases external goods or services at a price that is above the marginal cost of the supplier. This is worth it, if the difference between price and marginal cost is small enough so that the supplier's price is still less than the marginal cost of the purchasing firm's producing the good itself.

If, however, there is a very high degree of vertical division of labor among many firms that are involved in the production process almost one after another, then it will be possible to reduce the total cost of the end product by vertically integrating. Thus, it can also be empirically established that there is no tendency toward ever greater vertical division of labor. This is indicative of the fact that the optimal period of production is not infinitely large.

4.1.11   Real Interest Rates of Zero as Price Signal for the Negative Marginal Productivity of More Roundabout Production

If we take the risk-free capital market interest rate as our standard, then for a long time now, there have been real interest rates of zero or even negative real interest rates in the eurozone. And it would appear that this very low interest rate level is not the consequence, but rather the cause of the monetary policy of the European Central Bank (ECB). As Wicksell already showed, the monetary policy of a central bank has to be guided by the "neutral" equilibrium rate of interest. For if the lower rates were merely the consequence of a particular policy orientation of the ECB, then in light of how long they have persisted, there would have to be the onset of massive inflation in the eurozone. But this has not come to pass.

Hence, the evolution of the rate of interest in the eurozone shows that in a hypothetical closed economy consisting of the euro countries, the natural rate of interest is negative. The hypothetical closed eurozone economy has a hypothetical "neutral" rate of interest that is lower than the empirically observed rate. This is so for two reasons: Firstly, the real eurozone enjoys a current account surplus; secondly, there is not full employment in the eurozone. In order to achieve full employment, with given fiscal policy and given economic policy in other respects, the interest rate level would have to be lower than what it actually is. In order to offset the hypothetical disappearance of the current account surplus, the real full-employment rate of interest would have to be even lower. This hypothetical neutral, real full-employment rate of interest is thus already negative. But the natural rate of interest of this economic area is even lower than the neutral full-employment rate. For the level of public debt in the eurozone is equivalent to several years of consumption. Hence, the hypothetical "neutral" rate of interest of this hypothetical closed economy is considerably higher than the natural rate corresponding to a hypothetical steady state without public debt.

We do not want to engage here in speculations about where exactly this natural rate of interest of the eurozone is situated. In our thought experiment on the losses in prosperity of a steady state with a natural rate of interest, we assumed a real natural rate of interest of -2% per year. In keeping with our empirical analysis, we had the OECD plus China region in mind here. Already for demographic reasons alone, the eurozone is among the less dynamic parts of the larger OECD plus China region. Hence, we can presume that the natural rate of interest is algebraically even less than -2% per year. It is, then, even further from zero than -2%.

If, in the tradition of Böhm-Bawerk, we insist, at least for the purpose of a steady-state analysis, on the idea that the real rate of interest is a price signal for the marginal productivity of roundabout production, then we come to the conclusion that an economy without public debt, like the hypothetical closed eurozone, would be characterized by considerably *decreased productivity* of additional round-aboutness of production. It would represent a massive squandering of wealth for the purpose of maintaining full employment. In Chaps. 10 to 13, we will provide better answers, from the point of view of economic policy, to the problem of the structural private savings glut. These answers are related to public debt.

Estimating a real natural rate of interest that is conceived as negative is difficult, because peoples' behavior massively changes, if the returns that they are able to achieve on financial investments signal a risk-free real rate of interest that is no longer positive, but rather massively negative. A "flight to tangible assets" then occurs, which can take very different forms depending upon the investor's opportunities. But this flight is very harmful to the economy.

Buying gold may be a sensible strategy during a transition from higher to lower real interest rates. But in the steady state of a negative real rate of interest that is not, however, falling any further, gold appears to be a very risky investment. Buying real estate can also be a strategy for getting around negative real interest rates, but it too involves considerable risks. We will discuss them in greater detail in Chap. 5. If only due to the "counterparty risk," all these risks are difficult to eliminate by way of hedging with financial instruments. This is especially the case for people who have little wealth. On the whole, historical experience—for example, the experience of the "great inflations" of the 1920s in Europe or of inflation in Latin America—indicates that the losses in efficiency, and hence losses in prosperity, that occur when there are extremely negative real interest rates are even greater than our steady-state thought experiment suggests. If, for example, large parts of the German and Austrian middles classes lost practically all their wealth in the "great inflation," the upheavals to which this would later give rise point to the dangers for prosperity that lie in wait, if real interest rates slide too far into the minuses.

4.2 Determining the Value of Private Real Capital in the OECD Plus China Region

4.2.1 Definitions and Concepts

In this chapter and the following ones, we aim to determine the wealth of private persons. More specifically, the objective of Sects. 4.2, 5.2, 6.2 is to estimate the respective magnitudes of the particular types of private sector wealth that are discussed in greater detail in Sects. 4.1, 5.1 and 6.1. In our analytical framework, private sector wealth is composed of financial assets and non-financial assets in the form of real capital (a produced asset) and land (a non-produced asset) (cf. Table 4.1). The financial assets of the private sector consist exclusively of its financial claims on the state. For the state, there are corresponding liabilities of the same magnitude. The reason why the financial assets of the private sector only exist in this form becomes clear when we elucidate two matters. Firstly, within the private sector, the balance of reciprocal claims and liabilities is zero. Domestically,

Table 4.1 Basic structure of a balance sheet

Assets	Liabilities
Non-financial assets	Liabilities
Produced assets	
Non-produced assets	
Financial assets	Net wealth

Source Authors' own presentation

therefore, the private sector only has net claims vis-à-vis the state. Secondly, we are treating the OECD plus China region as a closed economic area (cf. Sect. 3.11). The balance of reciprocal foreign claims and foreign liabilities within this area is likewise zero.

Hence, the net wealth of the private sector consists of its net financial claims on the state and the two non-financial assets: real capital, the subject of the present chapter, and land, which we will examine in Chap. 5. The private sector's net claims on the state represent public debt, which is composed of explicit and implicit debt. We will deal with public debt in detail in Chap. 6. Excess value plays a special role. The excess value is the difference between the market and the book values of the real capital of the corporate sector in the sense of Tobin's Q. We will go into excess value separately below.

Thus, in our approach, private wealth (W_P) is, by definition, composed of the following four types of assets:

$$W_P = K_P + L_P + V + \tilde{D}$$

The meanings of the symbols are as follows:

K_P: private real capital (including buildings, etc.); L_P: private land (including subsoil reserves, water resources, etc.); V: excess value of the corporate sector; $\tilde{D}$: (explicit net and implicit) public debt.

All of the calculations we have carried out in this chapter and the following ones for estimating the magnitudes of these wealth components are ultimately based on data drawn from the official statistics. In this connection, the conversion of national accounting to the United Nations' 2008 System of National Accounts (2008 SNA) (European Commission et al. 2009) and the European System of Accounts 2010 (ESA 2010) (Eurostat 2013), which is used in all EU Member States, has brought about some significant improvements for our purposes. These improvements involve, in particular, conceptual changes and the expansion of the databases for compiling balance sheets. On the one hand, we should mention information on the present value of retirement benefit claims that have accrued in the context of social security; this data will serve as the basis for the estimation of implicit public debt that we undertake in Chap. 6.2. On the other hand, for some years now, the statistical offices of the OECD countries have been compiling national and sectoral balance sheets (Lequiller and Blades 2014, pp. 231–254).[1] A national balance sheet is a presentation of the assets and outstanding liabilities in an economy at a given point in time. The resulting balance is the net worth (Eurostat 2013, p. 193) or, in our (and Piketty's) terms, net wealth. "Only economic assets…to which institutional units have property rights and from whose use or possession the owner can obtain economic benefits count as assets in the balance sheet" (Schmalwasser and Müller 2009, p. 138). "Institutional units" here refers to the institutional sectors of an economy.

However, not all assets are included in the national and sectoral balance sheets. For instance, human capital, non-mineral natural capital (water, air, etc.), and national monuments are not covered (van de Ven and Fano 2017, pp. 281–283). It is particularly relevant for our investigation that the following three assets are likewise either not included at all or not fully included among the fixed assets:

1. The present value of future public retirement benefits (and medical services) in "pay-as-you-go" social security systems. Recently, however, a number of countries have provided data on entitlements to public retirement benefits separately from their balance sheets in so-called supplementary tables. At least for Eurostat, these tables are a standard part of the data delivery program. This only applies, however, for the public retirement plan. Up to now, it is not the case for other claims on social security systems (e.g., health insurance).

2. The consumer durables owned by households: such as motor vehicles, household appliances and furniture. The reason for this is that national accounting follows a predominantly production-oriented approach. Most statistical offices do not include consumer durables among assets in the balance sheets. Many countries, however, append the value of consumer durables to the balance sheets as a memorandum. For example, in Germany consumer durables owned by households were worth more than 1 trillion euros in 2019, which is equivalent to 12% of households' non-financial assets (Deutsche Bundesbank and Statistisches Bundesamt 2020). Since on our view, such assets form part of the wealth of households, we will add their value in later.

3. Certain intangible assets, like goodwill and marketing assets (brand names, mastheads, trademarks, logos, domain names, etc.) are only added, when they are included in a company balance sheet in the context of its sale (Eurostat 2013, p. 177). If the market values of companies that are not being sold differ from their book values, then excess value comes into being, which is not recorded in the official statistics, since fixed assets are included in the balance sheets at their book values.

---

[1]In Germany, complete sectoral and national balance sheets have been prepared since 2010. These are composed of data on fixed assets from the Federal Statistical Office [*Statistisches Bundesamt*] and the results of the calculation of monetary assets by the Bundesbank (Schmalwasser and Weber 2012, p. 944). Balance sheets are a key source of empirical data for Piketty and Zucman (2014) and Piketty (2014). Their analyses connect up with the pioneering work of Goldsmith (1985).

In this chapter and the following ones, we attempt to include the value of the three abovementioned types of assets, which are not included in private wealth as represented in the national and sectoral balance sheets. In doing so, we are able to draw on data that is available elsewhere, which is either directly or indirectly taken from official statistics. Various national statistical offices have published related data on certain of these assets (some of them having only begun to do so recently). We will use this data to the extent that it is helpful in making our estimates.

In order to make clear which of the national accounting figures correspond to the abovementioned types of assets that are relevant for us, we will now juxtapose the concepts we use and the terms from the national accounts.

- By real capital, we understand all produced assets. These include, in particular, buildings, machinery and equipment, infrastructure (roads, railway networks, etc.), inventories and intellectual property.
- Land is our generic term for all non-produced assets. The latter include, in particular, land in the strict sense of the term, but also exploitation rights and other natural resources (mineral and energy reserves and other natural assets). They are regarded as non-produced assets, because they are "discovered" and not produced by human beings (van de Ven and Fano 2017, pp. 283).[2]
- Excess value is what we call the intangible assets (goodwill and marketing assets) that do not appear in the balance sheet. Although they also figure among the non-produced assets, we want to separate them from the latter. These intangible assets become apparent when a company is sold and the price paid for it exceeds the reported value of its equity.[3] Excess value is the result of a difference between market value and book value.
- In the case of public debt, the focus of our interest is the balance of the state's liabilities and claims vis-à-vis the private sector. We are thus considering *net* public debt. Public debt includes both explicit public debt and the implicit public debt represented by the social security benefits to which households are entitled.

We assign these four types of wealth (real capital, land, excess value and public debt) to the various institutional sectors of the economy in a way that is guided by our research objectives. To this end, we subdivide the economy as a whole into the following institutional sectors, as is also done in the 2008 SNA and the ESA 2010:

- Private households (including the self-employed).
- Non-profit institutions.
- Financial corporations.

---

[2]In statistical practice, for certain assets, it is difficult or even impossible to determine what part of their value is produced and what part is not produced. Land improvements—thanks to cultivation—are an example. The value that they create represents a produced asset. But it is practically impossible to separate this value from the value of land as non-produced asset.

[3]In correctly determining the excess value, it should be taken into account that the value of the equity has to be reduced "for any subsequent reductions as the initial value is written down as an economic disappearance of non-produced assets" (Eurostat 2013, p. 177).

- Non-financial corporations.
- General government.
- Rest of the world.

Moreover, we combine financial and non-financial corporations under the generic category of firms, and we also subsume non-profit institutions under households. Since we are treating the OECD plus China region as a closed economy, the "rest of the world" can be dropped.

We are left, then, with the following three institutional sectors:

- Private households, H
- Firms, F
- Government, G

Table 4.2 shows how the abovementioned wealth components are apportioned among these sectors.

The three institutional sectors—households, firms and the government—each possess real capital (K) and land (L). In the case of firms, real capital is mostly composed of plant and equipment. In the household sector, residential buildings are particularly important. But since the self-employed are assigned to the household sector, equipment, commercial real estate, software, etc., are also included in the sector's real capital. In the case of the government, real capital consists almost entirely of non-residential structures, including public infrastructure (roads and waterways) and public buildings (schools, administrative buildings, etc.) (cf. Schmalwasser and Weber 2012, p. 945).

The household sector, firms and the government all possess land in the strict sense, which in most countries constitutes the greater part of land in the enlarged sense (L) adumbrated above. For instance, in Germany, the household sector, with a share of almost 80%, holds by far the most land (in the strict sense).[4]

In the corporate sector, there can also be negative excess value (V).[5] Excess value comes into being when the market and book value of firms diverge. The quotient of market and book value is known as Tobin's Q (Tobin 1969; Tobin and Brainard 1977). We are interested in a value quantity and hence define excess value as the difference between the market value and the book value of firms (Alvaredo

---

[4]Up to now, mineral and energy reserves and other types of natural assets are not included in the determination of the economic value of land in Germany. They are, however, in France: the country that, apart from Australia, provides the most complete account of its fixed assets. Non-produced assets like non-cultivated biological and water resources, mineral and energy reserves, and other natural resources are also covered in the French statistics. For more details, see Chap. 5.2.

[5]In our present context, it is irrelevant that discrepancies can also arise between the book and market values of the real capital of self-employed persons, who are included in the household sector.

Table 4.2 Wealth components and institutional sectors

Households (H)	Firms (F)	Government (G)
K_H	K_F	K_G
L_H	L_F	L_G
$\tilde{D}$		$-\tilde{D}$
	V	

Source Authors' own presentation

et al. 2017, pp. 45–47).[6] Different causes for a diverging of market values from book values are discussed in the relevant literature. We examine some of them in what follows. If book values are greater than market values, there is negative excess value in the aggregate corporate sector (Tobin's Q is then less than one). In this case, firms possess assets that are undervalued on the stock exchange in comparison to their book value. This can be a result of errors in assessing the book values of the assets, as well as of errors in assessing their market values. If, on the contrary, the market values are greater than the book values, there is positive excess value (Tobin's Q is then greater than one). The value of firms on the stock exchange is then higher than the value of the assets in their books. Different types of errors in assessment can likewise be responsible here. The overvaluation of the firms can also be due to the fact that in the market's view, they possess intangible assets, like rights, market power or reputation, that will increase their future profitability, but that are not included in their balance sheets.

Excess value is thus to be understood in the following sense. Since, in the final analysis, firms are owned by the other two domestic sectors (the household sector or the public sector) or by the rest of the world, positive excess value has to be added to the real capital of the corporate sector as measured in book values or, respectively, negative excess value has to be subtracted from the latter, in order for us to be able to determine the wealth of the other sectors as measured in market values. It is only when excess value is equal to zero (in which case, Tobin's Q equals one) that the market value of firms is already included in the wealth of the private or the public sector.[7]

In the developed economies, Tobin's Q was on average less than one on the macrolevel in the non-financial corporate sector from 1970 to 2010 (Piketty and Zucman 2013, p. 29). For many years now, however, there have been differences between individual countries that are difficult to explain. In Germany, France and Japan, Tobin's Q has been consistently less than one since the beginning of the 1970s (Piketty and Zucman 2013, p. 29). It is the common opinion that firms in these countries are undervalued. Expressed in the terms of our analysis, this means that the corporate sector exhibits negative excess value. By contrast, in some (above

---

[6]Piketty and Zucman (2014) and Alvaredo et al. (2017) call the difference between the book value and the market value of national income "corporate residual wealth." The concept of excess value that we employ here is equivalent to "corporate residual wealth," but with the plus or minus sign reversed. (For more on this, see below.)

[7]Since we are considering a closed economy, the rest of the world plays no role here.

all, Anglo-Saxon) countries, Tobin's Q has been greater than one on the macrolevel in the non-financial corporate sector for quite some time. This is so, above all, for the USA, where, apart from the years after the two stock market crashes in 2001 and 2008, Tobin's Q has been greater than one since around the middle of the 1990s (Hautle 2016, pp. 495–496).[8]

A whole series of factors could be responsible for the long-term divergence of market values from book values. A variety of hypotheses on the reasons for these differences are to be found in the relevant literature. Statistical offices' reporting too high a book value of company equity is presumed to be one key cause for a negative difference between market and book value. Gordon (1990) has shown that there is a tendency to underestimate quality improvements in capital goods, thereby overstating the evolution of their prices. Wright's (2004, p. 570) explanation has a similar tenor. He assumes that the reported depreciation of plant and machinery is too low, since the speed at which capital goods become technically obsolete is systematically underestimated. As consequence, the replacement costs of real capital are set too high. (Cf. also Hautle 2016, pp. 496).

Piketty and Zucman (2013, p. 31) explain the difference in Tobin's Q between the Anglo-Saxon countries, on the one hand, and the continental European countries and Japan, on the other, by the different degrees of shareholder control in the two groups of countries. They argue that in countries like Germany, France or Japan, shareholders have to cede some control to other stakeholders (such as trade unions and the government). Hence, they would have more limited opportunities for increasing the value of their capital and likewise could not simply liquidate all the company's assets, if they so wish. "According to this 'stakeholder' view of the firm, the market value of corporations can be interpreted as the value for the owner, while the book value can be interpreted as the value for all stakeholders" (ibid.).

On the other hand, there are a whole series of factors that cause the market value of firms to be greater than their book value. These include inadequate recording of intellectual property (patents, licenses, copyrights) or of the value of a corporate brand. The fact that a company as a whole is normally worth more than the sum of its parts would also lead to Tobin's Q being greater than one and hence to the corporate sector having positive excess value.

Whatever the reasons are for a long-term divergence of the market value of firms from their book value, the existence of positive as well as negative excess value has to be taken into account when calculating the wealth of households. If the corporate sector has positive excess value, the wealth of households is greater than what is shown in the official balance sheets; if the excess value is negative, the wealth of households is less.[9] Further on, we will discuss how we deal with this in the empirical analysis.

---

[8]It is interesting to note that some studies find that Tobin's Q is greater than one on the microlevel for both American companies and non-American companies (Fernandes et al. 2013, pp. 331–332). But American companies are shown to have a considerably higher Tobin's Q.

[9]This holds on the assumption that the fixed assets of the corporate sector are recorded in the official statistics at their book values.

We already pointed out above that the government's public debt corresponds to private household wealth of exactly the same magnitude.[10] The net claims of private households on the government ($\tilde{D}$) is the balance of the financial claims of households on the government minus the financial claims of the government on households. $\tilde{D}$ thus represents net public debt. Apart from the latter, the value of publicly owned real capital and of public land are decisive for the net wealth of the public sector.[11]

We have now examined all the assets that play a role in our analysis. Just one further step is required, in order to arrive at the concept of total private wealth. We need, namely, to take into account that households and the government are what could be called ultimate owner sectors. Firms—and hence their real capital and land —are owned by either the government or households. We combine the corporate sector with the household sector.[12] There thus remain only two sectors: the private sector, on the one hand, and the government (the public sector), on the other (cf. Table 4.3). What is of interest to us is the wealth of the private sector and hence also the reciprocal relationship between the private and public sectors with respect to their claims and liabilities.

Fixed assets are supposed to be included in the national accounts at their current replacement costs. The objective is to record "fixed assets…at market prices if possible." Since, however, market prices do not exist for most capital goods, "purchasers' prices at acquisition reduced by the accumulated consumption of fixed capital" are used instead (Eurostat 2013, p. 175). In accordance with international agreements, the so-called perpetual inventory method is applied (Schmalwasser and Weber 2012, p. 944).[13] This involves attempting to derive the current value of the stock of fixed assets from the past investment in the goods in question. For this

---

[10]For purposes of simplification, we abstract here from the fact that the government's creditors also include firms (especially financial firms). In the next step of our analysis, it will be made clear why this is an acceptable and unproblematic simplification.

[11]Like in many other developed countries, in Germany, public sector net wealth has tended constantly to decline in recent decades (IMF 2018). Under the previous 1993 SNA, the public "capital ratio" in Germany was still around 58% in 1991 and fell to 1.3% by 2011. Public sector fixed assets and hence public sector net wealth are now greater again in Germany: among other reasons, due to the classification of R&D and military weapons systems as fixed capital in the 2008 SNA. In 2019, German public sector net wealth was 1,145 billion euros (Deutsche Bundesbank and Statistisches Bundesamt 2020).

[12]In the 2008 SNA, publicly owned companies are assigned not to the government sector, but to the corporate sector. Thus, for example, a publicly owned railway network is included in the balance sheet of the *non-financial corporations* sector (Schmalwasser and Weber 2012, p. 945). This has the consequence of overstating private sector wealth. On the other hand, among other things, valuables, inventories and natural assets are not included in the calculation of fixed assets in the official statistics. This results, conversely, in underreporting the actual wealth of the private sector.

[13]"Ideally, observable market prices should be used to value non-financial assets. However, nonfinancial assets depreciate in value over time due to their use in the production process, and secondhand markets, from which one could derive market prices for assets of different ages, are often nonexistent" (van de Ven and Fano 2017, p. 287).

Table 4.3 Consolidated sectors and wealth components	Private sector (P)	Government (G)
	$K_p = K_H + K_F$	K_G
	$L_P = L_H + L_F$	L_G
	$\tilde{D}$	$-\tilde{D}$
	V	
	$\Sigma\ 1\text{--}4 = NW_P$	$\Sigma\ 1\text{--}4 = NW_G$

NW_P = Private Sector Net Wealth; NW_G = Public Sector Net Wealth

$NW_P + NW_G$ = National Net Wealth (NW)

Source Authors' own presentation

purpose, far-reaching assumptions about depreciation have to be made (ibid., pp. 934–938).

According to Piketty and Zucman (2014, p. 1269, footnote 13), the data on fixed assets reported in the 2008 SNA is essentially based on book values. Therefore, in what follows, we assume that the fixed assets and national wealth reported in the official balance sheets are determined according to the book value approach. Consequently, if market values diverge from book values, excess value (V) has also to be taken into account in calculating the net wealth of the private sector. Another way of determining the value of capital goods that is suitable for our purposes consists of assessing them according to their market prices. This renders it super-fluous to report excess value separately.

The *World Inequality Database* was developed by a team led by Facundo Alvaredo, Tony Atkinson and Thomas Piketty. It provides data on the value of capital goods and national net wealth that has been established using the market price approach. We will rely on this data for a large part of our calculations in the present chapter. In the *Guidelines* on the concepts and methods employed in the World Inequality Database, the decision generally to use market prices to assess wealth is justified as follows: "The main rationale for looking at market-value national wealth is the possibility of measurement error for non-financial corporate assets and the view that stock market values might provide a more accurate evaluation of the 'real' value of corporations (which is far from clear)" (Alvaredo et al. 2017, p. 47, footnote 28).

Accordingly, in our analytical framework, we will use data for real capital and net wealth that has been established using the *market price approach*. To this end, we can draw on different variables on wealth from the World Inequality Database.

In the final analysis, private sector wealth (NW_P) in the OECD plus China region is thus:

$$NW_P = \tilde{K}_P + L_P + \tilde{D}$$

The meanings of the symbols are as follows: $\tilde{K}_P$: real capital of the private sector in market prices, L_P: land owned by the private sector, $\tilde{D}$: explicit net and implicit public debt.[14]

4.2.2 Data

For the purpose of determining the value of the real capital of the private sector in the OECD countries plus the People's Republic of China, we use data from the World Inequality Database (WID.world). The World Inequality Database is an extensive and freely accessible database containing information on income and wealth in many countries and, in some cases, over very long periods of time. It is based on the work of Thomas Piketty and his colleagues. The database became known, however, especially thanks to the data on the distribution of income and wealth that it makes available for numerous countries. In addition, data is also to be found for many countries on the current state and historical evolution of wealth and its components.[15] The data provided by the World Inequality Database is partly based on modified classifications from the 2008 SNA and/or the ESA 2010. These modifications were essentially developed by Piketty and Zucman (2013, 2014). We can see from Table 4.4 how the database defines the wealth concepts for particular sectors and the economy as a whole that are of relevance for us.[16]

In contrast to our approach, Piketty and Zucman include neither explicit nor implicit public debt in the wealth of households or the private sector. As usual in national accounts, they also do not count the consumer durables owned by households as wealth (Piketty and Zucman 2014, p. 1268).[17]

We associate the wealth components of the WID.world database with our definitions of the real capital (K) and land (L) of the private and the public sectors as shown in Table 4.5.

The total net wealth (NW) of a closed economy—such as the closed economy that the OECD plus China region roughly represents—thus corresponds to the sum of the net wealth of the private sector (PW) and the net wealth of the public sector (GW). Thus

---

[14]Because of a lack of suitable data, the excess value of the corporate sector can only be assigned to private persons. In fact, the excess value of publicly owned companies that are not listed on the stock exchange should be assigned to the government sector when the corporate sector is combined with the household sector. If the excess value of these companies is positive, then we are overestimating private wealth; if it is negative, then we are underestimating it—in both cases, however, only to a relatively small extent.

[15]The OECD database also contains data reflecting the wealth concepts of the 2008 SNA. Nonetheless, for numerous reasons, the WID.world concepts are more suitable for our purposes. On the differences between the 2008 SNA wealth concepts and those in WID.world, see Piketty and Zucman (2013), Bauluz (2017), Alvaredo et al. (2017), Zwijnenburg (2017).

[16]Detailed information on the wealth concepts is to be found in Piketty and Zucman (2013, 2014) and Alvaredo et al. (2017).

[17]Since both of the latter are elements of private wealth for us, we will include them.

Table 4.4 Definitions of wealth concepts in WID.world

Net wealth	Nonfinancial assets + financial assets − liabilities[a]
Private wealth	Net wealth of households[b] + net wealth of NPISH[c]
Corporate wealth	Net wealth of corporate sector[d]
	= Book value of national wealth − market value of national wealth
Government wealth	Net wealth of general government sector
Market value of national wealth	Private + government wealth
Book value of national wealth	Sum of all non-financial assets (= domestic capital)[e] of all domestic sectors + net foreign asset position
Non-financial assets	1. Produced tangible capital
	1.1. Fixed assets
	1.2. Inventories
	1.3. Valuables
	2. Non-produced tangible capital
	2.1. Land (land underlying residential buildings, land underlying non-residential buildings, other land)
	2.2. Subsoil assets
	2.3. Other natural resources
	3. Intangible capital
	3.1. Research & Development
	3.2. Intellectual property other than Research & Development
	3.3. Non-produced intangible capital (goodwill and marketing assets)

Notes
[a]Includes balance sheets equities
[b]Includes capital stock of corporations through the equity holdings of households
[c]NPISH (= non-profit institutions serving households)
[d]Positive (negative), if Tobin's $Q < 1$ ($Q > 1$)
[e]Produced and non-produced tangible capital + intangible capital (incl. nat. resources like land, subsoil assets etc.)
Source Authors' own presentation following Piketty and Zucman (2013)

Table 4.5 Private and public sector net wealth

	Private sector (P)	Government (G)
1. Produced tangible capital + intangible capital	K_P	K_G
2. Non-produced tangible capital	L_P	L_G
Net wealth (NW)	Σ 1–2 = PW	Σ 1–2 = GW

Source Authors' own presentation
The meanings of the symbols are as follows
K_P: real capital of the private sector in market prices; $K_{G.}$: real capital of the public sector in market prices; L_P: Private sector land; L_G: Public sector land; PW: Private wealth (net wealth of the private sector at market values, without public debt); GW: Government wealth (net wealth of the government sector at market values, without public debt); *NW*: (national) net wealth

$$PW = NW - GW$$

holds for the net wealth of the private sector and

$$\tilde{K}_p = NW - GW - L_p$$

for the real capital of the private sector in market prices.

On the basis of these relationships, we will, in the next section, determine the value of private sector real capital in the OECD plus China region.

4.2.3 Determining the Value of Real Capital

For the purpose of determining the value of the real capital of the private sector in the OECD plus China region, we use data from the World Inequality Database (WID.world). The OECD plus China region that we are considering comprises 35 countries altogether: 34 OECD countries and the People's Republic of China.[18] The WID.world database contains data with which we can calculate real capital for 19 countries. They are: Australia, Denmark, Germany, Finland, France, Greece, Italy, Japan, Canada, Mexico, the Netherlands, Norway, Spain, Sweden, South Korea, the Czech Republic, the USA, the UK and the People's Republic of China. The share of these 19 countries in total consumption in the whole OECD plus China region is around 90%. The greater part of the region is thereby covered, such that the calculations for these 19 countries can roughly stand for the region as a whole.

The methodology and data for most of the countries in the WID.world database are based on the original studies by Piketty and Zucman (2013, 2014) and an update by Bauluz (2017). More recent data for countries of relevance for us comes from Waldenström (2017) for Sweden, Piketty et al. (2017) for the People's Republic of China, and Blanco et al. (2018) for Spain.

2015 is the reference year for our empirical calculations in this chapter and the following ones. We have chosen this year for two reasons. Firstly, data is available from statistical offices for 2015 on the present value of entitlements to social security retirement benefits. This data provides a good basis for our being able to estimate implicit public debt in Chap. 6.2. We want later to combine the main wealth components that are calculated in this chapter and in the empirical parts of the following two chapters. Since, if possible, the results should refer to the same year, we likewise calculate the values for real capital and land for 2015. Secondly, the chosen reference year is also a highly suitable year for data comparison, since no severe recession, which could have distorted the data, took place in 2015 in the group of countries under investigation.

For the reasons presented above, we relate the value of real capital not, as is customarily done, to the flow variable gross domestic product, but rather to the flow

---

[18]We include all the OECD countries that had joined the OECD by 2015 among the OECD countries (cf. Sect. 3.11).

variable total consumption. By "total consumption"—or, in what follows, also simply "consumption"—we understand the sum of the expenditures for the consumption of households (private consumption) and for the consumption of the state (public consumption) that were undertaken in the respective reporting year: i.e., for our purposes, in 2015. Thus, we will say, for instance, that the value of real capital in Japan corresponds to 2.58 times or 258% of (total) consumption in 2015.

In a first step, the value of national wealth in market prices (in WID.world terminology, "market value national wealth") is extracted from the database for each of the above-mentioned 19 countries. The value of national wealth is given in the respective national currency (LCU) (see Table 4.6, column A). The balance of domestic claims and liabilities vis-à-vis the rest of the world (net foreign assets) is subtracted from the national wealth (cf. column B).[19] We thus obtain overall national non-financial assets or net wealth (column C). Column D lists general government non-financial assets in the individual countries. We subtract the latter from the national non-financial assets, in order to arrive at the non-financial assets of the private sector (column E). In the WID.world database, land is reported in two data series (1. private land underlying dwellings and 2. private agricultural land); data for 2015 is not available for all countries, however. For some countries, we had to rely on data from prior years. If information was lacking on the value of land (which is the case for China, Canada, Italy and Great Britain), the figures in question were supplemented by estimates based on the average values for the countries for which the data in question is available.

As already mentioned above, most countries do not include consumer durables in non-financial assets in their balance sheets. This is also the case for the WID.-world database. Since in our view, such goods are to be regarded as assets, we have added them in. In Germany and France, consumer durables represent about ten percent of the total fixed assets of the economy as a whole (Deutsche Bundesbank and Statistisches Bundesamt 2020; van de Ven and Fano 2017). In the USA, this figure is significantly higher (Hautle 2016, Table 3.5).[20] Since information on the total value of consumer durables is available only for a small minority of the 19 countries, we have made a conservative estimate and only added a supplement of one percent to the countries' fixed assets for the value of consumer durables. Column F lists fixed assets plus consumer durables minus the value of land in the

---

[19]According to the Balance Sheets for Institutional Sectors of the Bundesbank and the Federal Statistical Office (Deutsche Bundesbank und Statistisches Bundesamt 2020), Germany had 1,180 billion euros in net foreign assets in 2015. Our table, on the other hands, shows 1351 billion euros. For Germany's "international investment position," the database uses Bundesbank figures that diverge from the other data sources. In the view of Piketty and Zucman (2013, pp. 71–72), the Federal Statistical Office underestimates Germany's net foreign assets. National wealth in market prices and the non-financial wealth of the private sector could in fact be considerably greater using the Bundesbank figures. In the authors' view, the underestimation could represent up to 20% of national income.

[20]In 2013, the value of consumer durables amounted to about 22% of the value of the non-financial assets of the household sector in the USA, 13.3% in Japan, 12.6% in Canada, 5.3%, in Australia, and 14.5% in Germany (Board of Governors of the Federal Reserve System 2020; OECD 2019b; Deutsche Bundesbank and Statistisches Bundesamt 2020).

Table 4.6 Private real capital in the OECD plus China region, 2015

Country	A Total national wealth Billions LCU	B Net foreign assets Billions LCU	C = A–B Total non-financial assets Billions LCU	D Government non-financial assets Billions LCU	E = C–D Private sector non-financial assets Billions LCU	F Private sector non-financial assets (minus land, plus consumer durables) Billions LCU	G = F/I Private sector real capital Billions Int'l $	H Total consumption Billions Int'l $	I Conversion factor LCU in Int'l $	J = G/H Private sector real capital In years of consumption
Australia	9,722.5	−886.9	10,609.4	2,061.2	8,654.3	4,953.5	3,360.4	829.1	1.47	4.05
Canada	8,741.9	234.1	8,507.8	872.3	7,720.6	5,184.6	4,154.3	1,252.1	1.25	3.32
Czech Republic	14,407.3	−1,074.4	15,481.7	5,696.7	9,939.8	8,793.0	692.2	230.1	12.70	3.01
Denmark[a]	7,621.0	797.0	6,824.0	923.6	5,968.6	4,309.8	588.1	197.2	7.33	2.98
Finland[a]	836.1	7.2	828.9	155.1	682.0	563.3	620.9	181.2	0.91	3.43
France[a]	10,871.8	−191.3	11,063.1	1,931.9	9,241.8	6,227.8	7,703.1	2,117.0	0.81	3.64
Germany	11,377.0	1,351.7	10,025.3	1,747.7	8,377.8	6,126.8	7,875.9	2,851.6	0.78	2.76
Greece	728.6	−218.5	947.1	115.4	841.2	841.2	1,332.5	261.0	0.63	5.11
Italy[b]	7,866.5	−338.4	8,204.9	479.1	7,807.8	5,156.6	6,982.5	1,785.2	0.74	3.91
Japan	2,642,741.4	351,336.0	2,291,405.4	689,088.4	1,625,231.0	1,048,967.9	10,139.9	3,929.5	103.45	2.58
Korea	9,293,346.7	−74,725.4	9,368,072.1	2,585,794.7	6,875,958.2	4,226,225.7	4,929.3	1,173.4	857.37	4.20
Mexico[c]	72,357.5	−5,958.3	66,399.2	6,004.2	60,395.0	61,059.0	7,333.6	1,537.8	8.33	4.77
Netherlands[b]	2,937.7	404.4	2,533.3	577.5	1,981.1	1,375.7	1,700.9	589.4	0.81	2.89
Norway	17,321.4	5,741.8	11,579.6	1,797.2	9,898.2	6,948.1	699.7	209.8	9.93	3.34
Spain	5,590.7	−972.2	6,562.9	850.4	5,778.1	3,074.5	4,641.7	1,224.0	0.66	3.79
Sweden[a]	19,743.3	111.7	19,631.6	3,678.9	16,149.0	13,113.2	1,481.4	336.2	8.85	4.41

(continued)

Table 4.6 (continued)

	A	B	C	D	E	F	G	H	I	J
			= A–B		= C–D		= F / I			= G / H
	Total national wealth	Net foreign assets	Total non-financial assets	Government non-financial assets	Private sector non-financial assets	Private sector non-financial assets (minus land, plus consumer durables)	Private sector real capital	Total consumption	Conversion factor	Private sector real capital
Country	Billions LCU	Billions LCU	Billions LCU	Billions LCU	Billions LCU	Billions LCU	Billions Int'l $	Billions Int'l $	LCU in Int'l $	In years of consumption
UK	9,608.0	–302.6	9,910.7	1,089.4	8,920.4	6,542.8	9,450.0	2,305.9	0.69	4.10
USA	75,580.1	–5,613.1	81,193.2	15,094.7	66,910.4	55,188.6	55,188.6	14,907.2	1.00	3.70
China	440,383.8	9,493.3	302,083.0	45,636.7	259,467.2	200,766.8	57,901.3	10,447.8	3.47	5.54
Total OECD							128,875.1	35,917.6		3.59
Total OECD plus China							186,776.4	46,365.4		4.03

Sources

Column A WID.world (2019). Market-value national wealth

Column B WID.world (2019). Net foreign assets

Column D WID.world (2019). Government non-financial assets

Column F WID.world (2019). Private land underlying dwellings; Private agricultural land

Column H World Bank (2019). World Development Indicators, Final consumption expenditure (current LCU)

Column I World Bank (2019). World Development Indicators, PPP conversion factor (GDP) (LCU per international $)

Authors' own calculations

Notes

[a]2014

[b]2013

[c]Data source for non-financial assets: OECD (2019a)

Land values partially estimated (China, Canada, Italy, UK)

LCU: Local currency unit

broader sense (including natural resources). This category of wealth corresponds to what we understand by private real capital.

Our objective in this chapter is to determine the total value of real capital in the OECD plus China region as expressed in years of total consumption. In order to achieve this objective, the values listed in the respective local currencies have to be converted into purchasing-power-adjusted "international dollars." Column G provides the real capital in international dollars. In total, the real capital in the 18 OECD countries listed came to around 128.9 trillion international dollars in 2015. Including China, the value of the real capital in the group of countries as a whole came to 186.8 trillion international dollars. Column H contains total consumption for 2015 in international dollars. The value of total consumption, consisting of the consumption of households and public consumption, came to 46.4 trillion international dollars in the OECD plus China region (without China: 35.9 trillion international dollars).

Column J shows the ratio of real capital to total consumption. The figures vary between the different countries: sometimes to a considerable extent. For the OECD countries, they range from 2.6 for Japan to 5.1 for Greece. As compared to the average for the OECD countries, the figure for China, at 5.5 times consumption, is considerably higher. On the one hand, there could be objective reasons for this, but, on the other hand, as experience shows, data collection errors in the database cannot be entirely ruled out either. In general, there is substantial uncertainty regarding the quality of economic data for China.[21]

4.2.4 The Value of Private Real Capital

In 2015, the value of real capital in Germany was nearly 2.8 times total annual consumption. In France, the corresponding figure was 3.8 times. In Germany, the value of real capital owned by firms is relatively low in comparison to other countries at a similar level of development. Van de Ven and Fano (2017, p. 411) explain this by the nature of so-called Rhenish capitalism, in which the participation of banks is relatively significant, while financing via capital markets does not play as great a role as elsewhere.

Our figures match the results of similarly oriented investigations (e.g., Piketty 2014). For France, the OECD also established a figure of 355% of gross domestic product for non-produced assets (van de Ven and Fano 2017). In light of a somewhat different system of classification with respect to wealth categories, the figures calculated, using the WID.world data, for French real capital (i.e., in relation to total annual consumption, which accounts for approximately 77% of French Gross Domestic Product) appear to be entirely plausible. The same holds for

---

[21]Piketty et al. (2017), from whom the data used for China originally comes, drew on official balance sheets and other national statistics of the People's Republic of China for their calculations (Piketty et al. 2017, pp. 11–13). Li and Zhang (2017) make clear the challenges involved in designing and compiling balance sheets for China.

Australia, for which we have calculated a figure of approximately four times total consumption in 2015, whereas the OECD arrives at a figure of 344% of gross domestic product (van de Ven and Fano 2017, Table 8.1).

On average, real capital in the OECD plus China region represented 4.03 times total consumption in 2015. As a look at the statistics shows, China raises the average for the region. Without China, real capital amounted to 3.59 times annual consumption in 2015.

> We thus find that, according to our calculations, private wealth in the form of real capital in the OECD plus China region comes to approximately four times total consumption.

References

Alvaredo, Facundo, Anthony B. Atkinson, Lucas Chancel, Thomas Piketty, Emmanuel Saez and Gabriel Zucman. 2017. *Distributional National Accounts (DINA) Guidelines: Concepts and Methods Used in the World Wealth and Income Database*. Version June 9th, 2017. WID.world Working Paper Series No. 2016/1. http://wid.world/document/dinaguidelines-v1/. Accessed: 20 March 2019.

Arrow, Kenneth J., Hollis B. Chenery, Bagicha S. Minhas and Robert M. Solow. 1961. Capital-Labor Substitution and Economic Efficiency. *Review of Economics and Statistics* 43 (3): 225–250.

Bauluz, Luis E. 2017. *Revised and extended national wealth series: Australia, Canada, France, Germany, Italy, Japan, the UK and the USA*. WID.world Working Paper Series No. 2017/23. https://wid.world/document/revised-extended-national-wealth-series-aust-ralia-canada-france-germany-italy-japan-uk-usa-wid-world-technical-note-2017-23/. Accessed: 20 March 2019.

Blanco, M. Artola, Luis E. Bauluz, Clara Martínez-Toledano. 2018. *Wealth in Spain, 1900–2014: A Country of Two Lands*. WID.world Working Paper Series No. 2018/5. https://wid.world/document/wealth-spain-1900-2014-country-two-lands-wid-world-wor-king-paper-2018-5/. Accessed: 3 May 2019.

Board of Governors of the Federal Reserve System. 2020. *Financial Accounts of the United States – Z.1, Flow of Funds, Balance Sheets, and Integrated Macroeconomic Accounts*, 3rd Quarter 2020. Washington (D.C.). https://www.federalreserve.gov/releases/z1/20201210/z1.pdf. Accessed: 20 January 2020.

Boettke, Peter J. 2018, *F.A. Hayek – Economics, Political Economy and Social Philosophy*. London: Palgrave-Macmillan.

Böhm-Bawerk, Eugen Ritter von. 1891 [1889]. *The Positive Theory of Capital*, trans. William Smart. London and New York: Macmillan.

Böhm-Bawerk, Eugen Ritter von. 1913. Eine „dynamische" Theorie des Kapitalzinses. *Zeitschrift für Volkswirtschaft, Sozialpolitik und Verwaltung* 22: 520–585 and 640-57.

Coase, Ronald H. 1937. The Nature of the Firm. *Economica* 4 (16): 386–405.

Coase, Ronald H. 1960. The Problem of Social Cost. *Journal of Law and Economics* 3: 1–44.

Deutsche Bundesbank and Statistisches Bundesamt (Federal Statistical Office). 2018. *Balance sheets for institutional sectors and the total economy 1999–2017*, Deutsche Bundesbank: Frankfurt am Main and Statistisches Bundesamt (Federal Statistical Office): Wiesbaden.

Deutsche Bundesbank and Statistisches Bundesamt (Federal Statistical Office). 2020. *Balance sheets for institutional sectors and the total economy 1999–2019*, Deutsche Bundesbank: Frankfurt am Main and Statistisches Bundesamt (Federal Statistical Office): Wiesbaden.

Deutsche Bundesbank. 2008. Integrated sectoral and overall balance sheets for Germany. In: *Monthly Report* January 2008, 31–45.

Epstein, Larry G. and Stanley E. Zin. 1989. Substitution, Risk Aversion and the Temporal Behavior of Consumption and Asset Returns: A Theoretical Framework. *Econometrica* 57 (4): 937–960.

European Commission, IMF, OECD, UN and World Bank. 2009. *System of National Accounts 2008*. https://unstats.un.org/unsd/nationalaccount/docs/SNA2008.pdf

Eurostat 2013. *European System of Accounts: ESA 2010*. Luxemburg: Publications Office of the European Union.

Fernandes, Nuno, Miguel A. Ferreira, Pedro Matos and Kevin J. Murphy. 2013. Are U.S. CEOs Paid More? New International Evidence. *Review of Financial Studies* 26(2): 323–367.

Fisher, Irving. 1906. *The Nature of Capital and Income*. New York (NY): Macmillan.

Fisher, Irving. 1907. *The Rate of Interest*. New York (NY): Macmillan.

Goldsmith, Raymond W. 1985. *Comparative National Balance Sheets, A Study of Twenty Countries, 1688–1978*. Chicago (IL): The University of Chicago Press.

Gordon, Robert J. 1990. *The Measurement of Durable Goods Prices*. Cambridge (MA): National Bureau of Economic Research.

Hautle, Willy. 2016. *Integrierte makroökonomische Konten und Stock-Flow konsistente Modelle: mit Anwendungen zur Grossen Rezession*. Norderstedt: BoD – Books on Demand.

Hayek, Friedrich A. von. 1937. Economics and Knowledge. *Economica* 4 (13): 33–54.

Hicks, John R. 1932. *The Theory of Wages*. London: Macmillan.

Hicks, John R. 1939. *Value and Capital*. Oxford: Clarendon Press.

Horvat, Branko. 1958. The Optimum Rate of Investment. *Economic Journal* 68 (272): 747–767.

IMF (International Monetary Fund). 2018. *Fiscal Monitor. Managing Public Wealth*. October 2018. Washington (D.C.): International Monetary Fund.

Jordà, Òscar, Katharina Knoll, Dmitry Kuvshinov, Moritz Schularick and Alan M. Taylor. 2019. The Rate of Return on Everything, 1870–2015. *Quarterly Journal of Economics* 134 (3): 1225–1298.

Kaldor, Nicholas. 1961. Capital Accumulation and Economic Growth. In *The Theory of Capital*, ed. F.A. Lutz and D. C. Hague, 177–222. London: St. Martin's Press.

Lequiller, François and Derek Blades. 2014. *Understanding National Accounts*. 2nd ed. Paris: OECD Publishing.

Li, Yang and Xiaojing Zhang. 2017. *China's National Balance Sheet: Theories, Methods and Risk Assessment*. Singapur: Springer. http://www.springer.com/cda/content/document/cda_download document/9789811043840-c2.pdf?SGWID=0-0-45-1608746-p180735840. Accessed: 18 July 2018.

Lutz, Friedrich. 1967. *Zinstheorie*. 2. ed. Tübingen: Mohr-Siebeck.

Luxemburg, Rosa. 1951 [1913]. *The Accumulation of Capital*. trans. Agnes Schwarzschild. London: Routledge and Kegan Paul.

Marx, Karl. 1976 [1867]. *Capital: A Critique of Political Economy*, vol. 1. trans. Ben Fowkes. London: Penguin/New Left Books.

Marx, Karl. 1981 [1894]. *Capital: A Critique of Political Economy*, vol. 3. trans. David Fernbach, London: Penguin/New Left Books.

Menger, Carl. 1871. *Grundsätze der Volkswirtschaftslehre*. Wien: Braumüller.

OECD. 2018. *National Accounts, Annual National Accounts, Detailed Tables and Simplified 9B. Balance sheets for non-financial assets, N1: Produced Assets; NS1: Total economy less NS13: General Government*. OECD, Paris. https://stats.oecd.org/Index.aspx?DataSetCode=SNA_ TABLE9B. Accessed: 22 August 2018.

OECD. 2019a. *Detailed National Accounts, SNA 2008 (or SNA 1993): Balance sheets for nonfinancial assets, OECD National Accounts Statistics (database)*. https://doi.org/10.1787/ data-00368-en. Accessed: 7 June 2019.

OECD. 2019b. *Households' financial and non-financial assets and liabilities – Annual and Quarterly – archived*. http://stats.oecd.org/OECDStat_Metadata/ShowMetadata.ashx?Dataset= 7HA_A_Q&ShowOnWeb=true&Lang=en. Accessed: 16 June 2019.

Piketty, Thomas and Gabriel Zucman. 2013. *Capital is Back: Wealth-Income Ratios in Rich Countries, 1700–2010. Data Appendix*. http://piketty.pse.ens.fr/files/PikettyZucman2013Appendix.pdf. Accessed: 15 January 2019.

Piketty, Thomas and Gabriel Zucman. 2014. Capital Is Back: Wealth-Income Ratios in Rich Countries, 1700–2010. *Quarterly Journal of Economics* 129 (3): 1255–310.

Piketty, Thomas, Emmanual Saez and Gabriel Zucman. 2018. Distributional national accounts: Methods and estimates for the United States. *Quarterly Journal of Economics*. 133(2): 553–609.

Piketty, Thomas, Li Yang and Gabriel Zucman. 2017. *Capital Accumulation, Private Property and Rising Inequality in China: 1978–2015*. WID.world Working Paper Series No. 2017/6. http://wid.world/document/t-piketty-l-yang-and-g-zucmancapital-accu-mulation-private-property-andinequality-in-china-1978-2015-2016/. Accessed: 20 April 2019.

Piketty, Thomas. 2014. *Capital in the Twenty-First Century*, Cambridge (MA): Harvard University Press.

Polanyi, Michael. 1958. *Personal Knowledge, Towards a post-critical philosophy*. Chicago (IL): Chicago University Press.

Sahlins, Marshall. 1968. Notes on the Original Affluent Society. In *Man the Hunter*, ed. R.B. Lee and I. Devore, 85-89. New York (NY): Aldine.

Samuelson, Paul A. 1958. An Exact Consumption-Loan Model of Interest with or without the Social Contrivance of Money. *Journal of Political Economy* 66 (6): 467–482.

Schmalwasser, Oda and Aloysius Müller. 2009. Gesamtwirtschaftliche und sektorale nichtfinanzielle Vermögensbilanzen. *Wirtschaft und Statistik* 2: 137–147.

Schmalwasser, Oda and Nadine Weber. 2012. Revision der Anlagevermögensrechnung für den Zeitraum 1991 bis 2011. *Wirtschaft und Statistik* 11: 933–947.

Schumpeter, Joseph. A. 1934 [1911]. *The Theory of Economic Development*. trans. Redvers Opie. Cambridge, MA: Harvard University Press.

Simon, Herrmann. 2012. *Hidden Champions – Aufbruch nach Globalia*. Frankfurt am Main: Campus.

Smith, Adam. 1776. *An Inquiry into the Nature and Causes of the Wealth of Nations*. London: W. Strahan and T. Cadell.

Solow, Robert M. 1957. Technical Change and the Aggregate Production Function. *Review of Economics and Statistics* 39 (3): 312–320.

Tobin, James and William C. Brainard. 1977. Asset Markets and the Cost of Capital. In *Economic Progress, Private Values and Public Policy: Essays in Honor of William Fellner*, ed. Bela Balassa and Richard Nelson, 235–262. Amsterdam: North Holland.

Tobin, James. 1969. A general equilibrium approach to monetary theory. *Journal of Money, Credit and Banking* 1: 15–29.

van de Ven, Peter and Daniele Fano (Ed.). 2017. *Understanding Financial Accounts*. Paris: OECD Publishing.

Waldenström, Daniel. 2017. Wealth-Income Ratios in a Small, Developing Economy: Sweden, 1810–2014. *Journal of Economic History* 77(1): 285–313.

Weizsäcker, Carl Christian von. 1974. Substitution Along the Time Axis. *Kyklos* XXVII (4): 732–756.

Weizsäcker, Carl Christian von. 1977. Organic Composition of Capital and Average Period of Production. *Revue d'Economie Politique* 87 (2): 198–231.

Weizsäcker, Carl Christian von. 2021. *Capital Theory of the Steady State – Or: T + L = Z–D*. https://www.coll.mpg.de/Weizsaecker/CapitalTheory2021 and https://www.springer.com/9783 658273620.

WID.world (World Inequality Database), ed. von Facundo Alvaredo, Anthony B. Atkinson, Lucas Chancel, Thomas Piketty, Emmanuel Saez and Gabriel Zucman. https://wid.world/. Accessed: March-July 2019.

World Bank. 2019. *DataBank – World Development Indicators.* https://databank.world-bank.org/data/home.aspx. Accessed: January–June 2019.

Wright, Stephen. 2004. Measures of Stock Market Value and Returns of the US Nonfinancial Corporate Sector, 1900–2002. *Review of Income and Wealth* 50(4): 561-584.

Zwijnenburg, Jorrit. 2017. *Unequal Distributions? A study on differences between the compilation of household distributional results according to DINA and EGDNA methodology.* Paris: OECD. wid.world/wp-content/uploads/2017/11/054-DNA_OECD.pdf. Accessed: 6 June 2019.

Land

5

Abstract

Private wealth is comprised in part of capitalized future land rents. The Golden Rule of Accumulation is preserved even if we introduce land into our meta-model. Urban land is far more valuable than agricultural land. The risk tied to land leads to a reduction in its value in the form of a "risk premium" $\alpha > 0$. Land rents can be taxed without any possibility of the tax being passed on to tenants and without loss of efficiency. If the tax is offset by a reduction in income tax, their taxation can even give rise to efficiency gains and positive distributive effects. The possibility of government intervention in the residential rental market represents a further risk for landowners. The sensitivity of the value of land to changes in the interest rate and hence the risk premium α rise with falling interest rates. In light of these many different risks, land as investment can only to a limited extent be a substitute for government bonds and hence for increasing private wealth by way of public debt. We calculate the value of land as asset category in the OECD plus China region. To this end, we primarily rely on data from statistical offices that provide figures for land in their national balance sheets. Our calculations show that the value of land in the countries of the OECD plus China region is about twice annual consumption in the region.

5.1 Land: Theoretical Foundations

5.1.1 The Formal Model

Assets in the form of land are the capitalized, discounted *future values* of land rents. But where do these future values come from? Economists are always well served by recalling the remark of one of the giants of political theory, Thomas Hobbes: "No man can have in his mind a conception of the future, for the future is not yet. But of

© The Author(s) 2021
C. C. von Weizsäcker and H. M. Krämer, *Saving and Investment
in the Twenty-First Century*, https://doi.org/10.1007/978-3-030-75031-2_5

our conceptions of the past, we make a future" (Hobbes 1651). Every prediction is based on an extrapolation of the past into the future.

Here, we will first present how we formally integrate the capitalized values of expected future rents into our steady-state model.

In the chapter on the natural rate of interest, we divided up the net national product per labor year into the interest (at the risk-free interest rate) on total assets $rv(r; \theta)$ and the "remainder" $w(r; \theta)$. We called this remainder the "net net product." As shown there, this net net product is the "more fundamental" variable as compared to the net national product y. At a given real allocation, the amount of the latter depends on the rate of inflation, whereas this is not the case for the net net product. Now, we divide up this net net product in turn into current rental income q and the "remainder," which is now comprised of labor income and other income and which we designate as $x(r; \theta)$. The labor income includes returns that can be understood as returns on "human capital." But $x(r; \theta)$ also includes risk premiums and "Schumpeterian" entrepreneurial profits. We thus obtain the following equation for the net national product per labor year.

$$y = x(r; \theta) + rv(r; \theta) + q(r; \theta).$$

We now look at the capitalized value of future land rents q. We first place q in relation to $w(r; \theta)$: the net net product. Let $\omega = q/w$ be the share of rental income in the net net product. For the capitalized value of future rents per labor year, we write $w(r; \theta)L$. The variable L has the dimension of "time," since it is a coefficient composed of a stock variable ($w(r; \theta)L$ and a flow variable ($w(r; \theta)$). We conceive this variable as the product of two other variables

$$L = \omega l(r; \theta).$$

Since the share of land rents, ω, in the net net product is dimensionless, $l(r; \theta)$ also has the dimension of "time."

Thus, total wealth per labor year, $\hat{v}$, in this economy is

$$\hat{v} = v(r; \theta) + w(r; \theta)(\omega l(r; \theta) + D)$$

The time variable $l(r; \theta)$ is, so to say, the average "*reliability index*" for land rents, as subjectively perceived from the point of view of the current owners of the rent stream. This reliability index will be very different for the many different individual parcels of land. The overall "reliability index" is a weighted average of these individual reliability indices. The latter do not tell us so much about the period of time during which rental income can be expected from each parcel of land. Rather, they tell us something, above all, about the period of time during which current owners of rental income streams can count on the flow of these rents *to themselves* (or to their heirs or to the purchasers of the income streams). We go into some of the details in the present chapter.

5.1.2 The Golden Rule of Accumulation Is Preserved

Before doing so, however, let us note that the Golden Rule of Accumulation is preserved in the model even when we include rental income. As in the chapter on the natural rate of interest, the following equation holds:

$$c(\theta) + gv(r;\ \theta) = w(r;\ \theta) + rv(r;\ \theta).$$

We partially differentiate this equation with respect to θ:

$$\frac{dc}{d\theta} + g\frac{\partial v}{\partial \theta} = \frac{\partial w}{\partial \theta} + r\frac{\partial v}{\partial \theta}.$$

Let θ^* be the value of θ at which consumption reaches its maximum in the set *Theta*. At θ^*, $dc/d\theta = 0$. Moreover, on the assumption of steady-state efficiency, for every r and the associated $\theta(r) = r$,

$$\partial w/\partial \theta = 0$$

holds. Hence, for θ^*, this gives the equation

$$0 + g\frac{\partial v}{\partial \theta} = 0 + r\frac{\partial v}{\partial \theta} = 0 + \theta^*\frac{\partial v}{\partial \theta}.$$

As shown in Chap. 2 on the natural rate of interest, it follows from the "Law of Demand" that $\partial v/\partial \theta < 0$. Hence, it follows from the above equation that

$$\theta^* = g.$$

The only complication that may arise in the land rent model is that *Theta* may not contain any θ that maximizes consumption. In mathematical terms, this means, in effect, that *Theta* is topologically an open set in which for each θ, it is possible that there is another $\hat{\theta}$ at which c is greater than at θ. We will discuss such a case in Sect. 5.1.3.

We can again partially differentiate $w(r;\ \theta) = x(r;\ \theta) + q(r;\ \theta) = x(r;\ \theta) + w(r;\ \theta)\omega$ with respect to r. We write

$$w(r;\theta) = \frac{x(r;\theta)}{1 - \omega}.$$

If ω is unaffected by a change in r, we obtain

$$\frac{\partial w}{\partial r} = \frac{1}{1 - \omega}\frac{\partial x}{\partial r} = -\frac{x(r;\theta)}{1 - \omega}T(r;\theta).$$

Here, as previously, we call $T(r; \theta)$ the "period of production," since it is equivalent in many models to the average time lag between labor inputs and the availability of consumer goods.

We can—making the necessary modifications—take over still more elements from the chapter on the natural interest rate. As in that chapter, it turns out that for a given work-consumption pattern η of the representative household, the equation

$$\frac{\partial \overline{w}(\eta; r)}{\partial r} = -Z(\eta; r)\overline{w}(\eta; r)$$

holds. From this equation, it follows, as previously, that

$$\frac{\partial U}{\partial r} = \frac{\partial U}{\partial \overline{w}} Z\overline{w}$$

As previously, we can then derive that at $r = g$,

$$T(g) + D(g) + L(g) = T(g) + D(g) + \omega l(g) = Z(g)$$

The left side of the equation stands for the wealth components real capital ($T(g)$), public debt ($D(g)$) and capitalized land rents ($\omega l(g)$). At $r = g$, the right side represents total wealth and desired wealth ($Z(g)$).

As a first approximation, we assume that when holding the interest rate constant at $r = g$, a change in $\omega l(g)$ and a countervailing change in $D(g)$ leave the period of production T unchanged. This means, however, that the two variables D (the public debt ratio) and L (the land rent share) are interchangeable without violating the conditions of the Golden Rule of Accumulation. We will put this finding to use further on.

5.1.3   Is the Steady-State Interest Rate Always Greater Than the Growth Rate?

It is the opinion of some economists that a steady-state interest rate r has always to be greater than the steady-state growth rate. Barro, for example, made this assumption when deriving "Ricardian equivalence" almost half a century ago (Barro 1974). According to this theory, on the assumption of citizens who are acting completely rationally and thinking in the long term, it is simply not possible to stimulate demand with additional public debt, since the increased debt causes citizens to restrict their current demand for consumer goods by exactly the present value of the additional taxes that it will bring about. In order to derive this result, however, Barro had to assume that fiscal authorities are subject to a binding intertemporal budget constraint. And this is only the case, if the relevant interest rate is greater than the growth rate of the economy.

The "generational accounting" method, which was developed by Kotlikoff and applied to Germany and Europe by Raffelhüschen, likewise depends on the assumption that the steady-state interest rate is greater than the steady-state growth rate (Kotlikoff 1992; Raffelhüschen 1999).

In the economic literature, there are models in which land plays a key macroeconomic role. Homburg (1991) is an example. Land is treated here as a homogeneous good. It is a factor of production in a macroeconomic production function. The two other factors of production are labor and capital. This is an expanded Solow production function to which the factor land has been added. In this production function, which also features a constant rate of technical progress, land rent equals the marginal product of land. The supply of land is fixed. If it is a Cobb–Douglas production function, the economy can grow at a constant rate. Land rent grows then proportionally to the national product, such that the share of land rent in the national product remains constant. If the future land rents are converted into a capitalized value of land at the prevailing steady-state interest rate, then this value of land is only finite when the interest rate is greater than the growth rate.

In Homburg's model, the addition of land leads the inequality $r > g$ to be treated as an equilibrium condition. Hence, the set Theta is half-open: For every $\theta \in$ Theta, there is a $\overline{\theta} \in$ Theta with $\overline{\theta} < \theta$. It then also holds that for every $c(\theta)$ with $\theta \in$ Theta, there is a $c(\overline{\theta})$ with $\overline{\theta} \in$ Theta, so that $c(\overline{\theta}) > c(\theta)$. We will show further on that the assumptions of the Homburg model are unrealistic. However, our argument below is different from the one developed by Kim and Lee (1997), criticized by Homburg (2014), but further refined by Hellwig (2020a and b).

5.1.4 Ponzi Scheme

A steady-state equilibrium with a constant interest rate that is lower than the growth rate is not a general equilibrium in the sense of Walras, Arrow and Debreu. For it obviously does not meet the criterion of Pareto optimality. Sustainably profitable Ponzi schemes are conceivable (Blanchard and Weil 2001). There are, however, good reasons why it is illegal for private actors to engage in Ponzi (or "pyramid") schemes. For they collapse as soon as there is competition. The only legitimate operator of a Ponzi scheme is the state, which possesses a *monopoly on the use of violence*. It is the "Leviathan" of Thomas Hobbes (1651). Thanks to this monopoly on the use of violence, the state can even be creditworthy when it has negative equity. This is at least the case as long as it has not completely exhausted its potential for raising tax revenue: i.e., as long as tax rates are low enough so that public finances are still on the rising part of the Laffer curve (Uhlig and Trabant 2011). For in this case, the state can convince its creditors that, "if needed," it can remain solvent by increasing tax rates.

What is decisive in this connection is that there is only *one* actor—the state—operating the Ponzi scheme. If the state were competing with other operators of Ponzi schemes, then this competition would drive interest rates so high that the

Ponzi scheme would no longer work. Inasmuch as we are considering a world in which there are many coexisting states, it is clear that the various fiscal authorities have to coordinate with one another, in order to prevent "cutthroat competition" among the Ponzi schemes operators. We will return to this question of the international co-existence of states as public operators of Ponzi schemes in Chap. 10 on free trade. (On the same topic, cf. also Hellwig and Lorenzoni 2009).

5.1.5 Financial Risks of Land Ownership 1: Agriculture

The question is whether we can regard the outcome of a model like Homburg's as a realistic description of the real world. We doubt it, and in the following, we explain why.

Models always represent real life in a simplified way. In order for them realistically to represent those points that are crucial for the issue under examination, it must be possible to show, using our economic judgment, that the simplification does not already transport the conclusions to be proven into the model itself.

In our present context, one crucial assumption is that we are dealing in the Homburg model with three factors of production—labor, capital and land—each of which is per se homogeneous. In Chap. 4, we discussed the question of capital as homogeneous factor of production in detail. We do not want to repeat that discussion here. Here, we will be looking at land as factor of production.

Land is far from being a homogeneous good. The location of a piece of land is important, as are its physical properties. In the case of land that is used in agriculture, the fertility of the soil is especially important. In Germany, this characteristic is even measured by a so-called "land value index" [*Bodenwertzahl*]. How land is used is decisive in determining its market value. As a rule, land designated for construction and land that has already been developed has a much greater market value per square meter than land that is used for agriculture or forestry. We will go into this matter in greater detail in Sect. 5.2 using some concrete numerical examples. The reason for this greater value is that the right to build on a piece of land is granted by public authorities in a restrictive manner. Urban and environmental planning play a major role in this connection. But there are also enormous differences in value within the category of urban land-use. The location of the land is decisive. Centrally located urban land is far more valuable than land on the urban periphery. Land for construction in a major metropolis is far more valuable than land for construction in a provincial town. All of this is well known.

In the case of land that is used for agriculture or extractive industries, in addition to the relevant physical characteristics, proximity to transportation links is also important. The potential for or current exploitation of returns to scale by connecting a parcel of land to neighboring land is also significant. In the context of our analysis, it is important that these latter factors are dependent upon decisions that are not made by the owner, but rather by other persons and institutions. These decisions are associated with a large number of externalities that have a positive or negative impact on the land in question.

This means, however, that property in land used for agriculture or extractive industries is, as an asset, connected to considerable *financial risks*. The expected value of the flow of future land rents from any given parcel of land can change "unexpectedly" from year to year: whether upward or downward. Thus in Germany, for example, the value of a great deal of agricultural land has risen, because German energy policy has for some time now been prioritizing renewable energies: including bioenergy. But no one can guarantee that this energy source will continue to be heavily subsidized in future. The risks for landowners posed by agricultural policy are also, of course, well-known: whether due to the reinforcement of protectionist measures or their weakening. But what is at issue is precisely not only such "macrorisks." Highly local decisions about transportation networks or connection to the power grid, and highly local developments, like family matters in the neighboring farm, can sometimes have a massive impact on the expected flow of rental income. And these third-party decisions cannot be predicted with certainty.

5.1.6 Financial Risks of Land Ownership 2: Urban Land

Much the same applies for urban or peri-urban land that has been built on or on which construction is taking place or that has been designated for construction. Apart from macrorisks, like those tied to legislation, there are also a large number of micro- and "meso"-risks involved here. Among the mesorisks, we include events or decisions that affect a city as a whole. The Bundestag's 1991 vote to make Berlin, instead of Bonn, the capital of reunified Germany had an influence, of course, on land prices both in Berlin and the surrounding area and in Bonn and the surrounding area, as well as in Karlsruhe and its surroundings: in the latter case, because Karlsruhe averted the danger of all the country's highest courts being moved to Leipzig. But the unforeseeable establishment or failure to establish a link to the highway system or to high-speed railway lines also contains risks for land values in a city as a whole. Whether and when the Elbe River will be deepened is an issue that affects all property owners in Hamburg and its surroundings.

The microrisks of land ownership include local decisions on public transportation or decisions that bring about positive or negative changes in noise pollution: whether from traffic, flight paths or the construction of nearby wind turbines. The "demographics" of the neighborhood can also undergo both positive and negative change. "Gentrification" is an example.

Building regulations and the urban planning of the municipality in question are, in principle, changeable, and they are not under the control of landowners. How many floors may be built? What landmark preservation restrictions will there be in future?

In short, there are a large number of both risks to which owners of urban land are exposed and opportunities from which they can benefit.

It is also important that risk diversification is not so simple in the real estate sector. If they are to retain their value, buildings cannot be divided up into smaller parts in any way the owner wants. Joint property of many owners is always associated with considerable transaction costs. As a wide variety of experience shows, real estate funds can give rise to massive principal-agent problems. As compared to the possibilities for diversification presented by share-ownership in publicly listed companies, risk diversification is far more expensive in the case of real estate. Just the transaction costs involved in transfer of ownership are already far greater in the case of real estate than in that of publicly traded shares.

5.1.7   A Dual Model of Land Use

Most of the value represented by land is nowadays related not to agricultural land, but rather to urban land that has been built on or on which construction is taking place or that has been designated for construction. This is significant for our analysis, because the supply of land for development is not a fixed quantity, but depends rather on private and public decisions. The model of a fixed supply of land, which came into the economic literature with the Ricardian theory of rent (and has antecedents in the Physiocrats), is at most suitable for agricultural land. It is not appropriate for the far more valuable land used for building.

It might be instructive to draw a parallel here to the subject of labor supply. There has long been a literature on the "dual economy" (Lewis 1954). In the "dual economy" model, which is meant to describe developing countries, there is a "traditional" sector and a "modern" sector. The latter is far more tightly connected to the global economy than the traditional sector and is modeled on the economy of the wealthy countries. The only difference is that, unlike in wealthy countries, the traditional sector, with its lower standard of living, makes a practically unlimited reservoir of labor available to the modern sector. In an analogous manner, we can argue that land that is currently used for agricultural purposes represents a large reservoir of land that can be used to increase the supply of land for construction. We will come back to this point in Sect. 5.2.2. Historically, of course, agricultural land has constantly been converted into land for development. Otherwise, it would have been impossible to satisfy the growing need for built space due to population growth—and, in particular, the growth of the urban population and the increase in its standard of living.

In considering the value of land, it is thus misleading to treat the supply of land as constant regardless of its use.

5.1.8   Macrorisks of Urban Land Ownership 1: Taxation or Increasing Supply

We now turn to the macrorisks faced by the owner of built-up land or land for development. We call such land *urban land*.

We should first point to a fact that is well known to specialists in public economics: Precisely when working with a model in which the quantity of urban land is given, land rents are pure rents in the economic sense. Taxation of the land or a reduction of its value due to other regulations cannot be passed on to others. For by assumption, supply remains the same with or without the taxes or regulations. As every trained economist knows, this is not the case for capital and—up to a certain point—labor as factors of production. If capital income is either directly or indirectly taxed, then, with given saving behavior and constant interest rates, the supply of capital shrinks. This has the effect of increasing interest rates, such that the tax burden can, to a large extent and perhaps even entirely, be shifted to others. Increased taxation of the labor supply that is offset by other tax benefits for households leads to a lower labor supply (a pure substitution effect). But, other things being equal, labor thus becomes scarcer and hence more expensive. Wages rise. The tax can at least be partially shifted to others.

This general finding about tax incidence gets an additional twist in the case of urban land. We are referring here to Arnott and Stiglitz's "Henry George Theorem" (Arnott and Stiglitz 1979). The authors grasp differential urban land rents as the result of the city's making a transport and information infrastructure available to the landowners. They show that in a city of optimal size, aggregate land rents are exactly equal to the costs of the optimal infrastructure. The positive externalities (to the benefit of the landowners) of the municipal infrastructure can, in effect, be internalized, inasmuch as the municipality imposes a land tax on the owners that drains off the entirety of the differential rent.

The more one is stuck in the theoretical universe of a fixed supply of urban land, the more compelling the idea becomes that the economic allocation of resources could be massively improved by heavily taxing land rents and using the tax revenues thus generated to reduce distorting taxes on income and sales proportionally.

Of course, the model of a fixed supply of land—especially of a fixed supply of urban land—is an unrealistic simplification. We are not suggesting here that differential urban land rents should be completely drained off by equivalent taxes. But an important reason why the taxation or regulation of urban land should not be pushed too far is the incentive that is created for private firms to increase the supply of urban land and to improve its quality, if they are allowed to retain part of the increase in value that this brings about.

Anyone who is considering investing their wealth in urban land in the form of real estate will keep in mind that there are good reasons why taxes imposed on land rents either cannot be passed on or can only be passed on with difficulty (if the supply of land is fixed or highly inelastic). Or they will understand that urban land is perhaps not so heavily taxed only because of the potential for additional supply, which will come into competition with the existing mass (if the supply of land is relatively elastic).

The Damocles sword of either increased taxation or increased supply hangs over the head of every owner of urban land. As consequence, considerable risk premiums are expected whenever urban land changes hands.

5.1.9 Macrorisks of Urban Land Ownership 2: Restrictions on the Freedom of Contract—In Particular, Rent Control

This analysis is reinforced by government interference in the freedom of contract between landlord and tenant (also in the case of commercial properties, though to a far lesser degree). All over the world, wherever they occur, these interventions always take the form of regulating rents in the name of "tenants' rights," never in the name of "landlords' rights." The political–economic reason for this universal constant is obvious. Even if, in the long term, there is considerable elasticity of supply for urban land, in the short term, there certainly cannot be. In the short term, introducing freedom of contract on the residential rental market would only have a minor impact: Such a measure cannot be expected to produce much additional supply by the time of the next elections. In all urban agglomerations, wherever rent control is already in place, there is excess demand for residential rental space. Due to rent control, rents are below the level at which supply and demand match. Hence, the first effect of such a legislatively sanctioned transition to freedom of contract would be to raise rents. But it is thus a sure thing that the party that abolished rent control and introduced freedom of contract will lose the next elections—and, as consequence, rent control will be reintroduced. In political–economic terms, rent control, and the excess demand for residential rental space that goes with it, is thus a stable system.

In countries in which rent control has been pushed to an extreme, the private rental market for dwellings has largely dried up, because private investors keep away from investing in rental properties.

As a general phenomenon, rent control is a global constant. But the specific form it takes is variable. This is the case both from country to country and in terms of its evolution over time. Anyone renting out a residential property must thus live with the risk of stricter rent control. Hence, investors will demand a considerable risk premium before investing in rental properties.

In order to encourage more private investment in the construction of rental properties, tax authorities in many countries offer generous tax rules on depreciation for investment in buildings. These are, in effect, tax subsidies, which lead real capital assets in the form of built structures to receive preferential tax treatment as compared to assets in the form of urban land. Since, however, urban land and real capital in the form of buildings are complementary factors of production, if the supply of urban land is inelastic, its value rises with every tax benefit given to investment in urban construction. Thus, a large part of the tax benefit accorded to residential development flows to the landowners and far less than 100% of it to the tenants who rent the residential units. This preferential tax treatment accorded by the government can also be changed, however; hence, it too is laden with risk that figures into a risk premium.

5.1.10 Rent Control as Shared Land Rent

Rent control can also be understood as a legally enforced dividing up of the rent on urban land between landlord and tenant. As already discussed, it regularly leads to excess demand for rental units in urban agglomerations, since the legally permitted rents are below the price level at which supply and demand match. For the property owners, urban land rent is thus less than it would be under conditions of freedom of contract. Consequently, capitalized future land rent is also lower, even if we do not include the risk premium discussed above.

A part of the urban land rent that property owners lose due to rent control is a sort of quasi-rent for tenants, which takes the form of their having to pay lower rent than they would under conditions of freedom of contract. This quasi-rent for the tenant is, however, less than the landlord's loss of rent. For rent control also entails inefficiencies in resource allocation. These are accepted by the majority of voters: In the view of the public, they are the price that the economy has to pay for a "fairer" housing market.

Moreover, if rent control is not pushed to such an extreme that, in the long term, no owners are willing to rent out their property, it no longer holds that land taxation, as taxation of a pure rent, cannot be passed on by landlords. For, in this case, the government must generally allow the periodic taxation of land (or property tax) to be transferred to the tenant in the form of increased rent. Otherwise, even more property owners will flee the rental market. Therefore, even the tenant's quasi-rent is indirectly taxed. In political–economic terms, the fear of rent increases as a consequence of increased property taxes is the common weapon used by landlords and tenants in urban areas to ward off efficiency-increasing tax increases on urban land combined with proportional reductions in income taxes and sales taxes – to the detriment of those who do not have any share in urban lands rents. And hence to the detriment of the regional "equality of living conditions."

5.1.11 The Role of Interest Rate Risk in the Capitalization of Land Rents

We now turn to the specific effect of interest rates in the valuation of land and other rental assets. It is generally accepted that a given expected stream of future land rents or other rental income leads to a higher capitalization, the lower the discount rate that is applied. This discount rate is derived from the market interest rate. In Homburg's simple model (Homburg 1991), this effect of the interest rate is sufficient to show that the long-term equilibrium rate of interest is always higher than the growth rate of the economy. But if, for the reasons discussed above, current and potential landowners use a discount factor consisting of the sum of the risk-free real market rate r and a risk premium $\alpha > 0$, then the risk-free real market rate can also be less than the growth rate of the economy in general equilibrium.

We can, however, go one step further here: The risk borne by the owner of land also includes the risk of a change in interest rate. As we showed in Chap. 2 on the natural rate of interest, a steady-state analysis does not mean that we ignore the risk of interest rate changes (See Sect. 2.9).

Let us assume that a landowner's expected value for future land rent is R $(t) = e^{gt}\overline{R}$. The owner calculates the value of the land part of his or her real estate using the risk-free market rate of interest r plus a risk premium α. The value of his or her land A is thus

$$A = \frac{\overline{R}}{r + \alpha - g}.$$

For a given g and a given α, we are interested in the sensitivity of the value of this asset A to changes in the interest rate. We calculate

$$\frac{\partial A}{\partial r} = -\frac{\overline{R}}{(r + \alpha - g)^2} = -A\frac{1}{r + \alpha - g}.$$

The proportionate sensitivity to changes in the interest rate is thus equal to

$$\frac{1}{r + \alpha - g}.$$

We obtain the same result for the proportionate sensitivity of the asset value with respect to the expected growth rate. This proportionate sensitivity to the interest rate is thus nothing other than the average time gap between the future land rents and the present as weighted by risk-adjusted present values.

Now, we can see from the formula that this proportionate sensitivity to the interest rate is greater, the lower the rate. But this has consequences in turn for the risk premium. The latter, has, after all, to take into account the risk of an interest rate change. Let us assume that the subjective probability distribution for future risk-free interest rates exhibits a spread (e.g., variance) that is independent of the current steady-state real interest rate. Since, however, the relative sensitivity to the interest rate of the value of a parcel of land is greater the lower the rate, there is good reason to think that the risk premium α rises with a falling steady-state interest rate. If purchases of real estate are often financed with loans, this negative sign of the derivative of α with respect to r is already to be expected from the fact that the banks will also take into account the interest rate sensitivity of the market value of the collateral in setting the interest rates on their loans.

There is also a political–economic reason why the lower the interest rate, the higher is the risk premium. For the greater the asset value that results from the capitalization of land rents, the more willing the government will be to do something to lower them: i.e., to lower ω. In other words: *High real estate prices give the government an incentive to do something for tenants and at the expense of landlords.* The current debate and atmosphere in Germany exemplify this political–economic relationship. Inasmuch as buying real estate is becoming more and more difficult and risky for persons with limited savings, due to high prices, rents in urban agglomerations are being targeted by policymakers—and, as a result, rent controls are being introduced or tightened. Thus, the political risk involved in owning real estate rises as interest rates fall.

Finally, fiscal authorities also have in interest in responding to very high real estate prices for the purpose of stabilizing the economy. If, as demonstrated, real estate prices are very sensitive to interest rate changes when interest rates are low, high real estate prices can lead the fiscal authorities to use higher deficits to ensure that the steady-state interest rate rises. In this way, the danger of real estate crises with macroeconomic consequences can be reduced, since both real estate prices and their sensitivity to interest rate changes decrease as a result. Landowners' knowing about these relationships contributes to the fact that the lower is r, the higher is α.

It is worth re-emphasizing that the inverse relationship between interest rate and risk premium presented here is not the same thing as the common argument to the effect that "When interest rates are low, people expect them to rise; when interest rates are high, people expect them to fall." Empirically, this may well be true. Nonetheless, the inverse dependence of the risk of interest rate change on the interest rate level still holds, even if the expectations for interest rates are such that their average expected value is equal to the prevailing rate.

We thus write

$$\frac{\partial \alpha}{\partial r} < 0.$$

In an entirely analogous fashion, we can, using similar arguments, show that

$$\frac{\partial \alpha}{\partial g} > 0$$

holds.

This analysis can be transferred to the macroeconomic level. Here (cf. Sects. 5.1.1 and 5.1.2), we found that

$$\hat{v} = v(r; \theta) + w(r; \theta)(\omega l(r; \theta) + D)$$

and, when $r = g$, that

$$T(g) + D(g) + L(g) = T(g) + D(g) + \omega l(g) = Z(g)$$

Purely formally, we now replace the overall "reliability index" $l(r; \theta)$ by a formula corresponding to the one we have just derived:

$$l(r; \theta) = \frac{1}{r + \alpha - g}.$$

Here, g *is* the growth rate of the economy. It is thus a kind of "average" of the growth rates of land rents assumed by individual property owners as expected values. This equation *defines* the average α for the economy as a whole at empirically observed values for $l(r;\ \theta)$, r and g respectively. In the case of the Golden Rule of Accumulation ($r = g$), we obtain

$$l(g; \theta^*) = \frac{1}{\alpha}.$$

On the Golden Rule path, the macroeconomic risk premium defined in this way is thus the inverse of the reliability index. Or vice versa: On the path of the Golden Rule of Accumulation, the reliability index is the inverse of the average risk premium.

We can now undertake a first-order Taylor approximation, in order to estimate the value of $l(r;\ \theta(r))$ for $r \neq g$. At every r, we have

$$\frac{\partial l}{\partial r} = -\frac{1}{(r + \alpha(r) - g)^2}\left(1 + \frac{\partial \alpha}{\partial r}\right) = -l^2\left(1 + \frac{\partial \alpha}{\partial r}\right).$$

If we designate the risk premium that holds at $r = g$ as α^* and the derivative of α at $r = g$ as $(\alpha^*)'$, then the first-order Taylor approximation reads as follows:

$$l(r; \theta(r)) \approx -\frac{r - g}{(\alpha^*)^2}(1 + (\alpha^*)') + \frac{1}{\alpha^*} = \frac{1}{\alpha^*}\left\{\frac{g - r}{\alpha^*}(1 + (\alpha^*)') + 1\right\}.$$

The proportionate deviation of $l(r;\ \theta(r))$ from its value at $r = g$ is thus

$$\frac{g - r}{\alpha^*}(1 + (\alpha^*)').$$

If, for example, $(\alpha^*)' = -1$, the first-order Taylor approximation implies that the reliability index is invariant with respect to a change in the steady-state interest rate. If the absolute value of $(\alpha^*)'$ is less than one, then the reliability index rises with a falling interest rate, but it does so more slowly than it would if the risk premium were not dependent on the interest rate.

We now provide a sensitivity analysis. We are making an estimate for when $r = g$. In this case, the equality of total consumption and net net income also holds. As will be shown in the second part of the present chapter, we estimate the value of $L = \omega l$ to be 1.94 years of total consumption and hence 1.94 years of net net income. The variable ω represents the share of land rents in net net income w. In the following calculations, we assume that $\omega = 1/9$. We thus obtain

$$l(r; \theta(r)) = \frac{L}{\omega} = 17.46 \text{ years}.$$

The one-ninth estimated share of land rent in net net income for the OECD plus China region as a whole is nothing more than an educated guess. Further research is required, in order for us to be able to be more precise. Here, we offer just some very simple considerations. Residential rents are found to represent around one-third of disposable income. Rental income from commercial tenants has to be added to this. We also have to add a hypothetical rent from owner-occupied residential properties, which is not included in the determination of income in the national accounts. Hence, a one-third share of rent in net net product may not be entirely off-track, since, as we have defined it, the net net product is greater than disposable income. Now we have to subtract both the landlord's running costs and the return on the real capital share. If we assume that these two items each account for one-third and hence combined for two-thirds of rents (less in the city centers of major metropolitan areas, more in the countryside or on the urban periphery), then net rental income is equal to approximately one-ninth of the net net product.

The result, a reliability index of around 17½ years, appears to be entirely realistic.

This equation holds for $r = g$. Thus, at $r = g$, we obtain the following value for the risk premium:

$$\alpha^* = \frac{1}{l(g; \theta(g))} \approx \frac{1}{17.5 \text{ years}} = 5.7\% \text{ p.a.}$$

This value seems plausible. It represents the risk premium on land assets when $r = g$. In making the following estimate, we assume a steady-state growth rate of 3% per year for the OECD plus China region. Hence, the hitherto estimated risk premium corresponds to a risk-free real interest rate that also equals 3% per year. We have to keep in mind here that we are considering the OECD plus China region, which includes both lower growth rates in Europe, in particular, and the much higher growth rates of China.

We are interested in estimating l at $r = 0$. If we use the first-order Taylor approximation presented above, we have now to determine a value for $\partial \alpha / \partial r$ at $r = g$ or, in other words, for $(\alpha^*)'$. From the above analysis, we can presume that it is somewhere between −1 and zero. Let us posit that

$$(\alpha^*)' = -\frac{1}{2}.$$

We can thus calculate

$$l(0; \theta(0)) \approx \frac{g}{(\alpha^*)^2} (1 + (\alpha^*)') + \frac{1}{\alpha^*} = l(g; \theta(g)) \left[1 + l(g; \theta(g)g \frac{1}{2}) \right]$$

$$= l(g; \theta(g)) \left[1 + \frac{17.5}{100} 1.5 \right] = l(g; \theta(g)) 1.2625 = 22 \text{ years.}$$

The reliability index is 26.25% greater at a real interest rate of zero than at a rate equal to the growth rate. In our calculations of total wealth, we round up to a 30% increase in assets.

At $r = 0$, per our assumptions, the risk premium is

$$\alpha(0) = 5.7\% + 1.5\% = 7.20\% \text{ p.a.}$$

This is a plausible figure.

5.1.12 Distributive Aspects of Land Rent

The formula

$$T(g) + D(g) + L(g) = T(g) + D(g) + \omega l(g) = Z(g)$$

for the Golden Rule of Accumulation is also of interest in light of its distributive implications. It contains two variables that are relatively easily susceptible to being influenced by government policy: ω, land rents as a share of net net product, and the public debt ratio D. The government can adjust the two variables to offset one another, such that the steady-state interest rate remains unchanged. As a first approximation, we can assume that the variables $T(g)$ and $Z(g)$ do not change, if the interest rate stays the same. These variables are, after all, the period of production and desired wealth. Now, it would be possible to increase $D(g)$ and offset this increase by reducing ω. This could take place, for instance, by increasing taxes on urban rents and offsetting the tax revenue thus generated by reducing income and sales taxes (with their well-known distorting effects). We have no need to discuss the details of such a tax reform here. It would to some extent resemble Arnott and Stiglitz's idea that we discussed above. The government has just to be careful not to go so far as to eliminate the incentive for private enterprise to convert agricultural land into land for urban development.

Here, we want only to call attention to the distributive effect of such a measure. The recipients of urban rents figure almost entirely among higher income groups. Fiscal authorities may use the increased tax revenues from the taxation of land rents to decrease income tax and sales tax rates, such that this lightening of the tax burden mainly benefits low-income groups. What is going on here then is a redistribution from "rich" to "poor," which also serves to reduce the distorting effects of the tax system as a whole. The consumer income that could be achieved in the Golden Rule steady state would thus be greater. At the same time, in the Golden Rule steady state, the greater public debt would not result in an additional burden for current or future taxpayers, since the interest on the debt is covered by the state's net borrowing (Weizsäcker 2018) .

Of course, the possibility of this redistribution presupposes that the Arnott-Stiglitz land tax was previously suboptimally low. This can be safely assumed for many of the countries in the OECD plus China region. On the political–economic background to this assumption, see the conclusion of Sect. 5.1.10 above. Owners of urban land will also be aware of the possibility of such a redistribution, so that it will already have an influence on the risk premium α.

In this book, we do not offer any estimate of the supply elasticity of urban land. Depending on the institutional environment, the latter will also vary from country to country. But it is clear that there is a politically explosive issue for future research here.

5.1.13 The Real Estate Inheritance Rate

It is a robust fact that privately owned real estate is left as an inheritance far more often than other types of wealth. It is legally impossible for wealth in the form of social security claims to be inherited. Financial assets are largely used, both directly and indirectly, for retirement: directly, inasmuch as they are amassed precisely for this purpose; indirectly, inasmuch as, for example, life insurance companies and corporate pension funds invest by far the greater part of their reserve funds in relatively liquid financial securities. A debt-free house is also used for retirement purposes. In the overwhelming majority of cases, it is not, however, mortgaged again in old age, but rather left debt-free to one's heirs. The owner-occupied debt-free house or apartment is almost the classic example for the model of making one's heirs into implicit life annuity insurers. We examined this dual use of property in Chap. 3, Sect. 3.6.

If, however, real estate is largely passed on as inheritance, then an erroneous estimate of the total value of real estate is not a serious problem when empirically deriving the negative natural rate of interest. If the total value of real estate is underestimated, then the share of total wealth that is passed on as inheritance will also be underestimated. In this case, however, as noted in Chap. 3, Sect. 3.6, we also underestimate desired wealth.

5.2 Determining the Value of Privately-Owned Land in the OECD Plus China Region

5.2.1 Concepts and Data Sources

In addition to real capital and explicit and implicit public debt, land is another important component of private wealth. The goal of this chapter is to estimate the value of land assets in the OECD plus China region. To this end, we primarily rely on data from statistical offices, which determine figures for land and sometimes for all natural resources in the context of national accounts and report them in the national balance sheets that are especially relevant for our purposes (Lequiller and Blades 2014, pp. 231–254).

In the national accounts, land is assigned to so-called *non-produced non-financial assets* (cf. Fig. 5.1). According to the 2008 SNA and the 2010 ESA, the latter include contracts, leases and licenses, goodwill, marketing assets and *natural resources* (Eurostat 2013, p. 171). In addition to land, natural resources

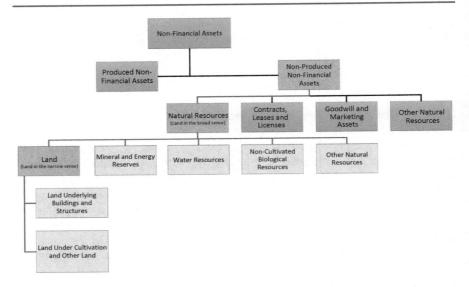

Fig. 5.1 Land in national accounts (2008 SNA). *Source* European Commission et al. (2009); Eurostat (2013). Authors' own presentation

include mineral and energy reserves, non-cultivated biological resources, water resources and other natural resources. Sometimes when discussing land in what follows, we in fact have this more extensive definition of natural resources in mind: what we could call "land in the broad sense." Most countries only include statistics on land in the narrow sense in their balance sheets, not statistics on the natural resources land comprises (like, e.g., mineral and energy reserves). To the extent that the official statistics of some countries in the OECD plus China region provide data on natural resources, we will use this data, but we will continue to designate this extended category of wealth simply as the "value of land."

In accordance with the ESA 2010, land is only regarded as an economic asset and included in the balance sheets, if there are ownership rights to it and these rights confer an economic benefit upon the owner (Eurostat 2013, p. 171). Land that confers no economic benefit is described as *barren land* and consequently does not represent an economic asset. This criterion also applies for other non-produced non-financial assets. Thus, for example, open seas and air are not counted as natural assets, because there are no ownership rights in them (ibid.). Hence, only data on assets that meet these criteria are to be found in the national balance sheets.

One of the major methodological difficulties involved in measuring the value of land consists of separating the value of the assets on the land (buildings, other built structures, trees and plants, etc.) from the value of the land itself, in order to determine just the latter. The value of parcels of land underlying buildings and other structures is, in principle, the difference between the replacement cost of a built structure (as determined, for instance, for insurance purposes) and the market price of the real estate as a whole (including the land) (Ryan-Collins et al. 2017, p. 6).

But such figures are only sometimes available. Hence, it is often difficult in practice to carry out this separation. The official statistics make use of special methods of assessing value and report the value of the land without the assets found on it (Schmalwasser and Brede 2015, p. 44).

A large part of the data on the value of land in the developed economies that we use is provided by the OECD in one of the datasets available under *Annual National Accounts: Detailed Tables and Simplified Accounts* (OECD 2019). In addition, for a limited number of European Union member states, Eurostat (2019) publishes data that is, in part, identical with the data from the above-mentioned OECD dataset. The German figures, which are reported by the Bundesbank and the Federal Statistical Office in the sectoral and national balance sheets (Deutsche Bundesbank and Statistisches Bundesamt 2020), are included in both datasets. Since 2015, the data available for Germany has improved thanks to an expansion of the data on land in the balance sheets. Previously, only estimates of the value of land underlying built structures were published in Germany (Deutsche Bundesbank and Statistisches Bundesamt 2015). Using benchmarks based on actual purchase prices, now data is also provided on the total value of land. But since market prices are not available for all land, estimates are still indispensable. The precise assignment of land to the different institutional sectors is also sometimes difficult (Schmalwasser and Brede 2015, pp. 49–50; Schmalwasser and Müller 2009).

Land is owned both by the state and by households and firms. What is of interest for us is the land that is privately owned. In calculating its value in the OECD plus China region, we will again combine households and firms. For the reasons that we have already presented, we relate the value of land not, as is customarily done, to the flow variable gross domestic product, but rather to the flow variable total consumption. By "total consumption"—or, in what follows, also simply "consumption"—we understand the sum of the expenditures for the consumption of households and for the consumption of the state (public consumption) that were undertaken in the respective reporting year. Thus, we will say, for instance, that the value of land in Great Britain is equivalent to 2.83 times or 283% of (total) consumption.

5.2.2 Land Values and Land Use in Germany

Whereas especially in the last three decades, the value of land has risen sharply in many developed countries, the rise of land values in Germany during this period has been relatively modest by comparison. Nonetheless, in Germany too, land values have clearly increased in recent years. Figure 5.2 shows how the value of all land and of land underlying built structures has evolved in the German economy as a whole and in the private sector from 1999 to 2019. The value of all land in Germany rose from nearly 2.4 trillion euros in 1999 to 5.3 trillion euros in 2019. The value of privately owned land more than doubled in value, reaching around 4.7 trillion euros, during this time. The value of underlying or "built-up" land similarly increased. The accelerated increase in the value of both categories of land

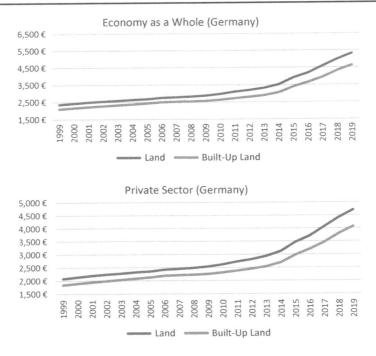

Fig. 5.2 Evolution of total land value and value of built-up land in Germany in Billions of Euros, 1999–2019. *Source* Deutsche Bundesbank and Federal Statistical Office (2020). Authors' own calculations

that began in around 2012 is clearly visible in both graphs. More than half of the growth in value that occurred between 1999 and 2019 thus took place in the last seven years of the 20-year period 1999–2019.

The graphs show the evolution for both total land and built-up land. It should not be forgotten, however, that the value of land varies considerably depending on its economic use (European Union and OECD 2015). The use of land can be roughly subdivided into its use for settlement, transportation, vegetation and bodies of water. The national land use statistics provide detailed information on how land is used.[1] They show that agricultural land accounts for the largest share of economically usable land in Germany, representing somewhat more than half of the total land area. Woodland accounts for the second largest share, representing nearly one-third of the total area. Land underlying and adjoining buildings (approximately

---

[1]Within the framework of its so-called minimum publication program, the Federal Statistical Office (Statistisches Bundesamt 2020) distinguishes between the following types of land use on the federal level: land underlying and adjoining buildings (for residential, commercial and industrial purposes), recreational land (parks, etc.), (undeveloped) land for industrial operations (including land for mines and quarries), land for traffic (roads, paths, squares), agricultural land (including moor and heath), woodland, surface water, land for other uses (cemetery, barren land).

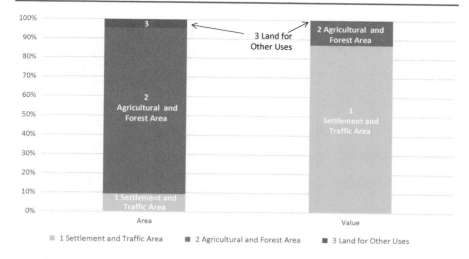

Fig. 5.3 Area and value: shares by type of land use. *Source* Schmalwasser and Brede (2015); Statistisches Bundesamt (2020). *Note* Area shares refer to 2019, value shares refer to 2012. Authors' own calculations

7%) and traffic area (approximately 5%) are far less significant. At barely 2.5%, the share of the total economically usable land area covered by water is roughly equal to that of recreational land, (undeveloped) space for industrial and commercial use and land for other uses combined.

As is well known, land is most valuable when it has been built-up or is designated for construction. Such land has considerably greater value than, for example, land that is covered by woods or that is used in agriculture. In 2012, agricultural land and woodland had a value of, on average, only 1.35 euros per square meter in Germany. By contrast, in the same year, the price of land used for residential buildings was 152.51 euros per m^2. Land used for residential buildings was thus 114 times more expensive than woodland or agricultural land. Land used for non-residential buildings cost, on average, 20.16 euros per square meter in 2012. This is equivalent to less than one-seventh of the value of land used for residential buildings.[2]

Figure 5.3 shows the difference between share of total land area and share of total value of land for the most important types of land use in Germany.[3] No less than 80% of Germany's total land area is covered by agricultural land and woodland; but their share in the total *value* of all land is only around 12%. By contrast, settlement area and traffic area together account for more than 87% of the total value of land in Germany, although they only represent about 9% of the total area. In terms of size, but, above all, in terms of value, land for other uses (e.g., recreational land and associated surface water) plays practically no role.

---

[2]The cited average prices for the various types of land use are each for one square meter of land and refer to 2012. The data is taken from Schmalwasser and Brede (2015, p. 54).
[3]Total land refers here to total economically usable land. So-called barren land [*Unland*] is not included.

Table 5.1 Value of land in Germany

	1999	2019	Change in value in relation to 1999	1999	2019
	Billions of euros		In %	In years of consumption	
Economy as a whole					
Total land	2,367.7	5,314.6	125.3	1.4	1.9
In particular built-up land	2,101.6	4,616.8	120.6	1.3	1.7
Private sector					
Total land	2,064.8	4,703.9	127.3	1.2	1.7
In particular built-up land	1,823.5	4,062.4	122.2	1.1	1.5

Sources Deutsche Bundesbank and Federal Statistical Office (2020), World Bank (2020). Authors' own calculations

Notes Consumption = Total consumption

As already discussed in Sect. 5.1.7, it is not only an increase in unit price (land price per hectare or square meter) that can give rise to increases in the value of land. Since the value of a parcel of land is heavily influenced by its use, an increase in the value of land can also be the result of the conversion of land from one use to another: for instance, agricultural land being converted into land for settlement. To illustrate this with a concrete example: From 2011 to 2012, the value of built-up land in Germany rose by 78.1 billion euros. This was due both to changes in price and changes in quantity. According to Schmalwasser and Brede (2015, p. 55), the increase in the value of built-up land was largely the result of the increase in land prices, which accounted for nearly four-fifths of the total increase in value. However, the remaining 22.6% of the rise in the value of land can be attributed to an increase in land for settlement and traffic, which was brought about, above all, by the conversion of agricultural land and woodland. Although the total supply of land has to be regarded as more-or-less fixed, this shows that (economically more valuable) land can certainly be obtained by converting existing land to new uses. Over time, such changes in land use can give rise to significant increases or losses in wealth.[4]

We now come back again to the evolution of the value of land in general and of built-up land in particular in Germany. From 2000 to 2019, the value of land rose in Germany by 123% (from 2359 billion euros to 5315 billion euros; cf. Table 5.1). The value of land in Germany thus increased from 1.4 times to 1.9 times the value of consumption.

The most important type of land use in terms of value is built-up land, representing nearly four-fifths of the total value of land. At 121%, the increase in value was somewhat less for built-up land than for land in general. Nonetheless, here too

---

[4]Change in socio-economic relations also brings about change in the value of the different types of land. According to Piketty and Zucman (2014), land used in agriculture accounted for more than half of total national wealth in Great Britain at the beginning of the eighteenth century. Today, its share is almost totally insignificant.

the growth was considerable. The value of built-up land increased from 1.3 times consumption in 1999 to 1.7 times in 2019.

With a share of 89%, most land in Germany is privately owned. In 2019, its value came to 4704 billion euros. According to the sectoral balance sheets of the Bundesbank and the Federal Statistical Office (Deutsche Bundesbank and Statistisches Bundesamt 2020), the value of privately owned land thus increased by 127% from 1999 to 2019. Private sector wealth invested in land grew by some two and a half trillion euros during this time.[5] Within the private sector, households and non-profit institutions predominate. In 2019, they owned land worth 3500 billion euros, representing two-thirds of the total value of land in Germany. Corporations accounted for about one-fifth of the value of land in 2019. The rest of the land, which is not privately owned, is public land. Its share in the total value of land fell from barely 13% in 1999 to around 11% in 2019.

Expressed in years of total consumption, in 2019, the German private sector as a whole owned land worth 1.7 times consumption. This is a considerable increase as compared to 1999, when the value of land represented only 1.2 times consumption. The value of built-up land also increased. At somewhat more than 1.5 times consumption (1999: 1.1 times), built-up land is, in value terms, the largest component of the land that is privately owned. The evolution that the value of land has undergone in the last 15 years or so in Germany represents a significant increase in the wealth of the private sector.[6] But as we will see in the following section, the growth of private wealth in land has (up to now) been relatively modest in Germany by comparison to the corresponding evolution in France.

5.2.3 Land as a Component of Real Assets: A Franco-German Comparison

Table 5.2 makes clear the growth in the value of land and its increasing importance as a component of all real assets. In 2000, land accounted for about one-quarter of total non-financial assets in the German economy as a whole. This share continually increased up to 2019, when it reached 31.7%. With an increase of nearly 120%, the value of land (here in the narrow sense) thus rose much more sharply than the value

---

[5]In the view of Baldenius et al. (2019, Footnote 3), the Federal Statistical Office's estimates of the value of real estate assets in Germany are "certainly" too low, "since the price index used does not match market data and deviates from the usual international methods of calculation." According to their information, the Statistical Office itself also regards "an undervaluation as likely." Consequently, the 4.7 trillion euros figure for the value of land in 2019 should also undoubtedly be regarded as the lower limit for any estimate.

[6]Land and the real estate situated on it are very unevenly distributed in Germany. According to Bundesbank data (Deutsche Bundesbank 2019, p. 27), only 44% of households own the dwelling in which they live. The first five deciles in the wealth distribution have almost no real estate assets (Krämer 2021). Hence, it can hardly be surprising that the recent increase in real estate prices in Germany has had appreciable distributive effects. According to the calculations of Baldenius et al. (2019), half of the increase in wealth brought about by the rise in real estate prices since 2011 has gone to the richest 10%.

Table 5.2 Value and percentage shares of land in all non-financial assets in Germany and France, 2000–2019

	2000		2005		2010		2015		2019	
	In years of consumption	In %	In years of consumption	In %	In years of consumption	In %	In years of consumption	In %	In years of consumption	In %
Germany										
Economy as a whole										
Total non-financial assets	5.7	100	5.7	100	5.9	100	6.2	100	6.7	100
In particular land	1.5	26.4	1.5	27.1	1.5	26.1	1.8	28.5	2.1	31.7
Private sector										
Total non-financial assets	4.9	100.0	4.9	100	5.1	100	5.6	100	5.8	100
In particular land	1.3	27.0	1.3	27.5	1.3	26.5	1.7	29.0	1.9	32.1
France										
Economy as a whole										
Total non-financial assets	5.3	100	7.7	100	8.3	100	8.0	100	8.7	100
In particular natural resources[a]	1.3	24.9	3.5	45.3	3.7	44.6	3.3	40.8	3.8	43.7
In particular mineral and energy reserves and other natural assets[b]	0.01	0.19	0.01	0.12	0.01	0.10	0.01	0.09	0.01	0.07
Private sector										
Total non-financial assets	4.4	100	6.6	100	7.1	100	6.9	100	7.5	100
In particular land	1.1	25.6	3.1	46.0	3.2	45.1	2.8	41.1	3.3	44.0

Sources OECD (2020); World Bank (2020); Deutsche Bundesbank and Federal Statistical Office (2020), Authors' own calculations

Notes: [a]Land and other natural resources (mineral and energy reserves, non-cultivated biological resources, water resources, etc.)

[b]Mineral and energy reserves and other natural assets (non-cultivated biological resources, water resources, etc.)

Consumption = Total consumption

of all non-financial assets, which merely increased by some 81% during the same period.

Expressed in years of total consumption, the value of non-financial assets, which was equivalent to 5.7 years of consumption in 2000, came to 6.7 years of consumption by 2019. The growth in the value of land, one of the most important components of real assets in value terms, significantly contributed to this increase. The value of land rose from 1.5 years of consumption in 2000 to 2.1 years of consumption in 2019.

If we turn now to the private sector, we can observe that the importance of land as an asset in relation to all non-financial assets is somewhat greater in the private sector than in the economy as a whole. The share represented by land in all non-financial assets also grew considerably in the private sector between 2000 and 2019: increasing from 27 to 32.1%. As a result, the value of privately owned land increased from 132% of consumption to 187% in 2019.

France is one of the few countries whose official statistics also cover mineral and energy reserves and other natural assets and that hence can provide data for all natural resources (i.e., for land in the narrow sense plus mineral and energy reserves and other natural assets). If we compare Germany and France, it is striking that the growth in the value of natural resources in France from 2000 to 2019 is considerably greater than the growth in the value of land in Germany. As shown in Table 5.2, the value of all natural resources in the French economy—99% of which is contributed by the value of land—increased from 1.3 times consumption in 2000 to 3.8 times in 2019. This is equivalent to an increase of around 192%. In the same period, all non-financial assets as measured in yearly consumption only increased by around 66%.

As can be seen, the French figures are significantly higher than the corresponding German numbers. This has nothing to do with the fact that the official French statistics also cover mineral and energy reserves and other natural assets, since the value of the latter is too low to make a significant difference. From the point of view of the economy as a whole, the value of mineral and energy reserves and other natural assets in France is minimal, amounting to barely 12 billion euros or 0.01 years of consumption. In the period under consideration, moreover, this value remained practically unchanged.[7] On the other hand, the higher real estate price level in France provides a clue to what is presumably the main source of the increase in value recorded in the French statistics.[8] It is safe to assume that not only total real estate prices, but also the prices, in particular, of land have risen far more

---

[7]At around 11 billion euros, the value of other natural assets in France is estimated to have been somewhat higher in 2015 than that of mineral and energy reserves, for which a value of only 658 million euros is shown (OECD 2019).

[8]Lower house prices in Germany as compared to France and other countries like Great Britain is often attributed to relatively low demand for owner-occupied homes and condominiums and the large number of inexpensive houses that were added to German supply after reunification in 1989 (cf. van de Ven and Fano 2017, p. 411).

sharply in France than in Germany in recent decades.[9] If we compare German and French land values in 2000, we see that at 1.5 times annual consumption, the German figure was still higher than the French Fig. 1.3 at the time. Subsequently, in the last one-and-a-half decades, land values have undergone far more rapid increase in France than in Germany. This can also be noted for the French as compared to the German private sector. In 2000, the value of privately owned land in France was only 110% of consumption. By 2019, this figure had risen to 330% of consumption. The share of land in total non-financial assets increased accordingly: from 25% in 2000 to around 44% in 2019.

A considerable part of the increase in private wealth that took place in France in recent years can be attributed to the evolution of the value of land. Strong growth in the value of privately owned land also occurred in some other countries; but this does not apply to the same extent for all countries (Homburg 2015; Piketty 2014; Piketty and Zucman 2014; van de Ven 2017).

5.2.4 The Value of Privately Owned Land

We now turn to the calculation of the value of privately owned land in the OECD plus China region. In order to preserve comparability to the other types of assets we are considering, viz., real capital and public debt, in what follows, we calculate the value of privately-owned land in 2015. We can use data from Eurostat (2019) and the OECD (2019) to determine the value of privately owned land in the countries of the OECD plus China region. Data on the value of land is available for 26 countries from this region, of which data for 23 of them comes from the OECD or Eurostat. The latter countries are: Australia, Belgium, Denmark, Germany, Estonia, Finland, France, Greece, Great Britain, Ireland, Italy, Japan, Canada, Luxembourg, Mexico, the Netherlands, Norway, Austria, Poland, Sweden, Slovakia, South Korea and the Czech Republic. For the USA, we rely on calculations done by the Bureau of Economic Analysis (Larson 2015). We also have data for China and Spain, which we have taken from the WID.world database.[10] No data on land is available for nine, mostly smaller, OECD countries. Nonetheless, with the data from the above-mentioned countries, we have enough data to be able roughly to estimate the value of land in the whole OECD plus China region. The 26 countries for which data is available accounted, after all, for around 93% of the total consumption of all the countries of the OECD plus China region in 2015.

Columns A to C in Table 5.3 show the value of land in 2015 in the respective local currency. Only some of the countries—namely, Australia, France, Japan, Canada, Mexico, South Korea and the Czech Republic—provide data on all natural

---

[9]Land prices in fact fluctuate more than house prices, which are principally determined by production costs. In many countries, their tendency is also to rise more rapidly than house prices. In Great Britain, for example, house prices have approximately doubled since the beginning of the 1990s, whereas land prices have increased around sixfold (Ryan-Collins 2017, p. 8).

[10]The figure for China comes from a study on wealth and its distribution in the People's Republic of China by Piketty et al. (2017) and was included in the WID.world database.

Table 5.3 Privately owned land in the OECD plus China region, 2015

Country	A Land economy as a whole Billions LCU	B Public land Billions LCU	C Private land[d] Billions LCU	D Total consumption Billions LCU	E = C / G Land Billions Int'l $	F = D / G Total consumption Billions Int'l $	G Conversion factor LCU in Int'l $	H = E / F Private sector land In years of consumption
Australia[a,c]	5,799.0	986.0	4,813.0	1,222.2	3,265.1	829.1	1.5	3.94
Austria	554.8	63.3	491.4	249.4	615.4	312.3	0.8	1.97
Belgium	...	...	851.3	308.1	1,064.4	385.2	0.8	2.76
Canada[a,c]	4,014.5	253.8	3,760.7	1,562.6	3,013.4	1,252.1	1.2	2.41
Chile	...	...	...	...	...	...	...	...
Czech Republic[c]	9,508.2	7,518.3	1,989.9	3,035.3	153.8	234.7	12.9	0.66
Denmark	...	...	1,491.6	1,478.0	204.2	202.4	7.3	1.01
Estonia	54.1	5.3	48.8	14.7	90.8	27.4	0.5	3.32
Finland	195.3	36.4	158.9	167.1	175.1	184.1	0.9	0.95
France[c]	5,613.0	745.4	4,867.6	1,711.6	6,020.7	2,117.0	0.8	2.84
Germany	3,835.7	427.7	3,408.1	2,218.3	4,381.1	2,851.6	0.8	1.54
Greece[a]	...	...	269.2	159.1	442.1	261.2	0.6	1.69
Hungary	...	...	...	...	...	...	...	...
Iceland	...	...	...	...	...	...	...	...
Ireland	...	...	217.7	119.2	55.5	30.4	3.9	1.83
Israel	...	...	...	...	...	...	...	...
Italy	...	...	3,421.9	1,318.3	4,633.6	1,785.2	0.7	2.60
Japan[a,c]	1,157,359.8	115,761.5	1,041,598.3	406,507.6	10,068.6	3,929.5	103.4	2.56
Korea[a,c]	6,614,467.3	1,739,147.7	4,875,319.6	1,006,005.6	5,686.4	1,173.4	857.4	4.85
Luxembourg	...	...	113.0	24.6	128.3	27.9	0.9	4.60
Mexico[a,c]	32,762.8	14,401.2	18,361.5	14,450.4	2,205.4	1,735.6	8.3	1.27
Netherlands	982.3	31.1	951.3	483.2	1,174.8	596.7	0.8	1.97
New Zealand	...	...	...	...	...	...	...	...

(continued)

Table 5.3 (continued)

Country	A Land economy as a whole Billions LCU	B Public land Billions LCU	C Private land[d] Billions LCU	D Total consumption Billions LCU	E = C/G Land Billions Int'l $	F = D/G Total consumption Billions Int'l $	G Conversion factor LCU in Int'l $	H = E/F Private sector land In years of consumption
Norway[f]	...	...	2,901.2	2,083.0	292.2	209.8	9.9	1.39
Poland	...	...	695.4	1,376.2	394.1	779.9	1.8	0.51
Portugal	...	...	...	...	...	...	...	...
Slovak Republic	71.6	20.5	51.1	58.5	104.0	119.1	0.5	0.87
Slovenia	...	...	...	...	...	...	...	...
Spain[b]	...	...	2,703.6	834.9	4,068.3	1,256.4	0.7	3.24
Sweden[c]	6,557.0	763.1	5,793.9	2,975.7	654.5	336.2	8.9	1.95
Switzerland	...	...	...	...	...	...	...	...
Turkey	...	...	...	...	...	...	...	...
United Kingdom[c]	4,681.7	158.7	4,522.9	1,596.5	6,532.6	2,305.9	0.7	2.83
United States[e]	22,982.0	1838.6	21,143.4	14,907.2	21,143.4	14,907.2	1.0	1.42
China[b]	...	...	58,700.4	36,226.7	16,929.2	10,447.8	3.5	1.62
Total OECD					76,567.6	37,850.0		2.02
Total OECD plus China					93,496.8	48,297.8		1.94

Notes Unless otherwise indicated, the original data comes from Eurostat (2019)

[a]Data from OECD (2019)

[b]Data from WID.world (2019)

[c]Land and other natural resources (mineral and energy reserves, non-cultivated biological resources, water resources, etc.)

[d]Belgium, Denmark, Ireland, Italy, Luxembourg, Canada, Norway, Poland: only households and non-profit institutions

[e]2009. Lower 48 states. Data from Larson (2015)

[f]2014

Authors' own calculations

Sources Columns A-C Eurostat (2019). Balance sheets for non-financial assets; OECD (2019): Dataset 9B, Balance sheets for non-financial assets; WID.world (2019); cf. notes

Column D World Bank (2019). World Development Indicators, Final consumption expenditure (current LCU)

Column G World Bank (2019). World Development Indicators, PPP conversion factor (GDP) (LCU per international $)

LCU: Local currency unit

resources: i.e., not only land, but also mineral and energy reserves and other natural assets.[11] For some of the countries, data is only available on the land owned by households. This is the case for Belgium, Denmark, Ireland, Italy, Luxembourg, Canada, Norway and Poland.[12] Where additional data is available, we are also able, in columns A and B respectively, to provide data on the value of land in the economy as a whole and land that is publicly owned. The individual national figures for land belonging to the private sector can be found in column C in the respective local currency. Column D contains data on total consumption (the sum of private and public consumption) in the respective local currency. Column E and column F show the value of land and total consumption in purchasing-power-adjusted international dollars. The conversion rates used come from the World Bank.

Finally, column H shows the value of privately owned land in each of the individual countries, as expressed in years of consumption. As can be seen, the total value of privately owned land varies greatly from country to country. The lowest figures are found for three Eastern European countries: namely, Poland, the Czech Republic and Slovakia, where private land assets represent 51, 66 and 87% of their respective annual consumption. South Korea and Luxembourg have the highest figures for privately owned land assets, at more than four times their respective annual consumption. At more than three times the value of their consumption, Australia, Estonia and Sweden also have a relatively large amount of private land assets by international standards. On average, the value of land in the OECD countries is *twice annual consumption*. If we add China, we obtain average private land assets for the OECD plus China region of 194% of consumption.

At 1.54 times and 1.42 times their annual consumption respectively, Germany and the USA are below the average for the OECD countries, whereas European countries like France and Great Britain are above it. We can assume that the clear difference between France and the UK, on the one hand, and Germany and the USA, on the other, is due to the fact that house and land prices are lower in Germany and the USA than in France and Great Britain. Whereas in Germany, the lingering consequences of both the Second World War and the country's roughly 40-year-long division into East and West Germany are responsible for these low prices, land assets in the USA were always relatively low by international standards due to the abundance of land available (Piketty 2014; van de Ven 2017, p. 211). In addition, German economic activity is regionally more broadly distributed than economic activity in France and Great Britain, where the overall value of land is especially heavily influenced by the greater metropolitan areas of Paris and London, respectively.

---

[11]In Australia's case, the value of mineral and energy reserves and other natural assets in 2015 was quite considerable, accounting for 11% of all natural resources.

[12]For the USA as well, the OECD only provides data on the value of land owned by households. Hence, we draw on a study in which the value of all land and the value of land owned by the US federal government is calculated for the period 2000–2009. In the value of land for 2009, we are using the last number from a period that was heavily marked by the formation and bursting of the last real estate bubble in the USA. The value of land in 2009 roughly corresponds to the average for the period (Larson 2015, Fig. 3).

To sum up:

Our calculations for 2015 show that the private wealth invested in land is equivalent to 1.94 times total consumption in the countries of the OECD plus China region.

We are presumably more likely to be underestimating the actual figure here than overestimating it. We can cite the following three reasons in support of this supposition. Firstly, less than one-third of the countries of the OECD plus China region collect data on their mineral and energy reserves and their other natural assets.[13] Secondly, around one-quarter of the countries only provide the value of land owned by households and non-profit institutions. Land belonging to firms is thus not included in the statistics. The value that is thus missing from the statistics should not be negligible.[14] And, thirdly, for the USA, which has great significance for the region as a whole, we can only provide a figure for 2009. We can assume that land prices have risen again since the end of the great recession. Hence, it is highly probable that the value of land in the USA is somewhat greater than the 142% of US total consumption that we determined for 2009. Finally, there are also general data collection and valuation problems in determining the value of natural resources (including land), which could lead most statistical offices in our region to tend to understate their value (Schmalwasser and Müller 2009; Schmalwasser and Weber 2012).

As already discussed above, a certain degree of error in estimating the value of land would not be all that problematic, because privately owned land is largely passed on debt-free to heirs, along with the real estate on it. This is to say that an erroneous estimate of land assets would entail an erroneous estimate of the assets that are supposed to be reserved as an inheritance and that are not intended for consumption in old age. Hence, an erroneous estimate of land assets would not have a major impact on calculating the wealth required for retirement planning.

References

Arnott, Richard J. and Joseph E. Stiglitz. 1979. Aggregate Land Rents, Expenditure on Public Goods, and Optimal City Size. *Quarterly Journal of Economics* 93 (4): 471-500.

Baldenius, Till, Sebastian Kohl and Moritz Schularick. 2019. *Die neue Wohnungsfrage: Gewinner und Verlierer des deutschen Immobilienbooms*. Bonn: Macrofinance Lab.

Barro, Robert J. 1974. Are Government Bonds Net Wealth? *Journal of Political Economy* 82 (6): 1095-1117.

Blanchard, Olivier and Philippe Weil. 2001. Dynamic Efficiency, the Riskless Rate, and Debt Ponzi Games Under Uncertainty. *Advances in Macroeconomics* 1 (2): 1-23.

---

[13]However, the impact of this underreporting presumably only concerns private wealth to a small extent. We can draw this conclusion based on the OECD countries that do report data on mineral and energy reserves and other natural assets, since by far the greater part of the latter are assigned to the public sector.

[14]In Germany, for example, land owned by financial and non-financial corporations accounts for 20% of the value of all domestic land.

Deutsche Bundesbank. 2019. Vermögen und Finanzen privater Haushalte in Deutschland: Ergebnisse der Vermögensbefragung 2017. *Monatsberichte der Deutschen Bundesbank* April 2019: 13–44.

Deutsche Bundesbank and Statistisches Bundesamt (Federal Statistical Office). 2015. *Balance sheets for institutional sectors and the total economy 1999–2014.* Deutsche Bundesbank: Frankfurt am Main and Statistisches Bundesamt: Wiesbaden.

Deutsche Bundesbank and Statistisches Bundesamt (Federal Statistical Office). 2020. *Balance sheets for institutional sectors and the total economy 1999–2019.* Deutsche Bundesbank: Frankfurt am Main and Statistisches Bundesamt: Wiesbaden.

European Commission, IMF, OECD, UN and World Bank. 2009. *System of National Accounts 2008.* https://unstats.un.org/unsd/nationalaccount/docs/SNA2008.pdf. Accessed: 15 April 2019.

European Union and OECD. 2015. *Eurostat-OECD compilation guide on land estimation.* Luxembourg: European Union and OECD.

Eurostat. 2013. *European System of Accounts: ESA 2010.* Luxembourg: Publications Office of the European Union.

Eurostat. 2019. *Balance sheets for non-financial assets.* http://ec.europa.eu/eurostat/web/products-datasets/-/nama_10_nfa_bs. Accessed: 16 June 2019.

Hellwig, Christian and Guido Lorenzoni. 2009. Bubbles and Self-Enforcing Debt. *Econometrica* 77 (4): 1137-1164.

Hellwig, Martin F. 2020a. *Dynamic Inefficiency and Fiscal Interventions in an Economy with Land and Transaction Costs.* Discussion Paper 2020/07, Max Planck Institute for Research on Collective Goods, Bonn.

Hellwig, Martin F. 2020b. Property taxes and dynamic inefficiency: A correction of a "correction". *Economics Letters* 197: 109603.

Hobbes, Thomas. 1651. *Leviathan, or, The Matter, Forme and Power of a Common-wealth Ecclesiasticall and Civil.* London: Printed for Andrew Crooke.

Homburg, Stefan. 1991. Interest and Growth in an Economy with Land. *Canadian Journal of Economics* 24 (2): 450-459.

Homburg, Stefan. 2015. Overaccumulation, Public Debt and the Importance of Land. *German Economic Review* 15(4): 411-435.

Kotlikoff, Laurence. 1992. *Generational Accounting: Knowing Who Pays and Knowing When for What We Spend.* New York (NY): The Free Press.

Krämer, Hagen M. 2021. *Einkommens- und Vermögensverteilung in Deutschland. Entwicklungen, Ursachen, Maßnahmen.* Wiso Diskurs, Analysen und Konzepte zur Wirtschafts- und Sozialpolitik. Bonn: Friedrich-Ebert-Stiftung.

Larson, William 2015. *New Estimates of Value of Land of the United States.* April 3, 2015. Washington (D.C.): Bureau of Economic Analysis. https://www.bea.gov/system/files/papers/WP2015-3.pdf. Accessed: 15 March 2018.

Lequiller, François and Derek Blades. 2014. *Understanding National Accounts.* 2nd ed. Paris: OECD Publishing.

Lewis, W. Arthur. 1954. Economic Development with Unlimited Supplies of Labour. *The Manchester School* 22 (2): 139-191.

OECD. 2019. *National Accounts, Annual National Accounts, Detailed Tables and Simplified Accounts. 9B. Balance sheets for non-financial assets.* https://doi.org/10.1787/data-00368-en. Accessed April-June 2019.

Piketty, Thomas. 2014. *Capital in the Twenty-First Century.* Cambridge (MA): Harvard University Press.

Piketty, Thomas and Gabriel Zucman. 2014. Capital Is Back: Wealth-Income Ratios in Rich Countries 1700–2010. *Quarterly Journal of Economics* 129 (3): 1255-1310.

Piketty, Thomas, Li Yang and Gabriel Zucman. 2017. *Capital Accumulation, Private Property and Rising Inequality in China: 1978–2015.* WID.world Working Paper Series No. 2017/6. http://wid.world/document/t-piketty-l-yang-and-g-zucmancapital-accu-mulation-private-property-andinequality-in-china-1978-2015-2016/. Accessed: 20 April 2019.

Raffelhüschen, Bernd. 1999. Generational Accounting in Europe. *American Economic Review: Papers and Proceedings* 89 (2): 167-170.

Ryan-Collins, Josh, Toby Lloyd and Laurie Macfarlane. 2017. *Rethinking the Economics of Land and Housing*. London: Zed Books.

Schmalwasser, Oda and Aloysius Müller. 2009. Gesamtwirtschaftliche und sektorale nichtfinanzielle Vermögensbilanzen. *Wirtschaft und Statistik* (2): 137-147.

Schmalwasser, Oda and Nadine Weber. 2012. Revision der Anlagevermögensrechnung für den Zeitraum 1991 bis 2011. *Wirtschaft und Statistik* (11): 933-947.

Schmalwasser, Oda and Sascha Brede. 2015. Grund und Boden als Bestandteil der volkswirtschaftlichen Vermögensbilanzen. *Wirtschaft und Statistik* (6): 43-57.

Statistisches Bundesamt. 2020. *Fachserie 3: Land- und Forstwirtschaft, Fischerei, Reihe 5.1 Bodenfläche nach Art der tatsächlichen Nutzung 2019*. Statistisches Bundesamt: Wiesbaden.

Uhlig, Harald and Mathias Trabandt. 2011. The Laffer Curve Revisited. *Journal of Monetary Economics* 58 (4): 305-327.

van de Ven, Peter. 2017. A full accounting for wealth. Including non-financial assets. In *Financial Accounts*, eds. Peter van de Ven and Daniele Fano, 279–302. Paris: OECD Publishing.

Weizsäcker, Carl Christian von. 2018. Verteilungswirkungen von Staatsschulden. *List Forum für Wirtschafts- und Sozialpolitik* 44 (2): 143-152.

World Bank. 2019. *DataBank – World Development Indicators*. https://databank.world-bank.org/data/home.aspx. Accessed: January-June 2019.

World Bank. 2020. *World Bank Open Data*. https://data.worldbank.org/. Accessed: 23 December 2020.

Public Debt

6

Abstract

More than a third of private wealth in the OECD plus China region consists of entitlements to public retirement benefits. If the state covered these future obligations using a reserve fund, an insoluble problem of investment would arise. It is only by doing without reserve funds that the twenty-first century welfare state is compatible with price stability at non-negative real interest rates. In calculating government obligations according to the ADL method, statistical offices acknowledge the implicit public debt deriving from the retirement system. Systems of public health insurance and public nursing care insurance also generate considerable implicit public debt and corresponding private wealth. The TRILL system advocated by Robert Shiller can make an important contribution to stabilize the high public debt that will be necessary in the future at low real interest rates. We undertake an empirical estimation of the level of public debt in the OECD plus China region. To determine explicit public debt, we use data on net public debt from the International Monetary Fund. Implicit public debt is mainly comprised of the state's capitalized financial obligations deriving from the public retirement system and public health insurance. Some statistical offices publish data on the retirement benefit entitlements that have accrued within social security systems. This data provides an important basis for our calculations. We estimate that total public debt in the OECD plus China region is equivalent to more than 600% of total annual consumption in the region.

C. C. von Weizsäcker and H. M. Krämer, *Saving and Investment in the Twenty-First Century*, https://doi.org/10.1007/978-3-030-75031-2_6

6.1   Public Debt: Theoretical Foundations

Part 1: What Is Public Debt?

6.1.1   Introduction

Our objective is to estimate the size of the net private wealth of people in the OECD plus China region. A large part of this wealth consists of the state's future payment obligations vis-à-vis its citizens. We subtract from this the state's claims on its citizens in the form of a wide variety of loans. Our analysis is guided by the balance sheets that are commonly used in the private sector. Since we are treating the OECD plus China region as a closed economy (cf. Sect. 3.11), we can also say that we are preparing a consolidated balance sheet of all the citizens in this area and calculating the citizens' "equity" reflected in this balance sheet. As a mirror image of the latter, we are also compiling a consolidated balance sheet of the public sector in the OECD plus China region. This also includes para-governmental organizations (like, for instance, the insurance providers forming part of the public health insurance system in Germany). The resultant state equity—with the "state" being understood here as the collective of the individual national states in the region—is negative nowadays, since in the OECD countries plus China, public debt vis-à-vis citizens is, on average, greater than the sum of the state's real and financial assets.

This way of calculating net public debt is the equivalent of calculating wealth by the "Accrued-to-Date Liabilities" approach (ADL approach), which has also been employed in the official national accounts recently. This method will be presented in detail in Chap. 6.2. Roughly speaking, it corresponds to the accounting practices that are commonly used in the private sector. On this approach, welfare state obligations also form part of public debt. For analogous future obligations of a firm vis-à-vis its employees have to be recorded as liabilities in the balance sheet under the heading of "retirement provisions."

This accounting method is not the same thing as the forecasts that are made in connection with the concept of the "sustainability" of public finances. "Generational accounting," which was developed by Kotlikoff and applied to Europe by Raffelhüschen and others, is an example (Kotlikoff 1992; Raffelhüschen 1999). The analysis by Werding (2011), which was commissioned by the German Council of Economic Experts, and the Council report based on it (SVR 2011) follow a similar approach. The point of these studies is to juxtapose the state's future expenditure and revenue. The private sector analogy is a "business plan," not a balance sheet drawn up on a given date. Another way of recognizing the difference between the approaches is that the temporal horizon of the ADL method we use is finite, inasmuch as only the claims of current contributors and retirees are recorded. By contrast, generational accounting and sustainability analyses always depend on taking all future generations into account. Hence, they have an "infinite" time horizon. Since, however, they ultimately have to employ finite values, they only work if the discount rate used is greater than the growth rate of the economy in question. These methods have then to rule out in advance that there can be an interest rate that remains lower than the growth rate in the long run. They are thus not appropriate for our purposes.

But as a solvent borrower that, as experience shows, has privileged access to the capital market, how is it possible for the state to have negative equity? The explanation is the state's monopoly on the use of violence. Thanks to a sort of "quasi-mortgaging" of future tax revenue, the latter allows the state to convince the capital market that public debt will be serviced. The citizen's ability to enjoy wealth that is perhaps twice national wealth per capita presupposes that Hobbes's idea of the Leviathan is correct: Only the state can legitimately use violence. And as collector of taxes, the state demands obedience from citizens: demands that taxes are in fact paid. (For more on this, cf. Sect. 5.1.4.)

6.1.2 Explicit Net Public Debt

In Sect. 6.2.1, we present the size of the explicit net public debt of the OECD plus China region. It comprises around three-quarters of the annual consumption of the area as a whole. But there are, of course, significant differences from one country to another. We will not go into their causes here. We will come back to them in the policy-oriented second part of this book: in particular, in Chaps. 10 and 11.

When interest rates are high, explicit public debt gives rise to a significant fiscal burden. If, however, interest rates are persistently lower than the economy's growth rate, no positive primary surplus is required to hold the public debt ratio constant. The analytical details were presented in Chap. 2.

Explicit public debt represents wealth for citizens: and indeed liquid wealth—at least in normal times. In Sect. 5.1.12, we showed that as a component of wealth, public debt is also in a sort of competitive relationship with land and that this relationship has interesting distributive repercussions.

6.1.3 Implicit Public Debt 1: Social Security Retirement Benefits

We estimate that at least one third of private wealth consists of implicit public debt in the OECD plus China region. This means that this considerable share of total wealth is included in the official national accounts neither as wealth nor as public debt. The state's obligations to pay social security retirement benefits represent the most significant part of implicit public debt. How we calculate these obligations is different from how we calculate explicit public debt. But this difference is no reason not to recognize that the modern welfare state creates obligations for the state to pay out considerable sums in the future and that for the beneficiaries, on the other hand, these sums already represent "wealth" today. How they currently live their lives is strongly influenced by the size and security of the entitlements that they have already earned in the context of the social security system. For workers who are covered by social security, the resulting entitlements have much the same effect on their saving and consumption behavior as pension claims that have, however, to be paid by a private person or a private business. But the latter claims undoubtedly form part of the assets of the beneficiaries, corresponding to liabilities of the same amount for the party required to pay them. Hence, analogously, the state's obligations resulting from social security should likewise be seen as liabilities.

In the introduction to this book in Chap. 1, we already noted that those entitled to future social security retirement benefits behave as if these future claims were wealth when making their saving and consumption decisions. The balance they strike between current consumption and voluntary current saving is such that without the future retirement benefits, many of them would fall into poverty in old age. The debates about retirement benefits and the threat of seniors living in poverty only make sense if we regard the expected benefits as something comparable to savings deposits or stock ownership. Hence, an economic approach requires us to treat these entitlements as wealth—just as Germany's constitutional court, the *Bundesverfassungsgericht*, has done.

The form taken by the state's obligation to pay social security retirement benefits is different than that involved in government bonds with a fixed-rate coupon. It has a greater resemblance to a private life annuity. But, exactly like fixed-rate bonds, the latter constitutes wealth for the beneficiary and a liability for the insurer. Hence, the different form taken by the state's obligations to pay retirement benefits is no reason for us not to recognize them as a part of public debt.

However, the payment of future social security retirement benefits—just like in the case of a private life annuity—is only an obligation to the extent that the required contributions have been paid into the social security system up to the date on which the balance sheet is compiled. Thus, the claims of people who are starting out in their careers, and have only just begun to pay into social security, are zero. If today they stop paying into the system, they have no claims to retirement benefits. By contrast, an employee who has been earning a salary for 45 years and now retires has claims to retirement benefits whose capitalized value comes to several times the value of his or her annual salary. The state—in particular, the social security retirement fund—owes him or her this amount. Hence, the latter should be considered as part of the stock variable "public debt."

An additional factor has to be taken into account when calculating this value. In most OECD member states, retirement benefits are continually adjusted to average wages. This is, in particular, a kind of protection against inflation, and it works as long as the evolution of nominal wages runs parallel to that of the price level. But, apart from this protection against inflation, there is also an adjustment—whose form varies from country to country and that is often only partial—to average real wages. Germany's "dynamic retirement benefits," which were first introduced in West Germany in 1958, are an example. The present value of these expected future adjustments to retirement benefits is, on average, considerable, because some of the claims they affect are far in the future and hence will undergo many such adjustments.

Claims to social security retirement benefits thus bear a certain resemblance to the "TRILLS" that have been proposed by Robert Shiller and others for explicit public debt (Shiller and Kamstra 2010). Shiller proposes that the government issue securities whose holders will every year receive one-trillionth of the previous year's national product. These securities would be negotiable, and hence, their market value would be determined by supply and demand. The name "TRILLS" comes from "trillion" and rhymes, moreover, with "bills": hence, Robert Shiller's call for "TRILLS instead of T-bills." A major difference between TRILLS and claims to social security retirement benefits is, of course, that the latter come to an end with the death of the beneficiary, whereas the claim to TRILL-income is transferable and inheritable. We will come back to the TRILLS in greater detail in a section especially devoted to them below.

There is, of course, another significant difference between claims to social security retirement benefits and traditional government bonds. Claims to retirement benefits either are non-negotiable or can only be transferred with great difficulty. In keeping with the very idea of social security, they represent a kind of "forced saving." They are also supposed to prevent workers from becoming dependent on public assistance once they stop working, due to insufficient voluntary saving. It would be incompatible with this function, if claims to social security retirement benefits were negotiable like ordinary securities.

Social security was initially conceived and also implemented (on the model of private insurance) with a reserve fund, which was supposed to cover payment obligations as they come due. If it had endured, such a funded scheme would have been a form of social security that did not increase net public debt. Like it or not, when the reserve fund disappeared in Germany due to the war and the resulting inflation, a transition had to be made to a so-called pay-as-you-go system, in which current retirement benefits are principally paid using the contributions of active members and their employers. In the meanwhile, however, the system also receives considerable subsidies from the federal budget. A "pay-as-you-go" system can be understood as a sort of funded social security minus the reserve fund, which is precisely lacking here. This makes it particularly clear that the state's obligations to pay future retirement benefits are a form of public debt. The considerations developed here on the basis of the German example essentially apply for all OECD countries, although there are, of course, quantitative differences from one country to another.

6.1.4 Implicit Public Debt 2: Public Health Insurance

To the implicit public debt resulting from the social security retirement plan, we have also to add the implicit public debt resulting from public health insurance. In Germany, most employees and employers make contributions to public health insurance that are only slightly less than their contributions to the public retirement plan. These contributions finance a large part of the healthcare system, whose services are provided to members of the public healthcare plan free-of-charge in the overwhelming majority of cases. Since the contributions are proportionate to the gross wages of beneficiaries, public health insurance is not in fact insurance: The contributions are more like taxes. De facto, they are a kind of second income tax. The "tax revenue" from this second incomes tax is, however, tied to a particular purpose, since it can be used only for funding the healthcare system. The level of the contributions is determined such that they can cover the healthcare costs of all members of the public health insurance plan. Now, for both public and private health insurance, healthcare costs rise with the increasing age of beneficiaries. On the other hand, the contributions paid by beneficiaries—since they are proportionate to their wage income or, respectively, their social security retirement benefits—are, on average, higher for younger, still economically active beneficiaries than for retirees. Consequently, every public health insurance plan involves a considerable transfer of resources from young to old. In Germany, we could, in principle, calculate the size of this transfer for every insurance provider or *Krankenkasse* forming part of the public health insurance system.

On closer inspection, however, this "transfer" from one population group to another is in fact something else. It is rather a particular form of forced saving. A comparison with private health insurance makes this clear.

Private insurance providers "smooth" their premiums by collecting premiums from younger age cohorts that are greater than the costs to which they give rise and collecting premiums from older age cohorts that are not sufficient to cover their healthcare costs. But the private insurers are required to invest the surpluses that they generate from younger beneficiaries on the capital market and to form client-specific old-age provisions. These resources are then used to finance a discount in the form of a reduced premium for these same beneficiaries, so that premium payments are more evenly distributed over the course of a lifetime than would correspond to the costs incurred. Hence, a part of the premiums paid by younger beneficiaries serves as saving for their old age.

Private health insurance providers are thus in debt to their clients for the amount of the old-age provisions they form. In their case, however, these old-age provisions correspond to the resources they have invested on the capital market. In the same way, the public health insurance system is in debt to its younger beneficiaries, who are required to pay premiums greater than the costs to which they give rise, but who thus can count on having their healthcare costs taken care of in their old age, even though their contributions will then, on average, be insufficient to cover these costs. In this sense, the state is in debt to citizens enrolled in public health insurance—just as private insurance providers are in debt to their clients for the amount of their old-age provisions.

The only difference is that the public insurance providers do not form any reserve funds to cover these debts—and they also do not include any corresponding provisions in their balance sheets. This missing reserve fund thus corresponds to additional public debt of the same amount—exactly like the missing reserve fund in the case of the public retirement plan.

Entirely analogous considerations also apply for public nursing care insurance. The latter is also taken into account in our calculations in Sect. 6.2.2.

6.1.5 Implicit Public Debt 3: An Exotic Example in the Form of Germany's Renewable Energy Act

It is not possible for us to count all implicit public debt. We concentrate here on the three most significant items: the public retirement plan, public health insurance and nursing care insurance. Similar institutions exist in almost all the member states of the OECD and are starting to develop also in China.

We want to mention just one exotic example of implicit public debt that is peculiar to Germany, in order to make clear to the reader how it is possible to find implicit public debt in many different forms. This exotic example will not be included in our calculation for the OECD plus China region as a whole, however. We are talking about Germany's Renewable Energy Act or EEG (*Erneuerbare Energiengesetz*). Like in the case of public health insurance, the Renewable Energy Act also involves a tax-like charge that is also connected to hidden public debt. This charge is a kind of "electricity tax," to which practically every consumer of electricity is subject in proportion to his or her usage.

The law promotes certain investments in electricity production that would not be profitable without subsidies and hence would not take place. The purpose of the legislation is to create incentives for an energy transition: a shift away from fossil fuels and toward renewable energies. A private investor who builds a wind park or a solar energy installation does not only receive priority rights to feed the produced electricity into the grid: For a period of 20 years, the investor also receives compensation per kilowatt-hour that is fixed by the state and that is significantly higher than the wholesale price of electricity that gets established every day on the energy exchange. But the burden of paying this additional compensation is not ultimately borne by the grid operator to whom the electricity is supplied. Rather, the grid operators are themselves compensated for buying the electricity at an elevated price, inasmuch as the price that end-users pay to them includes a surcharge on every kilowatt-hour consumed.

This web of payments within the framework of the EEG occurs entirely outside of the public budget, and hence, according to the official statistics, it also does not form part of the public sector share in the national product. Nonetheless, this should not obscure the fact that, from an economic point of view, the EEG surcharge is nothing other than a tax: in effect, an "electricity tax." For the EEG arrangement is economically no different than a hypothetical arrangement that would work by way of the budget. In this hypothetical alternative arrangement, the government imposes an electricity tax. This tax is always set such that it is just enough to finance the subsidies that the government provides to operators of wind and solar energy installations by paying a fixed price per kilowatt-hour for the electricity they supply for 20 years after the installations first come into operation.

The obligations vis-à-vis the owners of wind and solar energy installations that are assumed by the government in this alternative arrangement are comparable to the obligations that, as discussed above, the government assumes for the old age of beneficiaries covered by public health insurance. The fact that Germany chose a mechanism, in the form of the EEG, that takes place outside of the public budget is no reason not to speak here of implicit public debt.

The EEG has achieved its goal of establishing massive incentives for investment in wind and solar energy installations, and these incentives have also been extensively acted upon. Investment has been triggered. Exactly as in the case of debt-financed public investment, this investment can be financed by loans.

The amount of the public debt that is hidden behind the EEG can be estimated as follows. The investor in a wind park or a photovoltaic power station receives a share of the electricity tax for 20 years. In exchange, at time zero, he or she has made an investment of a certain sum. At the outset, the present value of the expected income from the electricity tax is thus (on a rough calculation that ignores interest rate effects) 20 times the annual income from the electricity tax. This value then declines over time, in more or less linear fashion, until it reaches zero in year 20. The average present value over time is thus ten times the annual income from the electricity tax, and public debt vis-à-vis this investor is also, on average, ten times the annual income from the electricity tax. If we add up the debt from all the energy installations that have been subsidized under the EEG in this way, then we obtain a figure for EEG-induced implicit public debt in the hundreds of billions.

6.1.6 Public Debt When the Real Interest Rate Is Zero

In Sect. 6.2.2, we arrive at an estimate of the size of implicit public debt. Our point of departure is the calculation of the present value of entitlements to social security retirement benefits. Each European Union member state calculates the present value of entitlements, and these national figures are published by Eurostat, the statistical office of the European Union. In accordance with uniform requirements, these present values are calculated at a real interest rate of 2% per year, 3% per year and 4% per year by discounting the future benefit payments.

The interest rate sensitivity of a stock variable like retirement benefit entitlements is great, since what is involved is the adding-up of future payments that are spread out over decades. This raises the question of the appropriate discount rate to use. For our purposes, there is a clear answer. Our analysis is based on the hypothesis that the natural rate of interest is negative in the twenty-first century. This means that positive net public debt is indispensable, if we want to achieve a non-negative real interest rate that is compatible with full employment.

In this context, it is interesting to know how great the share of net public debt is, when the real interest rate reaches its lowest possible non-negative level. Hence, we ask: How great is the present value of future claims to social security retirement benefits (and of analogous public health insurance and nursing care insurance claims), if we work with a real interest rate of zero?

We can also put this another way: If someone was to claim that a non-negative real interest rate is sufficient to satisfy people's saving requirements simply through the formation of private real assets, then he or she would have to show what is to be done with the money forming the hypothetical reserve fund for current public debt that is available at the lowest possible non-negative real interest rate—hence at the interest rate that is most favorable for this claim. At a hypothetical real interest rate of zero, however, this hypothetical reserve fund is the net public debt. This hypothetical reserve fund is the explanatory hurdle that anyone doubting our thesis has to overcome.

Moreover, the real interest rates at which countries with the highest possible credit rating can borrow have not in fact been higher than zero for quite some time already. The European calculations at a real interest rate of 3% or 2% per year are based on long-term averages. There is reason to think that the discount rates will be set lower in the future.

The leveraging effect of the discount rate on the present value can be identified with the average amount of time separating the payment obligations from the present. If this average time gap is 28 years, for example, then the present value of the total flow of these payment obligations increases by 28% with a reduction of the discount rate from 3 to 2% per year. The procedure employed for converting from present values at 2% per year to present values at zero percent per year will be explained in a methodological excursus in Sect. 6.2.2.1.

At a discount rate of zero percent, the present value of entitlements to social security retirement benefits for the OECD plus China region comes to nearly five times annual consumption. An estimated present value of the "savings" involved in public health and nursing care insurance of more than half of annual consumption has to be added to this.

In this calculation with a real interest rate of zero, explicit net public debt is only the "tip of the iceberg," representing around one-eighth or approximately 12.5% of total net public debt. (The visible tip of an iceberg in the North Sea accounts for around 11% of the iceberg's total mass.)

Part 2: High Public Debt as a Problem for Stability

6.1.7 The Discounting Discrepancy Problem

A little over a decade ago, Reinhart and Rogoff's *This Time is Different* came out (Reinhart and Rogoff 2009). Their book is about the large number of historically demonstrated debt crises that have occurred in the past. Again and again, powerful states have had to admit their inability to repay their debts and pay the interest on them. Again and again, the creditors have had to write off their claims as uncollectible. As the title of the book suggests, again and again, creditors have fallen for the assurances of loan-seeking governments that *this time* the new debt will certainly be paid back.

Twice in the twentieth century, Germany also failed to repay its debt. Once, creditors were expropriated by the Great Inflation from 1921 to 1923; the second time, the old currency had to be replaced by a new one, the *Deutschmark*, in order to restore orderly monetary conditions. This change of currency also amounted to a debt cancelation, as a consequence of which the state's creditors were largely expropriated.

Our aim here is not to investigate why countries have so often defaulted on their debt. What we want to examine are the conditions of a functioning global capital market in a world in which substantial public debt is required, because privately desired wealth is far greater than the level of real assets that it is reasonable to maintain, i.e., since they can be productively used: in a world, in other words, in which people's desired waiting period Z is far greater than the productively usable period of production T plus the present value of land rents $l\omega$—even when the interest r is zero.

Firstly, we can note that at a very low real interest rate that is close to zero, the primary surplus needed for stabilizing the public debt ratio D is negative, since, in this case, the steady-state growth rate of the economy is greater than the rate of interest the government has to be pay. At a constant public debt ratio, net borrowing is greater than the government's interest payments. We have discussed this in detail in Chap. 2.

Now, this condition applies when the capital market is willing to lend money to the government without a risk premium. If the capital market demanded a risk premium, then the interest rate the government has to pay could be greater than the sustainable long-term growth rate of the economy. To this extent, the inequality $g > r$ discussed above in fact merely says the following:

Public debt can be serviced without difficulty, if the capital market believes that a country can service its public debt without difficulty.

Hence, we have to investigate what conditions are required, such that a country does not have to pay any risk premium or only has to pay a very low one.

We can assume that a country normally has an interest in being regarded as a reliable borrower on the capital market. A good reputation is important to its fiscal authorities. A country pays to have its outstanding debt rated by rating agencies. Inasmuch as the creditor (often a bank) wants to use government bonds as collateral for its own borrowing (e.g., from the central bank), it is usually obligatory to have them rated by rating agencies.

On the other hand, we have to keep in mind that a country's politicians in the legislature and the executive branch are under pressure to be able to show results in the very short term. Their reelection depends on it. But this means that the subjective discount rate on which politicians base their decisions is far higher than the risk-free capital market interest rate. This *discounting discrepancy* can give rise to problems for a country's reputation on the capital market.

Some countries have adopted measures against this discounting discrepancy. Thus, the bicameral system in the 1788 US constitution can already be seen as basically an institution that was meant to address the problem of politicians' high subjective discount rates. Although the House of Representatives is elected every two years, members of the Senate are elected for six years. The principle of an independent central bank also serves to ensure that monetary policy is not abandoned to the short-term goal of a quick-fix economic stimulus at the expense of long-term monetary stability. Finally, "debt brakes," such as those found in the

Swiss or the German constitution, are institutional measures for hindering political decisions that favor short-term results to the detriment of long-term success. This sort of politics is often described as "populism" nowadays.

The theory of the negative natural rate of interest presented in this book and the consequent necessity of public debt make it more difficult to develop institutional measures for overcoming the discounting discrepancy problem. For simple constitutional rules, like the German and Swiss debt brakes, no longer work in a world with a negative natural rate of interest. Another way of putting this is that we can observe a secular trend toward a growing discounting discrepancy. Because people are living longer and longer and more and more people also want to leave large parts of their wealth as an inheritance, people's effective subjective discount rate has become smaller and smaller—or has even, as it were, become "negative." (We will dispense with formalizing this conclusion here.) At the same time, however, high subjective discount rates in politics represent just as big of a problem today as they were in the past. For their own private well-being and for the well-being of their descendants, people think in the long term, and this long term is getting longer and longer; but political institutions force politicians to act in a way that is just as short-term-oriented as in the past.

6.1.8 The Relative Size of the Public Sector

We will discuss the welfare state at length in Chap. 9 on the need for monetary stability. Our essential point will be that, in order to fulfill its social functions, the welfare state should not be too small, but, in the interest of preserving a liberal-democratic order, it also must not be oversized. There should be redistribution within the framework of the welfare state and a progressive income tax system; but it must not go so far as massively to undermine the incentive to contribute to the creation of the national product.

Here, we have now to examine a requirement for stability that is imposed by the international capital market. This requirement is closely connected to the question of the right size of the welfare state. This relationship is all the more important, the greater the public debt ratio D required to satisfy the population's desired wealth.

Every economist is familiar with the "Laffer curve," which was named after an adviser to the former US President Ronald Reagan. Arthur Laffer used his ideas to justify the massive tax cuts that were characteristic of the Reagan era (Fig. 6.1).

At low tax rates, a country's fiscal authorities can count on tax revenue rising with a moderate increase in tax rates. At very high tax rates, a further increase in tax rates is counterproductive for tax revenue in the long run, since economic incentives decline so much that, in percentage terms, the tax base shrinks more than the average tax rates have risen. When tax rates are too high, the allocation of resources is so heavily distorted that the steering function of relative prices is excessively impeded.

At given tax rates, the state can increase its tax revenue by greater surveillance of its citizens. Thus, for example, the system of surveillance that is currently being implemented in China can be expected to lead to an obedience toward the authorities that will also bring about increased tax revenue. In every country, there is, in

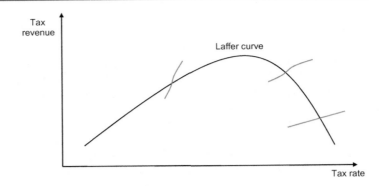

Fig. 6.1 Laffer curve. *Source* Authors' own presentation. *Notes* Black line: relationship between tax rate and tax revenue (long-term); Red lines: relationship between tax rate and tax revenue (short-term)

principle, a trade-off between privacy and the fiscal yield of the tax system. More "1984" creates higher government revenue. Better anti-corruption measures are one way in which stricter government surveillance can be brought about. More powerful tools of government surveillance can also be used to reduce crime. Less crime increases the efficiency of the economic system and hence also the yield of the tax system. This is not the place, however, for a detailed analysis of these relationships.

The Laffer curve is of significance for our analysis of public debt, because it also entails a relationship between the stability of public finances and the relative size of the public sector. In order to present this relationship, we have to distinguish between the short-term and long-term impact of changes in tax rates. As long as the economy has not yet adjusted to a tax increase, tax revenue will usually rise and net borrowing will fall commensurately. We speak here of the *short-term impact* of tax rate changes. The short-term impact of tax cuts is a decline in tax revenue and an increase in net borrowing.

As already discussed above, what ultimately determines the overall impact of tax rate changes on tax revenue is how economic actors adjust their behavior in response to them. These adjustments take place over a longer period of time. Whether the *long-term impact* of a tax increase on tax revenue is positive or negative depends on whether taxes were low or high before. If taxes were previously low, a modest increase in taxes can increase tax revenue. If taxes were previously high, a modest tax cut can–not right away, but *in the long run*–increase tax revenue.

As long as the tax burden of economic actors is low, a country's fiscal authorities can convince the capital market that public debt is a risk-free investment. For in the event of a shock that drives interest rates upwards, the fiscal authorities can increase tax revenue not only in the short term, but also in the long term, by increasing taxes. They are thus well-equipped for an interest rate shock. But other kinds of shock, which have a negative impact on tax revenue or require increased public spending, can also be cushioned by raising taxes, since doing so increases tax revenue not only immediately, but also in the long run.

The situation is different, if taxes are so high that the top of the Laffer curve has already been passed. Here, it would be a good idea, in any case, to cut taxes. But the adoption of such a policy could be hindered by the short-term orientation of the political instances, as well as by the capital market. For, in the short term, the fiscal authorities would have to accept higher net borrowing. This, however, could be misinterpreted by the capital market as indicating a danger that outstanding bonds and loans may not be repaid. In addition, some of a country's citizens who are dependent on welfare benefits could interpret a tax cut as a redistribution from the poor to the rich—with the consequence that the government refrains from undertaking one (Uhlig and Trabandt 2011). But, in this case, the capital market would be right to demand a risk premium on government bonds.

> There is, therefore, a causal relationship between how much wealth is redistributed via taxes and charges and the risk premium on outstanding government bonds.

The upshot of this analysis is that the share of national product represented by distorting taxes and charges must not be too great. An oversized welfare state has such a powerfully distorting effect on the price system and the system of economic incentives that it corresponds to a point on the descending part of the Laffer curve. But, if this is the case, then a country's fiscal authorities have to accept that they can only place its government bonds on the capital market with a considerable risk premium.

Thus we can ask, for example, whether the relative size of the public sector in France is not already beyond the maximum of the French Laffer curve. The country could, however, have massive difficulties, if its government tried to improve the situation by cutting taxes. For, in the short-term, this would lead to net borrowing that massively exceeds the Maastricht criterion. The Maastricht straitjacket would thus represent an obstacle to French economic recovery.

The considerations presented here would be irrelevant, if the public debt ratio was very small. For, in that case, shocks that raise the interest rate for government bonds would not be a problem for the capital market. But if, for the reasons discussed in Chap. 3 on desired wealth, the public debt ratio is high and its tendency is rising, then these considerations are extremely relevant. The interdependence between the level of desired wealth and the extent of reasonable redistribution within the framework of the welfare state has to be kept in mind.

6.1.9 Refining the Concept of the Relative Size of the Public Sector

As regards their effect on resource allocation, the different parts of government revenue are very heterogeneous. There are taxes that are not distorting, but essentially corrective. The fuel tax is an example. It serves, in the first place, to fund road infrastructure. To this extent, it can be seen as the price for using a scarce, but expandable resource. Hence, by way of the tax, "the market" can ultimately decide how extensive road infrastructure will become. If correctly calculated, the tax on carbon emissions that is advocated by many economists can also be understood as a corrective "Pigou tax."

The taxes that yield the most revenue are the sales tax in the modern form of the "value-added tax" and the income tax. These taxes have a distorting effect. They amount to taxes on the market-mediated division of labor. Work in which producer and consumer are identical—for instance, domestic work like cooking, cleaning, etc., that is performed by the housewife or househusband—is not subject to sales tax or income tax. The work involved in parents' bringing up children is likewise not subject to these taxes. If someone prefers a more "pleasant" job with a lower wage to a less pleasant, but better paid job, this choice is subsidized by the government, since, as a consequence, the tax base is smaller—assuming that the marginal contribution of the employee to national product is proportionate to the wage. Another way of putting this is that "greed" for a higher standard of living is effectively "punished" by the tax authorities.

In Sect. 3.3 of the chapter on desired wealth, we provided an overview of the different charges and taxes to which German employees are subject. Since the retirement benefits that employees will later receive under the public retirement plan depend on the amount of the contributions that they and their employers have paid into the plan, as a first approximation, these contributions are not to be regarded as taxes, but rather as saving. That said, how good of an approximation this still is would have to be tested in detail in light of the currently used benefits formula, as well as other legislative changes. But something else, in any case, is clear: The employee and employer contributions to public health insurance have the character of a tax and hence a distorting effect.

It would be useful in connection with our research if a documented, modified measure of the relative size of the public sector was available for the OECD countries and for China. This would differ from the traditional measure inasmuch as payments to the government would be excluded, if they function, in effect, like "prices" for an equivalent government service. Examples would be elements of the fuel tax and (in Germany) contributions to the public retirement plan, to the extent that the plan's character as a sort of insurance is largely retained.

6.1.10 Shiller's "TRILLS" Proposal

Apart from noting that governments should try to limit distorting taxes, so that their bonds do not bear any default risk, we should also consider whether, in parallel to fixed-rate bonds, there are other forms of public debt that are less exposed to default risk. By definition, firms whose shares are traded on the stock exchange are not only financed with fixed-rate bonds, promissory notes or bank loans. Part of their financing consists of equity, which participates in both corporate risk and corporate profits. We understand Robert Shiller's TRILLS proposal as a public version of this private form of equity financing (Shiller and Kamstra 2010).

Shiller has been arguing for this idea for a number of years now. He has also found a number of co-authors who, like himself, have been thinking about the exact form such a security could take. A "TRILL" gives its holder the right to one-trillionth of the nominal national product of the country whose government has issued the security. We can, in principle, imagine that this claim is preserved over time. It is also conceivable, however, that a TRILL lays claim to one-trillionth of the national product in the year of its issue, 95% of one-trillionth, for example, in the following year, 90.25% of one-trillionth in the year after that, etc. This type of gradually shrinking claim would have the advantage of allowing a country's fiscal authorities also to reduce the total number of outstanding TRILL claims. Note that if there is this kind of "radioactive" decay, then all outstanding TRILLs are perfect substitutes for one another, much like what we know is the case for substances like, for instance, a particular isotope of uranium. This would also assure that TRILLS have high liquidity.

Shiller sees his TRILLS proposal as an expansion of the choices available to the investor. Using calculations, he argues that thanks to the inclusion of TRILLS, the typical American investor could achieve a far better ratio of average returns to return variance than is currently possible without them. For this reason, he predicts that there would be great demand for TRILLs.

But, in addition, he emphasizes the contribution of TRILLS to a greater stability of public finances. If the actual evolution of nominal national product deviates, either upwards or downwards, from what was expected, then the payouts to TRILL holders would move in the same direction. The behavior of tax income is pro-cyclical. Thus, TRILL payouts rise and fall in parallel to tax revenue.

We now provide a brief formal presentation of the TRILL within the framework of a steady-state analysis. As concerns the present, a TRILL entitles its holder to a dividend worth one-trillionth of the national product. In order to connect this discussion to the formal apparatus used in the other chapters of this book, we will work with a different unit, but retain the designation "TRILL." As concerns the present, one TRILL unit entitles its holder to obtain w units of money, whereby w represents net national product per labor year minus the interest on capital employed. Hence, as shown, for example, in Chap. 2, the formula for w is:

$$w = y - rv(r;\ \theta)$$

As in Chap. 2 on capital theory, the growth rate of the economy per labor year, g, is given. A TRILL "shrinks" at a relative speed of δ. Thus, calculated from today, at time t it has come to be $e^{-\delta t}$ units. Accordingly, at time t, the dividend is $\overline{w}\,e^{(g-\delta)t}$, where $\overline{w}$ is the current value of w. If, as before, r is the risk-free interest rate and α is the risk premium, then the present value of all cash flows from a current TRILL is

$$p = \int_{0}^{\infty} \overline{w}e^{(g-\delta-r-\alpha)t}dt = \frac{\overline{w}}{\delta - g + r + \alpha}.$$

We can assume that p is the market price of a TRILL.

It is possible to calculate the yield on this security by, for example, imagining an investor who wants to keep the value of the TRILLs in his or her portfolio constant. The TRILLs shrink at the rate δ; on the other hand, the dividend grows at the rate g. If $\delta > g$, then the investor has to buy TRILLs, in order to keep the value of the TRILLs in the portfolio constant. If N is the number of TRILLs that the investor owns, then his or her current "cash flow" is

$$CashFlow = N\overline{w} - Np(\delta - g) = Np(\delta - g + r + \alpha - \delta + g).$$

The return on the investment is thus $r + \alpha$. This is also the return if $g > \delta$: i.e., if the investor is constantly selling TRILLs, in order to keep his or her TRILL assets constant.

This return is the expected return. The risk premium α makes this clear. Inasmuch as the risk premium is the same as that applied by the capital market in the case of fixed-rate government bonds, both types of investment achieve the same expected return. We will come back to the question of the amount of the risk premium below.

The elasticity of tax revenue as a function of national product is empirically greater than one. This is because the tax system as a whole is progressive. In the case of income tax, marginal tax rates are consistently higher than the average tax rates. Moreover, certain of the government's required expenditures have a countercyclical effect: above all, unemployment and welfare. As concerns the modern period, this is a highly robust fact, and it is a fact that reinforces the impact of the government budget and social security as "automatic stabilizers" over the course of the economic cycle. Accordingly, the government's net borrowing has a countercyclical character.

This countercyclical character of net borrowing is somewhat weakened by TRILLS. The magnitude of this effect is modest, however. If we assume that half of explicit public debt takes the form of TRILLs, then at an explicit debt ratio of 200% in relation to net national product or to private and public consumption, the value of the stock of TRILLs is precisely equivalent to the annual net national product (or to annual consumption). If we assume a figure of 5% for δ, a (nominal) growth rate g of 3%, a nominal risk-free interest rate r that is also 3%, and a risk premium of 1%, then the price of a TRILL is normally fifty times greater than the annual payout w. Hence, the TRILL payments amount to 2% or one-fiftieth of net national product (or of private and public consumption).

Now, if the nominal growth of national product is only 1%, rather than the expected 3%, then the saving on TRILL dividend payments for this year is 2% of 2% of net national product (or of consumption expenditure): i.e., 0.04%. This is not a major contribution to the stabilization of public finances. This calculation can also be made plausible by way of the following reflection. At a risk-free steady state interest rate equal to the growth rate and a "risk premium" of 1% per year, citizens' holdings of public debt in TRILL-form worth one annual national product costs the government payment of a 2% "share" in this national product.

Given the stabilizing effect of TRILLS that we want to present now, we regard it as highly probable that the risk premium on TRILLs, α, will not be greater than 1% per year.

The real contribution of TRILLs to stabilize the economy does not come from the countercyclical payment of TRILL dividends, but rather from the change that they bring about in citizens' long-term arrangements. The problem of a stable currency plays an important role here. We will come back to this question in Chap. 9 on stable money. There, the focus is on the indispensable contribution that stable money makes to prevent voters from destabilizing the government with their demands. Here, we want to discuss how TRILLs can contribute to increase investment security under conditions of price stability.

Most people think in the long-term: among other reasons, because they can expect to live for a long time still and because they have, or can expect to have, children whose well-being is important to them. On the other hand, they also know that politics is more short-term-oriented due to elections. And it is inevitable that the overall economic situation at any given moment will have a strong influence on people's mood: hence, the danger of an inflationary economic policy. Moreover, institutional safeguards can never fully eliminate this danger.

Now, if it follows from our analysis in this book that a high level of public debt both is and will continue to be a requirement for prosperity, then we have to ask how we can deal with people's fear that the government will unload its "debt burden" via inflation.

One answer that has already been put into practice consists of inflation-linked bonds. If there is a developed market for these bonds, their nominal yield in comparison with conventional government bonds proves to be a good indicator of average expected inflation. But once their dissemination has reached a certain level, there is a catch: Such bonds represent a particularly heavy burden for public finances in critical situations in which, at least temporarily, price increases could represent a correct macropolicy response. One example is when there is a sharp rise in the prices of raw materials or even a cutoff of deliveries of raw materials that have to be imported. In this case, it can make sense for monetary and fiscal policy to allow the consequent increase in the domestic price level to take place, so as to ward off a massive drop in investment and a resulting collapse of economic activity. The possibly critical situation of public finances under these circumstances can be exacerbated by the claims of holders of inflation-linked bonds.

By contrast, as shown above, TRILLs are hardly a fiscal burden in the short term when there is a rise in prices. On the other hand, TRILLs are also themselves precisely a form of protection against inflation. A sustained increase in the nominal growth rate by 1% point per year may well drive the inflation rate up by around 1% point as well. At the same time, however, this increase means that the growth rate of the annual TRILL dividends also rises by 1% point, such that holders of TRILLS are not hurt by the higher rate of inflation.

In this respect, TRILLs are comparable to the "dynamic retirement benefits" that were introduced in Germany in 1958. If dynamic retirement benefits are applied in undistorted fashion, current and future recipients of benefits under the public retirement plan are protected against inflation so long as the average wage keeps pace with it.

There is also a second problem with inflation-linked bonds that does not arise with TRILLs. What is known to statisticians as the "index number problem" makes clear that the depreciation of the currency cannot be unambiguously measured in the long run—just as, in the same way, real growth cannot be unambiguously measured in the long run. But this measurement problem does not exist for the TRILLs, since only nominal quantities are involved.

Of course, even with the availability of TRILLs as investment, the individual saver cannot be given a guarantee that his or her invested wealth will yield a real return, as expressed in the prices relevant to this saver, at the current real interest rate. For the latter is calculated on the basis of the average rate of inflation for the country as a whole. But what interests the individual saver are the prices of the goods that he or she wants to consume, and the inflation rate for these goods differs from town to town and from region to region. Nonetheless, the TRILL holder can count on there being a tight correlation between the national rate of inflation and the respective regional rates.

The phenomenon of "loss aversion" is well known in behavioral economics. When we think about decisions relating to the distant future, the pressure "not to make a mistake" (and this is what "loss aversion" is) typically involves comparing oneself to other people. But for this purpose, investing in TRILLs is a good move— at least once TRILLs have become well-established. For the success or failure of such an investment never leaves the investor by him- or herself. All one's friends and neighbors have had the same success or failure. In this respect, TRILLs are the counterpart to ETFs on the stock market—except that the risk connected to TRILLs is far smaller.

Introducing TRILLs as an investment instrument would make an important contribution to reducing citizens' mistrust of the government when it comes to public debt. And reducing this mistrust requires a government that, due to the high level of citizens' desired wealth, cannot avoid high public debt, if it wants to ensure prosperity and full employment. TRILLs are a form of "outwitting" the structural short-term orientation of government policy: the discounting discrepancy we described above. In this respect as well, they appear to us to be a better instrument than inflation-linked bonds.

It would seem advisable for the fiscal authorities to choose a mix of traditional government bonds (plus bank loans), inflation-linked bonds and TRILLs in proportions that minimize the overall risk premium that the government has to pay. This roughly amounts to the three forms of investment generating the same expected return. Thus, it is up to investors, viz. to the capital market, to decide what the correct proportions will be.

But even with the TRILLs as investment instrument, the reflections on the relative size of the public sector that we undertook, using the Laffer curve, in Sect. 6.1.8 remain relevant.

6.1.11 TRILLs When the Interest Rate Is a Biased Price Signal

At the end of Chap. 2 on the natural rate of interest, we discussed the situation when the interest rate is a biased price signal. The focus was on the case in which the intertemporal rate of return on a current marginal foregoing of consumption in the form of additional future consumption is greater than the interest rate r. So long as the interest rate on the household side does not exhibit any bias ($\beta_2 = 0$), the steady-state optimal interest rate is less than the growth rate. Here, we go through a numerical example in which we suppose that the degree of bias on the production side is 2% per year: thus, $\beta_1 = 0.02$. But, unlike in Chap. 2, we assume, antici-pating the precautionary principle we discuss in Chap. 13, that this results in a steady-state optimal interest rate of 1% point below the growth rate. Like in the earlier numerical example, we can, furthermore, assume a growth rate of 3% per year and a risk premium for public debt, α, of 1% per year. In this case, the capital market return on public debt in the steady-state optimum is equivalent to the growth rate, viz. 3% per year: viz. $r = 2\%$ per year and $\alpha = 1\%$ per year.

This means that if the public debt ratio is constant over time, an increase in public debt of 3% per year is exactly enough to cover the interest payments. Hence, there is no need for any budgetary primary surplus.

This numerical example has been chosen in such a way that two complicating effects exactly offset each another: on the one hand, the price signal bias of the interest rate and, on the other, the risk premium. We do this with a clear conscience, because the experience of recent years shows that absolutely secure ten-year bonds that are not, however, inflation-linked—like, for instance, the corresponding German government bonds—have a nominal yield that is predominantly below 1% per year despite the inflation risk associated with them. In light of a eurozone inflation rate of 1% per year, this corresponds to a real yield of zero at most. Even if we believe that the officially measured rate of inflation in the eurozone overestimates the "actual" rate of inflation—the problem of the Laspeyre-Index, which, especially in light of the raging success of the products of the digital economy, fails to take adequate account of the hedonic price index, or the "Aghion effect" (Aghion et al. 2019)—the real yield of 10-year bonds is still very low. There is little room here for a risk premium.

In Germany, the popular argument against this finding is that interest rates are so low, because the European Central Bank is artificially suppressing them with its monetary policy. It has been nearly a decade now that this counterargument could be heard. But it is no longer plausible. Have we not known since Wicksell that interest rates that are kept artificially low give rise to an inflationary spiral? But no such inflationary spiral has occurred. The more plausible hypothesis is that the ECB policy is merely following the very low full employment equilibrium interest rates in the eurozone. We are thus on the safe side, if we set the risk premium for TRILLs and also for conventional government bonds at 1% per year in our calculations.

6.1.12   Central Bank Money

Central bank money is put on the liabilities side of the central bank balance sheet. Since the central bank is publicly owned, one can also, purely formally, record it on the liabilities side of a consolidated government balance sheet. But this is not enough to decide whether it is public debt. There is also no consensus on the matter in monetary theory, as far as we know. These differences of opinion have taken on a certain virulence with regard to the eurozone, since the national central banks have significant TARGET balances and they do not have to be periodically settled. We are not going to get involved in this controversy, but we can refer here to Hellwig (2019). In his article, Martin Hellwig adopts the position that in the current monetary conditions that prevail since the end of the Bretton Woods system, central bank money does not represent public debt, because it is not a liability according to the fair value principle. On the other hand, he finds that recording it as a liability is justified on political grounds, in order to prevent the emergence of hard-to-control "desires" to use the central bank's very considerable equity.

For our purposes, it is helpful to consider central bank money as public debt strictly for presentational reasons. The formal apparatus that we have developed for a steady-state analysis can thus remain as presented in Chap. 2 on capital theory, while also including central bank money. It is not necessary to introduce central bank money separately. As we showed in Chap. 2, the formal presentation set out there assumes, in any case, that economic actors optimize their portfolio with respect to the various investments. To the extent that their investments are negotiable, the subjective marginal rate of substitution between two types of investment is, then, equal to one. From this point of view, the liquidity preference of economic actors is, then, just one of many investment options. The same considerations also apply to banks and to their balances with the central bank: i.e., to central bank money. As long as we stick to a steady-state analysis, we also do not need, in our formal presentation, to distinguish between the different maturities of government bonds.

In a model of macroeconomic dynamics, money and central bank money have, of course, to appear as separate variables. But in this book, we are not developing any new model of macroeconomic dynamics. In our view, however, our ideas about the level and form of public debt are important for an adequate dynamic modeling of how the economy as a whole operates.

6.2   Determining the Value of Explicit and Implicit Public Debt in the OECD Plus China Region

6.2.1   Explicit Public Debt

When the state goes into debt to its citizens, the latter acquire wealth to the same extent. In order to be able to determine empirically the magnitude of this wealth, or, in other words, of the private sector's claims on the state, we will first discuss *explicit* public debt in the present section. Apart from this explicit debt, citizens also have claims on the state in their capacity as beneficiaries of the various branches of the social security system, which we here understand broadly to include not only the public retirement scheme, but also public health and nursing care insurance.[1] In the following section, we will then examine this form of *implicit* public debt. It is, on the one hand, far more difficult to determine, but, on the other, as we will show, also far greater than explicit public debt. Our ambitious objective in this empirical part of this chapter is to estimate the magnitude of both explicit and implicit public debt for the 35 countries of what we have described as the OECD plus China region. For the reasons already explained, we then express both the individual components and the sum of explicit and implicit public debt in units of total annual consumption (the sum of private and public consumption in the current year, which in our case is the reference year 2015).

There are certain relationships between explicit and implicit public debt that have to be kept in mind, in order to proceed correctly when empirically determining their magnitudes. Since the introduction of the 2008 System of National Accounts (SNA), some countries show their pension obligations vis-à-vis government employees in the core tables of their national accounts. To this end, the discounted present value of current and future pension payments (accrued-to-date entitlements) to government employees is calculated according to internationally agreed actuarial methods (IMF 2016). Some countries count the underfunded part of their contributions-based pension scheme for government employees as part of explicit public debt, but others do not.[2]

In this chapter, we assign the pension or retirement benefit entitlements of both public sector and private sector employees to implicit public debt. Hence, we will deal with them in detail further on. In order to avoid double counting when calculating total public debt, however, the data of the countries that count the present value of civil servant pension entitlements as part of their explicit public debt has to be adjusted accordingly (IMF 2018b, p. 10, Footnote 23).

For the purposes of our research, a further adjustment has to be made to the usual public debt figures. In this chapter, we want to determine the private sector's financial claims on the state. We need, therefore, to use *net* public debt rather than *gross* public debt. To this end, we take the difference between the state's liabilities vis-à-vis the private sector and publicly owned private sector financial assets. The IMF defines net public debt as "Gross debt minus financial assets corresponding to debt instruments" (IMF 2018b, p. 43). Table 6.1 shows these interrelationships.

The financial assets that have to be taken into account to get from gross to net public debt include monetary gold and special drawing rights, currency and deposits, debt securities, insurance, pension and standardized guarantee schemes, and other

---

[1]When, further on, we discuss the specific American program known as social security, we will mark the difference from this broader concept by always using capitals.

[2]Even in the former countries, however, the claims of private sector employees on the public retirement system are neither shown in the core national accounts nor is their present value counted as part of explicit public debt (IMF 2018b, p. 3). In the next section, we will try to estimate the implicit public debt to which they give rise.

Table 6.1 Determining explicit net public debt

A	B	$C = A - B$
Gross debt (liabilities in the form of debt instruments)	Financial assets corresponding to debt instruments	Net debt
SDRs	Monetary gold and SDRs	
Currency and deposits	Currency and deposits	
Debt securities	Debt securities	
Loans	Loans	
Insurance, pension, and standardized guarantee schemes	Insurance, pension, and standardized guarantee schemes	
Other accounts payable	Other accounts receivable	
Total gross debt	Total financial assets corresponding to gross debt	Total net debt

Source IMF (2013, p. 5)

accounts receivable. Table 6.2 contains the net public debt ratios for 35 countries in the OECD plus China region; for informational purposes, data on gross public debt ratios is also provided. All the data on explicit and implicit public debt in this chapter refers to 2015. As the table shows, public debt decreases considerably, when the financial assets of the public sector are taken into account. On average, the difference between the gross public debt ratio and the net public ratio amounts to no less than 20% points for the OECD countries (not including Estonia, Chile, Luxembourg and Norway). The difference between the gross and net public debt ratio is particularly great for Japan. In 2015, Japanese public debt amounted to 231% of gross domestic product (GDP). The net public debt ratio is less, however, since a significant part of the debt securities issued by the government to finance public expenditure during the last decade are held by the Japanese central bank, which is likewise part of the public sector. Another part of the difference between gross and net debt is a result of the fact that the Japanese government has made considerable financial investments via public pension funds. As consequence, far less that 231% of gross domestic product in 2015 can be attributed to Japanese public debt: namely, only 147%. We may only use this figure in calculating the claims of private persons on the state in Japan. Much the same applies for the USA. Like in Japan, the unconventional monetary and fiscal measures that were used to combat the effects of the great recession in the USA also led to massive purchases of government securities by the Federal Reserve. Due to the fact that the Federal Reserve and certain other public institutions have extensive holdings in government bonds, and because of the public pension fund for government employees, explicit net public debt in 2015 only came to about 80% of GDP. This is considerably less than the explicit gross public debt, which amounted to nearly 105% of GDP in the USA in 2015. Here too, only the explicit net public debt can be assigned to the private sector as assets.

In some countries, the financial assets even exceed gross debt, such that net wealth is positive. The remainder is particularly great in the case of Norway, which has invested a large part of its oil revenue in a sovereign wealth fund. As shown in Table 6.2 (column B), the net value of Norway's public sector financial assets

Table 6.2 Explicit net public debt in the OECD plus China region, 2015

	A	B	C	D = B · C	E	F = D/H	G = E/H	H	I = F/G
	Gross public debt	Net public debt	Gross domestic product	Net public debt	Total consumption	Net public debt	Total consumption	Conversion factor	Net public debt
	In % of GDP	In % of GDP	Billions LCU	Billions LCU	Billions LCU	Billions Int'l $	Billions Int'l $	LCU in Int'l $	In years of consumption
Australia	37.8	17.9	1,621.4	290.0	1,222.2	196.7	829.1	1.5	0.24
Austria	84.3	58.2	344.3	200.5	249.4	251.1	312.3	0.8	0.80
Belgium	106.1	92.9	411.0	381.8	308.1	477.4	385.2	0.8	1.24
Canada	90.5	27.7	1,985.8	550.0	1,562.6	440.7	1,252.1	1.2	0.35
Chile	17.3	-3.4	159,605.9	-5,489.0	122,001.4	-14.0	311.7	391.4	-0.04
Czech Republic	40.0	28.1	4,595.8	1,289.4	3,035.3	99.7	234.7	12.9	0.42
Denmark	39.9	16.5	2,036.4	336.7	1,478.0	46.1	202.4	7.3	0.23
Estonia	10.0	-2.2	20.7	-0.5	14.7	-0.9	27.4	0.5	-0.03
Finland	63.5	20.8	210.0	43.8	167.1	48.2	184.1	0.9	0.26
France	95.6	86.4	2,198.4	1,898.6	1,711.6	2,348.4	2,117.0	0.8	1.11
Germany	70.9	51.1	3,048.9	1,557.5	2,218.3	2,002.1	2,851.6	0.8	0.70
Greece[a]	178.8	87.6	177.3	155.3	159.1	255.1	261.2	0.6	0.98
Hungary	76.7	72.8	34,378.6	25,043.0	23,835.3	189.0	179.9	132.5	1.05
Iceland	66.0	47.8	2,288.0	1,093.5	1,681.8	7.7	11.8	141.9	0.65
Ireland	76.9	65.9	262.5	172.9	119.2	44.1	30.4	3.9	1.45
Israel	64.0	60.2	1,167.9	703.1	898.7	868.5	1,110.2	0.8	0.78

(continued)

Table 6.2 (continued)

	A	B	C	D = B · C	E	F = D / H	G = E / H	H	I = F / G
	Gross public debt	Net public debt	Gross domestic product	Net public debt	Total consumption	Net public debt	Total consumption	Conversion factor	Net public debt
	In % of GDP	In % of GDP	Billions LCU	Billions LCU	Billions LCU	Billions Int'l $	Billions Int'l $	LCU in Int'l $	In years of consumption
Italy	131.5	119.5	1,652.1	1,974.2	1,318.3	2,673.3	1,785.2	0.7	1.50
Japan	231.3	147.6	531,985.8	785,280.0	406,507.6	7,590.9	3,929.5	103.4	1.93
Korea	39.5	6.4	1,564,123.9	99,364.8	1,006,005.6	115.9	1,173.4	857.4	0.10
Luxembourg	22.0	-12.1	51.6	-6.2	24.6	-7.1	27.9	0.9	-0.25
Mexico	52.8	46.5	18,551.5	8,633.2	14,450.4	1,036.9	1,735.6	8.3	0.60
Netherlands	64.0	52.1	690.0	359.7	483.2	444.2	596.7	0.8	0.74
New Zealand	34.3	9.8	254.7	25.0	193.2	17.0	131.0	1.5	0.13
Norway	33.0	-86.9	3,118.1	-2,709.6	2,083.0	-272.9	209.8	9.9	-1.30
Poland	51.1	46.4	1,798.2	834.3	1,376.2	472.8	779.9	1.8	0.61
Portugal	128.8	113.9	179.8	204.7	150.3	350.1	257.0	0.6	1.36
Slovak Republic	52.3	25.7	79.1	20.3	58.5	41.3	119.1	0.5	0.35
Slovenia	82.6	50.4	38.8	19.6	28.0	32.9	47.0	0.6	0.70
Spain	99.4	85.4	1,081.2	923.6	834.9	1,389.7	1,256.4	0.7	1.11
Sweden	44.2	11.3	4,201.5	472.8	2,975.7	53.4	336.2	8.9	0.16
Switzerland	43.0	23.3	654.3	152.2	426.8	123.2	345.4	1.2	0.36
Turkey	27.6	23.0	2,338.6	537.0	1,736.4	462.0	1,494.1	1.2	0.31

(continued)

Table 6.2 (continued)

	A	B	C	D = B · C	E	F = D / H	G = E / H	H	I = F / G
	Gross public debt	Net public debt	Gross domestic product	Net public debt	Total consumption	Net public debt	Total consumption	Conversion factor	Net public debt
	In % of GDP	In % of GDP	Billions LCU	Billions LCU	Billions LCU	Billions Int'l $	Billions Int'l $	LCU in Int'l $	In years of consumption
UK	87.9	79.3	1,895.8	1,503.1	1,596.5	2,171.0	2,305.9	0.7	0.94
USA	104.8	80.1	18,219.3	14,601.8	14,907.2	14,601.8	14,907.2	1.0	0.98
China[b]	41.1	2.7	68,905.2	1,883.3	36,226.7	543.1	10,447.8	3.5	0.05
Total OECD						38,556.5	41,738.2		0.92
Total OECD plus China						39,099.6	52,186.0		0.75

Sources

Column A: IMF (2018b). Tables A7 and A15: General Government Gross Debt, 2009–23; IMF (2018c)

Column B: IMF (2018b). Tables A8 and A16: General Government Net Debt, 2009–23; IMF (2018c)

Column C: World Bank (2019). World Development Indicators, GDP (current LCU)

Column E: World Bank (2019). World Development Indicators, Final consumption expenditure (current LCU)

Authors' own calculations

Notes

IMF (2018b), p. 64, Footnote 1: "For cross-economy comparability, gross debt levels reported by national statistical agencies for economies that have adopted the 2008 System of National Accounts (Australia, Canada, Hong Kong SAR, USA) are adjusted to exclude unfunded pension liabilities of government employees' defined benefit pension plans."

[a]Net public debt: estimated value. A proportional reduction in gross debt in line with the average for OECD countries is assumed.

[b]Net public debt: IMF (2018b), p. 23, Box 1.3 "China—Revisiting the General Government's Balance Sheet"

LCU: Local currency unit

amounts to almost 87% of GDP. But the net wealth of the public sector is also positive in Chile, Estonia and Luxembourg. These countries are, however, exceptions in the OECD. As a rule, the OECD countries have positive net public debt. Among the OECD countries with positive net public debt, this debt was, on average, around 55% of GDP in 2015. With a net debt ratio of 51% of GDP, Germany was somewhat below the average for the OECD countries. China's net debt ratio is extremely small: In 2015, it came to only 2.7% of GDP. According to the IMF, China's gross public debt is 41%.[3]

The IMF shows net public debt for the OECD countries and for China as a percentage of GDP (cf. Table 6.2, column B). Multiplying this figure by the 2015 value of GDP for each country (column C), we obtain, in column D, the explicit net public debt in the respective local currency. Our objective is to determine explicit public debt for the whole OECD plus China region. To this end, the figures in the respective local currency are converted into international dollars (purchasing power parities). Column F shows explicit net public debt, which we will simply call explicit public debt from now on, in international dollars. Since we ultimately want to express the wealth of private households in units of total annual consumption, we also convert the country-specific consumption figures in the respective local currencies (column E) into international dollars. At the bottom of column F, we find, on the one hand, total explicit public debt for all the OECD countries, not including China: In 2015, this total came to 38.6 trillion international dollars. On the other hand, total explicit public debt for the OECD countries plus China is also shown. In 2015, the latter came to 39.1 trillion international dollars. In 2015, total consumption amounted to 41.7 trillion international dollars in all the OECD countries combined. If we add China, we arrive at a figure of 52.2 trillion international dollars. Finally, we relate the explicit public debt of the OECD countries or, respectively, of the OECD plus China region to annual consumption. The end result is that explicit net public debt in the OECD countries amounted to *92% of their annual consumption* in 2015. China's exceptionally low public debt, as compared to the average for the OECD countries, significantly reduces the overall figure due to the great weight that China has in the OECD plus China group. *Thus, explicit* net *public debt in the OECD plus China region came to around three-quarters of annual consumption in 2015.*

---

[3]On China, the IMF (2018b, p. 23) writes tersely: "Compiling China's general government balance sheet is a challenge." In its *Global Debt Database*, the IMF does not itself provide a figure for China's net public debt. However, in the focus box "China—Revisiting the General Government's Balance Sheet" (ibid.), the IMF undertakes some estimates of the liabilities and financial assets of the Chinese state. We have derived our figure of 2.7% for Chinese net public ratio from these estimates.

6.2.2 Implicit Public Debt

6.2.2.1 Public Retirement Schemes

Having determined the level of the *explicit* public debt of the OECD plus China region in years of total annual consumption in the previous section, we will now estimate the level of *implicit* public debt. What appears as debt from the point of view of the public sector is wealth for the private sector. In what follows, we will examine the claims of households on the state that have come into being as a result of contributions paid into pay-as-you-go social security systems. The present value of the future cash flows to which households are entitled, given the rules applicable at a given date and the contributions that have been paid until then, represents an extremely important component of their wealth. For the state, the present value of these future cash flows from the different branches of the social security system represents an implicit liability. We regard a pay-as-you-go social security scheme—the mechanism of which we have examined in detail in Sects. 6.1.3 and 6.1.4—as a kind of funded scheme without a reserve fund. The missing reserve fund for the different branches of social security represents the implicit public debt.

Among these different forms, the public retirement scheme makes by far the largest contribution to this implicit public debt. We need to add the implicit public debt represented by civil service pensions, which are directly funded from tax revenue.[4] The other branches of social security also add to implicit public debt. This is, above all, the case for public health insurance and nursing care insurance, with which we will deal in a later section.

The objective of the present section is to estimate the public debt that derives from the public retirement scheme. More specifically, what we want to do is to determine the present value of the future claims of beneficiaries of the public retirement scheme and the future pension claims of civil servants and to express this value in years of total consumption. These claims are also known as accrued-to-date pension entitlements in the international statistics, with "pensions" here covering both of the aforementioned categories. The basic data on which our calculations are based comes from a variety of sources. In what follows, we describe the data sources and the procedure used in our calculations for the European countries, for the USA and for the other countries of the OECD plus China region.

Europe

One of the innovations connected to the introduction of the 2008 System of National Accounts (2008 SNA) and the 2010 European System of Accounts (ESA 2010) consists of the fact that participating countries have set themselves the objective of regularly reporting retirement benefit and pension entitlements—here

---

[4]In Germany, the federal government and some of the individual states or *Bundesländer* have begun to build up reserves for the future financing of civil service pensions. These reserves have to be subtracted from implicit public debt. Up to now, however, they are nowhere near adequate to cover the future pension claims of retired civil servants. In the USA, only about half of the pension obligations owed to public sector employees are currently covered. The section below on the USA provides more details on this.

designated uniformly as "pension entitlements"—arising from unfunded systems (European Commission et al. 2009; Eurostat 2013[5]). Every three years, European Union member states are required to calculate "accrued-to-date pension entitlements in social insurance" and to report them to Eurostat, the statistical office of the European Union. Since 2018, data is available on the level of retirement benefit and pension entitlements for the year 2015 for 26 European Union countries, as well the EFTA countries Switzerland, Norway and Iceland.[6] 22 of these 29 countries belong to the OECD plus China region that we are investigating.

Retirement entitlements are here understood as the present value of future retirement benefit and pension payments (projected benefit obligation) based on already acquired claims as of the balance sheet date. The method thus follows the accrued-to-date-liabilities (ADL) principle: The only claims that are taken into account are those that have been acquired in the past by current retirees or workers paying into the scheme. Claims acquired after the balance sheet date are left out. We thus establish the present value of the entitlements that exist if the retirement scheme were to be wound up on the balance sheet date (Holzmann et al. 2004; Freudenberg 2017, p. 328). Figure 6.2 shows the different approaches used in calculating the present value of benefit entitlements in a retirement scheme.

The ADL method is a method that only takes into account already acquired entitlements of current members of the retirement scheme. Future payments into the system (both retirement scheme contributions and other contributions), i.e., payments made after the balance sheet date, are not taken into account by the ADL method (cf. Box 1 in Fig. 6.2). If, in the context of a closed system, payments that current workers will make in the future are also taken into account, then we speak of a CWL (projected current workers' and retirees' liabilities) method (cf. Box 2 in Fig. 6.2). We say the system is "closed," because both methods only calculate the present values of the entitlements of workers or retirees who are already part of the system. In calculating the projected benefit obligation, open systems also take into account the present value of future benefit payments to future members. This is known as the open-system liabilities or OSL method (cf. Box 3 in Fig. 6.2).[7] Like the statistical offices, we base our reflections and calculations in what follows on the ADL method.

What interests us here are social security retirement schemes and pension schemes providing benefits to civil servants and other government employees. According to Germany's Federal Statistical Office, the present value of households' social security retirement entitlements in Germany came to 6843.9 billion euros at the end of 2015 (Haug 2018). The Statistical Office calculated a present value at the end of 2015 of 1235.2 billion euros for civil service pensions to be paid by the

---

[5]Cf., in particular, the section titled "Supplementary Table for Accrued-to-Date Pension Entitlements in Social Insurance" in Chap. 17 (Eurostat 2013, pp. 379).

[6]Due to the fact that 2015 is the first year for which data on pension entitlements was published by Eurostat and the OECD, we have used this year as the reference year for the empirical estimates of all wealth components in this book.

[7]Holzmann (1998); Braakmann et al. (2007, pp. 1169); Freudenberg (2017, p. 329); van der Ven and Fano (2017, pp. 319).

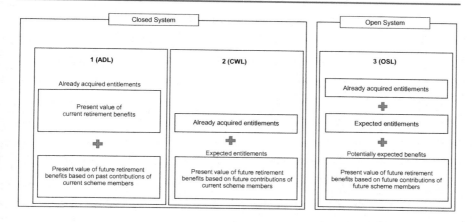

Fig. 6.2 Methods for determining projected benefit obligations. *Sources* Modified diagram following Braakmann et al. (2007, p. 1169), Freudenberg (2017), Holzmann (1998)

federal government, the states (the *Bundesländer*) and municipalities (ibid., p. 87, Table 1).[8]

When determining the present value of future cash flows, the discount rate is of decisive importance. The usual assumption is that a positive real interest rate should be used to discount to a present value. The results of the calculations of the European statistical offices provided below are derived from a base case scenario that assumes a nominal discount rate of 5%. The discount rate is the same for all Eurostat countries and is applied for "a very long period of time" (ibid., p. 89). The discount rate is set by an EU working group, which makes a series of assumptions about the future development of significant economic parameters like demographic change, productivity, wage growth and so on (ibid., p. 89).[9] Since the calculated present value is highly dependent on the discount rate applied, each of the European statistical offices responsible for determining the retirement benefit and pension entitlements for their respective countries is required by the ESA 2010 to perform so-called sensitivity analyses using other discount rates. The base case scenario, from which the abovementioned figures for Germany's retirement claims are derived, assumes a rate of inflation of 2% per year, such that the base case

[8]Haug (2018, p. 88) notes that "accrued-to-date social security retirement entitlements…are not to be interpreted as public debt." He argues, on the one hand, that future contributions are not set off against them and, on the other, that the full amount of the entitlements "is not legally guaranteed": "Thus, legislative reforms can affect the scope of social security benefits." These are legitimate points. Nonetheless, the approach that we have adopted in this book grasps such entitlements as implicit public debt for reasons that we have laid out in detail in Sects. 6.1.1–6.1.5. A further important reason is that Germany's constitutional court, the *Bundesverfassungsgericht*, has accorded such entitlements the protection given to property under Article 14 of Germany's constitution.

[9]A number of other assumptions are needed, some of which have a major impact on the amount of the present value. These include assumptions on mortality, the rate of inflation, wage growth, etc. (Braakmann et al. 2007).

scenario's real discount rate comes to 3% per year. In two alternative scenarios, present values of retirement entitlements are calculated using a discount rate 1% point over and 1% point under the discount rate in the base case scenario (i.e., at nominal rates of 4 and 6% per year, respectively). Since a rate of inflation of 2% is assumed here too, the real discount rates in the two alternative scenarios come to 2% and 4% per year, respectively.

Table 6.3 shows the level of retirement benefit and pension entitlements deriving from social security retirement schemes and pension schemes for public sector employees (mainly civil service pensions) for each of the European countries. For some of the countries, however, no data is available on the level of pension obligations owed to public sector employees. Hence, the total column on the right underestimates the amount of accrued benefit claims in the European countries. The economic importance of the entitlements, and hence the implicit public debt deriving from retirement benefit and pension claims, varies significantly among the countries we are considering here. But this can only be made clear once the amount of the entitlements has been converted into a common currency and placed in relation to each country's annual consumption. This will be done further on.

USA

To estimate the implicit public debt in the US, we need to distinguish between the pension entitlements of public sector employees and the retirement entitlements of private sector employees who receive social security benefits in old age. For both calculations, we can draw on data from official statistics.

Pension Entitlements of Public Sector Employees in the USA

Data on the present value of pension entitlements of federal, state and local government employees is available for the USA. Since the transition to the 2008 System of National Accounts in the USA, these pension entitlements of public sector employees are shown in the *National Income and Product Accounts* (NIPA) (Reinsdorf et al. 2014; Stefanescu und Vidangos 2014). They are accordingly recorded as assets in the household sector. In order to determine what part of this must be regarded as implicit public debt, a few preliminary considerations are necessary.

Two different types of schemes can be distinguished in the US pension system. On the one hand, there are defined contribution plans, in which plan members' agreed contributions are invested in one or more selected funds, whereas the resulting income and hence the amount of the future pension payments is not fixed. The capital market risk is principally borne by the plan members. Besides these defined contribution plans, there are also defined benefit plans. In the case of the latter, the amount of future payments is guaranteed by the plan or by the employer, which thus bears the capital market risk. In the USA, both private and public retirement plans are either completely or at least partially funded. If a defined benefit plan is only partially covered by financial assets (if there are, in other words,

Table 6.3 Accrued-to-date social security retirement benefit and civil service pension entitlements in Selected European Countries, 2015

Country	Social security retirement schemes	Defined benefit pension schemes for general government employees[b]	Total retirement benefit and pension claims
	Billions LCU	Billions LCU	Billions LCU
Belgium	941.46	181.93	1,123.39
Bulgaria[a]	140.55	n.a	140.55
Czechia	10,549.00	n.a	10,549.00
Denmark	84.10	567.95	652.05
Germany	6,843.92	1,235.22	8,079.14
Estonia	50.84	1.54	52.38
Ireland	231.00	114.50	345.50
Spain	2,792.23	310.09	3,102.32
France	6,948.00	1,160.00	8,108.00
Croatia[a]	807.24	n.a	807.24
Italy	5,631.63	n.a	5,631.63
Cyprus[a]	32.71	7.33	40.04
Latvia[a]	41.77	1.63	43.40
Lithuania[a]	99.59	1.62	101.21
Hungary	82,349.20	n.a	82,349.20
Malta[a]	21.93	2.91	24.84
Netherlands	1,153.29	11.01	1,164.30
Austria	1,044.41	211.12	1,255.53
Poland	4,381.93	426.09	4,808.03
Portugal	370.84	190.91	561.75
Romania[a]	1,295.48	n.a	1,295.48
Slovenia	121.71	n.a	121.71
Slovakia	223.93	24.12	248.05
Finland	631.53	n.a	631.53
Sweden	8,490.59	289.22	8,779.81
UK	4,027.15	916.80	4,943.95
Iceland	1,605.90	n.a	1,605.90
Norway	7,480.00	690.60	8,170.60
Switzerland	1,350.40	n.a	1,350.40

Source Eurostat (2020), Authors' own calculations
Notes Retirement benefit and pension claims that are not included in the core national income accounts. Closing balance sheets
[a]Not part of the OECD plus China region (see Chap. 3.11)
[b]General government employees classified in general government
LCU: Local currency unit
n.a: not available

unfunded liabilities), then the invested capital is not sufficient to cover all future benefit payment commitments.[10]

The contributions paid into pension schemes by public sector employees are also invested to a large extent on the capital market. In the case of civil servants enrolled in defined benefit schemes, any emerging gap between the capital income from invested contributions and promised pensions has to be covered by the government (Novy-Marx and Rauh 2011). For us, the amount of the unfunded liabilities vis-à-vis public sector employees represents the part of implicit public debt in the USA that derives from the civil service pension scheme. For the public sector employees themselves, on the other hand, the unfunded liabilities represent assets that they are guaranteed by the government.[11]

Since the 2007–08 financial crisis, the share of unfunded liabilities in the US retirement system has increased significantly. Around twenty years ago, state and local government pensions were still fully funded. At the time, assets even exceeded liabilities by 7.8% (Lenze 2013, p. 2). By contrast, in 2019, state and local government pension funds had assets that still covered only 54% of the overall liabilities under the defined benefit plans (cf. Fig. 6.3). The financial crisis made itself felt on the assets side especially, as Fig. 6.3 clearly shows in comparing the value of financial assets before and after 2008.

According to the calculations of the Federal Reserve, the liabilities of state and local government defined benefit pension plans, expressed as pension entitlements, amounted to 7754.4 billion dollars at the end of 2015 (Board of Governors of the Federal Reserve System 2020b). The assets came to 3679 dollars. The difference between the liabilities and the assets of defined benefit pension plans are unfunded liabilities. They represent claims on the state or "claims of pension fund on sponsor" (ibid., table L.119 and table L.120, line 17; Munnell et al. 2014). At the end of 2015, these came to 4075.3 billion dollars. To this, we need to add the claims from the corresponding pension plans for federal government employees. In 2015, the present value of unfunded pension obligations owed to federal government employees in the USA came to 1732.3 billion dollars. The total present value of public sector employee pension entitlements in the USA thus amounted to 5807.6 billion dollars in 2015.

---

[10]The situation is different for people who receive their retirement benefits from private retirement plans and/or from the social security program. Private pensions represent claims and liabilities within the private sector. They thus play no role in the context of interest to us, in which what is at issue are the claims of the private sector on the state.

[11]According to the Center for Retirement Research (CRR), a large number of American public sector pension funds are significantly underfunded. For example, Kentucky's scheme for so-called non-hazardous workers is now only 12.8% funded. This is due, among other things, to the fact that the fund has not recovered the losses suffered in the dotcom bust. The deficit of all public sector pension funds monitored by the CRR was more than 1.6 trillion US dollars in 2018 (The Economist 2019, p. 65).

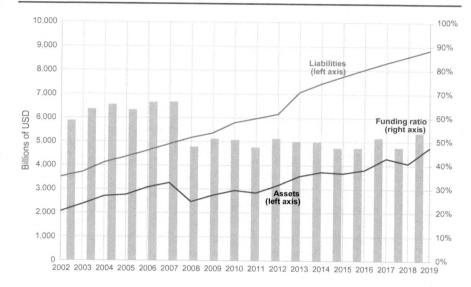

Fig. 6.3 Liabilities, Assets and Funding Ratio for Public Sector Employee Pensions in the USA, 2002–2019. *Source* Board of Governors of the Federal Reserve System (2020a). *Notes* Liabilities and assets of defined benefit pension plans are for state and local government employees only. Funding ratio: assets as percent of liabilities

The US Social Security Scheme

The US social security program is responsible for the retirement benefits of private sector employees. Like in many other OECD countries, it is largely conceived as a pay-as-you-go system.

Social security in the USA consists of the Old-Age and Survivors Insurance and the Disability Insurance programs (together OASDI[12]) (Board of Trustees OASDI 2020). In the following, we summarize the expenditure for both programs and refer to it as social security expenditure for the sake of simplicity.[13] In 2015, our reference year for calculating explicit and implicit public debt, the USA spent around 910 billion dollars on social security (Board of Trustees OASDI 2016); this is equivalent to around 5% of the US GDP in 2015.

Since part of employee contributions are paid into a corresponding Trust Fund, social security is a so-called partially funded retirement scheme. The deposits in the Trust Fund have been declining in recent years, however, such that the fund is

---

[12]"The OASDI program consists of two parts. Retired workers, their families and survivors of deceased workers receive monthly benefits under the Old-Age and Survivors Insurance (OASI) program. Disabled workers and their families receive monthly benefits under the Disability Insurance (DI) program" (Board of Trustees OASDI 2020, p. 1).

[13]Among other things, social security is responsible for the provision of "monthly benefits designed to replace, in part, the loss of income due to retirement, disability, or death. Entitlement to benefits and benefit levels are related to earnings in covered work and defined by law. Coverage is nearly universal; about 96% of U.S. jobs are covered" (OECD 2020bb, p. 10).

expected to be depleted, on the Trustees' intermediate assumptions, by the mid-2030s (Board of Trustees OASDI 2020, p. 3).

The US has recently started to provide data on social security retirement schemes to the OECD. From this data, we can obtain information on accrued-to-date entitlements. The methodology used to calculate US retirement entitlements differs in some respects from that used by Eurostat. This relates, in particular, to some key actuarial assumptions (Board of Trustees OASDI 2020; OECD 2020a, b).[14] However, we follow the OECD's approach of combining the data of the Eurostat countries and those of the US in a supplementary table on what are here called, in keeping with the ESA/Eurostat terminology, "social insurance pension schemes." We take the data for accrued-to-date social security retirement benefit entitlements from this table.

The supplementary table was introduced as part of the 2008 SNA. It is intended "to provide a comprehensive overview of liabilities of all social insurance pension schemes in an economy..." (OECD 2020a, p. 1). One of its essential purposes is to create "...a framework for compiling and presenting comparable balance sheets and transactions and other flow data of all types of pension entitlements. The table also covers stock and flow data not fully recorded in the core national accounts for specific pension schemes such as government-unfunded defined benefit schemes with government as the pension manager, and social security pension schemes" (Eurostat 2013, p. 379).

The USA calculates the value of government-unfunded defined benefit pension schemes and social security retirement (here also called "pension") schemes as follows: "The pension entitlements for the Federal OASDI fund are calculated as the sum of the value of assets in the fund and the maximum transition cost based on a 100 year projection period. The maximum transition cost is equivalent to the unfunded accrued obligation of a plan designed to be fully advanced-funded at the time of plan termination" (OECD 2020b, p. 10).

Based on this methodology, the relevant agencies in the USA calculated the value of accrued-to-date retirement benefit entitlements in social security and reported it to the OECD. The data that the USA submitted to the OECD indicates that the current value at the end of 2015 of accrued-to-date social security retirement benefit entitlements not fully recorded in the core national accounts is 34,812.5 billion US dollars. We will use this figure in our further calculations.

In our opinion, the unfunded portion of the pension liabilities of public sector employees in the USA would have to be added here. As shown above, their present value was 5835.5 billion US dollars in 2015. However, the USA did not submit data to the OECD for the category "Defined benefit schemes for general government employees—administered by general government—not included in the core SNA accounts." Therefore, we only use the official data published by the OECD in its table 2900 on "Social Insurance Pension Schemes" (OECD 2020a).

---

[14]In the USA, different discount rates are applied for different time periods (OECD 2020b, p. 10). In contrast, Eurostat uses a uniform discount rate, but also performs a so-called sensitivity analysis (cf. the above section on Europe; OECD 2019, p. 8; Mink and Rodríguez-Vives 2010, p. 90).

The value for retirement benefit entitlements of US social security schemes of 34,812.5 billion US dollars is equivalent to 234% of 2015 US total consumption. According to our approach, this amount would correspond to the implicit public debt from the public retirement scheme in the USA at a positive real interest rate of about 3%.

The Other Countries in the OECD plus China Region

In addition to the USA and the European OECD countries listed above, Israel and Mexico have also recently submitted related data on "accrued-to-date pension entitlements in social insurance" to the OECD. Other OECD countries, however, have not provided data despite a basic agreement reached within this institution. These countries include Australia, Canada, Chile, Greece, Japan, Luxembourg, New Zealand, South Korea and Turkey.[15] In addition, there is China, which is not a member of the OECD, but which is part of the OECD plus China region we are looking at. We are thus faced with the task of undertaking a rough estimate to determine the present values of social security retirement benefit entitlements for nine countries (eight OECD countries plus China).

To this end, we draw on a study of entitlements in international retirement systems that were carried out by Müller et al. (2009). It found that one of the most important determinants influencing the level of country-specific entitlements deriving from the retirement system is the country's current level of retirement benefit expenditures. According to the study, currently paid benefits are an expression of the generosity of each retirement system and the age structure of the population (Freudenberg 2017, p. 332; Kaier and Müller 2015). If retirement-related entitlements are calculated according to the accrued-to-date-liabilities principle, as is done by Eurostat and in the USA, then current retirement benefit expenditures represent a sound basis for calculation. This is because around half of all benefit claims are attributable to persons who are already retired.

The entitlements calculated by Müller et al. (2009) using the accrued-to-date-liabilities method exhibit a high correlation to benefit expenditures in the reference year. The authors determined that the present value of future benefit flows is equivalent to approximately 28-times the benefit expenditures (in both cases, as a percentage of GDP) in the reference year.[16] Thus, for example, in 2006, retirement benefit expenditures in Germany amounted to approximately 12% of GDP and entitlements came to around 340% of GDP. A country like Lithuania, on the other hand, only spent 6.5% of its GDP on retirement benefits in 2006, whereas retirement-related entitlements amounted to around 180% of Lithuania's GDP in the same year (Freudenberg 2017, p. 332).

---

[15]Greece and Luxembourg do not transmit their data to Eurostat or the OECD, as they are supposed to remain confidential. New Zealand indicated that there are no social insurance pension schemes in the country (OECD 2019, p. 9).

[16]Just like in the Eurostat base case scenario, a real discount rate of 3% is used here. Since the ADL approach is applied in the form of the *Projected Benefit Obligation* (PBO) method, in which expected future wage increases are included in the calculation of entitlements, the figures determined here are in principle compatible with the Eurostat calculations.

The correlation between retirement benefit expenditures and present value of retirement-related entitlements is given by the equation $y = 28.052x + 0.0333$ (ibid., p. 332).[17] Only Finland, Latvia and the Netherlands deviated somewhat more clearly from this relationship in the study. But the deviations in the case of these countries were distributed both upwards and downwards. Since in what follows we will apply this method of estimation to a group of countries, we assume that, on average, we arrive at a reasonably acceptable result by using it. We are aware, of course, that this is only a very rough method for estimating the present value of entitlements in countries for which we do not have any other data. It seems to us, nonetheless, to be an acceptable one for our purposes.

The retirement benefit expenditures of these countries vary considerably (OECD 2017a). As a percentage of GDP, their average for the period 2013–2015 ranged from 4% in Australia to over 10% in Japan. Whereas the unweighted average for all OECD countries came to about 9% in this period, the unweighted average for the nine countries we are considering here was only 7%. Five of the countries were under the OECD average. Greece represents an outlier at around 16%. This can be attributed to the contraction of Greek GDP in the period in question. As described above, the present value of retirement benefit entitlements in relation to GDP was determined by multiplying benefit expenditures as a percentage of GDP by a fixed factor taken from the study by Müller et al. (2009). The present values of retirement benefit entitlements for the individual countries are given in the respective local currencies (LCU) in column A of Table 6.4.

Aggregating the Retirement Benefit Results Using a Positive Discount Rate

The countries for which data on retirement-related implicit public debt could be obtained from the described official statistics include 29 European countries (of which 22 belong to the OECD plus China region that we have defined) and three non-European OECD countries (the USA, Mexico, Israel). For the remaining eight OECD countries plus China, we estimated retirement benefit entitlements using a simple method taken from the relevant literature. We are conscious of the fact that this procedure only allows for a rough estimate. We assume that the existing gaps in the data will be closed shortly, since at least the eight still missing OECD countries are likewise constructing their national accounts on the basis of the 2008 SNA and the latter stipulates that countries should regularly report figures on the stocks and flows of their retirement benefit and pension entitlements.

We now want to determine the implicit public debt arising from retirement systems for the entire OECD plus China region on the assumption of a real interest rate of three percent (USA: about 2.5%) and as measured in years of total consumption. We start from the individual country figures for implicit public debt that have been established as previously described. Table 6.4 presents the intermediate steps and the results of the calculations. Column A shows the implicit public debt

---

[17]Here, x stands for retirement benefit expenditures and y for the present value of entitlements, in each case as a percentage of GDP.

Table 6.4 Implicit retirement-related public debt in the OECD plus China region, 2015 (real discount rate of 3%)

	A	B	C = A / E	D = B / E	E	F = C / D
	Implicit public debt	Total consumption	Implicit public debt	Total consumption	Conversion factor	Implicit public debt
	Billions LCU	Billions LCU	Billions Int'l $	Billions Int'l $	LCU in Int'l $	In years of consumption
Australia[a]	1,819.9	1,222.2	1,234.6	829.1	1.5	1.49
Austria	1,255.5	249.4	1,572.2	312.3	0.8	5.03
Belgium	1,123.4	308.1	1,404.6	385.2	0.8	3.65
Canada[b]	830.0	1,562.6	665.1	1,252.1	1.2	0.53
Chile[a]	228,393.7	122,001.4	583.6	311.7	391.4	1.87
Czech Republic	10,549.0	3,035.3	815.6	234.7	12.9	3.48
Denmark	652.0	1,478.0	89.3	202.4	7.3	0.44
Estonia	52.4	14.7	97.5	27.4	0.5	3.56
Finland	631.5	167.1	695.9	184.1	0.9	3.78
France	8,108.0	1,711.6	10,028.7	2,117.0	0.8	4.74
Germany	8,079.1	2,218.3	10,385.7	2,851.6	0.8	3.64
Greece[a]	805.3	159.1	1,322.5	261.2	0.6	5.06
Hungary	82,349.2	23,835.3	621.4	179.9	132.5	3.45
Iceland	1,605.9	1,681.8	11.3	11.8	141.9	0.95
Ireland	345.5	119.2	88.0	30.4	3.9	2.90
Israel	991.1	898.7	1,224.4	1,110.2	0.8	1.10
Italy	5,631.6	1,318.3	7,625.8	1,785.2	0.7	4.27
Japan[a]	1,522,350.2	406,507.6	14,715.8	3,929.5	103.4	3.74

(continued)

Table 6.4 (continued)

	A	B	C = A / E	D = B / E	E	F = C / D
	Implicit public debt	Total consumption	Implicit public debt	Total consumption	Conversion factor	Implicit public debt
	Billions LCU	Billions LCU	Billions Int'l $	Billions Int'l $	LCU in Int'l $	In years of consumption
Korea[a]	1,141,317.7	1,006,005.6	1,331.2	1,173.4	857.4	1.13
Luxembourg[a]	135.7	24.6	154.0	27.9	0.9	5.53
Mexico	1,621.2	14,450.4	194.7	1,735.6	8.3	0.11
Netherlands	1,164.3	483.2	1,437.8	596.7	0.8	2.41
New Zealand[c]	–	–	–	–	–	–
Norway	8,170.6	2,083.0	822.8	209.8	9.9	3.92
Poland	4,808.0	1,376.2	2,724.6	779.9	1.8	3.49
Portugal	561.8	150.3	960.6	257.0	0.6	3.74
Slovak Republic	248.1	58.5	504.8	119.1	0.5	4.24
Slovenia	121.7	28.0	204.5	47.0	0.6	4.35
Spain	3,102.3	834.9	4,668.2	1,256.4	0.7	3.72
Sweden	8,779.8	2,975.7	991.8	336.2	8.9	2.95
Switzerland	1,350.4	426.8	1,093.0	345.4	1.2	3.16
Turkey[a]	4,724.2	1,736.4	4,065.1	1,494.1	1.2	2.72
UK	4,944.0	1,596.5	7,140.7	2,305.9	0.7	3.10
USA	34,812.5	14,907.2	34,812.5	14,907.2	1.0	2.34

(continued)

Table 6.4 (continued)

	A	B	C = A / E	D = B / E	E	F = C / D
	Implicit public debt	Total consumption	Implicit public debt	Total consumption	Conversion factor	Implicit public debt
	Billions LCU	Billions LCU	Billions Int'l $	Billions Int'l $	LCU in Int'l $	In years of consumption
China[a]	79,273.0	36,226.7	22,862.4	10,447.8	3.5	2.19
Total OECD			114,288.5	41,607.3		2.75
Total OECD plus China			137,150.9	52,055.1		2.63

Sources

Column A: Eurostat (2020), OECD (2017a), van de Ven and Fano (2017)

Column B: World Bank (2019). World Development Indicators, Final consumption expenditure (current LCU)

Column E: World Bank (2019). World Development Indicators, PPP conversion factor (GDP) (LCU per international $)

Authors' own calculations

Notes

Closing balance sheets

[a]Estimated value based on data from OECD (2017a) and method by Müller et al. (2009)

[b]2012. "Net present value for Canada Pension Plan. Unfunded liabilities, closed group approach. The projected cash flows over an extended time period of 150 years are used." Billig (2016, p. 6); van de Ven and Fano (2017, p. 320)

[c]"New Zealand explained that the table is not relevant for them, as there are no social insurance pension schemes in New Zealand" (OECD 2019, p. 9)

LCU: Local currency unit

and column B the total consumption of each of the countries in 2015 in the respective local currency.

For the purpose of determining an aggregate value for the region as whole, the individual country figures for implicit public debt (column C) and total consumption (column D) are converted into international dollars (World Bank purchasing power parities). Column F shows implicit public debt in years of total consumption for each country. Luxembourg and Austria have the highest figures at 5.5 times and five times their total annual consumption, respectively. The lowest figures are found for Mexico (0.1 times) and Denmark (0.4 times). Germany's implicit public debt from the retirement system is equivalent to 3.6 times total annual consumption. The figures for the USA and China are equivalent to 2.3 times and 2.2 times their total annual consumption respectively. If we place aggregate implicit public debt in international dollars in relation to aggregate total consumption in international dollars, we obtain the result that implicit public debt from retirement systems in the OECD countries at a positive discount rate is equivalent to *2.75 times total annual consumption*. Implicit public debt from retirement systems in the OECD plus China region is equivalent to *2.63 times total annual consumption*.

Implicit Retirement-Related Public Debt at a Real Discount Rate of Zero

In Sect. 6.1.6, we showed in detail why we will be calculating private assets in the form of net public debt at a real interest rate of zero. We will now undertake an estimation of retirement-related implicit public debt, in which we do not—like in the official estimates—assume a nominal interest rate of 5% or a real rate of 3% for the European countries and a nominal interest rate of 5% or a real rate of 2.5% for the USA. Since the zero percent interest rate scenario is relevant for our purposes, in a next step, we use an extrapolation method to calculate the present value of retirement-related liabilities on the basis of a real rate of zero. We first undertake this calculation only for the Eurostat countries, since more data is available to us for these countries. Using a simple procedure, we will then transfer the results obtained to the other countries.

Extrapolation Procedure
On the basis of the deliveries of the national statistical offices, Eurostat (the statistical office of the European Union) has compiled data on public retirement benefit claims that will come due in the future for most of the European countries. We symbolize the real temporal progression of these claims in a given country as $F(t)$. The present value of these claims G at a real discount rate r is given, then, by

$$G(r) = \int_0^\infty e^{-rt} F(t) dt$$

If we differentiate with respect to r, we obtain

$$\frac{dG}{dr} = -\int_0^\infty te^{-rt}F(t)dt$$

The percentage rate of change of G due to a marginal increase in the interest rate is thus

$$\frac{dG/dr}{G} = \frac{-\int_0^\infty te^{-rt}F(t)dt}{\int_0^\infty e^{-rt}F(t)dt} = -S(r)$$

whereby $S(r)$ is the temporal "center of gravity" of the future payments.

The national statistical offices are required to perform so-called sensitivity analyses (Haug 2018, p. 86). In these analyses, they calculate present values of entitlements for a higher and a lower annual interest rate than in the base case scenario (5% nominal rate = 3% real rate).

Eurostat shows the level of $G(r)$ for $r = 2, 3$ and 4%. For Germany, for example, the results are 8,281,610 million euros at $r = 2\%$, 6,843,920 million euros at 3% and 5,760,220 million euros at $r = 4\%$. Based on these figures, we can estimate that the temporal center of gravity at $r = 2\%$ is around 21 years and at $r = 3\%$ around 18.8 years.

We can now differentiate the temporal center of gravity $S(r)$ with respect to r. In so doing, we obtain:

$$\frac{dS}{dr} = \frac{\left[\int_0^\infty e^{-rt}F(t)dt\right]\int_0^\infty -t^2e^{-rt}F(t)dt + \left[\int_0^\infty te^{-rt}F(t)dt\right]^2}{\left[\int_0^\infty e^{-rt}F(t)dt\right]^2}$$
$$= -\text{Variance}\{e^{-rt}F(t)\} < 0$$

We thus find that $S(r)$ increases when r falls. The numbers of the statistical offices implicitly provide an approximation of ds/dr, inasmuch as G is reported for three different values of r. We thus obtain $S(2\%) \approx (G(2\%) - G(3\%))/G(3\%)$ and $S(3\%) \approx (G(3\%) - G(4\%))/G(4\%)$. By subtraction we arrive at an estimate for ds/dr.

$$dS/dr \approx 100(S(3\%) - S(2\%))$$

We now use this estimate of the first derivative dS/dr for a linear extrapolation.

$$S(1\%) \approx S(2\%) - 1/100 \, dS/dr \approx S(2\%) + ((S2\% - S(3\%)))$$
$$= 2S(2\%) - S(3\%)$$

and
$$S(0\%) \approx S(1\%) - 1/100 \, dS/dr \approx S(1\%) + (S1\% - S(2\%)$$
$$= 2S(1\%) - S(2\%)$$

We then extrapolate the values for G from these estimates for S using the equation
$$dG/dr = -GS(r)$$

If we only had the value of G for two interest rates r, then we would have been able to perform a linear extrapolation of G. This would, however, have been less precise than proceeding by way of the linear extrapolation of S, for which the value of G for three values of r is required. In our case, we are, in a sense, using the first and the second derivate of G with respect to r.

For the other countries, for which we do not have data on present values of retirement benefit entitlements, we estimate the values by taking the change in the average value of the implicit public debt, as expressed in years of total consumption, that results from using the zero interest rate scenario as opposed to the 3% scenario for the 20 Eurostat countries that provide such data and then applying it also to them.[18] In the extrapolation for the zero interest rate scenario, the implicit public debt of the 25 countries for which we have data on the present value of retirement benefits amounts, on average, to 5.19 times their respective annual consumption. Using a real discount rate of 3%, implicit retirement-related public debt for these countries is, on average, only 2.79 years of total consumption. In the zero interest rate scenario, the implicit public debt of these 25 countries is thus 1.86 times higher than in the 3% scenario. This multiplier is now applied to the individual country figures for the remaining nine countries[19] in column A in Table 6.4, in order to generate the corresponding entries in column A of Table 6.5.

Table 6.5 shows the results obtained for all the countries of the OECD plus China region at a discount rate of zero percent. The structure of Table 6.5 is like that of Table 6.4. Hence, following the table, we can move on directly to the overall result for the region as a whole.

The consequence of assuming a discount rate of zero percent is that retirement-related implicit public debt increases considerably for all the countries. On average, there is nearly a doubling of the amount as compared to the base case scenario using

---

[18]Denmark and Sweden did not report data for present values of retirement benefit entitlements except in the baseline scenario. We therefore had to estimate values for these two countries. In doing so, we applied the average change in the present value of entitlements resulting from zero percent interest in the other 20 Eurostat countries. This is exactly how we proceeded in the case of the three non-European OECD countries: the USA, Mexico and Israel.

[19]As mentioned above, there are no comparable retirement programs or "social insurance pension schemes" in New Zealand. Therefore, we only consider 34 out of 35 countries in the OECD plus China region in our estimations for implicit retirement-related public debt.

Table 6.5 Implicit retirement-related public debt in the OECD plus China region, 2015 (real discount rate of 0%)

	A	B	C = A / E	D = B / E	E	F = C / D
	Implicit public debt	Total consumption	Implicit public debt	Total consumption	Conversion factor	Implicit public debt
	Billions LCU	Billions LCU	Billions Int'l $	Billions Int'l $	LCU in Int'l $	In years of consumption
Australia[a]	3,384.3	1,222.2	2,295.9	829.1	1.5	2.77
Austria	2,248.5	249.4	2,815.5	312.3	0.8	9.02
Belgium	2,040.5	308.1	2,551.3	385.2	0.8	6.62
Canada[b]	1,543.5	1,562.6	1,236.8	1,252.1	1.2	0.99
Chile[a]	424,725.9	122,001.4	1,085.3	311.7	391.4	3.48
Czech Republic	19,382.0	3,035.3	1,498.5	234.7	12.9	6.39
Denmark	1,212.5	1,478.0	166.0	202.4	7.3	0.82
Estonia	112.9	14.7	210.0	27.4	0.5	7.67
Finland	1,096.9	167.1	1,208.7	184.1	0.9	6.57
France	15,174.1	1,711.6	18,768.7	2,117.0	0.8	8.87
Germany	14,948.5	2,218.3	19,216.2	2,851.6	0.8	6.74
Greece[a]	1,497.5	159.1	2,459.3	261.2	0.6	9.41
Hungary	156,869.3	23,835.3	1,183.8	179.9	132.5	6.58
Iceland	2,890.8	1,681.8	20.4	11.8	141.9	1.72
Ireland	667.4	119.2	170.1	30.4	3.9	5.60
Israel	1,824.3	898.7	2,253.7	1,110.2	0.8	2.03
Italy	9,491.0	1,318.3	1,2851.8	1,785.2	0.7	7.20

(continued)

Table 6.5 (continued)

	A	B	C = A / E	D = B / E	E	F = C / D
	Implicit public debt	Total consumption	Implicit public debt	Total consumption	Conversion factor	Implicit public debt
	Billions LCU	Billions LCU	Billions Int'l $	Billions Int'l $	LCU in Int'l $	In years of consumption
Japan[a]	2,830,995.7	406,507.6	27,365.9	3,929.5	103.4	6.96
Korea[a]	2,122,419.3	1,006,005.6	2,475.5	1,173.4	857.4	2.11
Luxembourg[a]	252.4	24.6	286.5	27.9	0.9	10.27
Mexico	3,074.5	14,450.4	369.3	1,735.6	8.3	0.21
Netherlands	2,054.5	483.2	2,537.2	596.7	0.8	4.25
New Zealand	–	–	–	–	–	–
Norway	15,303.6	2,083.0	1,541.2	209.8	9.9	7.35
Poland	8,886.4	1,376.2	5,035.8	779.9	1.8	6.46
Portugal	1,004.4	150.3	1,717.6	257.0	0.6	6.68
Slovak Republic	529.9	58.5	1,078.4	119.1	0.5	9.05
Slovenia	234.1	28.0	393.4	47.0	0.6	8.37
Spain	5,459.6	834.9	8,215.3	1,256.4	0.7	6.54
Sweden	16,625.3	2,975.7	1,878.1	336.2	8.9	5.59
Switzerland	2,547.9	426.8	2,062.3	345.4	1.2	5.97
Turkey[a]	8,785.3	1,736.4	7,559.6	1,494.1	1.2	5.06
UK	11,114.1	1,596.5	16,052.4	2,305.9	0.7	6.96
USA	66,017.4	14,907.2	66,017.4	14,907.2	1.0	4.43

(continued)

Table 6.5 (continued)

	A	B	C = A / E	D = B / E	E	F = C / D
	Implicit public debt	Total consumption	Implicit public debt	Total consumption	Conversion factor	Implicit public debt
	Billions LCU	Billions LCU	Billions Int'l $	Billions Int'l $	LCU in Int'l $	In years of consumption
China[a]	147,417.9	36,226.7	42,515.4	10,447.8	3.5	4.07
Total OECD			214,577.6	41,607.3		5.16
Total OECD plus China			257,093.0	52,055.1		4.94

Sources

Column A: Eurostat (2020), OECD (2017a), van de Ven and Fano (2017)

Column B: World Bank (2019). World Development Indicators, Final consumption expenditure (current LCU)

Column E: World Bank (2019). World Development Indicators, PPP conversion factor (GDP) (LCU per international $)

Authors', own calculations

Notes

Closing balance sheets

[a]Estimated value based on data from OECD (2017a) and method by Müller et al. (2009)

[b]2012. "Net present value for Canada Pension Plan. Unfunded liabilities, closed group approach. The projected cash flows over an extended time period of 150 years are used." Billig (2016, p. 6); van de Ven and Fano (2017, p. 320)

[c]"New Zealand explained that the table is not relevant for them, as there are no social insurance pension schemes in New Zealand" (OECD 2019, p. 9)

LCU: Local currency unit

On methodology. see too "Extrapolation Procedure" on pp. 176

a real rate of 3%. In the base case scenario, retirement-related implicit public debt in 2015 was about 2.7 times annual consumption in the OECD countries and 2.6 times annual consumption in the OECD plus China region as a whole (cf. Table 6.4). Now, at a real discount rate of zero percent, retirement-related implicit public debt in the OECD countries comes to slightly more than *five-times total annual consumption*. If we add China, then retirement-related implicit public debt (including the pension claims of civil servants and other public sector employees) in the OECD plus China region as a whole is *4.9 times total annual consumption*—thus not so far from the OECD average. The overall result is especially heavily influenced by the big economies of the USA and China. In both countries, implicit retirement-related public debt as a percentage of annual consumption is below the OECD average of 5.2 years of consumption. In the zero interest rate scenario, we calculate retirement-related implicit public debt for the USA of about 4.4 times and for China about 4 times their respective annual consumption (cf. Table 6.5, column F).

> We thus estimate that, for 2015, private sector wealth deriving from the public retirement system in the OECD plus China region is the equivalent of about 490 percent of annual consumption.

6.2.2.2   Public Health Insurance

Public health insurance also adds to implicit public debt. This is because a large part of health-related expenses are typically incurred in old age, but, unlike in private health insurance, no age-group-specific old-age provision funds are formed, as we have discussed in greater detail in Sect. 6.1.4. For estimating the implicit public debt arising from public health insurance, no data comparable to that for the public retirement system is available to us. Moreover, the 2008 SNA and the ESA 2010 do not provide for determining the present values of entitlements arising from public health insurance as part of the national accounts.

Since, along with nursing care insurance, public or national health insurance also contributes significantly to implicit public debt, we do not want to forego making a rough estimate of its magnitude.[20] The reason for this is that a large part of healthcare expenditures are typically incurred in the final stages of a beneficiary's life. But, unlike private insurers, public health insurance systems usually do not form any reserves for younger beneficiaries. Hence, there is a similarity to the pay-as-you-go retirement system with respect to the absence of a reserve fund, and

---

[20]According to a study by Germany's Council of Economic Experts (SVR 2011), the public retirement system accounted for around 71% of Germany's implicit public debt in 2011. Public health insurance and nursing care insurance together accounted for 26%. Unemployment insurance, which we will not be taking into account, contributed just under 3%. But the focus of the Council in estimating the implicit public debt arising from the various branches of the social security system was, above all, the sustainability of public finances. Moreover, the methodology used evidently did not follow the ADL principle and hence was different from ours. Therefore, the calculations of implicit public debt of the Council are not suitable for our purposes.

public health insurance also involves implicit public debt. Like in the case of the retirement system, this implicit public debt is found by capitalizing future payments arising from the claims of beneficiaries enrolled in public health insurance and nursing care insurance.[21]

In the absence of international data, we will have to use an estimate for Germany as a guide when subsequently determining the value of implicit public debt arising from public health and nursing care insurance in the OECD plus China region. In so doing, we will make the highly simplifying assumption that a similar type of public health insurance system exists in the other 34 countries of the OECD plus China region as exists in Germany. This allows us also to estimate the implicit public debt from health insurance for the other countries by analogy with Germany. We will take into account here the different levels of healthcare expenditure by the relevant public agencies in the individual countries relative to their respective GDP. We are well aware that the estimate that we make for the OECD plus China region as a whole using this simple procedure can only serve as a rough approximation of the actual magnitude.

Public Health and Nursing Care Insurance in Germany

If, as we have suggested, a pay-as-you-go social security scheme can be regarded as a kind of funded scheme without a reserve fund, then the task at hand is to estimate the size of the missing reserve fund for public health and nursing care insurance. For we understand the missing reserve fund as an expression of the implicit public debt arising from this insurance. We begin with Germany.

Unlike the pay-as-you-go public health and nursing care insurance, private health insurance providers in Germany form old-age provisions for their policy-holders. In the glossary in its 2015 report, Germany's Association of Private Health Insurance Providers (PKV) explains the concept of "old-age provision funds" as follows:

"Old-age provisions: private health and nursing care insurance providers form old-age provisions in anticipation of the fact that with increasing age, healthcare benefit claims also increase. Insurance premiums are calculated in such a way that they are higher in younger years than the benefits actually claimed. The difference is initially invested in old-age provision funds. When, in later years, the calculated costs of health care are then greater than the premium paid, the shortfall is made up by withdrawals from the old-age provisions…" (PKV 2017, p. 118).

These provisions thus represent a reserve fund for covering future healthcare costs of privately insured persons that are predominantly incurred in old age. In order to make adequate provision, in light of predicted demographic changes and expected additional expenditure, private health insurance companies allocate a certain amount to their old-age provisions each year, so that the reserve fund can

---

[21]Since 2010, however, the public insurance providers and their associations in Germany are legally required "to build up a sufficient capital fund, by the end of 2049 at the latest, to be able to meet their old-age benefit obligations (both pensions and health and nursing care benefits)" (Bundesversicherungsamt 2017, p. 2).

Table 6.6 Calculation of hypothetical old-age provisions for public health and nursing care insurance in Germany

Health insurance	2005	...	2014	2015	2016
Private insurance provisions (actual value)[a]	88,748	...	177,706	189,045	200,165
Private insurance premium income[a]	24,748	...	32,642	32,822	33,159
Ratio of private insurance provisions to premium income	3.59	...	5.44	5.76	6.04
Public insurance premium income[a]	145,740	...	204,240	212,560	224,350
Public insurance provisions (estimated value)[a]	522,625	...	1,111,892	1,224,267	1,354,281
Nursing care insurance	2005	...	2014	2015	2016
Private insurance provisions (actual value)[a]	14,623	...	28,487	31,038	32,555
Private insurance premium income[a]	2,038	...	2,913	3,205	3,281
Ratio of private insurance provisions to premium income	7.18	...	9.78	9.69	9.92
Public insurance premium income[a]	17,490	...	25,910	30,690	32,030
Public insurance provisions (estimated value)[a]	125,526	...	2,3,423	297,259	317,856
Ratio of total provisions to current consumption	2005	...	2014	2015	2016
Total consumption[a]	1,751,547	...	2,158,105	2,218,284	2,291,063
Total hypothetical provisions: public health and care insurance[a]	648,152	...	1,365,315	1,521,526	1,672,137
Hypothetical provisions in years of total consumption	0.37	...	0.63	0.69	0.73

Sources
PKV (2015, 2016)
The Information System of the Federal Health Monitoring, www.gbe-bund.de
World Bank (2019). World Development Indicators, Final consumption expenditure (current LCU)
Authors' own calculations
Notes
[a]In millions of euros
Public health insurance premium income without federal funding
Private health insurance premium income from full health insurance, supplementary insurance to public health insurance coverage, per diem sickness insurance, hospitalization per diem insurance
Private care insurance premium income from nursing care insurance, complementary nursing care insurance, subsidized nursing care insurance (since 2013)

constantly grow (cf. Table 6.6). In 2015, according to the association, the old-age provisions of private health insurance providers came to around 189 billion euros. Up to 2015, old-age provisions of around 31 billion euros were formed for private nursing care insurance.

In what follows, we estimate *hypothetical* old-age provisions for public health and nursing care insurance in Germany. To this end, we first determine the ratio of the old-age provisions of the private health insurance providers to their income from insurance premiums. As Table 6.6 shows, in 2005, the old-age provisions of private health insurance providers came to around 3.6 times their annual income from insurance premiums. Over the years, this ratio has constantly and significantly increased. By 2016, the amount of the old-age provisions had grown to six times the income from premiums. The ratio of old-age provisions to premium income is even far greater in the case of private nursing care insurance. Whereas in 2005, old-age provision funds amounted to seven times the premium income of private nursing care insurance providers, this figure had risen to ten times by 2016.[22]

In order to determine the hypothetical old-age provisions of public health and nursing care insurance, we now make a highly simplifying assumption. We assume that the ratio of old-age provisions to premium income is the same in the two sorts of public insurance as in private health insurance. This is a gross simplification, to which various objections can be raised. These objections, however, go in different directions. An argument for assuming a *higher* ratio of old-age provisions to premium income for the public insurance providers is that private insurers generally cover the "better risks" and can hence expect relatively lower expenditures for beneficiaries in old age. An argument for assuming a *lower* ratio of old-age provisions to premium income for the public insurance providers is that persons enrolled in public insurance schemes tend to pay lower premiums for their insurance in old age than persons with private insurance usually have to do. Since, in the absence of data, we have here to make an estimate, we regard the assumption of an equal ratio of old-age provisions to premium income in both private and public health and nursing care insurance as justifiable.

As can be seen in Table 6.6, in 2015, the public health insurance system in Germany collected around 212.6 billion euros in premiums. Assuming a ratio of old-age provisions to premium income of 5.76, there were hypothetical old-age provisions in public health insurance of around 1224.3 billion euros in 2015. The premiums that were collected in 2015 for public nursing care insurance came to around 30.7 billion euros. If we apply the 2015 multiplier of 9.69, we get hypothetical old-age provisions for public nursing care insurance worth approximately 297.3 billion euros.

We estimate that the combined hypothetical old-age provisions for public health and nursing care insurance in Germany in 2015 were around 1521.5 billion euros. This is equivalent to 0.69 years of total consumption in 2015. As Fig. 6.4 shows, hypothetical old-age provisions, as expressed in years of total consumption, have

---

[22]In accordance with actuarial principles, this increase must be attributable to increased life expectancy and to a lower discount rate.

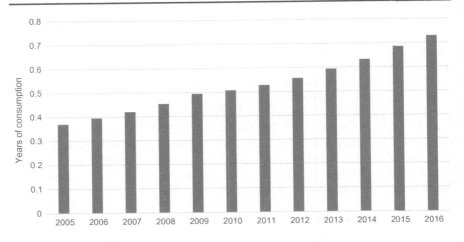

Fig. 6.4 Hypothetical old-age provisions for public health and nursing care insurance in years of total consumption. *Source* Authors' own calculations

risen significantly since 2005. In 2005, they amounted to only 0.37 times total annual consumption, in 2010 to half of annual consumption, and in 2016 to nearly three-quarters of annual consumption. In light of the clear rise in the numbers and in anticipation of the trend continuing in the future, the considerations set out in this book lead us to expect a further rapid increase in implicit public debt due to public health and nursing care insurance. Since, however, we have chosen 2015 as reference year in this book, in what follows, we merely assume 0.69 times total annual consumption for public debt arising from public health and nursing care insurance in Germany. This figure, moreover, forms the basis for applying the German result to the other countries and hence for the estimate of implicit public debt from health and nursing care insurance in the OECD plus China region as a whole.

6.2.2.3   Implicit Public Debt from Health Insurance in the OECD Plus China Region

In estimating implicit retirement-related public debt for those nine countries without OECD data on retirement benefit entitlements, we used the ratio of current benefit expenditure to GDP for each country. We want now to proceed in an analogous fashion for health and nursing care insurance. The OECD (2017b) divides the healthcare expenditure of the countries on which it reports into "voluntary/ out-of-pocket" and "government/compulsory" expenditure. By the latter category, the OECD understands expenditure that is undertaken, on the one hand, by public agencies, but also, on the other, by private health insurance providers.[23]

---

[23]In most OECD countries, health insurance is compulsory. Since one has either to be insured under the public health insurance scheme or by a private insurance provider, the OECD also classifies private health insurance as "government/compulsory health expenditure" (OECD 2017b).

Since what is of interest for us is the relationship of private persons to the state, in what follows, only *public* healthcare expenditure will be used.[24] Private health insurance expenditure will thus be purged from the OECD "government/compulsory" figure, in order to arrive at public healthcare expenditure.[25]

In 2015, approximately 252.4 billion euros were spent on public health services in Germany.[26] This is equivalent to around 11% of total annual consumption in the same year. If we now place the implicit public debt arising from German public health and nursing care insurance in 2015 (1521.5 billion euros) in relation to public healthcare expenditure, we obtain a ratio of 6.028. This multiple of current public healthcare expenditure is for us a proxy for the hypothetical old-age provisions of public health and nursing care insurance. We are thus, in principle, applying the same method of estimation that we used to infer implicit retirement-related public debt from current retirement benefit expenditure in the previous section and that was derived from the calculations of Müller et al. (2009).

Hence, we assume that the implicit public debt arising from health and nursing care insurance is equivalent to approximately six times a country's public health-care expenditure. For simplicity's sake, we refer to the ratio of the flow variable, healthcare expenditure, to the stock variable, hypothetical old-age provisions or the hypothetical capital fund, as the "capitalization factor." In what follows, public health and public nursing care insurance, as well as other forms of health-related public insurance (e.g., accident insurance), will simply be called "public health insurance" for short. Thus, for implicit public debt DI arising from public health insurance, DI_G^H, in Germany,

$$DI_G^H = HE_G \cdot CF_G^H$$

holds. HE_G stands here for public healthcare expenditure in Germany, which amounted to around 11% of total consumption in 2015.

Using the German figures for 2015, the "capitalization factor" (CF) from public health insurance is:

$$CF_G^H = \frac{DI_G^H}{HE_G} = \frac{0.61}{0.11} = 6.028$$

[24]This includes health-related expenditure of the public health insurance plan, public nursing care insurance, the public retirement plan (especially for rehabilitation), public accident insurance and expenditure from public budgets (in particular, investment in hospitals) (Bundesministerium für Gesundheit 2018).

[25]In 2015, private health insurance expenditure amounted to approximately 30.5 billion euros; this is equivalent to 8.9% of total health care expenditure in Germany. Together with employer expenditure (above all, for income replacement in the case of illness and company health services) and voluntary healthcare expenditure of households and non-profit institutions, private healthcare expenditure accounted for somewhat more than one-quarter of total expenditure.

[26]Authors' own calculations using data from Bundesministerium für Gesundheit (2018, 2019), p. 129.

We now assume that this ratio can also be applied to every other country i in the OECD plus China region:

$$CF_G^H = CF_i^H = CF^H$$

The implicit public debt deriving from the public health insurance of a given country i (DI_i^H) can thus be calculated as:

$$DI_i^H = HE_i \cdot CF^H$$

The meanings of the symbols are as follows:

DI_G^H, DI_i^H: implicit public debt from public health and nursing care insurance in years of total consumption in Germany and country i respectively.

$HE_G, HE_{i,}$: Healthcare expenditure in years of total consumption in Germany and country i, respectively.

CF_G^H, CF_i^H: "capitalization factor" for health and nursing care insurance in years of total consumption for Germany and country i, respectively.

We apply this "capitalization factor" of 6.028 for estimating implicit public debt from health and nursing care insurance to the other countries by multiplying the public healthcare expenditure of each of the countries in 2015 by this factor. An example for the USA can serve to illustrate the procedure. In 2015, the USA spent 2227.6 billion US dollars on health (OECD 2017b). Therefore,

2227.6 billion US dollars $\times$ 6.028 = 13,428.0 billion US dollars.[27]

Column D of Table 6.7 shows the implicit public debt calculated for each country using this procedure. For the purpose of aggregation, in the next step, both the implicit public debt and the total consumption of each country are converted from the respective local currency (LCU) into international dollars (purchasing power parities; cf. columns E and F) The aggregate implicit debt of all the countries divided by the aggregate total consumption of all the countries gives the overall result for the OECD countries and the OECD plus China region, respectively.

For the OECD countries, we estimate that implicit public debt from health and nursing care insurance is approximately 64% of total annual consumption. If we take China into account, then we obtain a figure of 57% of total annual consumption for the implicit public debt from health and nursing care insurance in the OECD plus China region.

Implicit Public Debt: Present Value of Changes in Healthcare Expenditure in the OECD plus China Region, 2015–2050

To test the plausibility of our results and the methodology underlying them, we want finally to present an alternative estimate based on data from the International Monetary Fund (IMF). In its report, the IMF notes that implicit public debt is of

---

[27]Discrepancy due to rounding.

Table 6.7 Implicit public debt from health insurance in the OECD plus China region, 2015

	A	B	C = A / B	D = A · CF	E = D / G	F = B / G	G	H = E / F
	Public healthcare expenditure	Total consumption	Public healthcare expenditure	Implicit public debt	Implicit public debt	Total consumption	Conversion factor	Implicit public debt
	Billions LCU	Billions LCU	In years of consumption	Billions LCU	Billions Int'l $	Billions Int'l $	LCU in Int'l $	In years of consumption
Australia	94.2	1,222.2	0.08	567.9	385.3	829.1	1.5	0.46
Austria	23.6	249.4	0.09	142.0	177.8	312.3	0.8	0.57
Belgium	29.0	308.1	0.09	174.8	218.6	385.2	0.8	0.57
Canada	130.2	1,562.6	0.08	785.0	629.0	1,252.1	1.2	0.50
Chile	6,942.4	122,001.4	0.06	41,848.7	106.9	311.7	391.4	0.34
Czech Republic	244.6	3,035.3	0.08	1,474.4	114.0	234.7	12.9	0.49
Denmark	156.4	1,478.0	0.11	942.8	129.1	202.4	7.3	0.64
Estonia	0.9	14.7	0.06	5.4	10.0	27.4	0.5	0.36
Finland	13.6	167.1	0.08	82.3	90.7	184.1	0.9	0.49
France	172.4	1,711.6	0.10	1,039.3	1,285.5	2,117.0	0.8	0.61
Germany	252.4	2,218.3	0.11	1,521.5	1,955.9	2,851.6	0.8	0.69
Greece	7.5	159.1	0.05	45.3	74.4	261.2	0.6	0.28
Hungary	1,457.8	23,835.3	0.06	8,787.6	66.3	179.9	132.5	0.37
Iceland	134.5	1,681.8	0.08	810.7	5.7	11.8	141.9	0.48
Ireland	12.4	119.2	0.10	74.7	19.0	30.4	3.9	0.63
Israel	48.0	898.7	0.05	289.1	357.2	1,110.2	0.8	0.32
Italy	98.8	1,318.3	0.07	595.6	806.6	1,785.2	0.7	0.45

(continued)

Table 6.7 (continued)

	A	B	C = A / B	D = A · CF	E = D / G	F = B / G	G	H = E / F
	Public healthcare expenditure	Total consumption	Public healthcare expenditure	Implicit public debt	Implicit public debt	Total consumption	Conversion factor	Implicit public debt
	Billions LCU	Billions LCU	In years of consumption	Billions LCU	Billions Int'l $	Billions Int'l $	LCU in Int'l $	In years of consumption
Japan	43,382.6	406,507.6	0.11	261,511.1	2,527.9	3,929.5	103.4	0.64
Korea	57,930.0	1,006,005.6	0.06	349,202.9	407.3	1,173.4	857.4	0.35
Luxembourg	2.4	24.6	0.10	14.2	16.1	27.9	0.9	0.58
Mexico	496.6	14,450.4	0.03	2,993.4	359.5	1,735.6	8.3	0.21
Netherlands	51.4	483.2	0.11	309.6	382.3	596.7	0.8	0.64
New Zealand	16.7	193.2	0.09	100.7	68.2	131.0	1.5	0.52
Norway	240.5	2,083.0	0.12	1,449.5	146.0	209.8	9.9	0.70
Poland	71.3	1,376.2	0.05	429.6	243.4	779.9	1.8	0.31
Portugal	9.5	150.3	0.06	57.4	98.2	257.0	0.6	0.38
Slovak Republic	3.9	58.5	0.07	23.2	47.3	119.1	0.5	0.40
Slovenia	2.1	28.0	0.08	12.7	21.4	47.0	0.6	0.46
Spain	62.6	834.9	0.08	377.6	568.1	1,256.4	0.7	0.45
Sweden	343.7	2,975.7	0.12	2,071.9	234.1	336.2	8.9	0.70
Switzerland	43.9	426.8	0.10	264.9	214.4	345.4	1.2	0.62
Turkey	67.5	1,736.4	0.04	406.7	349.9	1,494.1	1.2	0.23

(continued)

Table 6.7 (continued)

	A	B	C = A / B	D = A · CF	E = D / G	F = B / G	G	H = E / F
	Public healthcare expenditure	Total consumption	Public healthcare expenditure	Implicit public debt	Implicit public debt	Total consumption	Conversion factor	Implicit public debt
	Billions LCU	Billions LCU	In years of consumption	Billions LCU	Billions Int'l $	Billions Int'l $	LCU in Int'l $	In years of consumption
UK	131.3	1,596.5	0.08	791.5	1,143.2	2,305.9	0.7	0.50
USA	2,227.6	14,907.2	0.15	13,428.0	13,428.0	14,907.2	1.0	0.90
China	1,877.0	36,226.7	0.05	11,314.8	3,263.2	10,447.8	3.5	0.31
Total OECD					26,687.1	41,738.2		0.64
Total OECD plus China					29,950.3	52,186.0		0.57

Sources
Column A: OECD (2017b)
Column B: World Bank (2019). World Development Indicators, Final consumption expenditure (current LCU)
Column G: World Bank (2019). World Development Indicators, PPP conversion factor (GDP) (LCU per international $)
LCU: Local currency unit
Authors' own calculations
Notes Public healthcare expenditure: Healthcare expenditure from public health, nursing care and accident insurance, as well as the public retirement plan and from public budgets
CF ("Capitalization Factor") = 6.028

great significance, given the aging of the population in many of its member countries (IMF 2018b, p. 12).

In contrast to our methodology, which is based on the accrued-to-date-liabilities (ADL) principle that we have described in detail above, the IMF (2018b) attempts to estimate the present values that result from the *changes* in healthcare expenditure in the IMF member countries that are projected to take place between 2015 and 2050. Future revenue is also taken into account here, as is usual in the Open Group Method that appears to have been used.[28] These present values are given as a percentage of each country's GDP (cf. column A of Table 6.8). As can be seen in the table, the countries are facing very different present values. Switzerland (116%) and the USA (122%) especially stand out.[29] A present value of 48% is calculated for Germany.

If we relate these individual present values of the countries of the OECD plus China region to their respective total annual consumption and aggregate them in the same way as has been done in Tables 6.2, 6.4, 6.5 and 6.7, then we obtain the following overall result. In accordance with the IMF data and methodology, the changes in healthcare expenditure that are projected for the OECD countries between 2015 and 2050 give rise to implicit public debt equivalent to just under one year of total consumption. For the OECD plus China region as a whole, the implicit public debt arising from changes in healthcare expenditure is estimated to be 91% of total annual consumption. Comparing these results with the results of the estimates that we have undertaken (OECD countries: 64% of total annual consumption; OECD plus China region: 57% of total annual consumption) shows that our approach has evidently not led to implausibly high estimates for implicit public debt from health insurance.

6.2.3   Explicit and Implicit Public Debt in the OECD Plus China Region: Summary of Estimates

Table 6.9 provides a concluding overview of all the figures on explicit and implicit public debt that have been calculated with zero percent interest rate in Sect. 6.2. We estimate that total public debt (the sum of explicit and implicit public debt) in the OECD is 6.72 times and in the OECD plus China area 6.26 times the respective total annual consumption. At 0.75 times total annual consumption, explicit debt, which has been calculated as net public debt, accounted for only a relatively small part of this. According to our estimates, implicit public debt in the OECD plus China region in 2015 came to 5.51 times total annual consumption. Implicit public

---

[28]The IMF does not provide any detailed information on methodology in its report. Like Germany's Council of Economic Experts in its expert opinion on demographic change (SVR 2011), the IMF's focus is clearly on analyzing the sustainability of public debt. Thus, the report states: "Taking a long-term view through the intertemporal balance sheet allows a comparison of current wealth against future fiscal pressures." On methodology, moreover, it specifies: "...the balance sheet is used to determine the long-term intertemporal net worth under current policies, combining discounted future flows of revenues and spending with the static balance sheet" (IMF 2018b, p. 17 and p. 33).

[29]On the status of the US healthcare system, cf. Gaudette et al. (2015).

Table 6.8 Implicit public debt, present value of healthcare spending change in the OECD plus China region, 2015–2050

	A	B	C = A · B	D	E = C / G	F = D / G	G	H = E / F
	Present value of healthcare spending change 2015–50	Gross domestic product	Present value of healthcare spending change	Total consumption	Implicit public debt	Total consumption	Conversion factor	Implicit public debt
	in % of GDP	Billions LCU	Billions LCU	Billions LCU	Billions Int'l $	Billions Int'l $	LCU in Int'l $	In years of consumption
Australia	59.6	1,621.4	965.8	1,222.2	655.2	829.1	1.5	0.79
Austria	59.0	344.3	203.3	249.4	254.5	312.3	0.8	0.82
Belgium	76.8	411.0	315.9	308.1	394.9	385.2	0.8	1.03
Canada	46.8	1,985.8	930.1	1,562.6	745.3	1,252.1	1.2	0.60
Chile	53.3	159,605.9	85,020.2	122,001.4	217.2	311.7	391.4	0.70
Czech Republic	25.1	4,595.8	1,152.9	3,035.3	89.1	234.7	12.9	0.38
Denmark	46.0	2,036.4	936.7	1,478.0	128.3	202.4	7.3	0.63
Estonia	21.1	20.7	4.4	14.7	8.1	27.4	0.5	0.30
Finland	50.8	210.0	106.7	167.1	117.6	184.1	0.9	0.64
France	30.6	2,198.4	672.2	1,711.6	831.4	2,117.0	0.8	0.39
Germany	47.8	3,048.9	1,456.9	2,218.3	1,872.9	2,851.6	0.8	0.66
Greece[1]	83.7	177.3	148.4	159.1	243.7	261.2	0.6	0.93
Hungary	40.1	34,378.6	13,795.3	23,835.3	104.1	179.9	132.5	0.58
Iceland	94.0	2,288.0	2,150.9	1,681.8	15.2	11.8	141.9	1.28
Ireland	38.3	262.5	100.6	119.2	25.6	30.4	3.9	0.84
Israel	15.4	1,167.9	179.4	898.7	221.6	1,110.2	0.8	0.20

(continued)

Table 6.8 (continued)

	A	B	C = A · B	D	E = C / G	F = D / G	G	H = E / F
	Present value of healthcare spending change 2015–50	Gross domestic product	Present value of healthcare spending change	Total consumption	Implicit public debt	Total consumption	Conversion factor	Implicit public debt
	in % of GDP	Billions LCU	Billions LCU	Billions LCU	Billions Int'l $	Billions Int'l $	LCU in Int'l $	In years of consumption
Italy	40.8	1,652.1	674.4	1,318.3	913.2	1,785.2	0.7	0.51
Japan	72.0	531,985.8	383,069.6	406,507.6	3,703.0	3,929.5	103.4	0.94
Korea	84.3	1,564,123.9	1,318,256.5	1,006,005.6	1,537.6	1,173.4	857.4	1.31
Luxembourg	74.1	51.6	38.2	24.6	43.4	27.9	0.9	1.56
Mexico	31.1	18,551.5	5,761.3	14,450.4	692.0	1,735.6	8.3	0.40
Netherlands	94.6	690.0	652.6	483.2	805.9	596.7	0.8	1.35
New Zealand	66.4	254.7	169.0	193.2	114.6	131.0	1.5	0.87
Norway	78.2	3,118.1	2,439.5	2,083.0	245.7	209.8	9.9	1.17
Poland	40.0	1,798.2	719.5	1,376.2	407.8	779.9	1.8	0.52
Portugal	74.3	179.8	133.6	150.3	228.4	257.0	0.6	0.89
Slovak Republic	26.5	79.1	21.0	58.5	42.7	119.1	0.5	0.36
Slovenia	42.9	38.8	16.6	28.0	28.0	47.0	0.6	0.59
Spain	60.0	1,081.2	648.3	834.9	975.5	1,256.4	0.7	0.78
Sweden	25.0	4,201.5	1,052.2	2,975.7	118.9	336.2	8.9	0.35
Switzerland	116.1	654.3	759.4	426.8	614.7	345.4	1.2	1.78
Turkey	33.6	2,338.6	785.8	1,736.4	676.2	1,494.1	1.2	0.45
UK	65.0	1,895.8	1,233.2	1,596.5	1,781.2	2,305.9	0.7	0.77

(continued)

Table 6.8 (continued)

	A	B	C = A · B	D	E = C / G	F = D / G	G	H = E / F
	Present value of healthcare spending change 2015–50	Gross domestic product	Present value of healthcare spending change	Total consumption	Implicit public debt	Total consumption	Conversion factor	Implicit public debt
	in % of GDP	Billions LCU	Billions LCU	Billions LCU	Billions Int'l $	Billions Int'l $	LCU in Int'l $	In years of consumption
USA	122.3	18,219.3	22,274.4	14,907.2	22,274.4	14,907.2	1.0	1.49
China	31.9	68.905.2	21,954.0	36,226.7	6,331.5	10,447.8	3.5	0.61
Total OECD					41,127.4	41,738.2		0.99
Total OECD plus China					47,458.9	52,186.0		0.91

Sources

Column A: IMF (2018b)

Column B: World Bank (2019). World Development Indicators, GDP (current LCU)

Column D: World Bank (2019). World Development Indicators, Final consumption expenditure (current LCU)

Column G: World Bank (2019). World Development Indicators, PPP conversion factor (GDP) (LCU per international $)

LCU: Local currency unit

Authors' own calculations

Note Present value of healthcare spending change 2015–2050: IMF (2018b) forecast

Table 6.9 Overview of the estimates of explicit and implicit public debt in the OECD plus China region, 2015

Results of the empirical estimates of public debt in years of total consumption (with zero percent interest rate)	USA	Germany	OECD	OECD plus China
Explicit public debt	0.98	0.70	0.92	0.75
Implicit public debt (pensions)	4.43	6.74	5.16	4.94
Implicit public debt (health and care insurance)	0.90	0.69	0.64	0.57
Total	6.31	8.12	6.72	6.26

Source Authors' own calculations

debt is thus much more significant for the claims of private persons on the state. By far the largest part of this debt derives from the public retirement system, for which we have calculated implicit public debt of 494% of total consumption in the OECD plus China region in 2015. A closer look at the table reveals that at 631%, the US total public debt figure is about the average for both the OECD countries and the OECD countries plus China. Whereas, at 812% of annual consumption, the corresponding figure for Germany is significantly higher than these averages. The difference is especially pronounced for the public retirement system (180% points above the total area average), while the US figure is about 50% points below the total area average (i.e., the OECD plus China). The situation is somewhat different for implicit public debt from public health and nursing care insurance. Both the USA and Germany have a higher implicit public debt from these sources than the total area average of 57% of total consumption. However, the USA has a higher figure than Germany at 90% as compared to 69% of total consumption.

References

Aghion, Philippe, Antonin Bergeaud, Timo Boppart, Peter J. Klenow and Huiyu Li. 2019. Missing Growth from Creative Destruction. *American Economic Review* 109 (8): 2795-2822.

Billig, Assia. 2016. *Compiling the actuarial balance sheet for the Canada Pension Plan – methodological overview. Presentation to the Eurostat/ILO/IMF/OECD Workshop on Pensions. Paris, 9.3.2016.* http://www.osfi-bsif.gc.ca/Eng/Docs/OCA-Assia-Billig-03092016-Slides.pdf. Accessed: 12 May 2019.

Board of Governors of the Federal Reserve System. 2020a. *Enhanced Financial Accounts, State Pensions, State and Local Pension Funding Status and Ratios by State, 2002–2018.* https://www.federalreserve.gov/releases/z1/dataviz/pension/comparative_view/table/. Accessed: 12 December 2020.

Board of Governors of the Federal Reserve System. 2020b. *Z1-Financial Accounts, L.119.b Federal Government Employee Retirement Funds: Defined Benefit Plans.* https://www.federalreserve.gov/apps/fof/DisplayTable.aspx?t=l.119.b/. Accessed: 12 December 2020

Board of Trustees OASDI. 2016. *The 2016 Annual Report of the Board of Trustees of the Federal Old-Age and Survivors Insurance and Federal Disability Insurance Trust Funds.* Washington (D.C.): U.S. Government Publishing Office.

Board of Trustees OASDI. 2020. *The 2020 Annual Report of the Board of Trustees of the Federal Old-Age and Survivors Insurance and Federal Disability Insurance Trust Funds.* Washington (D.C.): U.S. Government Publishing Office.

Braakmann, Albert, Jens Grütz and Thorsten Haug. 2007. Das Renten- und Pensionsvermögen in den volkswirtschaftlichen Gesamtrechnungen. Methodik und erste Ergebnisse. *Wirtschaft und Statistik* 12: 1167-1179.

Bundesministerium für Gesundheit. 2018. *Daten des Gesundheitswesens 2018.* Berlin: Bundesministerium für Gesundheit.

Bundesministerium für Gesundheit. 2019. *Finanzierungsgrundlagen der gesetzlichen Krankenversicherung.* Berlin: Bundesministerium für Gesundheit. https://www.bundesgesundheitsministerium. de/finanzierung-gkv.html. Accessed: 30 May 2019.

Bundesversicherungsamt. 2017. *Leitfaden zur Altersrückstellungsverordnung für die gesetzlichen Krankenkassen und ihre Verbände, Version: 8 December 2017.* https://www.bundesver sicherungsamt.de/fileadmin/redaktion/Krankenversicherung/Altersversorgungsverpflichtungen/ Leitfaden_KK-AltRueckV_Stand_8._12.2017.pdf. Accessed: 1 June 2019.

Economist. 2019. Public Pensions - State of Denial. 16 November 2019: p. 65–66.

European Commission, IMF, OECD, UN and World Bank. 2009. *System of National Accounts 2008.* https://unstats.un.org/unsd/nationalaccount/docs/SNA2008.pdf. Accessed: 2 April 2019.

Eurostat. 2013. *European System of Accounts: ESA 2010.* Luxembourg: Publications Office of the European Union.

Eurostat. 2020. *Pensions in National Accounts (nasa_10_pens).* https://ec.europa. eu/eurostat/ web/pensions/data/database. Accessed: 30 December 2020.

Freudenberg, Christoph. 2017. Alterssicherungssysteme in der Finanzierungsrechnung. In *Die gesamtwirtschaftliche Finanzierungsrechnung. Revision und Anwendung in ökonomischen Analysen*, Berliner Beiträge zu den Volkswirtschaftlichen Gesamtrechnungen, vol. 1, eds. Reimund Mink and Klaus Voy, 323–347. Marburg: Metropolis-Verlag.

Gaudette, Étienne, Bryan Tysinger, Alwyn Cassil and Dana P. Goldman. 2015. Health and Health Care of Medicare Beneficiaries in 2030. *Forum for health economics & policy* 18 (2): 75-96.

Haug, Thorsten. 2018. Berechnung der Pensions- und Rentenanwartschaften in den volkswirtschaftlichen Gesamtrechnungen. Berechnungsmethodik und Ergebnisse. *Wirtschaft und Statistik* 2: 77-90.

Hellwig, Martin. 2019. Target-Falle oder Empörungsfalle – Zur deutschen Diskussion um die Europäische Währungsunion. *Perspektiven der Wirtschaftspolitik* 19 (4): 345-382.

Holzmann, Robert, Robert Palacios and Asta Zviniene. 2004. *Implicit pension debt: Issues, measurement and scope in international perspective.* Social Protection Discussion Paper No. 0403. Washington (D.C.): World Bank.

Holzmann, Robert. 1998. *Financing the Transition to Multi-Pillar.* Social Protection Discussion Paper No. 9809. Washington (D.C.): World Bank.

IMF (International Monetary Fund). 2013. *Public sector debt statistics: guide for compilers and users.* 2nd ed. Washington (D.C.): International Monetary Fund.

IMF (International Monetary Fund). 2016. *Implementing Accrual Accounting in the Public Sector.* Technical Notes and Manuals. Prepared by Joe Cavanagh, Suzanne Flynn, and Delphine Moretti. Washington (D.C.): International Monetary Fund.

IMF (International Monetary Fund). 2018a. *Fiscal Monitor. Capitalizing on Good Times.* April 2018. Washington (D.C.): International Monetary Fund.

IMF (International Monetary Fund). 2018b. *Fiscal Monitor. Managing Public Wealth.* October 2018. Washington (D.C.): International Monetary Fund.

IMF (International Monetary Funds). 2018c. *Global Debt Database.* https://www.imf.org/∼/ media/Files/Publications/fiscal-monitor/2018/April/data/gdd121318.ashx?la=en. Accessed: 27 May 2019.

Kaier, Klaus and Christoph Müller. 2015. New figures on unfunded public pension entitlements across Europe: concept, results and applications. *Empirica* 42 (4): 865-895.

Kotlikoff, Laurence. 1992. *Generational Accounting: Knowing Who Pays and Knowing When for What We Spend*. New York (NY): The Free Press.

Lenze, David G. 2013. *State and Local Government Defined Benefit Pension Plans: Estimates of Liabilities and Employer Normal Costs by State, 2000–2011*. Working paper. Washington (D. C.): Bureau of Economic Analysis.

Mink, Raimund and Marta Rodríguez Vives (eds.). 2010. European Central Bank and Eurostat Workshop on Pensions, 29-30 April 2009. Frankfurt am Main: European Central Bank.

Müller, Christoph, Bernd Raffelhüschen and Olaf Weddige. 2009. *Pension obligations of government employer pension schemes and social security pension schemes established in EU countries*. Studie im Auftrag der Europäischen Zentralbank. Freiburg: Forschungszentrums Generationenverträge, Universität Freiburg.

Munnell, Alicia H., Jean-Pierre Aubry and Mark Cafarelli. 2014. *The Funding Of State And Local Pensions: 2013–2017*. Boston (MA): Center for Retirement Research at Boston College.

Novy-Marx, Robert and Joshua D. Rauh. 2011. Public Pension Liabilities: How Big Are They and What Are They Worth? *Journal of Finance* 66 (4): 1207-1246.

OECD. 2017a. *Pensions at a Glance 2017: OECD and G20 Indicators*. Paris: OECD Publishing.

OECD. 2017b. *Health at a Glance 2017: OECD Indicators*. Paris: OECD Publishing.

OECD. 2019. The OECD Collection of Annual Estimates of Pension Entitlements in Social Insurance: First Main Findings, Working Party on Financial Statistics, COM/SDD/DAF(2019) 4. Paris: OECD. http://www.oecd.org/officialdocuments/publicdisplaydocumentpdf/?cote= COM/SDD/DAF(2019)4&docLanguage=En. Accessed: 1 January 2021.

OECD. 2020a. Guidelines for the OECD Table on Social Insurance Pension Schemes (Table 2900). https://www.oecd.org/statistics/datacollection/Guidelines%20on%20the%20OECD%20table%20 on%20social%20insurance%20pension%20schemes.pdf. Accessed: 1 January 2021.

OECD. 2020b. Notes to OECD Pension Metadata Sheet. OECD: Paris. https://www.oecd.org/sdd/ na/OECD-Social-Pension-Scheme-Metadata-United-States.pdf. Accessed: 3 January 2021.

PKV (Verband der Privaten Krankenversicherung). (various years) *Zahlenbericht der Privaten Krankenversicherung*. Cologne: Verband der Privaten Krankenversicherung e.V.

Raffelhüschen, Bernd. 1999. Generational Accounting in Europe. *American Economic Review: Papers and Proceedings* 89 (2): 167-170.

Reinhart, Carmen M. and Kenneth S. Rogoff. 2009. *This Time is Different: Eight Centuries of Financial Folly*. Princeton (NJ): Princeton University Press.

Reinsdorf, Marshall, David Lenze and Dylan Rassier. 2014. *Bringing Actuarial Measures of Defined Benefit Pensions into the U.S. National Accounts*. Paper prepared for the IARIW 33rd General Conference, Rotterdam, the Netherlands. August 2014. http://www.iariw.org/papers/ 2014/ReinsdorfPaper.pdf. Accessed: 23 May 2019.

SVR (German Council of Economic Experts). 2011. *Herausforderungen des demografischen Wandels – Expertise im Auftrag der Bundesregierung*. Occasional Report. Wiesbaden: Statistisches Bundesamt.

Shiller, Robert J. and Mark J. Kamstra. 2010. Trills Instead of T-Bills: It's Time to Replace Part of Government Debt with Shares in GDP. *The Economists' Voice* 7 (3): Article 5.

Stefanescu, Irina and Ivan Vidangos. 2014. *Introducing Actuarial Liabilities and Funding Status of Defined-Benefit Pensions in the U.S. Financial Accounts*. Finance and Economics Discussion Series Note. 2014–10–31. Washington (D.C.): Board of Governors of the Federal Reserve System.

Uhlig, Harald and Mathias Trabandt. 2011. The Laffer Curve Revisited. *Journal of Monetary Economics* 58: 305-327.

van de Ven, Peter and Daniele Fano (eds.). 2017. *Understanding Financial Accounts.* Paris: OECD Publishing.

Werding, Martin. 2011. Demographie und öffentliche Haushalte – Simulationen zur langfristigen Tragfähigkeit der gesamtstaatlichen Finanzpolitik in Deutschland, Arbeitspapier 03/2011 des Sachverständigenrats zur Begutachtung der gesamtwirtschaftlichen Entwicklung, Wiesbaden: Statistisches Bundesamt.

World Bank. 2019. DataBank – World Development Indicators. https://databank.world-bank.org/data/home.aspx. Accessed: January-June 2019.

Investment, Saving and Stagnation from a Keynesian Perspective

7

Abstract

It can also be shown from a Keynesian perspective that planned investment and saving are diverging in the twenty-first century and that there is a risk of sustained (secular) underemployment unless appropriate countermeasures are taken by the state. In this chapter, we look at the arguments that Keynesian authors have used, in both older and more recent writings, to demonstrate the possibility of secular stagnation and at the possibilities they considered for overcoming tendencies toward stagnation. We make clear that, despite general differences in the theoretical framework and some differences in detail, there are a number of parallels between the Keynesian view and the new capital-theoretical conception presented in this book. This applies both for the causes of the structural divergence between planned private saving and private investment and for its consequences.

7.1 The Disparity Between Capital Supply and Capital Demand and the Divergence Between Saving and Investment

In the previous chapters of this book, we have argued that long-term structural factors are responsible for the fact that the supply of private capital and the demand for private capital are not in equilibrium at a non-negative interest rate and full employment. Under the conditions in question, in our view, private capital supply is greater than private capital demand. In particular, the trend toward significantly higher life expectancy is, on the one hand, increasing the population's desire to save, whereas, on the other hand, due to a number of factors, private demand for capital is not increasing relative to national product or total consumption. In other words, the argument of this book is that under the given circumstances, the natural

© The Author(s) 2021
C. C. von Weizsäcker and H. M. Krämer, *Saving and Investment in the Twenty-First Century*, https://doi.org/10.1007/978-3-030-75031-2_7

interest rate mechanism is no longer able to bring saving and investment into an equilibrium that is compatible with prosperity. Our approach thus forms part of the neoclassical tradition, in which the interest rate is of central importance for capital supply and demand. Since John Maynard Keynes, however, there are also other views on the mechanisms that bring investment and saving into equilibrium and on the conditions that have to be fulfilled to eliminate macroeconomic imbalances and to achieve full employment. Nonetheless, it can also be argued from a Keynesian perspective that investment and saving are diverging in the twenty-first century and that there is a risk of sustained underemployment and stagnation unless appropriate countermeasures are taken by the state. In this chapter, we will look at the arguments used by some Keynesian authors, in both older and more recent writings, to demonstrate the possibility of secular stagnation and at the measures they recommend for preventing tendencies toward stagnation from being realized. Despite the different theoretical approach, we will see that both the finding of a divergence between saving and investment and the analysis of its consequences exhibit important similarities to the arguments developed in this book.

7.2　Public and Private Saving and Public and Private Investment in a Macroeconomic Context

We have essentially worked with stock variables in our analysis up to now. Stocks have a definite relationship to flows, which will be our focus in what follows. Households that would like to accumulate wealth can only succeed in doing so, if a portion of their income is not spent for consumption purposes, but rather saved.[1] Overall, firms have to invest more than is required just to replace plant and equipment in order to increase their capital stock: i.e., they have to undertake net investment (in what follows, simply "investment" for short). Saving and investment are flows, which affect the stock of household wealth and capital stock, respectively.

On the macrolevel, the equality of saving and investment is a key equilibrium condition. To show this, we start from the national income equation:

$$Y^d = C_P + C_G + I_P + I_G + (EX - IM) \tag{7.1}$$

Y^d: aggregate demand; C_P: private consumption; C_G: public (or "government") consumption; I_P: private investment; I_G: public (or "government") investment; EX: exports; IM: imports.

In equilibrium, aggregate demand Y^d on the goods market is equal to aggregate supply Y^s. For national income Y, $Y^d = Y^s = Y$ holds in equilibrium. Equilibrium national income is thus determined by:

---

[1]We abstract here from changes in stocks due to changes in valuation.

$$Y = C_P + C_G + I_P + I_G + (EX - IM) \tag{7.2}$$

In Sect. 3.11, we were able to show that the OECD plus China region has a nearly balanced current account vis-à-vis the rest of the world ($EX = IM$). If, moreover, we define national saving as the part of national income Y that is not used up by private consumption C_P or public consumption C_G, i.e.,

$$S = Y - C_P - C_G \tag{7.3}$$

then Eq. 7.2 gets reduced to the well-known identity of aggregate saving and aggregate investment:

$$S = I \tag{7.4}$$

When this equilibrium condition is satisfied, then supply and demand are in equilibrium on the goods market. We now divide saving, just like investment, into private and public saving. In equilibrium, then,

$$S_P + S_G = I_P + I_G \tag{7.5}$$

holds. Household saving consists of the part of current income that households do not consume. The taxes that private individuals pay to the state have to be subtracted from income Y, and the subsidies that private individuals receive from the state have to be added to it. If we designate net taxes (taxes minus transfer payments) as $\tilde{T}$, then the following holds for private saving S_P:

$$S_P = Y - \tilde{T} - C_P \tag{7.6}$$

Public saving S_G is equivalent to the sum of the state's net acquisition of financial and non-financial assets. The state's net acquisition of financial assets equals the difference between its revenues $\tilde{T}$ and its expenditure $G = C_G + I_G$. Its net acquisition of non-financial assets is equal to its net investment I_G. Public saving is thus the sum of the budgetary surplus or deficit and public investment:

$$S_G = (\tilde{T} - G) + I_G \tag{7.7}$$

As discussed at length above, in the OECD plus China region, on the one hand, especially due to rising life expectancy, households increasingly want to accumulate wealth, but, on the other, private demand for capital is hardly increasing relative to the national product. Consequently, private saving S_P is persistently and increasingly greater than the more slowly growing private investment I_P:

$$S_P > I_P.$$

This is what we call the "Great Divergence."

We have argued, furthermore, that the endogenous process of adjustment via the real interest rate, which could restore the balance between saving and investment, does not work under the specific conditions of the twenty-first century. In order to restore equilibrium, such that there can be prosperity with full employment and price stability, the state has to take measures to ensure that a substantial—and, given the continuing rise in life expectancy, growing—part of the desired saving of private individuals can be realized. This can be seen by inserting Eq. 7.7 into Eq. 7.5 and then rearranging:

$$I_P - S_P = (\tilde{T} - G) \tag{7.8}$$

This presentation in terms of flow variables is the counterpart to the presentation in terms of stock variables that, for theoretical reasons, we have preferred in this book: $Z - T = D$. Equation 7.8 makes clear that the difference between current private investment and current private saving can be made up in the current period by commensurate net borrowing by the state. If private saving and private investment come to diverge again, the budgetary deficit in the subsequent equilibrium becomes greater. Public debt increases accordingly.

A permanent budgetary deficit thus becomes a *conditio sine qua non* for sustained prosperity. We argue that it is only thanks to such a deficit that the equality of saving and investment can be restored without bringing about undesirable economic consequences. But the restoration of equilibrium without adverse consequences requires the relevant political institutions to intervene in the economy. The willingness to offset a gap between planned investment and planned saving by net borrowing (expressed as a flow) or corresponding public debt (expressed as a stock) thus becomes an indispensable condition for economic stability.

7.3 The Adjustment Mechanism in Disequilibrium

The equilibrium condition $S = I$ is derived from the well-known definitional relationships of national accounting and it is always satisfied ex post. Ex ante, however, it is possible for this condition not to be met. In this case, there is no equilibrium on the goods market and no equality between aggregate voluntary saving S^v and aggregate investment I^v. Instead, $S^v \neq I^v$ holds. Theories are then needed to explain how an economy that has fallen into disequilibrium can return to equilibrium. The different paradigms in economic theory provide different explanations. Both between and within the various macrotheoretical paradigms, the following questions are given sometimes very different answers.

1. What long-term factors lead to a situation in which $S^v \neq I^v$?
2. What happens when $S^v \neq I^v$?
3. Is government intervention necessary, useful or harmful when $S^v \neq I^v$?
4. If the government should intervene, in what way should it do so and using what instruments?

Our aim in the following is to show how our finding in this book that $S^v \neq I^v$ and its possible consequences appear from the perspective of Keynesian theory.

In considering the relationship between saving and investment, the natural rate of interest has been our main focus thus far. In our approach, the interest rate is key, because both the levels of (private) investment and that of (private) saving are dependent upon the interest rate (r): $S_P(r)$, $I_P(r)$. We have argued that under the different conditions that prevailed in earlier times, a sufficiently flexible interest rate could bring investment and saving into equilibrium.

A further distinguishing feature of our reflections up to this point was that saving and investment are to some extent in a hierarchical relationship to one another. Given a certain interest rate level, the preferences of households for more or less current consumption as compared to future consumption are decisive for the supply of capital (in the form of savings).[2] The interest rate mechanism then ensures that investment adjusts in such a way that saving and investment are brought into equilibrium in the long run and there is prosperity (full employment). The level of saving thus "determines" the level of investment. We could also describe this figuratively and in highly simplified fashion as follows: Saving and investment are in equilibrium in the same car and are thus moving at the same speed—but saving is in the driver's seat.[3]

Since Keynes, however, there is also an entirely different view of the relationship between saving and investment. In Keynes too—but for entirely different reasons—planned investment and planned saving do not come into balance. For Keynes, the interest rate does not, in general, have the function of harmonizing saving and investment that it is assigned in neoclassical economics. In the Keynesian system, the failed coordination of saving and investment is at the origin of the employment problem of a monetary economy. The second important difference concerns the direction of causality in the relationship between investment and saving. Like Marx and Schumpeter, Keynes was of the opinion that it is not saving that dominate investment, but, on the contrary (innovation or profit-driven) investment that plays the key role and the level of saving adapts to the latter: "But we have shown that the extent of effective saving is necessarily determined by the scale of investment..." (Keynes 1936, p. 375).

In Keynes, this is due to the fact that in a monetary economy, the banking system can, as it were, create money or credit "out of thin air" (fiat money). This creates the additional liquidity required for financing investment without there having first to

---

[2]In an economic model in which only goods are exchanged and there is no money, investment necessarily presupposes a foregoing of goods and hence of consumption in the present. In Wicksell (1936 [1898]), a kind of intertemporal lending of goods take place. The real interest rate is understood as the relative price of a homogeneous good in the future and in the present. For Wicksell, the real interest rate is determined by the time preference of consumers.

[3]This is not to deny that the interest rate simultaneously affects both investment and saving in neoclassical theory. But at least for full employment equilibrium, James Meade's famous metaphor of the dog wagging its tail applies: "...a dog called savings wag[s] his tail labelled investment" (Meade 1975, p. 62).

be an equivalent foregoing of consumption (= saving).[4] The fact that in Keynes, investment and saving are not, in principle, brought into equilibrium by the interest rate mechanism, as in neoclassical theory, is important to keep in mind. Keynes developed a theory of a monetary economy in which the interest rate is determined on the money market, which Keynes explained by his theory of liquidity preference.[5] Instead, the adjusting of saving and investment to one another comes about by way of the level of production, since saving is dependent on income. Apart from the prevailing monetary interest rate, the profit expectations that entrepreneurs connect to a planned investment are a key factor for determining the level of investment in turn. These expectations can be extremely volatile, however. They can easily change and, with them, so too does investment demand. It is thus highly uncertain whether aggregate investment is enough to create sufficient effective demand to bring about full employment. For Keynes, a situation in which planned full-employment saving and planned investment are equal was not fundamentally inconceivable, but it was not assured. Hence, the analysis of a situation in which ex ante saving and investment are unequal, i.e., $S^v \neq I^v$, was highly relevant for him.

The path to an equilibrium of saving and investment—which Keynes, however, only analyzed using a comparative static approach—principally takes place, as already discussed, via a change in aggregate income that brings saving and investment into equilibrium ex post. The adjustment takes place, above all, by way of the income multiplier.[6] If consumer demand is lacking, for example, more will be saved at a given income, whereby the additional saving can also trigger interest rate cuts. In Keynes, however, this path does not necessarily lead to the restoration of an equilibrium between saving and investment with full employment. On the one hand, the profit expectations of entrepreneurs can become so troubled in this sort of situation that, despite lower interest rates, investment falls instead of rises. The consequence is a further decline in income, consumption, investment and hence, ultimately, also saving. On the other hand, the interest rate can be at its lower limit (in a "liquidity trap"), since there is speculation on falling prices on the bonds

---

[4]Citing criticism of the treatment of financial resources as loanable funds, Bofinger and Ries (2017) critically examine recent theories of stagnation in which the natural rate of interest plays an important role. They emphasize that private saving is not a precondition for investment in a monetary economy and hence reject the savings glut approach for fundamental theoretical reasons. Palley (2019), for whom a shortage of demand likewise cannot chiefly be eliminated by interest rate changes, makes a similar argument. But such criticism ignores the fact that the high propensity to save is the result of an active desire to accumulate wealth and not a "passive" reaction to insufficient effective demand.

[5]The interest rate in Keynes and the natural rate of interest that is our focus are thus based on entirely different conceptions. In the *General Theory*, Keynes distanced himself from Wicksell's natural rate of interest, which he had previously used: "If there is any such rate of interest, which is unique and significant, it must be the rate which we might term the *neutral* rate of interest..." (Keynes 1936, p. 243; emphasis in the original). This rate must be "consistent with full employment" and is in this sense an "optimum rate," as Keynes also called it (ibid.).

[6]In Keynes, the process of adjustment of demand and supply in disequilibrium is generally characterized by quantities reacting faster than prices. Nonetheless, price adjustments also play a role in Keynes.

market. In this case, the additional savings are hoarded and no cut in the interest rate takes place.[7] Here too, the adjustment takes place via a decline in production and falling income.

Precisely on the question of whether saving tends to dominate investment or vice versa, Keynesian theory clearly differs from neoclassical theory. Keynes puts the focus on the autonomous investment decisions of entrepreneurs. In analytical terms, investment is there "first" and aggregate saving adjusts to the latter. Saving is determined by income and income is determined by investment, such that ultimately saving is dependent on investment. To return to the image we used previously: In the Keynesian paradigm, entrepreneurs are in the driver's seat thanks to their autonomous investment decisions, whereas savers become passengers in the same car.

In the following, we want to examine to what extent the analysis of (dis)equilibrium between saving and investment on Keynesian premises differs from the basic approach of this book. We will see that—even though the direction of causality between saving and investment is viewed precisely the other way around —the situational analysis and, above all, the economic policy prescriptions exhibit a very large overlap with what we have argued thus far.

In Keynes and the Keynesian economists who have followed him—first and foremost, Alvin Hansen—the inability of an economic system to reach a level of production at which sustained full employment prevails is explained, above all, by a permanent insufficiency of (effective) demand. An economy that is characterized by such an insufficiency is in a situation of stagnation or, from a long-term perspective, in a state of *secular stagnation*.[8]

7.4 John Maynard Keynes as Spiritual Father of the Modern Theory of Stagnation

Though often regarded as a pure analyst of the short term, Keynes dealt with questions of the long-term evolution of the economy at many places in his work. In Keynes's view, this long-term evolution is characterized by tendencies toward stagnation. This is why Joseph A. Schumpeter described Keynes as the spiritual father of the modern theory of stagnation in his *History of Economic Analysis*: "Keynes must be credited or debited, as the case may be, with the fatherhood of modern stagnationism" (Schumpeter 1954, p. 1172).

---

[7]There is talk is of a "zero lower bound" in the current discussion about possibilities of stimulating demand by means of an expansionary monetary policy, since, in practice, the nominal central bank rate cannot be reduced (much) below zero. The zero lower bound plays an important role in the argumentation of some current stagnation theories: for example, in Summers (2014); cf. Sect. 7.5.
[8]Keynes and Hansen were by no means the first economic theorists to regard stagnation as possible. The major representatives of classical political economy already discussed the causes and consequences of stagnation. For contemporary overviews of the historical precedents in economic theory, cf. Anselmann (2020, pp. 25–149).

Keynes was firmly convinced that highly developed economies would sooner or later encounter a problem with full employment and prosperity, since they would one day have exhausted all their profitable investment potential:

> [S]ooner or later, we shall be faced, if not with saturation of investment, at any rate with increasing difficulties in finding satisfactory outlets for new investment. (Keynes 1943, p. 360)

One of Keynes's most important works in which he takes a very long-term perspective is his essay on "The Long-Term Problem of Full Employment" (Keynes 1943). Here, Keynes elaborated a forecast of future economic development, which he divided into three phases. Whereas the first phase is characterized by full employment, inflationary pressures and greater investment than saving, the second phase would be distinguished by investment and saving being more or less equal while preserving full employment. After this Golden Age, however, Keynes expected a phase of stagnation on the demand side, since the demand for capital goods would at some point be saturated and hence planned investment would be less than full-employment saving. As a solution, Keynes recommended economic policy measures that make saving less attractive and stimulate household consumption.

Keynes provided the theoretical grounds for his expectation of stagnation in his *General Theory of Employment, Interest and Money* (Keynes 1936). In Chap. 21, he listed the factors that he believed were responsible for investment being great enough to keep employment at a high level during the nineteenth century:

> During the nineteenth century, the growth of population and of invention, the opening-up of new lands, the state of confidence and the frequency of war over the average of (say) each decade seem to have been sufficient, taken in conjunction with the propensity to consume, to establish a schedule of the marginal efficiency of capital which allowed a reasonably satisfactory average level of employment to be compatible with a rate of interest high enough to be psychologically acceptable to wealth-owners. (Keynes 1936, p. 307)

This period, Keynes continues, is about to come to an end, and he also did not expect any such favorable conditions for economic development to prevail in the future:

> To-day and presumably for the future the schedule of the marginal efficiency of capital is, for a variety of reasons, much lower than it was in the nineteenth century.[9] (Keynes 1936, p. 308)

---

[9]It is understandable, in light of these remarks, why Schumpeter saw the origin of the modern theory of stagnation in Keynes's work. On the above-cited passage from the *General Theory*, Schumpeter (1954, p. 501) writes verbatim: "Here, then, we have the origin of the *modern* stagnation thesis." But Schumpeter finds that the basic idea of Keynes's stagnation theory was already present in Keynes (1919) *The Economic Consequences of the Peace* (Anselmann 2020, p. 44).

Keynes thus expressed his doubts that the favorable economic conditions that he identified for the nineteenth century would continue to exert their influence. At the same time, this allows us to deduce what Keynes regarded as the crucial determinants of long-term economic development (Kurz 2017, p. 121):

1. Firstly, he assumed that, due to a fundamental psychological law, saving rises disproportionately as compared to income, which brings about a decline in consumer demand. This argument exhibits certain parallels to classical under-consumption theories.
2. Keynes was convinced that "the demand for capital is strictly limited" (Keynes 1936, p. 375). Hence, he expected that the possibilities of profitable investment would diminish in the long term, resulting in a tendency for the marginal efficiency of capital to decline.[10] Here, Keynes's argument is similar to those of Smith, Marx, Walras and other theorists of stagnation before him, who, for various reasons, assumed a long-term fall in the profit rate.
3. Finally, there is his view on the function of the interest rate that has already been mentioned above. Keynes argues that the interest rate reacts either not at all or at least not enough to the oversupply of private savings.

All this contributes to the fact that there is insufficient effective demand, resulting in a long-term weakening of growth. Elsewhere, Keynes listed other factors that also point in the direction of tendencies toward stagnation. He was concerned, in particular, about the expected decline in population growth (Keynes 1937). In his view, positive growth in population is a highly significant stimulus for capital investment, since population growth raises business expectations and directly increases demand: above all, for buildings and capital goods like plant and equipment. Thus, in various places, Keynes made clear that in his opinion, investment would grow more or less at the same pace as the population. He assumed, however, that population growth could come to a standstill and finally even become negative: resulting, on the one hand, in a decline in investment demand and, on the other, in a rise in the propensity to save due to an increase in average incomes and the decline in the size of families (Keynes 1937, p. 15).[11] Moreover, the nature of future technological change would also have a negative impact on demand for investment goods. Keynes expected, namely, that technological change would be capital-saving, which would lower the capital-output ratio

---

[10]He even considered the possibility that a situation could arise in which, little by little, no more net investment would be undertaken, leading growth in the aggregate capital stock to come to a complete standstill (Keynes 1936, pp. 323–324).

[11]For a number of reasons, however, it is questionable whether fewer persons per household really does increase the propensity to save. In equipping themselves with certain consumer goods, larger households benefit from economies of scale, which, other things being equal, results in lower consumption per capita. If demographic change is responsible for the decreasing household size, then one should consider that in old-age savings are normally used up.

and also, for this reason, weaken investment demand in the long run.[12] In the end, Keynes argued, insufficient effective demand for investment and consumer goods will lead to a contraction of production, which would come to be below the full-employment level.

If we consider Keynes's overall expectations for the long-term tendencies of developed economies, falling into stagnation appears unavoidable for him. According to Keynes, a downward spiral can lead to the establishing of a new equilibrium of saving and investment at a level of production at which there is no full employment. In his view, this level of production can persist over a long period of time. Even if Keynes did not use the expression "secular stagnation," his description of this condition is very close to what will later be the usual definition of the term:

> In particular, it is an outstanding characteristic of the economic system in which we live that, whilst it is subject to severe fluctuations in respect of output and employment, it is not violently unstable. Indeed it seems capable of remaining in a chronic condition of sub-normal activity for a considerable period without any marked tendency either towards recovery or towards complete collapse. (Keynes 1936, p. 249)

Since, according to Keynes, there is no endogenous mechanism that restores full-employment equilibrium, government intervention via monetary and/or fiscal policy is required. Since monetary policy quickly comes up against its limits here, essentially just fiscal measures are available. At most, the stabilization of entrepreneurs' investment expectations or—as a last resort—public steering of investment could represent other appropriate responses in Keynes's view (Keynes 1936, p. 378).

Supposing that it is possible to solve the problem of employment in a stagnating economy (for example, by reducing labor time), Keynes—like, for example, John Stuart Mill—by no means regarded stagnation as a threat. In his essay on "Economic Possibilities for Our Grandchildren" (Keynes 1930), in particular, he gave expression to the idea that a highly developed economy that is no longer growing could be seen as one that has solved humanity's economic problem. In such a society, it would be possible to live a comfortable life and work only a few hours per week, for example. Despite this optimistic assessment, Keynes repeatedly pointed out the risks for prosperity and employment that are inherent to the expected tendencies toward stagnation. He took the view, however, that it is possible actively to counter these tendencies. To this extent, Keynes was not a stagnation pessimist like Marx, for example, who regarded the decline into stagnation and, ultimately, the collapse of the capitalist economic system as inevitable.

---

[12]"Many modern inventions are directed towards finding ways of reducing the amount of capital investment necessary to produce a given result..." Drawing on Böhm-Bawerk's terminology, Keynes continues, "I do not believe, therefore, that we can rely on current changes of technique being of the kind which tend of themselves to increase materially the average period of production" (Keynes 1937, p. 14).

Keynes's views on the long-term perspectives of economic development had a strong influence on Alvin H. Hansen. Hansen was described by Samuelson (1976, p. 25) as "the American Keynes." In the 1940s, he made what was undoubtedly the most important contribution to the development of the modern theory of stagnation. In his "rediscovery" of the problem of stagnation in 2013, Larry Summers explicitly referred to Alvin Hansen, who, like Summers today, once taught at Harvard University. It will come as no surprise, then, that Hansen's theory of stagnation, which we will examine in the next section, exhibits strong similarities to Keynes's reflections.

7.5   Alvin Hansen and Secular Stagnation

Alvin H. Hansen was initially very skeptical about Keynes's new economic thinking and only became a Keynesian in the later part of his academic career (Samuelson 1976, p. 25).[13] In a 1936 review of Keynes's *General Theory*, Hansen (1936) still had a very reserved reaction to Keynes's claim that he had developed a new general economic theory. But a few years later, his attitude to Keynes's main work had fundamentally changed. In order to contribute to the dissemination of Keynesian ideas, he even wrote a popular introduction to Keynes for economics students (Hansen 1953).

It was Alvin Hansen who introduced the term "secular stagnation" into the literature. He made clear what he meant by it when he wrote:

This is the essence of secular stagnation—sick recoveries which die in their infancy and depressions which feed on themselves and leave a hard and seemingly immovable core of unemployment. (Hansen 1939, p. 4)

The secular stagnation hypothesis is clearly based on the same theoretical principles as Keynes's analysis of equilibrium with underemployment. According to Hansen, the key problem is

... a lack of planned investment as compared to desired saving at the full-employment level of output. (Hansen 1966, p. 7)

Unlike in the approach of the present book, for Hansen, the decisive trigger for the diverging of planned saving and planned investment is not an increased propensity to save or, in other words, a growing desire to accumulate wealth on the part of households. For Hansen, the primary cause for the appearance of tendencies to stagnation is rather the deficient investment demand of firms. Constant or growing savings volume, but lack of investment opportunities are key features of what he called a mature "high-savings economy" (Hansen 1941, pp. 306–309).

---

[13]It would be reductive to classify the later Hansen as exclusively Keynesian. Institutional arrangements also play an important role in his analysis (Hansen 1941). Hence, Backhouse (2019, p. 454) rightly characterizes Hansen as "...a blend of Keynesian economics with American Institutionalism."

This interpretation is supported by the observation that Hansen discussed the possible causes of reduced investment at length, but only went into the determinants of saving more or less in passing. One hardly finds any remarks in Hansen on why the problem of a growing divergence between saving and investment could be exacerbated precisely by more saving. The main focus of his interest was clearly a lack of investment demand:

> For it is an indisputable fact that the prevailing economic system has never been able to reach reasonably full employment or the attainment of its currently realizable real income without making large investment expenditures. (Hansen 1939, p. 5)

Why did Hansen expect there to be a lack of profitable investment opportunities in the future? This becomes clear, when we recall what are, in his view, the key determinants of investment demand. He mentions: (1) The availability and discovery of new land and new resources, (2) population growth and (3) technical progress.

For Hansen, all three determinants are exogenous variables and they are necessary stimuli for investment demand. Given the economic and social developments that Hansen expected in the USA, he was skeptical, however, about the preconditions for the continued force of these factors. In light of the nearly complete settlement of the USA, the impetus that long came from expansion onto new land was going gradually to peter out.[14] Population growth rates would not always be able to remain as high as they were at the time when the USA was the most important magnet for immigration in the world. As regards technical progress, Hansen noted that its rate is negatively affected by the decline of the first two factors. He concluded that there is hence a risk of investment activity weakening in the long run. Consequently, Hansen spoke of a coming "period of investment stagnation" (Hansen 1939, p. 5). It can thus be seen that for Alvin Hansen, secular stagnation is primarily caused by a *stagnation of investment*.[15]

In his 1939 presidential address to the American Economic Association, in which he focused on the future growth prospects of the US economy in light of an expected weakening of population growth, Alvin Hansen also referred to the traditional idea that the economic system could come back into a full-employment equilibrium thanks to an endogenously triggered reduction in the interest rate. He explicitly mentioned Wicksell and Wicksell's analysis of the interest rate and the rate of profit, but he expressed strong skepticism about the interest rate being able to fulfill the function Wicksell assigns to it in light of the future evolution of the US economy (Hansen 1939, p. 5). Hansen was convinced rather that too much significance had hitherto been attached to the interest rate as a determinant of

---

[14]In this connection, Hansen often spoke of the closing of the "American frontier" (Hansen 1939, p. 9) or of the "western frontier" (Hansen 1941, p. 44). His recommendation to develop a "new economic frontier" was later frequently taken up by other authors as well (Backhouse 2019, p. 453).

[15]"The Hansen-Keynes version holds that stagnation is the result of a declining rate of return on investment" (Blaug 1962, p. 152).

investment, and he thus made clear that he intended to follow the new Keynesian point of view:

> Yet all in all, I venture to assert that the role of the rate of interest as a determinant of investment has occupied a place larger than it deserves in our thinking. (Hansen 1939, p. 5)

The only possible replacement that Hansen saw for the diminishing force of the extensive factors, land and population, was a substantial, but targeted, expansion of debt-financed public investment. He was very skeptical about the possibilities of an expansionary monetary policy. For Hansen, debt-financed public investment was thus the first choice: also because Hansen believed there were narrow limits both to what higher taxation could accomplish and—unlike Keynes—to the possibilities of income redistribution in a free market system.[16]

Hansen's address also includes a remark on the consequences of an aging population. It makes clear that Hansen considered private household demand as significant too, but that he connected this factor to investment as well:

> A stationary population with its larger proportion of old people may perhaps demand more personal services; and the composition of consumer demand will have an important influence on the quantity of capital required. (Hansen 1939, p. 7)

According to Hansen, an aging population also contributes to investment demand lagging behind the desired saving of households.

We can thus observe that Alvin Hansen expected highly developed economies to move toward secular stagnation due, above all, to diminishing investment opportunities.

It is important to stress here that Hansen did not see the decline into stagnation as inevitable. His objective was to identify the causes of a long-term weakening of growth, which he regarded as a realistic prospect, in order to be able to derive the necessary economic policy countermeasures. Paul Samuelson was Hansen's student at Harvard. In his obituary for Hansen, he addressed the still widespread misconception that Hansen, as a stagnation theorist, was automatically also a pessimist about growth:

> Those who have not read Hansen carefully have often misinterpreted him. He was never pessimistic about the growth potential of the system. Hansen believed productivity trends were as good as ever, and perhaps even better. Hansen never believed we had to stagnate: he believed that any tendency toward ineffective demand could be offset by macroeconomic policy. (Samuelson 1976, p. 30)

In order to ward off the threat of stagnation, the state can respond by increasing public investment. Hansen—like Keynes—called for public investment in this context not only as a temporary stimulus, but as the necessary precondition for long-term growth with full employment. The state has to develop new and profitable investment opportunities, in order to compensate for deficient private

---

[16]Hansen's skepticism in this regard has clear parallels to the view that we put forward, in particular, in Sect. 6.1.8 that excessively high taxes have distorting effects that can reduce growth even further.

investment. Hansen included investment in housing, transportation and resource development among such opportunities (Backhouse 2019, p. 453). According to Hansen, tax cuts could also be used to increase effective demand and stimulate investment. But he argued that the advantage of debt-financed public expenditure, as opposed to tax cuts, is that government bonds would represent stable and secure assets for private households, insurance companies and other financial institutions. In Hansen's view, it is also not a problem to place the additional bonds on the market, as they would meet with high demand in a prosperous society:

> Moreover, at higher income levels the volume of savings increases and it is possible to sell more bonds to savings institutions, government trust funds, and the public. (Hansen 1941, p. 432)

For Hansen, however, it was not only important for purely economic reasons to counteract tendencies toward stagnation. Similar to how we argue especially in the second part of this book, Hansen also pointed out that the state has an important stabilizing function for the economy and that this is a key precondition for personal freedom and real democracy (cf. Mehrling 1997, p. 121).

Keynes's and Hansen's predictions of stagnation, which originated in the 1930s and 1940s, did not come true in the further course of the twentieth century. On the contrary, starting in the 1950s, there was a historically unprecedented boom, which persisted into the 1970s. Ever since, theories of stagnation have often been dismissed as refuted by these developments. Defenders of stagnation theories counter with the argument that after Keynes and Hansen, several special factors came into play, which suspended the tendencies to stagnation or more than compensated for them. These included, in particular, the phase of rebuilding after the Second World War. Keynes had already alluded to the effect of wars, and Hansen had made it clear that his expectation of stagnation would only be fulfilled in the absence of countervailing forces. For many economies, the process of catching-up to the USA also created a growth impetus. Since many of these effects have, in the meanwhile, run their course and significantly weaker growth can be observed in most OECD countries for several decades now, it could be useful to have another look at the growth determinants identified by Keynes and Hansen. Even if Hansen's *prediction* of stagnation has turned out to be false, the course of empirical economic development after the Second World War cannot serve as proof that the theory is invalid, since Hansen always stressed that stagnation only occurs if there are no counteracting forces. "In the aftermath of the Second World War, however, such counteracting forces did exist. Among them were especially a large backlog of demand in the first post-war years, massive government spending…, and the post-war baby boom" (Anselmann 2020, p. 57). But the effects of such forces are not apparent today. In the recent past, it is rather exactly the opposite that can be observed.

7.6 Larry Summers' Rediscovery of Alvin Hansen's Stagnation Thesis

Already in 2010, Carl Christian von Weizsäcker first publicly called attention to the diverging of saving and investment that necessarily occurs under twenty-first-century conditions and to the role of the natural rate of interest (cf. the appendix to the present book). Unlike Larry Summers in his oft-cited speech at an IMF conference in 2013 (Summers 2013), von Weizsäcker did not make any reference to Alvin Hansen. Summers took up Hansen's concept of secular stagnation in his speech and connected it to the notion of the natural rate of interest, thus attracting greater public attention. He subsequently developed his reflections at somewhat greater length in several articles (Summers 2014, 2015). He himself describes his approach as the "new secular stagnation hypothesis." His point of departure is the natural rate of interest or a rate that he calls the "Full Employment Real Interest Rate" (FERIR). Summers is thus at least semantically close to the concept that already played a key role in Weizsäcker (2010, 2014) as an analytical tool for deriving a divergence of privately desired wealth and the demand for capital for investment purposes.

Summers wants to explain why, in light of a number of changed factors, there is no longer any FERIR coupled with low inflation. When Summers refers to "the interest rate" in his discussion, it is not always clear whether he referring to the money market rate, the natural rate of interest or some other interest rate. This does not make it particularly easy to follow the details of the arguments he puts forward for his hypothesis.

Summers holds the below factors responsible for tendencies toward stagnation and for a decline in the FERIR. He divides these factors into those that have a negative impact on the level of planned investment and those that have a positive impact on the level of planned saving (Summers 2014).

Among the factors dampening investment, he includes:

- demographic change,
- slower technological progress,
- a decline in the relative price of capital goods,
- a structural shift toward less capital-intensive sectors,
- less public investment and
- factors that are specifically connected to the major financial crisis of 2008–09.

According to Summers, factors that have increased households' propensity to save are:

- demographic change,
- an increasingly unequal distribution of income and
- factors specifically related to the financial crisis.

In addition, global current account imbalances would have both a negative impact on investment and a positive effect on the propensity to save.

Secular stagnation does not have a single cause for Summers, but is rather the result of a chain of different structural shocks, which emerge in an unconnected or only loosely connected fashion. The mutually reinforcing impact of these shocks has lowered the "natural rate of interest" below zero. The factors mentioned by Summers include some of the causes of stagnation that Hansen identified. Unlike Hansen, however, Summers does not put the focus on the investment side. For Summers, the causes that have brought about an increased propensity to save appear to be at least as significant as the reasons for a general weakness in investment. But the crucial difference between Hansen and Summers is that the latter makes his secular stagnation hypothesis revolve around the natural rate of interest. Although Summers explicitly refers to Hansen, he provides no justification for why he places the natural rate of interest so much at the center of his analysis. This can best be explained by the fact that the natural rate plays an important role in Neo-Keynesianism (Woodford 2003) and Summers is, broadly speaking, a Neo-Keynesian. In this sense, his having recourse to the concept is understandable. But, given the other arguments that Summers uses to support what he himself calls his demand-oriented stagnation hypothesis, is it also necessary?

Various Post-Keynesians have criticized Summers for integrating the natural rate into his stagnation thesis and accused him of having "forgotten Keynes' message that interest rates may not solve demand shortage" (Palley 2016, p. 7; Hein 2016). If we consider in detail the reasons why, on Summers' account, stagnation comes about, we cannot rid ourselves of the impression that he could have also formulated his stagnation hypothesis without referring to the natural rate:

> In contrast to Hansen, Summers's strong focus on the natural interest rate overshadows his otherwise Keynesian line of reasoning. One may say, in fact, that his secular stagnation theory could have done without the natural interest rate, as it can be maintained on purely Keynesian grounds. (Anselmann 2020, p. 86)

What Summers calls the "new secular stagnation hypothesis" can be described as new at most in the sense that he added a few more, specifically contemporary, factors to the factors that Hansen regarded as relevant. It is also new that Summers points to the danger of financial crises that could occur due to the formation of bubbles on asset markets, if central banks try to restore the balance between planned saving and investment by using monetary policy measures. But here too, it is not entirely clear why Summers assumes that the FERIR, which seems, after all, to be closely related to the concept of the natural rate, can be changed using monetary policy.[17]

---

[17]In the paper on secular stagnation that he jointly authored with Lukasz Rachel, Summers no longer uses the term "*natural* real interest rate" (Rachel and Summers 2019). Instead, already in the title, the authors speak of "*neutral* real interest rates." They thus suddenly use a term from Keynes's *General Theory* (Keynes 1936, p. 243). Just why the description and/or the concept of the interest rate has changed is not discussed in the paper.

Although for Summers there is no single cause for the new stagnation tendencies, there are, in his view, two key countermeasures for neutralizing or at least mitigating their impact. On the one hand, he advocates a more progressive tax system and transfer payments to reverse the trend toward sharply rising income inequality in the USA in recent decades. On the other, he calls for an expansionary fiscal policy, which is to be used for financing public investment. In a later paper, however, Summers and his co-author Rachel are skeptical about the prospects for success of these measures (2019, p. 44): "There is no guarantee that deficits sufficient to maintain positive neutral real rates will be associated with sustainable debt trajectories." They here allude to the important question as to whether the long-term interest rate will be above or below the growth rate, which is of decisive significance for the sustainability of public debt (Blanchard 2019).

In principle, Rachel and Summers (2019) see three possible ways in which the economy could be stabilized in the long run, given the inequality between planned saving and planned investment:

> Policymakers must, if they wish to avoid output being demand constrained, do some combination of accepting high and rising deficits and government debt levels, living with real interest rates very close to zero or negative, and finding structural policies that promote investment or reduce saving. (Rachel and Summers 2019, p. 44)

The authors suggest that these policy measures can be derived from their econometrically tested, theoretical model. But they have considerable doubts about their practical implementation: "We are not sure of their validity in practice" (ibid.). They explain their doubts by, among other things, a variety of considerations that are as much political as economic. Thus, unlike Alvin Hansen, who was an *optimist* about growth, it turns out that Larry Summers tends to be a *pessimist* about it.

Summers' contributions have triggered an intensive international debate about weaknesses in growth, stagnation and possible economic policy countermeasures. His causal analysis, like those of Keynes and Hansen, is clearly situated on the demand side.[18]

7.7 Keynes and the New Capital-Theoretical Approach

In conclusion, we want to return to the questions posed at the outset of Sect. 7.3 on the causes for the divergence between planned saving and planned investment and the consequences to which it gives rise. Our aim here was essentially to show some key differences and similarities between the core hypotheses of this book and Keynesian stagnation theories.[19] To this end, we presented the basic relationships in

---

[18]Demand-oriented stagnation hypotheses of this sort have been supplemented by significant supply-side considerations: like the arguments put forward, above all, by Gordon (2016). The latter contributions have likewise fueled the discussion about secular stagnation.

[19]On the relationship between the new capital-theoretical approach and Keynes, cf. Weizsäcker (2016).

terms of flows, in order to make the connection to the preferred analysis in this book in terms of stocks.[20]

(1) We first addressed the causes that the different theories identify for the divergence between ex ante investment I^{v} and ex ante saving S^{v}. In the previous chapters of this book, we argued in detail that the latter is primarily due to the rising desired saving of households. Private investment, on the other hand, does not increase commensurately in the long run, such that the Great Divergence between saving and investment comes about.

Keynesians look both at factors that influence saving and factors that affect investment. Nonetheless, the determinants of investment that lead to an imbalance between planned saving and planned investment are particularly frequently discussed by Keynes, Hansen and many of their followers. Whereas this book defends a specific variant of the savings glut hypothesis,[21] Keynes and first generation Keynesians tend to make the "investment drought" hypothesis the focus. Most of the recent (neo-)Keynesian secular stagnation theories, by contrast, do not place any emphasis on one side or the other.[22] They include all imaginable developments that could increase the propensity to save and reduce the propensity to invest in the long run.[23]

In Keynesian theory, it is not scarcity of natural resources that leads to weak growth, as in the stagnation theorists of classical political economy or in some neoclassical approaches (Spahn 1986; Anselmann 2020). On the contrary, from a Keynesian perspective, stagnation gives rise to a prolonged underutilization of economic resources. Whereas Keynes only discussed the problem of underemployment in the *General Theory*, post-Keynesians include underutilization of capital stock in their analysis.

Keynesian theorists highlight the characteristic features of mature, highly developed economies that can give rise to stagnation. Alvin Hansen also speaks of stagnation being typical of a "high-savings economy." The Austrian post-Keynesian and Kaleckian, Josef Steindl, assumed that the trend toward oligopolization of highly developed economies brings about a reduction in investment (Backhouse and Boianovsky 2016). In such advanced and affluent societies, saving exceeds the

---

[20]Rachel and Summers (2019, p. 43) have also alluded to the equivalence between the two approaches: "We believe that these trends are best analyzed in terms of changes in saving and investment propensities or equivalently in terms of trends in desired wealth holdings by consumers and desired capital accumulation by producers."

[21]The expression "saving glut" was made famous by a speech by then Fed chair Bernanke (2005).

[22]This is especially clear in Summers' collection of possible factors presented above. Still other factors are adduced by the authors of the contributions to a collective volume edited by Teulings and Baldwin (2014).

[23]"Three, Four... Many Secular Stagnations!"—this is how DeLong (2017) caricatures the wide variety of determinants that appear in the new debate on secular stagnation. He is also alluding to a certain arbitrariness in compiling the factors.

amount that firms need to finance their investment.[24] The fact that the planned saving of the private sector (households and firms) exceed the willingness to invest and borrow in an economy is thus "a phenomenon of prosperous, long-living societies," as Tichy (2016, p. 44) aptly observes.

(2) Secondly, we raised the issue of what happens when $S^v \neq I^r$. In orthodox neoclassical theory, the market mechanism ensures, primarily via the interest rate, that investment and saving balance and thus that a full-employment equilibrium is brought about. But there is no such automatic correction in either the new capital-theoretical approach or the Keynesian paradigm.

The reasons given to explain why the interest rate mechanism does not work are very different, but ultimately they lead to practically the same result. In the Keynesian analytical framework, household saving does not, *in principle*, free up funds for investment. An increase in saving merely redistributes already existing monetary resources: here, for example, from firms to households. The total liquid resources available are not changed, which is why interest rates will also not react to the increased saving of the household sector. In the new capital-theoretical approach for which we argue in this book, the private sector exhibits a structural excess of saving over investment even when the interest rate is zero. Since nominal interest rates cannot fall (much) below zero, a high level of employment can only be achieved by negative real interest rates or, in other words, inflation. Hence, whereas in the Keynesian paradigm, the interest rate cannot eliminate a disequilibrium between saving and investment for essential reasons, in the new capital-theoretical approach presented here, the interest rate de facto can no longer fulfill this function under the conditions prevailing in the twenty-first century.

The consequences that follow if fiscal policy fails to act are also described in an almost identical way. If there is a divergence between planned saving and investment—or, in other words, between desired wealth, on the one hand, and existing wealth, on the other—restoring the I-S equilibrium without additional public debt would mean an end to prosperity, price stability and full employment. The recessionary adjustment processes lead to what Keynes called an underemployment equilibrium: namely an economy that is characterized by persistent unemployment.

(3) Thirdly, we derived from this the question of whether government intervention is necessary, useful or harmful. In the orthodox view of a self-regulating market, the state's role is limited to just a few functions in the economy. Prolonged fiscal intervention is rejected on the grounds that productive private investment will be "crowded out" by public investment that tends to be less productive. This argument is based on the assumption of a fundamental scarcity of capital, requiring an efficient allocation of resources to maximize prosperity. The main focus of this book is the hypothesis that there is no longer any scarcity of capital under twenty-first-century conditions, but rather precisely the

---

[24]There is surprisingly little reference made to Steindl's stagnation theory in the current debate on secular stagnation. Hein (2016) and Anselmann (2020, pp. 195–239) represent recent exceptions.

opposite. The key challenge now is to confront the savings glut resulting from private individuals' increasing desire to accumulate wealth. We have argued that the state is the only actor capable of absorbing these savings. Moreover, there are few other ways for the state to respond, so long as its citizens are not interested in using their longer lifespans to extend their active *working* lives to the same extent. This is what gives rise to the desire of citizens to accumulate more private wealth—or the necessity for them to do so—and the state has to respond by a commensurate increase of explicit and/or implicit public debt to ward off the threat of depression.

There is a necessity for government intervention also from the Keynesian perspective. Since the market mechanism and the interest rate are not able to prevent an underemployment equilibrium from coming into being, economic policy countermeasures are needed. In the view of most Keynesians, monetary policy cannot do what is required; hence, fiscal policy instruments have to be used.

Thus, the response to the phenomenon of a structural excess of saving or—the other side of the coin that a Keynesian would perhaps prefer to show—the lagging of aggregate effective demand behind aggregate supply largely coincides in both the Keynesian and the new capital-theoretical approaches: The state has to fill the gap by going into debt!

(4) The fourth question addressed the specific instruments that the state should use in reacting to a structural excess of private saving over private investment. In this book, we concentrate on presenting the finding that there is an excess of saving, on deriving and situating it theoretically, and on providing empirical support for it. In our opinion, the only possible response to the Great Divergence between saving and investment in the twenty-first century is an increase in public debt that fills the gap. Public dis-saving can be brought about either by generalized tax cuts or by increasing public spending. The use to which additional public revenue is put is a secondary matter in this connection and is not the subject of this book. At one place, we will discuss what seems to us to be one sensible use for these funds in the international context (cf. Chap. 11). But beyond that, we will not deal any further with the issue of the possible uses of additional public revenue. The second part of the book will, however, examine other economic policy consequences and options resulting from the Great Divergence.

There is a need for government intervention also from the Keynesian perspective. Depending on what is considered to be the main cause of the I-S disequilibrium and the resulting threat of stagnation, different measures are required. These range from economic policy measures for stimulating consumption or diminishing the propensity to save to subsidies for private investment and increased public investment.

Almost all the possible public measures result in public debt also rising. Thus, in the Keynesian paradigm as well, the state is the key authority responsible for overcoming the threat of stagnation or at least mitigating tendencies toward it. An overview of the core Keynesian stagnation literature shows that the main aim in the Keynesian framework is to reduce the gap between planned investment and planned saving by way of public policy measures. In the Keynesian paradigm, the resulting public debt is more the *consequence* of government intervention, rather than, as in our case, the actual *instrument* for solving the problem.

To sum up, we can see that, despite all the differences in the theoretical framework and some differences in the details, there are a number of parallels between the Keynesian account of the causes and consequences of the structural divergence of planned private saving and investment, on the one hand, and, the new capital-theoretical conception, on the other. The key theoretical difference concerns the concept of the natural rate of interest, which does not even exist in the former and is analytically fundamental for the latter. But there are similarities especially in the view that, under twenty-first-century conditions, it is essential for the state to act to avoid instability and long-term underemployment. There is also large agreement on the important role that has to be played by public debt to close the gap between planned private saving and investment.

References

Anselmann, Christina. 2020. *Secular Stagnation Theories. A Historical and Contemporary Analysis with a Focus on the Distribution of Income.* Cham: Springer.

Backhouse, Roger E. 2019. Alvin Harvey Hansen. In *The Elgar Companion to John Maynard Keynes*, eds. Robert W. Dimand and Harald Hagemann, 451–455. Cheltenham: Edward Elgar.

Backhouse, Roger E. and Mauro Boianovsky. 2016. Secular stagnation: The history of a macroeconomic heresy. *European Journal of the History of Economic Thought* 23 (6): 946–970.

Bernanke, Ben. 2005. *The global saving glut and the U.S. current account deficit.* Speech 77. Washington (D.C.): Board of Governors of the Federal Reserve System.

Blanchard, Olivier. 2019. Public Debt and Low Interest Rates, AEA Presidential Lecture 2019. *American Economic Review* 109 (4): 1197–1229.

Blaug, Mark. 1962. *Economic Theory in Retrospect.* Homewood (IL): Richard D. Irwin.

Bofinger, Peter and Mathias Ries. 2017. *Excess saving and low interest rates: Theory and Empirical Evidence.* CEPR Discussion Paper 12111. London: Centre for Economic Policy Research. https://cepr.org/active/publications/discussion_papers/dp.php?dpno=12111. Accessed: 29 December 2018.

DeLong, J. Bradford. 2017. *Three, Four... Many Secular Stagnations!* https://www.brad-ford-delong.com/2017/01/three-four-many-secular-stagnations.html. Accessed: 28 October 2018.

Gordon, Robert J. 2016. *The Rise and Fall of American Growth. The U.S. Standard of Living since the Civil War.* Princeton (NJ): Princeton University Press.

Hansen, Alvin H. 1936. Mr. Keynes on Underemployment Equilibrium. *Journal of Political Economy* 4 (5): 667–686.

Hansen, Alvin H. 1939. Economic Progress and Declining Population Growth. *American Economic Review* 29 (1): 1–15.

Hansen, Alvin H. 1941. *Fiscal Policy and Business Cycles*. London: Allen and Unwin.

Hansen, Alvin H. 1953. *A Guide to Keynes*. London: McGraw Hill.

Hansen, Alvin H. 1966. Stagnation and Under-Employment Equilibrium. *Rostra Economica Amstelodamensia*. 15 November 1966: 7–9.

Hein, Eckhard. 2016. Secular stagnation or stagnation policy? Steindl after Summers. *PSL Quarterly Review* 69 (276): 3–47.

Keynes, John Maynard. 1919 [1971]. The Economic Consequences of the Peace. In *The Collected Writings of John Maynard Keynes*, vol. 2: The Economic Consequences of the Peace, eds. Elizabeth Johnson and Donald Moggridge. London and Basingstoke: Macmillan.

Keynes, John Maynard. 1930 [1972]. Economic Possibilities for Our Grandchildren. In *The Collected Writings of John Maynard Keynes*, vol. 9: Essays in Persuasion, eds. Elizabeth Johnson and Donald Moggridge, 321–332. London and Basingstoke: Macmillan.

Keynes, John Maynard. 1936. *The General Theory of Employment, Interest and Money*. London: Macmillan.

Keynes, John Maynard. 1937. Some economic consequences of a declining population. *The Eugenics Review* 29 (1): 13–17. Reprinted 1973. In *The Collected Writings of John Maynard Keynes*, vol. 14: The General Theory and After (Part II: Defence and Development), eds. Elizabeth Johnson and Donald Moggridge, 124–133. London and Basingstoke: Macmillan.

Keynes, John Maynard. 1943 [1980]. The Long-Term Problem of Full Employment. In *The Collected Writings of John Maynard Keynes*, vol. XXVII: Activities 1940–1946. Shaping the Post-War World: Employment and Commodities, eds. Elizabeth Johnson and Donald Moggridge, 320–325. London and Basingstoke: Macmillan.

Kurz, Heinz D. 2017. *Economic Thought: A Brief History*. New York: Columbia University Press.

Meade, James. 1975. The Keynesian Revolution. In *Essays on John Maynard Keynes*, ed. Milo Keynes, 82–88. New York (NY): Cambridge University Press.

Mehrling, Perry G. 1997. *The Money Interest and the Public Interest: American Monetary Thought, 1920–1970*. Cambridge (MA): Harvard University Press.

Palley, Thomas I. 2016. Why Negative Interest Rate Policy (NIRP) Is Ineffective And Dangerous. *Real-World Economics Review* 76. http://www.paecon.net/PAEReview/issue76/Palley76.pdf. Accessed: 31 October 2018.

Palley, Thomas I. 2019. The fallacy of the natural rate of interest and zero lower bound economics: why negative interest rates may not remedy Keynesian unemployment. *Review of Keynesian Economics* 7 (2): 151–170.

Rachel, Lukasz and Lawrence H. Summers. 2019. On Falling Neutral Real Rates, Fiscal Policy, and the Risk of Secular Stagnation. *Brookings Papers on Economic Activity* March 4: 1–66.

Samuelson, Paul A. 1976. Alvin Hansen as a Creative Economic Theorist. *Quarterly Journal of Economics* 90 (1): 24–31.

Schumpeter, Joseph A. 1954. *History of Economic Analysis*. New York (NY): Oxford University Press.

Spahn, Heinz-Peter. 1986. *Stagnation in der Geldwirtschaft. Dogmengeschichte, Theorie und Politik aus keynesianischer Sicht*. Frankfurt am Main and New York (NY): Campus.

Summers, Lawrence H. 2013. *Speech at IMF Fourteenth Annual Research Conference in Honor of Stanley Fischer*. 8 November 2013. Washington (D.C.): International Monetary Fund.

Summers, Lawrence H. 2014. US Economic Prospects: Secular Stagnation, Hysteresis, and the Zero Lower Bound. *Business Economics* 49: 65–73.

Summers, Lawrence H. 2015. Demand Side Secular Stagnation. *American Economic Review: Papers and Proceedings* 105 (5): 60–65.

Teulings, Coen and Richard Baldwin (eds.). 2014. *Secular Stagnation: Facts, Causes and Cures.* London: CEPR Press. http://www.voxeu.org/sites/default/files/Vox_secular_stagnation.pdf. Accessed: 6 December 2014.

Tichy, Gunther. 2016. Vom Kapitalmangel zum Savings Glut: Ein Phänomen der Wohlstands-gesellschaft. In *Keynes, Schumpeter und die Zukunft der entwickelten kapitalistischen Volkswirtschaften*, eds. Harald Hagemann and Jürgen Kromphardt, Schriften der Keynes Gesellschaft, vol. 9, 33–68. Marburg: Metropolis-Verlag.

Weizsäcker, Carl Christian von. 2010. Das Janusgesicht der Staatsschulden. *Frankfurter Allgemeine Zeitung*. 4 June 2010: 12 (published in the appendix to this book as "The Two Faces of Public Debt").

Weizsäcker, Carl Christian von. 2014. Public Debt and Price Stability. *German Economic Review* 15 (1): 42–61.

Weizsäcker, Carl Christian von. 2016. Keynes und das Ende der Kapitalknappheit. In *Keynes, Schumpeter und die Zukunft der entwickelten kapitalistischen Volkswirtschaften*, eds. Harald Hagemann and Jürgen Kromphardt, Schriften der Keynes Gesellschaft, vol. 9, 21–31. Marburg: Metropolis-Verlag.

Wicksell, Knut. 1936 [1898]. *Interest and Prices: A Study of the Causes Regulating the Value of Money*, trans. R. F. Kahn. London: Macmillan.

Woodford, Michael. 2003. *Interest and Prices: Foundations of a Theory of Monetary Policy.* Princeton (NJ): Princeton University Press.

Concluding Remarks on the Negative Natural Rate of Interest

8

Abstract

The Great Divergence: The period of production T is not rising anymore. The "waiting period" Z is rising over time with the rising standard of living and rising life expectancy, and this is the case worldwide. In the interest of full employment, the public debt period D has to compensate for this divergence: $T = Z - D$. Using an extrapolation procedure that we have developed and the available empirical data, we calculate total private wealth in the OECD plus China region. Net public debt already accounts for nearly half of private wealth today. COVID-19 increases the optimal steady-state public debt period. Both our theory and our empirical findings are increasingly confirmed by the work of other economists: for example, by Lawrence Summers' secular stagnation thesis and by the study of Jordà, Schularick and others on the secular evolution of private wealth.

8.1 The Great Divergence

In the first part of our book, we have found that almost one half of private wealth in the OECD plus China region consists of net claims on the state. Using our analytical method, we arrived at the conclusion, moreover, that there is a secular increase in the share of net public debt in total private wealth. We will first summarize the procedure that leads to this result. Given the numerous trees, this review is also intended to help the reader still to recognize the forest as such.

Our point of departure is the reflection that we can use the method of steady-state analysis that is commonly employed in capital theory. (Cf. Chap. 2 and Weizsäcker 2021.) Steady-state analysis has a long tradition in economic theory: starting with the Physiocrats, whose most important representative, François Quesnay, published the *Tableau Économique* (Quesnay 1758), and continuing through Adam Smith,

© The Author(s) 2021

C. C. von Weizsäcker and H. M. Krämer, *Saving and Investment in the Twenty-First Century*, https://doi.org/10.1007/978-3-030-75031-2_8

who used the physics of Isaac Newton as his model, in order to derive the "natural prices" of commodities in his *Wealth of Nations* (Smith 1776). This tradition went on then via Ricardo, John Stuart Mill, Marx, Walras, Marshall, and Böhm-Bawerk up to Solow (1956) and Debreu (1959) and finally to the present day. But this sort of steady-state analysis or equilibrium analysis is also a pillar of every natural science. We can mention ecology as an example. Ecology is the science of equilibria in living nature. The concept of sustainability, which has become a key objective of government policy nowadays, is derived from it.

On the basis of a steady-state analysis, it is possible to recognize secular trends. We do this by using *two time concepts*: the period of production T and the waiting period Z. The equilibrium between supply of and demand for capital gets established via the real interest rate r and the public debt period D. The latter is the third time concept and it serves as the bridge between the first two: At the optimal interest rate $r = g$, the equation $T = Z - D$ corresponds to full employment equilibrium.

We find that the *Great Divergence* is a secular trend: Whereas the period of production, i.e., relative capital requirements, is almost constant over time, the waiting period Z, i.e., relative capital supply, has a secular tendency to increase. Over time, a gap thus comes into being: a growing divergence between Z and T. This has to be bridged by a growing public debt period D.

There are two reasons for the *Great Divergence*:

One is the limit to the "greater productivity of more roundabout production" (Böhm-Bawerk). We also call this the "*limit to the greater productivity of more complexity.*" There is a danger of overcomplexity. There is the danger of excessive division of labor, of overspecialization. And it seems that an average time lag of a few years between the original input (labor and land) and the ultimate output (consumer goods) marks the degree of roundaboutness that maximizes the yield of the original factors of production. Beyond this point, productivity goes downhill again.

One of the reasons for this in turn—perhaps indeed the main reason—is technical progress: the increase in useful knowledge to which human civilization constantly gives rise. Due to this constant changing of our knowledge, the intermediate products comprising the real capital stock become outdated. Hence, they cannot be allowed to become "too old," and they are replaced. This is why there are limits to how much capital can be usefully tied up in the production process, and this is why *the capital coefficient tends to be constant over time*: which is to say, why *the period of production tends to be constant over time*. The low interest rates that have prevailed for some time now suggest that the OECD plus China economic area that we are examining is already close to the degree of roundaboutness of production that maximizes the yield of the original factors of production, labor and land.

The second reason for the Great Divergence also has to do with change or progress in our knowledge. This is the "*law of the increasing future-directedness of human action as prosperity increases.*" The higher the level of prosperity, the greater is relative desired wealth: i.e., the ratio between planned wealth and current consumption. We call this ratio the *wealth coefficient*. This law of a growing wealth coefficient is the same as the law of a growing private waiting period Z. At the prosperity-maximizing rate of interest $r = g$, the overall period of production T is equal to the *overall waiting period $Z - D$*. The latter is the sum of the private waiting period Z and the public waiting period—D, which corresponds to the normally negative net asset position of the state. Since the period of production and the overall economic waiting period are equal in the optimum, we also call the corresponding equation $T = Z - D$ the *Fundamental Equation of Steady-State Capital Theory*. (Cf. Chap. 2 and Weizsäcker 2021.)

The rising private waiting period reflects the rise in *life expectancy* as prosperity increases. For nowhere in the world is there a parallel rise in the average retirement age. Hence, the time during which people receive retirement benefits is rising, and parallel to it, so too is the saving rate during their active working lives. The savings triangle gives graphic expression to these relationships (cf. Sects. 3.1 and 3.2). Despite the simplification it involves, it provides, for example, a good approximation of the facts for Germany.

Globally rising life expectancy is thus a key aspect of the Great Divergence. At the same time, it is also a side effect of the rising standards of living in many poorer countries: in particular, in developing countries. This is the part of the world that does not belong to the OECD plus China region that is the focus of our investigations. In the course of the twenty-first century, however, we can expect that private desired wealth in a significant number of countries in this part of the world will also come to exceed capital requirements. It is already the case today that more wealth is exported from these countries into the OECD plus China region than vice-versa (cf. Sect. 3.11).

8.2 Implicit Public Debt

Even today, the Great Divergence is far from being acknowledged as such by all economists. This is because up to now implicit public debt has not generally been recognized as public debt, including in the official statistics. As our investigations show, especially in Chap. 6, explicit net public debt for the OECD plus China region is merely the tip of the iceberg. Floating in the water underneath it is the far larger remainder of the iceberg in the form of implicit public debt. The latter is to a great extent a reflection of the welfare state that has been developed in this area.

Social security protection for old age, illness and unemployment is a core component of the modern welfare state. The protection that citizens are afforded by social security is tantamount to protection by way of property ownership. Social security retirement benefits make this particularly clear. The retirement system creates property in the form of entitlements vis-à-vis the state. If, analogously to private insurers, the state had formed reserve funds to cover these entitlements, then the former would offset the latter and social security would not have led to additional net public debt. But in the overwhelming majority of cases, no such reserve funds have been formed. And for good reason, in our opinion. Such reserve funds would have caused a massive investment crisis in the OECD plus China region. They would have become a threat to the very people they were supposed to help. The market system would not have been able to cope with the investment pressure. Individual citizens would have found it difficult or downright impossible to plan for their futures. At best, considerable and prolonged inflation could have transformed *this* particular investment crisis into a *different sort of* investment crisis. Instead of an oversupply of capital, the high inflation would have made it impossible to secure the value of assets. Real capital would have flowed massively into economically unproductive investments.

8.3 The Natural Rate of Interest Is Negative

On our estimate, the net position of citizens vis-à-vis the state is about six times the annual consumption of the population in the OECD plus China region (cf. Sect. 6.2) —at a real discount rate of zero, in any case. We can infer from this that the natural rate of interest is negative. The natural rate is, after all, the real full-employment rate that would apply, if citizens did not have any net position vis-à-vis the state (cf. Chap. 1). At a real interest rate of zero and without any net position of citizens vis-à-vis the state, there would be an enormous excess of capital supply as compared to capital demand at full employment. This excess would put pressure on returns, which would thus fall into the negative.

It is pointless to speculate about how far into the minuses the real interest rate would slide. Once the real rate becomes clearly negative, peoples' investment behavior changes. High inflation changes their subjective perception of what a relatively safe investment is. So long as inflation plays no role or only a minor one, investment in financial assets like savings accounts, fixed term deposits or highly rated bonds is regarded as the safest investment. If investors are very conscious of inflation, then certain tangible assets, like gold or real estate, are regarded as the safer investments. The "flight to tangible assets" often leads to investments that do not only have a negative overall economic impact, but whose "best available" return for the investor is in fact negative as well. If the state does not offer a better alternative by way of a policy of stable money and public deficits, people's strong orientation toward the future comes to nothing, disappointments are a foregone conclusion, inequality in the distribution of wealth is exacerbated, and the market economy will be voted out at the ballot box. Paradoxically, this failure of government then drives people into the arms of "Big Brother." Like in times of need, their attitude toward the future gets transformed from that of carefully planning for far-off goals to "run for your lives!": from an attitude of personal responsibility and providing for one's family to an attitude of doing whatever it takes to survive even at the expense of one's fellow citizens.

Under these conditions, when the Great Divergence has already come about, it is pointless to speculate about where exactly the negative natural interest rate is situated.

8.4   The Distribution of Wealth

The conventional view of wealth that has prevailed up to now also means a distorted view of the *distribution of wealth*. For implicit wealth in the form of entitlements to future retirement benefits and healthcare services is obviously distributed differently than the wealth that has been hitherto considered.

In a cross-sectional view, the saving rate for voluntary saving rises with disposable income and already available wealth. This applies even if we take into account the "permanent income hypothesis." These observations hold for all the OECD countries and also for China. The facts they describe stabilize or exacerbate the unequal distribution of wealth. This is reinforced by the fact that, on average, greater wealth also generates higher returns due to a greater willingness to assume risks and to economies of scale in portfolio management (Piketty 2014, Chap. 12).

Progressive income, property and estate taxes dampen the tendency toward greater inequality (Krämer 2020). But the existence of tax havens creates opportunities for avoiding progressive taxation. It is, above all, the very wealthy who can make use of these opportunities. Persons whose wealth is medium-sized and is often tied up in a family-owned business have far fewer opportunities of this sort.

Entitlements to future retirement benefits are, however, much more equally distributed than the classical wealth that we have just discussed. We are not able to provide any data here on the Gini coefficient for entitlement assets in the OECD plus China region. Nonetheless, it is clear that it must be considerably lower than for conventionally defined wealth. Determining the overall distribution of wealth in the OECD countries and China is an important research project that remains to be done. We are aware, however, of a comparative study on Germany and the USA that refers to 2013 (Bönke et al. 2019). According to this study, the Gini coefficient for conventionally defined wealth is 0.889 in the USA and 0.755 in Germany. For all wealth, including public retirement benefit entitlements, the Gini coefficient is 0.700 in the USA and 0.508 in Germany.

Given the secular trend toward an increasing share of implicit wealth in total wealth, it cannot be ruled out that, contrary to the claims of many commentators (cf., for example, Piketty 2014), inequality in the distribution of wealth has not increased as much as is often presumed.

8.5   Private Wealth at a Real Interest Rate of Zero

In the context of our thesis of a negative natural rate of interest, we are especially interested in the situation of the smallest possible non-negative real interest rate: i.e., a real rate of zero. For, as Carl Christian von Weizsäcker has demonstrated in

Weizsäcker (2021), every equilibrium rate above the natural rate is connected to positive net public debt and every equilibrium rate below the natural rate is connected to negative net public debt (Weizsäcker 2021, Theorem 4). Hence, positive public debt at a real interest rate of zero means that the natural rate must be negative.

In Chap. 6 on private wealth in the form of net public debt, we were able to provide a fairly reliable estimate of public debt at a zero real interest rate using a second degree Taylor approximation. This extrapolation from a real interest rate of three percent per year to a real interest rate of zero percent was possible, because the statistical offices of the European Union member states have reported present values of retirement benefit entitlements not only for a real discount rate of three percent per year, but also for four percent and two percent. In an excursus in Chap. 6, we showed how, on the basis of this data, a second-order Taylor approximation can be used to estimate the value at a real interest rate of zero. The result for the OECD plus China region is that if we take the sum of explicit public debt and the zero interest rate value of assets in the form of entitlements to public retirement and healthcare benefits, the total comes to 6.26 times annual consumption in this area.

We stress that this is only an estimate. The level of entitlements as a function of the steady-state real interest rate is not a quadratic function. Hence, a second-order Taylor approximation always deviates from the real values. Experience has shown, however, that the approximation error in an extrapolation over only two percentage points (from 2% annually to zero percent) is not very big.

We are not able to undertake a similar approximation for real capital and land, the other components of private wealth, because the relevant data is not available. In both cases, however, we are able to make other estimates by way of a more detailed analysis of the facts.

Let us start with land. The valuation of land sometimes includes natural resources it contains, like coal, oil, natural gas and ores, among other things. The estimate of a value of land amounting to 1.94 times annual consumption is based on official national figures on land value. The latter are derived from transaction prices when property changes hands. We presume that these valuations correspond to a real interest rate of two percent or three percent per year. In what follows, we assume that the official land value figures thus correspond to an interest rate that is equal to the growth rate in the OECD plus China region: i.e., $r = g$. We can expect higher values to result, if we use a risk-free real interest rate of zero. We undertook an estimate in Sect. 5.1.11. The following point is important here: The risk premium α on land is higher, the lower the risk-free rate of interest. This is because the lower the risk-free rate of interest is, the greater is the valuation risk due to possible interest rate changes. Thus, in our mathematical example in Sect. 5.1.11, the risk premium rises from 5.7% per year at a risk-free interest rate $r = g$ to 7.2% per year at a real interest rate of zero. It follows that in moving from $r = g$ to a zero real interest rate, the valuation of land in the OECD plus China region rises by 30%—and thus amounts to 2.52 times annual consumption instead of 1.94 times.

Similarly great revaluations are not to be expected in the case of real capital. It is useful to recall here that when $r = g$, the capital coefficient (= real capital divided by steady-state annual consumption) is equal to the period of production T (cf.

Sect. 2.5). Now, it is of interest to know how the period of production reacts when the interest rate changes. There are two conflicting effects here. On the one hand, there is a substitution effect. Using the concept of the coefficient of intertemporal substitution ψ, Carl Christian von Weizsäcker has shown in Weizsäcker (2021) that, as a result of a substitution effect, the period of production has the tendency to rise when the interest rate is falling (Weizsäcker 2021, Chap. 3, Sect. 2). Since, however, the period of production is calculated using present values, changes in interest rates also have a valuation effect on it. This valuation effect (which, by the way, has something to do with the Sraffa school's "Wicksell effect," but is not identical to it) goes in the opposite direction: With a falling interest rate, and bracketing the substitution effect, the period of production falls. (See Weizsäcker 2021, Chap. 2, Sect. 5.)

It is conceivable that these two effects exactly offset each another, so that the period of production T turns out to be constant. As shown in Weizsäcker (2021), this is not a far-fetched assumption: a Solow production function with a constant intertemporal coefficient of substitution ψ entails that, *empirically*, this ψ must be around 1 (Weizsäcker 2021, Chap. 3, Sect. 7). This is connected to the fact that, as discussed here at numerous points, the capital coefficient does not exhibit any secular trend. But precisely if this is so, then it is also the case that T is no longer dependent on r: that the substitution effect and the valuation effect neutralize each other. The relevant Solow production function runs as follows:

$$Tf(k) = k\{1 + \ln \bar{k} - \ln k\}$$

Here, k is the capital stock per worker (or the capital intensity). In the case of Harrod-neutral technical progress, k refers to a labor "efficiency unit." The variable $\bar{k}$ is the value of k at which labor productivity is maximized. T is the period of production, which is a constant in this case. The marginal productivity of capital is zero when $k = \bar{k}$. Now, let k^* be the value of k at which the marginal productivity of capital is equal to the growth rate of the economy. Let c^* be consumption per worker when $r = g$. Now, $rT = f'(k)T = (\ln \bar{k} - \ln k)$ is thus $gT = (\ln \bar{k} - \ln k^*)$. It follows that

$$ln\bar{k} = lnk^* + gT \text{ or } \bar{k} = k^* e^{gT}$$

In Chap. 4, we found that $k^*/c^* = 4.03$. By the Böhm-Bawerk formula in Weizsäcker (2021), however, this is equivalent to the period of production T (Weizsäcker 2021, Chap. 2, Sect. 3). The growth rate of the economy is set at three percent per year. This results in a value of $gT = 0.1209$ or, rounded, 0.12. Thus, at $r = 0$, we have the following approximation for the capital stock:

$$\bar{k} = k^* e^{012} \approx k^*(1 + 0.12) = k^* 1.12$$

Hence, at a real interest rate of zero, we obtain an addition to the real capital stock of around 12%, bringing its number to 4.51 in units of annual consumption.

If we take the sum of the two estimates for the values of real capital and land at a real interest rate of zero, we thus obtain *4.51 + 2.52 = 7.03 annual consumption units*, whereby consumption is here consumption at a zero real interest rate.

8.6   The Shift in Optimal Public Debt After COVID-19

As we have seen, the optimal public debt period D equals the difference between the waiting period Z and the sum of the production period T and the land value period L, all three evaluated at the optimal risk free rate of interest $r = g$. How does the COVID-19 pandemic influence Z, T and L? How does COVID-19 thereby influence the optimal level of D? The answer comes from a steady-state analysis, which differs from the analysis of the optimal stabilizing fiscal policy. The latter is important for short-term fiscal operations. However, steady-state analysis provides guidance on the likely path of long-term real rates of interest. This guidance is necessary for the optimal stabilizing fiscal policy.

Due to the pandemic, for any given r we expect the steady-state level of Z to shift upward and the steady-state level of T and of L to shift downward. We then should observe a higher steady-state optimal public debt period D.

We first discuss steady-state Z. The pandemic is an unexpected shock for effective demand and for effective supply. On average, people have lost money and welfare. Their "animal spirits" adapt to a world of substantially higher uncertainty. This should raise the ratio between wealth and annual consumption to which they aspire. But, at a real rate of interest $r = g$, this ratio equals the waiting period Z. In short, the pandemic induced shift in animal spirits raises the waiting period Z. A different way of expressing the same conclusion is as follows. Due to the pandemic, the representative consumer expects a lower level of future well-being, mainly because of a higher subjectively felt uncertainty regarding developments to come. The representative consumer thereby restricts present day consumption. He or she will only come back to the old level of consumption after having accumulated additional reserves.

What about a shock to T? The pandemic provides a heavy push toward digitalization. Home office is an example. "Amazonization" of shopping habits is a second example. A substantial portion of this digitalization push will remain after the pandemic has receded.

The secular trend toward increased digitalization is technical progress. In this respect, economists interpret it analogously to the industrial revolution of the last 250 years. Like the latter, digitalization steadily, step by step, changes our lives; and, most of the time, in hindsight, we do not want to go back by repeating the steps in reverse.

Does technical progress in the case of digitalization have a bias? And if so, is it labor-saving or is it capital-saving technical progress? If, on the macrolevel, we use the Solow production function, the answer is not clear. To put it differently, it is difficult to find out whether, on average, digitalization is neutral or labor-saving or capital-saving according to the Hicks definition of these terms.

However, as we will now show, the answer is very clear for the Harrod definitions of bias in technical progress. The Harrod approach fits our Neo-Böhm-Bawerkian theory. Using our theory, we can show that digitalization is capital-saving and land-saving.

We separate the production system of the economy into two sectors: sector 1 is the "analog" sector; sector 2 is the digital sector. We may then construct a two-by-two input/output matrix, showing the input/output coefficients from one sector to itself and to the other sector. Both sectors also have labor-input coefficients and land-input coefficients. In addition, the sectors are characterized by a period of production T_1 or, respectively, T_2. And there is a "direct labor + land-input period of production" τ_1 or, respectively, τ_2. The direct labor + land-input period of production of a sector shows the average time lag between the direct labor and land inputs and the sector output. In our Neo-Böhm-Bawerkian model, we work with continuous time. Let a_{ij} be the steady-state input/output coefficient of industry j for input i. Let b_i be the direct labor and land-input coefficient of industry i. We then obtain the following system of linear equations for the two industry-specific periods of production

$$T_1 = b_1\tau_1 + a_{11}T_1 + a_{21}T_2$$

$$T_2 = b_2\tau_2 + a_{12}T_1 + a_{22}T_2$$

We should note that the steady-state coefficients b_i and a_{ij} are not the technical coefficients of a Leontief input/output system, although they are related to the latter. The best way to understand them is by considering them as the economic value of the deliveries from workers and landowners to the industry per value unit of industry output (for b_i) and, respectively, from industry i to industry j per unit of output of industry j (for a_{ij}). This means that these coefficients also depend on the rate of growth g of the system and on r, the rate of interest. (Remember that the period of production defined in Chap. 2 and in Weizsäcker 2021 also depends on the steady-state rate of interest.) But for our present purposes, we do not have to go into the details of that dependence on g and on r, the rate of interest.

We also want to point out that the "direct labor and land inputs" b_i are not the same as those in the Leontief input/output system. There, they can be identified with the direct labor inputs of the firms in sector i. In a Leontief system, one frequently uses discrete time periods and then models the economy as if the inputs would have to be available exactly one period earlier than the corresponding outputs. Here, in our system, the direct labor and land input coefficient b_i is the ratio between the "wages and land rents" paid in sector i and the output value of the sector. Correspondingly, the industry specific period of production τ_i is the average time lag between the labor and land input in this sector and the final output of the sector. Thus, if for example, the sector would comprise the economy at large, the "direct" labor and land-input period of production τ_i would be equal to the period of production of the economy at large, T. The mix of labor and land inputs is no problem in this set-up. The direct period of production τ_i is a weighted average of the direct labor period of production and the land period of production. The weights are the values of these two inputs, expressed as present values. Indeed, since both labor inputs and land inputs are heterogeneous goods anyway, the same weighing procedure has already been implicitly applied for an aggregate of the labor period of production and of the land period of production.

Above, we have a system of two linear equations with the unknowns T_1 and T_2 and the given direct labor and land-input periods of production τ_1 and τ_2. The solution then is this

$$T_1 = \frac{b_1\tau_1(1 - a_{22}) + a_{21}b_2\tau_2}{(1 - a_{11})(1 - a_{22}) - a_{12}a_{21}}$$

$$T_2 = \frac{b_2\tau_2(1 - a_{11}) + a_{12}b_1\tau_1}{(1 - a_{11})(1 - a_{22}) - a_{12}a_{21}}$$

The period of production for the production system as a whole is then

$$T = (1 - \delta)T_1 + \delta T_2$$

with δ symbolizing the value share of the digital sector 2 in the production system in terms of its final output (consumption goods).

We now investigate the following special case: the relative "digital content" of the consumption goods is the same as the relative "digital content" of all intermediate goods, including intermediate digital goods. This assumption implies the following equations for the input/output coefficients. For some common value $\mu \geq 0$ we have

$$a_{11} = \mu(1 - \delta)^2; \quad a_{12} = \mu(1 - \delta)\delta$$

$$a_{21} = \mu\delta(1 - \delta); \quad a_{22} = \mu\delta^2$$

Moreover, the "labor" coefficient b_i of sector i must fill the gap between unity and the costs of the intermediate inputs: remember that the coefficients are expressed in money units, and the "labor" coefficients include land rents, as well as profits beyond the interest costs of the capital employed. Thus

$$b_1 = 1 - a_{11} - a_{21} = 1 - \mu(1 - \delta)$$

$$b_2 = 1 - a_{12} - a_{22} = 1 - \mu\delta$$

Using these equations, by some straightforward calculation, we can obtain the following three results.

For $\delta = 0$ we obtain $T = \tau_1$. For $\delta = 1$ we obtain $T = \tau_2$.
For $\delta = \frac{1}{2}$ we have $T = \frac{\tau_1 + \tau_2}{2}$.

This looks like a linear relation between δ and T. We may then approximate other values of T by linear interpolation. The equation then is

$$T \approx (1 - \delta)\tau_1 + \delta\tau_2$$

We now show that τ_2 is substantially smaller than τ_1.

Output of the digital sector mainly consists of software and a little bit of associated hardware like smartphones, PCs and fiberglass communication lines. The overwhelming part of the workforce employed in sector 2 produces and manages software. And thus the main part of the capital employed consists of software. One thing is important: the production function of software is quite different from the production function of hardware.

The main part of physical capital produced in sector 1 (the "analog" sector) consists of buildings, which tend to be long-lived. The construction cost of a single building is roughly half the construction cost of two buildings of the same size; and it is roughly one percent of the construction cost of one hundred buildings of the same size. Due to wear and tear and due to obsolescence, maintenance costs are unavoidable, if the owner wants to keep the building functional. These annual maintenance costs are a rather small fraction of the original construction costs. The annual service value provided by a building (like, e.g., annual rental of residential buildings) is a small fraction of its original construction costs. This is the main reason why any product requiring a large fraction of its total costs in terms of building services is associated with a high capital intensity and thus with a high period of production.

The service provided by standardized software (like operating systems, programming languages, apps, etc.) has a completely different cost structure. Once the software program is written, it can be used with negligible marginal cost in a very large number of devices like smart phones, PCs, etc. Software has a cost structure similar to that of patented inventions obtained by research and development. Once available to the market, the marginal cost of the service provided to an additional user is quite small.

This difference in the cost structure has decisive implications for maintenance costs: in particular, with respect to the rate of obsolescence. Obsolescence occurs everywhere; but in the case of buildings, it results in a rather slow speed of degradation. In a year's time, buildings that are more modern can replace only a very small fraction of existing ones. On the other hand, new software, once available, threatens to replace existing software everywhere. Just as in the case of medical drugs: A new and better performing medical drug can replace the earlier one with every patient. To maintain the market position of given software, its owner has to undertake great efforts to modernize it all the time.

The very successful firms of Silicon Valley and other places are a good example. Their original programming effort to provide a product turns out to be quite small in comparison with their later effort to maintain and expand their position in the market. Their customers receive a steady flow of upgrades.

Compatibility with other software is important for the market success of any given software product. However, this other software is changing all the time. Therefore, the effort involved in maintaining compatibility is quite substantial. Without this effort, the software product rapidly becomes obsolete due to a lack of compatibility.

Similar results obtain if we look at the protection of the functionality of the item under consideration. Burglary is an attack on the functionality of a building. Its owner thus spends resources to protect the building against burglary. The likelihood of burglary is small whenever the owner spends a reasonable amount of money to protect against such attacks. The main reason for this minute likelihood is the cost structure of the burglary business: To break into two houses is about twice as expensive as to break into one house. To break into one hundred houses is approximately one hundred times as expensive as to break into one building. The production function for making a virus intruding into pieces of standardized operating software is quite different. After the setup cost of developing the virus, spreading it over many of its users is almost independent of their number. This is particularly the case for a virus, which, like in a pandemic, is automatically sent on from one software user to all of his or her correspondents. There are then huge economies of scale in manufacturing viruses designed to attack users of standardized software. The incentive to enter this business of virus manufacturing thus rises with the number of users of a given piece of standardized software.

Therefore, the manufacturer of such standardized software needs continually to employ a large amount of skilled labor, in order to protect the software against successful intrusion by viruses.

The upshot of all this is the quite high rate of obsolescence of capital in the digital sector. This indicates a low value of τ_2.

However, we have to consider two further consequences of a higher production share of digitalization. They work in opposite directions.

First consequence: Interaction between different users of software generates a strong incentive to use the same software product. Everybody uses "Word" from Microsoft. Text thereby can be sent from one user to the next one and changed to be sent back to the first user—without any compatibility problems. The "quality" of such a software product thus rises with the number of its users. Similar effects apply to the Google search engine. This "frequency of use -> quality" effect generates a very high profitability for the original developer of this kind of software. Shares of these firms exhibit very high Tobin's Q values. In relation to their annual turnover, their balance sheet shows low values of their real capital. On the other hand, their market value is a high multiple of their reported equity. This high Tobin's Q is not so much the result of hidden reserves. Rather, it signifies a substantial level of market power. Given that these companies are traded on the stock market, every citizen can buy into this market power. To the extent that a higher level of digitalization raises the opportunity to buy into market power, this effect raises investment opportunities for citizens and thereby works to dampen the loss of investment opportunities due to the reduced period of production T.

Second consequence: Digitalization is not only capital-saving technical progress, but also land-saving technical progress. Our measure of the period of production is a weighted average of the time lag between labor and final output and the time lag between land and final output. The weights are the values of their respective services. Due to digitalization, the use of land is substantially reduced. We only have to mention the increased use of home–office labor and the higher share of mail-order purchases, led in particular by Amazon. In both cases, one labor year does not only use a reduced number of square meters of office space and/or shopping space: In addition, and this is perhaps quantitatively more important, digitalization replaces expensive office space and shopping space by much cheaper building space—away from the expensive inner city locations. Digitalization increases the space of possibilities of where one can work. The competition between locations rises: to the benefit of consumers and workers, but at the expense of landowners. We have discussed land in Chap. 5. We are aware of the fact that land enters the value of real assets twice: first—as it were, looking backwards—as a part of the historical cost of real capital and thus as a contributing part of the period of production T; second—as it were, looking into the future—as land value discounting future land rents. A higher level of digitalization thus not only reduces the period of production T, but also the relative discounted value of future land rents, L.

Given that land is a real asset for investment, its diminished value (at a given rate of interest) reduces the share of private wealth that can be invested in real assets. This raises the optimal public debt period.

8.7 Real Assets in Comparison with an Estimate by Jordà et al. (2019)

Our estimate of the value of real assets is somewhat higher than the estimate for 31 December 2015 that Jordà et al. (2019) have presented in their study on rates of return from 1870 to 2015 (Jordà et al. 2019, Fig. 4 in the appendix, p. 63). The value of real assets is given there as around three times annual GDP. This is the equivalent of approximately four times annual consumption. The estimates for the period from 1870 to 2015 are made assuming the prevailing interest rate level. If we use our extrapolation factors to calculate for a hypothetical real interest rate level of zero, then, starting from the Jordà et al. (2019) estimate, we obtain real assets worth around five years of total consumption. This is less than our estimate of 7.03 years of total consumption. This difference cannot be attributed to the fact that the area that we are examining includes China, whereas China is left out in Jordà et al. (2019).

Further research is required to explain this discrepancy. We suspect that both groups of researchers have tried to be conservative in their estimates. Our focus is the thesis of the need for high net private claims on the state. In this case, a conservative approach could lead us to overestimate alternative ways of investing wealth. Jordà et al. (2019) want, among other things, to point to the great significance of home ownership for growth in the wealth coefficient. A conservative approach would thus lead them perhaps to underestimate real estate ownership as a component of wealth.

8.8   Total Private Wealth at a Real Interest Rate of Zero

On the assumption of a zero interest rate, in addition to their real assets, private persons have entitlements vis-à-vis the state amounting to 6.26 annual consumption units. On this calculation, the value of the real assets, consisting of land and real capital, is 12–13% greater than the net financial claims on the state.

At a steady-state real interest rate of zero, total private wealth in the OECD plus China region thus adds up to 7.03 + 6.26 = 13.29 or around 13 annual consumption units. 47.10% of this sum comprises private net claims on the state; 33.94%, private real capital; and 18.96%, privately owned land. We can also write that approximately 7/15 is net public debt, 5/15 or one-third is private real capital and 3/15, i.e., one-fifth, is land and the mineral and energy reserves it contains.

8.9   Recent "Secular Stagnation" Literature: An Example

Even if Carl Christian von Weizsäcker can claim to have already made similar observations in earlier publications (Weizsäcker 2010, 2011, 2014), it was, above all, thanks to public statements by the former US Secretary of the Treasury and well-known economist, Lawrence Summers, that the secular stagnation thesis became a subject of academic reflection again. Summers (2013, 2014), and Rachel and Summers (2019) should be mentioned, in particular. Thanks to Olivier Blanchard's Presidential Lecture on "Public Debt and Low Interest Rates" at the 2019 AEA Annual Meeting (Blanchard 2019), positions that are clearly related to the position on the Great Divergence that we have argued for in this book have become almost mainstream in the USA.

As already touched upon in Sect. 8.1 above, the description "secular stagnation" does not reflect our fundamentally optimistic attitude to the economic future of the world. (On the debate on secular stagnation, also see Chap. 7 and Kurz 2021.)

The robust optimism that is apparent in the UN's population forecasts and especially its forecasts of life expectancy is more reflective of our attitude. It is true that the Great Divergence, which we have described in Sect. 8.1 above, requires wise economic and financial policy. If we can depend on the latter, however, the Great Divergence appears as a journey into abundance from an economic point of view: less and less onerous labor combined with a constant or even increasing material standard of living.

Our approach is based on steady-state capital theory and its empirical anchoring is provided by the careful examination and adaptation of data on the components of private wealth, such as one can find in the official statistics. We consider a particular *point in time*: namely December 31, 2015 or the average values for 2015. We thus abstain from undertaking an econometric time series analysis. We examine the situation from the vantage point of the hypothetical natural rate of interest that would be compatible with full employment in the steady state without net public debt. Our comparative empirical analysis involves comparing different hypothetical steady states on the date in question, whereby we *extrapolate*, in particular, from the interest rates that are implicitly or explicitly used in the official statistics to a real interest rate of zero. (For a summary, cf. Sect. 8.5 above.) Using this analysis based on steady-state properties, we find that net public debt at a real interest rate of zero is very substantial for the OECD plus China region. We derive the thesis of a negative natural rate of interest from this finding. The temporal depth dimension of our approach is, *firstly*, the narrative concerning *the exhaustion of the greater productivity of more roundabout production* and, *secondly*, the narrative concerning *the increase in relative desired wealth as prosperity increases*—or, expressed in formulas, the narrative about the secular constancy of the period of production T and the narrative about the secular rise in the private waiting period Z. (In general on narratives, also see Shiller 2017.) We do *not* connect these two narratives to an econometric time series analysis. Nonetheless, the UN world population forecast up to 2100 provides "quasi-empirical" *future-oriented* backing for our thesis of the rising private waiting period Z; just as the empirical constancy of the capital coefficient over time provides *past-oriented* backing for our thesis of the exhaustion of the greater productivity of more roundabout production. The fact that our starting point is a steady-state analysis based on capital theory allows us to use a "meta-model." This has the advantage of allowing us to do without many specific assumptions: especially about the production sector, but also about the consumption sector.

We want here again to compare our approach with the study by Rachel and Summers (2019). The latter consists of a theoretical and empirical analysis of the evolution of the neutral rate of interest or, in other words, the real equilibrium rate over the past five decades. Like in our approach, the authors try to cover a large geographical area, in order to be able realistically to work with a model of a closed economy. In their case, the countries examined comprise the members of the OECD. The situation circa 1970 is the point of reference. A number of time series are now introduced, in order to establish causal relationships between the different variables. The main interest is the evolution of the neutral interest rate. The latter has fallen by a few percentage points over these nearly five decades. Nonetheless, a number of variables whose rise economists expect to push the interest rate upwards have increased. Thus, for example, the conventionally measured public debt ratio in the OECD countries has increased from around 20% of GDP in 1970 to around 70% today. If we assume, based on the econometric analysis, that a rise in the debt ratio by one percentage point (e.g., from 30 to 31% of gross domestic product) raises the equilibrium interest rate by 3.5 basis points, the increase in the public debt ratio from 20 to 70% will have raised the neutral interest rate by 1.75%.

The authors examine a number of other factors that have an influence on the neutral rate. These include factors of a demographic nature, factors related to income distribution and, finally, policy-related factors: in particular those, as in the case of the public debt ratio, that are affected by fiscal policy and social policy, with special attention being given to the funding of the healthcare system. The model created with these variables serves to estimate the influence of the various parameters on the neutral interest rate using time series analysis.

The point estimates of Rachel's and Summers' model suggest that change in the directly policy-related variables has pushed up the neutral interest rate by around 4% (Rachel and Summers 2019, p. 13). Given that the neutral interest rate is today much lower than four percent, the authors conclude that were it not for the change in the directly policy-related variables, the neutral rate would be negative.

Now, it should be added that the reference point, the neutral rate in 1970, was higher than the natural rate at the time, i.e., the hypothetical neutral rate with zero public debt. Hence, the results of Rachel and Summers (2019) provide all the more reason to conclude that the natural rate must be negative today.

A brief comparison of the two approaches follows. The two most important points are the same in both cases, viz. the following qualitative points: 1. The natural rate of interest today is negative; 2. The natural rate is falling over time. Neither approach attempts to make a precise estimate of the negative natural rate. The analytical methods of the two approaches are complementary. The econometric time series approach of Rachel and Summers (2019) is able—also by drawing on numerous prior studies by other economists—to provide a graphic representation of the downward trend in the neutral interest rate while holding the public policy parameters constant. We mention here just two related studies: the above-cited paper by Jordà et al. (2019) and Eggertsson et al. (2019). But Rachel and Summers are conscious of the fact that the confidence intervals are very large. The "real" trend parameter of the neutral interest rate while holding the public policy parameters constant may be quite different from their point estimate. To this extent, our simplified illustration using the savings triangle is no less instructive than the parameter estimates of Rachel and Summers (2019)—especially since it matches the reality for employees covered by the German social security system very well.

Our meta-model-based approach does not require such special assumptions as the approach of Rachel and Summers (2019). Thus, in specifying their model, they use a Cobb–Douglas production function with Hicks- and Harrod-neutral technical progress from the outset. They thus find, like practically all such models, that there is a secular decline in technical progress. By contrast, our meta-model can also cope with the hypothesis that technical progress has not decreased at all, but is merely directed nowadays toward reducing the "disutility of labor" that is ignored in the conventional way of measuring technical progress.

Our "*Fundamental Equation of Steady-State Capital Theory*" ($T = Z - D$) (or also: $Z = T + L + D$) provides insight into secular trends, without our having to enter into complicated time series analyses that are fraught with uncertainty. There is no doubt, however, that by using such econometric methods, it is possible to answer more specific questions that cannot be answered by way of steady-state analysis.

It thus seems to us that the two approaches are complementary. It could prove worthwhile to try to combine them.

8.10   Sensitivity Analysis on the Negative Natural Rate of Interest

Our finding that the state has substantial net debt vis-à-vis its citizens at a zero real interest rate is sufficient to prove that the natural rate of interest is negative. In fact, we do not need any estimate of citizens' real assets in the zero interest rate scenario. We have, nonetheless, undertaken such an estimate, in order, among other things, to call attention to the robustness of our thesis. Purely hypothetically, we could well have imagined that net public debt at a zero interest rate only represents a small fraction of citizens' total wealth. We would have had then to show that people's desired wealth could not also have been completely covered by real assets. Just a small error in estimating real assets would then have been sufficient to call into question the positive result for the zero interest rate estimate of net public debt. As an example: If up to 90% of privately desired wealth could be covered by real assets, miscalculating real assets by 20% would be enough to arrive at a situation in which real assets in the zero interest rate scenario are greater than desired wealth. In this case, the natural rate of interest would be positive, since net public debt would not be needed to satisfy the desired level of wealth.

But at real interest rates of zero, the desired wealth of the population is almost twice private real assets. In order then for desired wealth to be exclusively covered with private real assets, we would have to consider the possibility that the estimate of real assets is too low by a factor of two. This seems very unlikely—especially since other estimates come to even lower figures (Jordà et al. 2019).

Moreover, a further fact has to be kept in mind here: We have not even undertaken any direct estimate of relative desired wealth. All we have done is to make it plausible that relative desired wealth rises with rising life expectancy. This is the main message of the "savings triangle." Apart from that, we have relied on the measured private wealth coefficient roughly corresponding to relative desired wealth. The background to this is the consideration that the government will intervene in compensatory fashion to stabilize employment, if desired wealth is considerably greater than actual private wealth. If desired wealth massively exceeds actual wealth, then voluntary private saving is significantly greater than private investment. Without government intervention, however, this means recession or even depression. If, in this case, interest rates cannot be cut any further, because they have already reached the lower bound, then the state will have to ensure, by way of additional "dis-saving," that aggregate saving is brought into line with aggregate investment (cf. Chap. 7). This increases the net position of citizens vis-à-vis the state and thus desired wealth and actual wealth come together again.

We can ask, furthermore, where underestimates of real assets primarily come from. The official statistics may have underestimated the actual value of firms and hence the value of citizens' shareholdings. But this can only concern shares that are not traded on the stock exchange. Statistical agencies make certain estimates of the value of shareholdings by inferring the value of firms that are not listed on the stock exchange from known market values. But it cannot be ruled out that underestimates occur when using this method.

It is possible that the "true" value of all firms that are not publicly traded is, on average, greater than the equity reported in their balance sheets. The latter is already taken into account on the liabilities side of the balance sheet in calculating real capital (Chap. 4) and the value of land (Chap. 5). What is at issue is thus the valuation of "family businesses."

If their value is, on average, underestimated, then we have also underestimated the value of real assets. But this does not have any great impact on our estimate of net private claims on the state. For in the overwhelming majority of cases, such businesses stay "in the family." In other words, they are inherited. And, as we have shown in Sect. 3.6, the wish to leave wealth to one's descendants has a one-to-one effect on increasing desired wealth. At least as an approximation, we can thus assume that an underestimation of the value of non-publicly traded firms entails an equivalent underestimation of desired wealth. The difference between privately desired wealth and private real assets that is bridged over by public debt thus remains practically untouched by possible errors in estimating the value of shares in non-publicly traded companies.

Thus, in short:

> The thesis of a negative natural rate of interest proves to be extremely robust.

8.11   A Summary of the Results of Our Empirical Estimates

Table 8.1 provides a final overview of our empirical estimates of the components of private wealth—real capital, land and public debt—in the OECD plus China region, as presented in Chaps. 4, 5 and 6.

Table 8.1 Overview: results of our main empirical estimates

Composition of private wealth in the OECD plus China region, 2015					
In years of total consumption					
With a positive real interest rate					With zero percent interest rate
	USA	Germany	OECD	OECD plus China	OECD plus China
Real capital	3.70	2.76	3.59	4.03	4.51
Land	1.42	1.54	2.02	1.94	2.52
Public debt	4.22	5.03	4.31	3.95	6.26
– Explicit public debt	0.98	0.70	0.92	0.75	0.75
– Implicit public debt (retirement)	2.34	3.64	2.75	2.63	4.94
– Implicit public debt (health insurance and care insurance)	0.90	0.69	0.64	0.57	0.57
Total	**9.34**	**9.33**	**9.92**	**9.92**	**13.29**

Note Health insurance: Public health insurance
Care insurance: Public nursing care insurance
Source Authors' own calculations

Real Capital

When calculated using a positive real interest rate, real capital in the OECD was equivalent on average to 3.59 times total annual consumption in 2015. The USA is above the OECD average at 370% of total annual consumption, while Germany is below the average at 276% of total annual consumption. In Chap. 4, we estimated real capital wealth in China, which is as high as 554% of China's total annual consumption—well above the OECD average. For the OECD plus China region as a whole, we estimate real capital wealth to be about 4.03 times total annual consumption. Applying our calculation method using a real interest rate of zero percent, we estimate private real capital wealth to be 4.51 times total annual consumption for the OECD plus China region as a whole.

Land

On average, the value of land in the OECD countries is twice total annual consumption. If China is added, the average private land wealth in the OECD plus China region is 194% of the consumption of the region as a whole. Germany and the USA are below the OECD average at 1.54 and 1.42 times their annual consumption, respectively. If we apply the zero interest rate, this results in a land value of 252% of total annual consumption for the OECD plus China region in 2015.

Public Debt

Using a positive discount rate, we arrive at the following results: In 2015, private citizens' net claims on the state accounted for the largest share of private wealth. In the USA it's value was at 422% of total annual consumption. As we argued in Chap. 6, pension and retirement benefit entitlements, as well as public health and nursing care insurance, give rise to implicit public debt. At 234% of total annual consumption, implicit public debt from retirement benefit entitlements deriving from social security retirement schemes accounted for the largest share of private citizens' claims on the state in the USA. The structure of claims vis-à-vis the state (explicit and implicit debt) is similar in Germany. At 364% of total annual consumption, implicit public debt from retirement benefit entitlements is even higher in Germany.

Using a positive discount rate, we estimate that total public debt (the sum of explicit and implicit public debt) is 4.31 times total annual consumption in the OECD and 3.95 times total annual consumption in the OECD plus China area. Explicit debt, calculated as net public debt, accounts for a relatively small fraction of these totals at 0.92 times (OECD) and 0.75 times (OECD plus China area) total annual consumption. According to our estimates, in 2015, implicit public debt was 339% of total annual consumption in the OECD and 320% of total annual consumption in the OECD plus China region. Implicit public debt is thus much more significant for the claims of private individuals on the state in these regions.

As we argued earlier, in a world with zero interest rates, we also need to calculate the present values of expected future income flows using a zero discount rate. The last row in Table 8.1 shows the results of our estimates for the three private wealth components. Public debt amounted to 626% of total annual consumption in the OECD plus China region in 2015. By far the largest contributor is implicit retirement-related public debt, which, according to our calculations, came to 494% of total annual consumption. Implicit retirement-related public debt thus accounts for nearly 80% of total public debt.

Total Wealth

Using a positive discount rate, total private wealth amounted to 9.92 years of total annual consumption in 2015 in the OECD countries and also in the OECD plus China region. Using a discount rate of zero percent, private sector wealth in the OECD plus China area totaled 13.29 years of total consumption. One-third of this was private wealth in the form of real capital (machinery, equipment, buildings), one-fifth was land, and just under half (more precisely: 7/15) was comprised of net financial claims on the state.

References

Blanchard, Olivier, 2019, Public Debt and Low Interest Rates, AEA Presidential Lecture, *American Economic Review*, 109 (4), 1197–1229.

Bönke, Tim, Markus M. Grabka, Carsten Schröder and Edward N. Wolff. 2019. A Head-to-Head Comparison of Augmented Wealth in Germany and the United States. *The Scandinavian Journal of Economics*. Online: 28 March 2019. https://doi.org/10.1111/sjoe.12364. Accessed: 15 June 2019.

Debreu, Gérard. 1959. *Theory of Value. An Axiomatic Analysis of Economic Equilibrium*. New Haven: Yale University Press.

Eggertsson, Gauti B., Neil R. Mehrotra und Jacob A. Robbins. 2019. A Model of Secular Stagnation: Theory and Quantitative Evaluation. *American Economic Journal: Macroeconomics* 11 (1): 1–48.

Jordà, Òscar, Katharina Knoll, Dmitry Kuvshinov, Moritz Schularick and Alan M. Taylor. 2019. The Rate of Return on Everything, 1870–2015. *Quarterly Journal of Economics* 134 (3): 1225–1298.

Krämer, Hagen M. 2020. Verteilungspolitische Interventionen. *List Forum für Wirtschafts- und Sozialpolitik* 46 (2): 117–155.

Kurz, Heinz D. 2021. The Spectre of Secular Stagnation Then and Now. In *Stagnations- und Deflationstheorien*. Schriften des Vereins für Socialpolitik, vol. 115/XXXVIII, Studien zur Entwicklung der ökonomischen Theorie, ed. Volker Caspari, 10–53. Berlin: Duncker & Humblot.

Piketty, Thomas. 2014. *Capital in the Twenty-First Century*. Cambridge (MA): Harvard University Press.

Quesnay, Francois. 1758. *Tableau Economique, et Maximes Générale du Gouvernement Economique*. Versailles.

Rachel, Lukasz and Lawrence H. Summers. 2019. On Falling Neutral Real Rates, Fiscal Policy, and the Risk of Secular Stagnation. *Brookings Papers on Economic Activity*. March 4: 1–66.

Shiller, Robert J. 2017. Narrative Economics. *American Economic Review* 107 (4): 967–1004.

Smith, Adam. 1776. *An Inquiry into the Nature and Causes of the Wealth of Nations*. London: W. Strahan and T. Cadell.

Solow, Robert M. 1956. A Contribution to the Theory of Economic Growth. *Quarterly Journal of Economics* 70 (1): 65–94.

Summers, Lawrence H. 2013. *Speech at IMF Fourteenth Annual Research Conference in Honor of Stanley Fischer*. 8 November 2013. Washington (D.C.): International Monetary Fund.

Summers, Lawrence H. 2014. US Economic Prospects: Secular Stagnation, Hysteresis, and the Zero Lower Bound. *Business Economics* 49: 65–73.

Weizsäcker, Carl Christian von. 2010. Das Janusgesicht der Staatsschulden. *Frankfurter Allgemeine Zeitung*. 4 June 2010: 12 (published in the appendix to this book as "The Two Faces of Public Debt").

Weizsäcker, Carl Christian von. 2011. *Public Debt Requirements in a Regime of Price Stability*. Preprint 2011/20. Max Planck Institute for Research on Collective Goods. Bonn: 1–59.

Weizsäcker, Carl Christian von. 2014. Public Debt and Price Stability. *German Economic Review* 15 (1): 42–61.

Weizsäcker, Carl Christian von. 2021. *Capital Theory of the Steady State – Or: T+L = Z–D*. https://www.coll.mpg.de/Weizsaecker/CapitalTheory2021 and https://www.springer.com/9783658273620.

Part II
Economic Policy

Monetary Stability and the Stability of the Open Society

Abstract

Historical experience shows that the welfare state is what holds democracy and the market economy together. Neither a welfare state that is too small nor one that is too large can fulfill this connective function. A "stability pact" between citizens and the state is needed: 1. A welfare state to provide citizens security even in their old age. 2. In order to preserve appropriate incentives, the retirement system has to be a form of "saving" (forced saving) for old age. 3. In addition, most citizens also undertake voluntary saving. 4. The state provides for monetary stability. 5. The state uses its fiscal policy to promote high employment. A modern understanding of personal freedom includes the security provided by a welfare state of appropriate dimensions. It follows that in the twenty-first century, a large part of the wealth of citizens consists of net claims on the state.

9.1 Authoritarian Tendencies, Complexity and Simplicity

Even today, the democratically constituted "open society" is threatened by authoritarian tendencies. Many democratically minded people fear a tendency toward authoritarianism in today's world. Religious fundamentalism is an example. But the highly successful combination of a partial market economy and one-party rule in China also has observers concerned. It is worth reflecting again on the conditions of a stable, democratically constituted society.

In *The Open Society and Its Enemies*, Karl Popper presented what is, up to now, the most convincing fundamental approach to how a liberal-democratic social order works (Popper 1945). It is not our intention to try to outdo him on the terrain of social philosophy in our book. We understand our contribution rather as being embedded in the basic structure of the "open society" outlined by Popper. The idea

© The Author(s) 2021
C. C. von Weizsäcker and H. M. Krämer, *Saving and Investment in the Twenty-First Century*, https://doi.org/10.1007/978-3-030-75031-2_9

of an open and therefore shapeable future and that of "piecemeal engineering" by "trial and error" form part of this basic structure.

Within this framework, what interests us are citizens' *mental and behavioral dynamics*. The stability of a liberal-democratic society depends on the outcome of these dynamics. We are engaging here in "political economy" in the sense that it has been practiced by economists like James Buchanan, Gordon Tullock, Amartya Sen, Alfred Müller-Armack, Mancur Olson, Peter Bernholz, Bruno Frey, Gebhard Kirchgässner and many others in modern times.

As already discussed in Chap. 2 on real capital, the success story of the West is closely linked to the development of the division of labor, which Karl Marx attributed to the "bourgeois epoch" under the heading of the "socialization of labor" (Marx and Engels 1967 [1848]; Marx 1976 [1867]). The historical process of "modernity" has led to an enormous increase in prosperity, but also in the *complexity* of human coexistence (cf. also Deaton 2013; Osterhammel 2010). It has always been the case that many people feel an instinctive rejection of this constantly growing social apparatus: a longing for truthfulness, "authenticity," simplicity, transparency, rootedness, and for an idealized past. In his excellent book on Romanticism in Germany, Rüdiger Safranski has revealed this common thread running from Novalis, by way of Richard Wagner, to Heidegger and Adorno (Safranski 2014). This longing—for simple truths, unshakeable beliefs, authority, for a vertical worldview with a clear "above" and "below"—is the source from which modern authoritarianism flows.

Simplicity is the opposite of complexity. Nonetheless, increased complexity, which increases prosperity in turn, comes from making use of *simplifications*. The abundance and variety of available goods would be inconceivable without the institution of money. Thanks to money, the transaction costs of consumers—whether those of end consumers or those of the productive consumers of intermediate products—can be reduced by orders of magnitude on the numerous goods markets they use. Money is the great simplifier. (Cf. also Simmel 1978 [1900]: *The Philosophy of Money*.) An important correlate is market asymmetry: On most markets for goods and services, there are many buyers, on the one hand, and a much smaller number of sellers, on the other. In keeping with the idea of the division of labor, the latter are specialized. Prices are almost always above marginal costs. Hence, in the overwhelming majority of cases, the buyer can count on the desired product being in stock. For even after a transaction has been concluded, sellers on the market in question remain hungry for more transactions, so that they have an incentive to be always ready to serve their master: the customer. By contrast, the buyer has stocked up on the product to the point that the monetary equivalent of the marginal utility that he or she derives from it is equal to its price (Gossen's Second Law): Hence, the buyer's hunger for transactions has been satiated for the time being. The simplicity of the transaction for the customer is one side of the coin. The other is the productive complexity of the market-mediated division of labor that is thus made possible (Weizsäcker 2005).

It is worth quoting Hayek here: "It is not thanks to anyone's specific instructions that we can count on finding the things that we need to live even in an unfamiliar city or that, despite all the changes that are constantly happening in the world, we still by and large know what we will be able to procure next week or next year. We are so spoiled about this that we are more likely to complain that we have not found exactly what we expected. But actually we should be astonished that our expectations are met to such a high degree as they in fact are, even though it is nobody's obligation to ensure that we find available the things we want" (Hayek 1967).

Since there is so much talk of artificial intelligence nowadays, let us recall one of its pioneers: Herbert Simon. In 1962, Simon published an article titled "The Architecture of Complexity" in the *Proceedings of the American Philosophical Society* (Simon 1962). In it, he shows that complex systems have always to exhibit a property that he calls "near-decomposability." They are split up into subsystems in such a way that the interaction of the elements within a subsystem is, on average, considerably more intense than the interaction of elements from different subsystems. Insofar as the highest order subsystems are still complex systems, they are themselves split up into even smaller subsystems: and so on, until the lowest level subsystems only contain so few elements or such homogeneous elements that they lose the property of the complexity.

Simon explains the property of near-decomposability of complex systems by the advantage of evolutionary stability that it confers on them. If a system is disturbed locally at a certain point, a subsystem may be disrupted. But due to near-decomposability, this has only a minor effect on the rest of the system. The evolutionary process of "trial and error" or, in Darwinian language, "mutation and selection" can thus work. A mutation is a local disturbance. Near-decomposability ensures that it remains local. When something new develops out of the mutation, then the result is a further evolutionary step. The ability to cope with mutations or disturbances increases the threshold of tolerance for the number of mutations per unit of time and thus increases the frequency of successful evolutionary steps per unit of time. In his article, Simon shows how this abstract systems—theoretical idea can be applied to chemical, biological and social systems, as well as purely symbolic ones. Moreover, this fundamental idea was also the basis for his pioneering work in the field of artificial intelligence.

The development of the division of labor in the historical process of "modernity" is a prime example of near-decomposability. By trial and error, knowledge gets tied together into different bundles, and these bundles tend to have the property that the elements of knowledge in each bundle support one another in the task of applying it for the benefit of society. At the same time, the possessor of this knowledge relies on the fact that both the other bundles of knowledge and the agents assigned to them will work dependably, so that his or her own bundle can demonstrate its usefulness in concert with the others. Money is the unifying bond in this division of labor and of knowledge.

This near-decomposability of an economic system based on the division of labor allows economists to earn their daily bread by doing partial analyses. If, for example, the vast majority of economists with expertise in the field call for a uniform, global price for carbon emissions, a closer analysis of the problem reveals that their reasoning involves implicit assumptions about the near-decomposability of the global economic system. In general, all partial cost–benefit analyses and other methods of "mechanism design" are based on implicit or explicit assumptions that are tantamount to assuming the near-decomposability of the economic system.

But this near-decomposability of knowledge introduces a vast distance between the bearers of knowledge and the beneficiaries of knowledge. The world of commodities (including services) is what connects them to one another. The social relationship between bearer and beneficiary of knowledge gets "reified" in the commodity. Both the early Marx and the Marx of *Capital* addressed the "alienation" arising from this reification of social relationships. The subsequent Marxist tradition retained this theme. It is a key aspect of the critique of capitalism. Heidegger's critique of the "forgetfulness of being" (*Seinsvergessenheit*) also relates to it.

9.2   Irenicism: The Symbiosis of Democracy and Market Economy I

The *modern welfare state* in the OECD countries is a realization of the basic idea that Alfred Müller-Armack called "social irenicism" (Müller-Armack 1950): of peace between the different strata (or "classes") comprised by the population. At the same time, however, it is also a kind of peace between two principles of social and political integration: that of liberal democracy and that of the free market economy.

Carl Christian von Weizsäcker's reflections on "The Normative Co-Evolution of the Market Economy and Democracy" take up this point (Weizsäcker 2014). Here is an abbreviated version of the argument. If, pursuant to the idea of individual liberty, we want decisions on the level of the state to be normatively anchored in the preferences of citizens (the social choice approach of Arrow, Sen and others), then it has to be taken into account that these preferences are not fixed, but change rather in response to external influences. A coherent concept of social *progress* assumes that every path of small step-by-step improvements, in the sense of Popper's piecemeal engineering, is non-circular. Otherwise, we would not speak of progress. Now, it can be shown mathematically that such a path of progress consisting of piecemeal engineering steps is always non-circular, if preferences are "adaptive." And vice versa: If all conceivable paths of progress of this sort are non-circular, then citizens' preferences are adaptive. (The fixed preferences of the *homo economicus* are a special case of adaptive preferences.) Adaptive preferences can be characterized intuitively as follows: The preferences induced by the prevailing status quo *valorize this status quo* as compared to the preferences induced by every other status quo.

If preferences are adaptive, a majority rule democracy would thus be massively hostile to change without a market economy. The market economy gives rise to decentralized, incremental changes. When they are successful, these changes are justified, ex post, as progress by the associated (adaptive) changes in preferences, even though, ex ante, they would have been rejected by the majority. This allows the progress-oriented dynamics to arise that are a hallmark of the Western success story. It should be noted that the empirical results of behavioral economics consistently confirm the hypothesis of adaptive preferences. But the success story of the West is also a kind of "proof" that preferences are adaptive.

Conversely, in order to enjoy legitimacy, the decentralized decision-making system of the market economy normatively requires its embedding in a democratic political order. Since there are interpersonal influences on preferences, these preferences are not in and of themselves legitimate sources for social decisions. They only become so by being submitted to "domination-free discourse" (Habermas) in society. In the context of this discussion, citizens are free, in particular, to choose the "influencers" to which they want to be exposed. Just as in the market economy, at the level of the choice of goods, consumers can usually choose between several competitors on the producer side, so too there is a choice of influencers (the "producers" of preferences, as it were) at the level of the formation of consumer and voter preferences; i.e., there is competition among the influencers. It is only on this condition that we want to speak of preferences as legitimate sources of social decision-making processes.

9.3 Irenicism: The Symbiosis of Democracy and Market Economy II—The Welfare State

The normative co-evolution of the market economy and democracy does not yet tell us everything there is to know about the possibility of a de facto symbiosis between the two principles. Experience has shown that when the modern market economy is embedded in a democratic political system, it leads to the welfare state. It can thus be presumed that the welfare state is an indispensable component of a successful symbiosis of market economy and democracy.

The core of the welfare state is social security in the broad sense or what can also be called forms of *social insurance*. Unlike private insurance, social insurance is *mandatory*. The beneficiaries are typically employees. The mandatory nature of social insurance avoids the well-known problem of *adverse selection*: If participation in the insurance plan were voluntary, then the likelihood of participation would be greater, the greater the risk of benefits being claimed. This, however, drives up insurance premiums, and, as a result, fewer and fewer people make use of the coverage, because it becomes too expensive.

Of course, mandatory insurance with uniform or at least highly schematized insurance premiums already brings about an implicit *redistribution* among beneficiaries: People whose ex ante probability of using the insurance is low subsidize people whose probability of claiming coverage is high.

In addition, like with all insurance, there is also the *moral hazard problem*. As compared to someone who is uninsured, people with good coverage reduce their efforts to avoid the harmful eventuality against which they are insured. People who are *over*-insured may even be tempted to bring about the damages in question deliberately. In such a case, we speak of "insurance fraud."

Redistribution and moral hazard reduce people's incentive to raise their standard of living by being economically productive.

These effects, which have been abstractly formulated here for every form of mandatory insurance and hence also for every form of social insurance, show that managing the welfare state is a challenging political task. Even if the great majority of voters express strong support for the basic idea of social insurance, the political system has to have the "wisdom" not to overextend such insurance to the point that the incentive to be economically productive is massively diminished. For if this happens, the state can no longer ensure the proper functioning of the social security system as a whole. The promised benefits will turn out then to have been illusory— a mirage—and the productive symbiosis of democracy and market economy will be destroyed.

9.4   The Intertemporal Aspect of Social Insurance

The intertemporal aspect of social insurance is of particular interest in connection with the main subject of this book. As shown in Chap. 6 on public debt, a considerable part of private wealth consists of beneficiaries' claims on the system of social security in the broad sense. Claims to retirement benefits as part of the public retirement system are the most important element of this wealth. In addition, public health insurance is connected to substantial claims to future health services, which have already been paid for by beneficiaries and their employers in the form of premiums. These assets of the beneficiaries correspond to implicit public debt of the same amount.

We have discussed the example of the German public retirement plan, which is a key component of the welfare state in Germany. The original idea behind it is closely linked to the institution of the life annuity in private insurance. This basic idea has been preserved to a large extent up to today. It is—still—very common for participants in the retirement plan to conceive of it as a "quid pro quo." As an employee, I pay (and my employer pays) into the plan, so that the latter will pay me retirement benefits in my old age. Most of the beneficiaries understand that the amount of their benefits depends on how long they have paid into the plan when they were working—and also on the size of their contributions. The contributions deducted from the gross wage of the employee and the contributions, in excess of the gross wage, paid by the employer can thus be regarded as employee saving—in the same way that the premiums paid by the beneficiary of a private life annuity contract can be understood as a form of saving. Both a private life annuity contract and the public retirement plan thus create comparable incentives to earn income for retirement by working.

In the case of the public retirement plan, however, these incentives have already been watered down some. This is, above all, due to publicly guaranteed minimum income in Germany. For people with little labor income and only irregular employment, the benefits formula can lead to retirement benefits being less than the subsistence minimum in old age. But since these benefits are deducted from the basic allowance, the earlier retirement contributions turn out to have been "for nothing." Inasmuch as one expects, or even plans, to have a low income, the mandatory contributions to the retirement plan do not work like a form of saving for the future, but simply like a "tax," which provides an additional incentive to withdraw from the labor market as much as possible. Things would be different, if, in addition to the basic subsistence allowance, people were allowed also to keep the retirement benefit claims they had acquired. We do not want, however, to enter into any detailed discussion of guaranteed minimum income here.

What is crucial is that the public retirement plan still be designed in such a way that there are not any massive incentives to withdraw from the official labor market, because legal work is burdened with high contributions (including the employers' contributions), but the benefits paid in old age bear hardly any relation anymore to the amount beneficiaries have worked.

The adoption of a populist retirement policy is a constant danger. By improving benefits, a parliamentary majority can "help out" current retirees, as well as voters who are about to reach retirement age. These electoral favors may be financed by increasing explicit public debt or by additional taxation on one or another form of value creation or by cutting public spending in other areas: for instance, on the development and maintenance of infrastructure. The full impact of the chosen method of financing increased benefits is only felt in the long term, and this impact is, moreover, distributed in a diffuse way over the whole population. Hence, the costs of such a policy may weigh less heavily in voters' current electoral choices than its immediate visible benefits.

Voters have to be kept aware of the dangers of this sort of populism.

9.5 Subsidiarity and Stable Money: A "Stability Pact"

As a general principle, we can say that the best way of preventing the system of social security from degenerating into a candy shop, which is no longer affordable and which is highly incompatible with economic incentives, is by following the long-established principle of subsidiarity. The state—i.e., here the system of social security in the broad sense—should only become active in providing support, and also monitoring, when self-help is insufficient. Making provision for their own future and, in particular, for their retirement years is part of individuals' helping themselves Forced saving due to employees' mandatory participation in the public retirement plan is consistent with the principle of subsidiarity—but only if the benefits formula is correctly designed, so that it does not give employees a massive incentive to withdraw from the rules of the labor market, which promote economic prosperity.

Subsidiarity in retirement planning also entails that, beyond a minimum, people secure their own future by way of voluntary saving.

The most important function of money with stable purchasing power is that it makes it much easier for individuals to provide for their own future by saving. This principle of stable money means that there is a risk-free real interest rate that is not negative. A non-negative, risk-free real interest rate is possible under conditions of inflation, but experience shows that the real interest rate is difficult to predict under these conditions. In this case, it is difficult for savers to foresee how great their wealth will be in the distant future.

These thoughts on the importance of price stability for preserving a free democratic social order reflect the first of the constituent principles in Walter Eucken's "Principles of Economic Policy": viz., the "primacy of monetary policy" (Eucken 1952, Chap. XVI).

A "stability pact" should thus be concluded between citizens and the state, and it should contain the following components: 1. The state provides for basic social security and a system of compulsory saving, so that employees will have a minimum level of retirement benefits adapted to their respective standard of living. 2. The state structures forced saving in the public retirement plan in such a way that for average employees it is really a matter of saving: i.e., the greater the contributions that have been paid in, the greater the retirement benefits. 3. In addition, citizens also undertake voluntary saving, so that most of them will enjoy a standard of living in their old age that goes beyond their social security retirement benefits. 4. The state commits itself to a policy of monetary stability to make it easier—and, in many cases, even just possible—for citizens to achieve a risk-free (after tax) rate of return of at least zero on their current foregoing of consumption. 5. In its macro- and labor market policies, the state is guided by the goal of high employment, so that every citizen who wants to work is also able to find work.

9.6   A Culture of Personal Responsibility and Future-Directedness

The welfare state, which serves as the hinge between democracy and the market economy, should neither be too extensive nor too sparse. It would be too sparse if it were only able to fulfill its most basic function poorly: viz., the function of protecting people against hardship in cases in which strictly private sector solutions cannot regularly be found. It would be too extensive if, due to effects of schematization and redistributive effects, it were severely to impair the incentive for citizens to take personal responsibility for their own future. In the first case, the majority of voters would turn against the status quo and possibly also fall for illusory authoritarian solutions. In the second case, the economic system would become overburdened, resulting in the welfare state no longer being able to keep its promises. This also could lead voters to seek refuge in authoritarian solutions.

In order to be able to keep to the productive middle way, there needs to be a *culture of personal responsibility and future-directedness* as an expression of the principle of subsidiarity.

When discussing inheritance in the chapter on desired wealth, we pointed to the "multiple uses" of wealth. Individuals' efforts to protect themselves against the "risk" of great longevity are made subjectively easier to bear by the fact that they can leave the savings not required for consumption during retirement to their descendants. The heir thus becomes an implicit insurer providing a life annuity. Hence, there is far less need for a commercial insurer to provide such an annuity.

But the basic idea of the "multiple uses" of savings is more general. There are different risks in life. You can get sick and hence be inhibited from having gainful employment, and social insurance cannot cover every such risk of losing income. You can lose your job and become temporarily unemployed, or even unemployed for a longer period of time, or only be able to find a job that does not pay as well. Your family situation can change in such a way as to increase the money you need for your daily life. Someone can die before reaching old age, creating financial duress for his or her descendants. You can end up separating from your partner, which usually also leads to higher living expenses. For whatever reason, your children may suddenly need more from you—including more financially. The business of a self-employed person can start to have difficulties, which can only be overcome by an injection of equity.

Even if people emphasize just *one* goal of saving in surveys, it is clear to everybody that savings can also be used for other purposes if needed. There can be a variety of ways of using savings in the form of money. A particular use does not have to be decided upon in advance. The multiple uses of savings in covering all sorts of different risks means that responding to any given risk requires much less of a sacrifice of current consumption. For you would have presumably foregone this consumption to a large extent in any case, even if the particular risk had not come about at all.

But this multiplicity of uses to cover very different risks can also be the basis for a *virtue of self-sufficiency*: for a self-image as someone who does not have to depend on the constant help of others—in particular, of taxpayers.

It is one of the functions of the state to promote this culture of personal responsibility and individual future-directedness by making it easier for people who want to work to find work—and by making it easier for people to plan for their future by saving. It is thus the state's responsibility to provide, on the one hand, for full employment and, on the other, for monetary stability.

An important criterion for the appropriate size of the welfare state is the public sector share in national product. The best way to illustrate this idea is by using the "Laffer curve" (Uhlig and Trabandt 2011). For the state to have the highest credit rating on the capital market, it must be able to show that tax revenues are on the rising part of the Laffer curve. It can thus make clear to creditors that, in an "emergency," it will be able to increase revenues for repaying debt by raising taxes. This Laffer curve criterion sets limits to the tax-funded public sector share.

9.7   Inflation or Public Debt?

If we conclude, in keeping with the foregoing analyses, that the natural rate of interest in the given tax system or in an optimal tax system is negative, then society has the choice between a *negative real interest rate without public debt* and *price stability with positive public debt*. We described price stability above as an element of the "stability pact" between state and citizens that is required for a successful symbiosis between democracy and economic dynamism in the form of the market economy.

Public debt is not a major problem, so long as the interest charged on it is not greater than the growth rate of the economy. At a negative natural rate, this condition is satisfied, so long as the state does not overdo its borrowing.

We should recall the Golden Rule of Accumulation here: In comparing different steady states, the lifetime utility of a representative citizen is maximized at the rate of interest that is equal to the growth rate. In addition to the considerations of political stability discussed in this chapter, considerations of optimal allocation also favor the "*price stability with public debt*" option over the "*inflation without public debt*" option.

But distributive considerations also speak in favor of this option. As experience shows, an inflationary environment causes greater problems for the naive saver and investor than for the astute, sophisticated investor. More affluent social strata can afford to be advised by people who have specialized in navigating through the depths and shallows of inflation. Small savers normally cannot. Rich people invest in tangible assets and shareholdings: investments that are "inflation-protected." Investment in fixed-rate financial assets is of greater relative importance for small savers. The risk aversion of small savers is greater than that of persons who possess great wealth. Eliminating the risk arising from inflation is thus far more important for small savers than for rich people (cf. Sect. 5.1.12).

9.8   The Aspect of Freedom

Individual freedom creates prosperity, but also heterogeneity, confusion and complexity. The longing people feel for simple solutions, clarity and security is understandable—but it can also be fertile terrain for the propagation of illusory solutions that are exploited by populist movements. The irenicism that is made possible by an appropriate dose of the welfare state is a response to the resulting political dangers for freedom. Thanks to the existence of a welfare state system that publicly ensures a certain level of private wealth, most people feel that they are on solid ground, and this enables them to accept the confusing, but also substantial benefits of personal and economic freedom. The final sentences of Karl Polanyi's *The Great Transformation* are fitting here: "As long as man is true to his task of creating more abundant freedom for all, he need not fear that either power or planning will turn against him and destroy the freedom he is building by their instrumentality. This is the meaning in a complex society; it gives us all the certainty that we need" (Polanyi 1944, p. 268).

And today this "complexity" of a liberal social order also includes the knowledge that securing peoples' futures via price stability and welfare state institutions entails the existence of significant private wealth in the form of net claims on the state.

References

Deaton, Angus. 2013. *The Great Escape: Health, Wealth, and the Origins of Inequality.* Princeton (NJ): Princeton University Press.

Eucken, Walter. 1952. *Grundsätze der Wirtschaftspolitik.* Tübingen: Mohr-Siebeck.

Hayek, Friedrich A. von. 1967. Rechtsordnung und Handelnsordnung. In *Zur Einheit der Rechts- und Staatswissenschaften,* ed. Erich Streißler, 195–230. Karlsruhe: C.F. Müller.

Marx, Karl. 1976 [1867]. *Capital: A Critique of Political Economy,* vol. 1, trans. Ben Fowkes. London: Penguin/New Left Books.

Marx, Karl and Friedrich Engels. 1967 [1848]. *The Communist Manifesto,* trans. Samuel Moore. London: Penguin.

Müller-Armack, Alfred. 1950. Soziale Irenik. *Weltwirtschaftliches Archiv* 64: 181–203.

Osterhammel, Jürgen. 2010. *Die Verwandlung der Welt – Eine Geschichte des 19. Jahrhunderts.* Munich: C.H. Beck-Verlag.

Polanyi, Karl. 1944. *The Great Transformation.* New York (NY): Farrar and Rinehart.

Popper, Karl. 1945. *The Open Society and its Enemies.* London: Routledge.

Safranski, Rüdiger. 2014. *Romanticism: A German Affair,* trans. Robert E. Goodwin. Evanston, Illinois: Northwestern University Press.

Simmel, Georg. 1978 [1900]. *The Philosophy of Money,* trans. Tom Bottomore and David Frisby. London: Routledge and Keegan Paul.

Simon, Herbert. 1962. The Architecture of Complexity. *Proceedings of the American Philosophical Society* 106 (6): 467–482.

Uhlig, Harald and Mathias Trabandt. 2011. The Laffer Curve Revisited. *Journal of Monetary Economics* 58 (4): 305–327.

Weizsäcker, Carl Christian von. 2005. Hayek und Keynes: Eine Synthese. *Ordo* 56: 95–111.

Weizsäcker, Carl Christian von. 2014. Die normative Ko-Evolution von Marktwirtschaft und Demokratie. *Ordo* 65: 13–43.

A New Era of International Economic Policy

10

Abstract

We distinguish between a "*Friedman world*" and a "*Keynes world*," the latter being characterized by the zero lower bound problem. With the natural rate of interest tending to fall over time, the Keynes world is becoming the norm. In the Keynes world, voters defend their interests as producers more than their interests as consumers. This strengthens protectionism at the ballot box. We are less and less able to rely on the USA to serve as the engine of the global economy via its high current account deficits. In addition to the WTO rules, an international fiscal order is needed to rescue free trade: 1. At low real interest rates, countries with current account surpluses undertake to eliminate them by increasing government net borrowing. 2. At high real interest rates, countries with current account deficits undertake to eliminate them by cutting fiscal expenditure or raising taxes.

10.1 Free Trade in Modernity

The struggle between free trade and protectionism is at least as old as the modern period itself. In his *The Wealth of Nations* (1776), Adam Smith wrote against mercantilism, which provided the theory for the protectionist practice of the then hegemonic power France. It took seventy years for his plea for free trade to be translated into legislation in Britain. It was in no small measure this late (and temporary) triumph of the idea of free trade that led John Maynard Keynes to include the following phrase in the last paragraph of his *General Theory*: "… the ideas of economists and political philosophers, both when they are right and when they are wrong, are more powerful than is commonly understood. Indeed the world is ruled by little else. Practical men, who believe themselves to be quite exempt from any intellectual influences, are usually the slaves of some defunct economist.

© The Author(s) 2021
C. C. von Weizsäcker and H. M. Krämer, *Saving and Investment in the Twenty-First Century*, https://doi.org/10.1007/978-3-030-75031-2_10

Madmen in authority, who hear voices in the air, are distilling their frenzy from some academic scribbler a few years back" (Keynes 1936, p. 383).

The classical school argued for free trade. Ricardo took up the thread from Adam Smith—and was even a member of the British House of Commons for a time. He developed his theory of comparative advantage as a justification for free trade. In Germany, Friedrich List wrote his *National System of Political Economy* (List 1841) as an argument against the free trade doctrine of the classical school. To use today's economic terminology, he pointed to the significant *positive externalities* of industrial activity, which would be denied a still backward country like Germany, if, in keeping with the classical doctrine, it had to compete with superior British industry on the basis of free trade. He thus argued for a German customs union with protective tariffs against British goods. We will come back to List's ideas in Chap. 12 on the developing countries and emerging economies.

In addition to purely economic considerations, freedom and international peace have always played an important role in the classical liberal arguments for free trade. Protectionist arguments, on the contrary, always also involve the idea that free trade is in reality a weapon of imperialism and colonialism. Hence, for centuries already, slogans like "prosperity through trade," "freedom through trade," and "peace through trade" have been facing off in public discourse against others like "(foreign) domination through trade," "colonization through trade," "free trade imperialism" and "exploitation through trade."

The free trade position predominates in modern economic theory. Among other reasons, this is due to the tremendous success that a regime of relatively free trade, under first the GATT rules and then the WTO rules, has had in fostering global prosperity—also precisely in many countries that were still very poor at the beginning of the postwar era in 1945 (cf. also Rosling et al. 2018). Nonetheless, economic theory has also, of course, contained indications that a simple, unnuanced free-tradism is inadequate. We can recall, in this connection, the Stolper–Samuelson Theorem (Stolper and Samuelson 1941) and the theory of international trade with imperfect competition (Krugman 1979).

The process of European unification got underway in the mid-1950s with the creation of a common market. On the model of domestic freedom of movement and domestic free trade in nation states, international, but still intra-European, free trade was used here as an instrument for establishing a peaceful European order. Even if emphasis was placed on the economic benefits of such a common market, the actual goal was the creation of an intra-European order that would end wars between the European nation states once and for all. The resiliency of European liberal democracy in the face of authoritarian or even totalitarian disturbances of external origin was also supposed to be heightened by the ongoing process of economically driven unification. We will come back to this point in the following chapter on the euro.

10.2   Free Trade or Import Barriers as Nash Equilibrium

It is not our intention here to present a comprehensive political economy of international trade. We only want to call attention to the relationship between the overall macroeconomic situation and more or less strong tendencies toward "protectionism."

To start our analysis off, we again refer to John Maynard Keynes. To the astonishment of many of his contemporaries, in a newspaper article of April 7, 1931, Keynes called for British import tariffs. He argued that they were needed because of the high unemployment that had also developed in Great Britain since the October 1929 crash: job creation by eliminating foreign competition or at least making it more difficult (Krämer 2011). The proposal did not only contradict the prevailing opinion among economists, but also what Keynes himself had previously argued in the spirit of free trade. With his talent for pointed formulations, he wrote: "I seem to see the elder parrots sitting round and saying: 'You can rely on us'. Everyday for thirty years, regardless of the weather, we have said: 'what a lovely morning'. But this is a bad bird. He says one thing one day and something else the next" (Keynes 1931).

We know, of course, that tariff barriers are not an appropriate means for increasing total global employment in recessions or depressions. Nonetheless, a unilateral increase in import tariffs can have a positive effect on domestic employment in this sort of situation, as long as other countries do not respond with corresponding tariff increases ("beggar thy neighbor"). In game-theoretical terms, a free trade regime is *not a Nash equilibrium* under conditions of global underemployment, if import tariffs can be changed unilaterally.

The political prospects for free trade are far better when the global employment situation is good. It is possible that import tariffs or other import barriers will still find supporters. Nonetheless, it is generally known in this case that real national product cannot be increased by imposing import tariffs: The price increases resulting from such tariffs force the central bank to raise interest rates, which, in turn, drain demand from other sectors of the economy.

In a certain way (without wanting here to provide a precise mathematical formulation), we can say that in a world with low global unemployment, free trade is nearly a *Nash equilibrium*.

Of course, the real world is more complicated than this juxtaposition of global underemployment and global full employment suggests. The phenomenon of *market asymmetry*, which we already discussed in Chap. 9, is of particular significance. Market asymmetry is also the basis of neo-Keynesian macroeconomics. The theory of interest groups developed by Olson (1982) can help us to explain its political effects. According to Olson, it is easier for small groups to come together to defend their interests than it is for large groups. It is easier to achieve the "public good" of a common representation of interests, if the number of participating members in the group is small. Given specialization based on the division of labor on the supply side and diversification on the demand side, the number of sellers is considerably smaller than the number of buyers in almost every market for produced goods. The supply side also possesses the technical know-how required for manufacturing the goods. For these reasons, the supply side can defend its interests in the political arena better than the demand side.

This is why, by and large, *import tariffs* play a role in the political system and not *export tariffs*. Similarly, there are often *export subsidies*, which as "dumping" may distort competition, but only rarely *import subsidies*.

In parallel to the market asymmetry that we have just discussed, individual citizens also have "*split personalities*": They are normally both producers and consumers and thus both part of the economy's system of production and part of its system of consumption. The weighting of their preferences as producers or as consumers also depends to a very large degree on the overall economic situation. If unemployment is high, their interests as producers are the focus. At full employment, most people can count on finding work again if they lose their current job. Hence, the interest in favorable buying conditions, especially low prices, increases relative to the interest in keeping their current jobs. As a rule, the same people will be more protectionist, both in their thinking and in their political action, the worse the employment situation.

Negative experiences with resurgent protectionism as a result of the Great Depression moved the spiritual fathers of the post-WWII global economic order to propose and to implement a system of international trade that was supposed to stabilize free trade. This was the purpose of both the GATT and the IMF, as well as the Bretton Woods system of fixed exchange rates. The architecture of this system of trade was supposed to make unilateral protectionist measures, like tariffs and devaluations, unattractive. The aim was to prevent the formation of a Nash equilibrium seeped in protectionism. The fact that this liberation from protectionism largely succeeded was due not only to the cleverly constructed architecture of the system and an initially overvalued US dollar, but also to the market-inspired dynamics of the rebuilding of Western Europe and Japan, which led to high employment and a massive increase in prosperity.

The system of fixed exchange rates ultimately broke down: among other reasons, due to the crisis into which the Vietnam War precipitated the USA as hegemonic power. Nonetheless, the progress made in liberalizing global trade ensured that the GATT/WTO system survived. The re-emergence of a global capital market after two world wars and the cross-border direct investment associated with it contributed to economic life adjusting to the rules of globalization, thus giving rise to significant gains in prosperity.

In recent years, the symptoms of crisis in the globalized economic system have been multiplying. These symptoms are often connected to the policies of Donald Trump in public discussion. In our opinion, attributing the crisis to the eccentricities of a single individual is too superficial. We will try to provide a deeper explanation in the following sections.

10.3 "Friedman World" or "Keynes World"

Every economist is familiar with the "liquidity trap." It is well known as an important building block of Keynes's *General Theory*. If the propensity to invest is low, even a nominal interest rate of zero may not be sufficient for private investment to absorb hypothetical private savings under conditions of full employment. The consequent "slump" is often exacerbated by the fact that price expectations are for deflation, so that potential investors may fear high real interest rates.

Locally or regionally deficient investment can then be offset at full employment, if there are other parts of the world where desired investment exceeds saving. In principle, the free movement of capital can thus serve to ensure that saving (S) matches investment (I) in the global economy even when employment is high. The interest rate level on the global capital market is then the pilot that brings the global "S" and the global "I" into line. If the interest rate can reach the "correct" level, a system of flexible exchange rates and free movement of capital is compatible with global prosperity at high global employment. We speak here of a "*Friedman world*" (Friedman 1953). Another feature of this world is that fiscal policy can be designed in a decentralized, i.e., autonomous, way and can vary from country to country. If one country has a restrictive public debt policy and if domestic saving is thus structurally greater than investment, this does not represent any danger to full employment, since the national surplus of savings can be invested on the international capital market to finance the excess investment of other countries. This then also corresponds to an excess of exports as compared to imports, which compensates for the domestic aggregate supply surplus. As a rule, however the price paid for this form of savings surplus is that domestic (real) interest rates are lower than the (real) rates in the recipient countries of the excess savings.

On the other hand, another country may run high deficits, so that domestic saving is not sufficient to finance domestic investment. The excess investment will then be made possible by capital imports, accompanied by a negative current account balance. Interest rates in this country are normally higher than in the countries of origin of the foreign savings.

But what happens if the level of the global full-employment real interest rate is so low that, due to the zero lower bound for the nominal rate, it can only be achieved through inflation? We assume that the goal of price stability should be maintained. In Chap. 9, we argued for this goal on the basis of the connection between monetary stability and the stability of the open society. If, with stable prices, the global full-employment real interest rate is so low as to be unattainable, then we are in a world that we will call a "*Keynes world*" (Keynes 1936).

In the Keynes world, *international coordination* of national macropolicies is required. Before going into the Keynes world in greater detail, we want to recall the well-known fact that there has always been a *reference currency* in times of free movement of capital. In the period before the First World War, the reference currency was the British pound. In the period since the Second World War, it is the

US dollar. Special rules apply for the country that controls the reference currency. It is, in particular, far less vulnerable than other countries to balance of payment crises, since there is no threat of its own currency being devalued against the reference currency. For the two currencies are one and the same. Of course, the country of the reference currency must preserve at least a certain degree of monetary stability. For its currency to discharge the function of reference currency, it is also useful for foreign investment to enjoy a high degree of security in this country. The pound before the First World War and the US dollar since the Second World War have more or less fulfilled these conditions.

It was understanding that international coordination could be needed that led to the international meetings of heads of state and government that have been held for decades now and that are known to the public nowadays as the "G7" (or "G8") and the "G20." But, up to now, the dichotomy between "Friedman world" and "Keynes world" that we have presented here is not used in international economic diplomacy.

International coordination of macropolicies must also, of course, encompass international coordination of fiscal policy. In the Keynes world, the fiscal policies in question run in two opposite directions. On the one hand, in the Keynes world too, there are constantly countries that have accumulated too much debt and hence run the risk of insolvency. In the view of many stakeholders in the global financial system, such insolvencies have to be prevented, in order to preserve the stability of the system. The traditional role of the IMF includes providing support in such cases, but also actively intervening in and monitoring countries. But sometimes support packages have also been put together that go well beyond the lending resources of the IMF. The Greek debt crisis is an example. Since the impending insolvency often escalates into a crisis situation in a matter of just days or weeks, it becomes the focus of public attention. The government of a country that finds itself in such a crisis has to commit itself to consolidating public finances, i.e., to imposing "austerity."

By contrast, the opposite international need for coordination, namely that which goes in the direction of more expansionary fiscal policy, is a slow-burning candle under the conditions of the Keynes world. There is no doubt that international pressure has sometimes led countries to pursue a more expansionary fiscal policy than they would have done otherwise. The means used to exert this pressure, however, are basically incompatible with the principles of free trade. We will come back to this matter later in the chapter. But there is often no general consensus that, on average, a more expansionary fiscal policy course should be pursued globally.

How can we explain this lack of consensus? To start with, there is already no consensus on whether we are in a Keynes world or in a Friedman world. Those who are inclined to view the situation as a Friedman world will not have any understanding for more fiscal expansion. They will tend to view low interest rates on the capital market as a consequence of central bank policy. And they will tend to believe that the full-employment equilibrium interest rate corresponding to current fiscal policy is higher than the actually prevailing rate. Conversely, those who take the view that we are in a Keynes world will regard much of what is officially proclaimed as the expression of a misguided austerity policy, which is partly to blame for the fact that many countries are far from full employment.

In principle, it can never be ruled out that the world will be transformed in the near future from a Friedman world into a Keynes world—or, conversely, that it will be transformed from a Keynes world into a Friedman world. Whether such a transformation goes in the one direction or the other depends in no small measure on the evolution of countries' fiscal policies.

When the overall situation of the global economy is so opaque, it is difficult to get countries like Germany or the "northern" eurozone countries in general to abandon their current fiscal policy. The latter can always argue that there is a high probability that we are in a Friedman world. In "normal" times, moreover, the need for action is not so urgent, so that there is also no hurry to find a consensus.

The result is an asymmetry in international macroeconomic cooperation. If we are in a Keynes world, the excessive public debt of certain countries leads to crises, the overcoming of which involves massive restrictions on the debt of the countries in question. But an expansion of the debt of countries with "healthy" public finances, which would be useful from the point of view of monetary stability and higher employment, cannot be implemented due to a lack of consensus. In a Keynes world, the useful shifting of public debt from the less competitive countries to the more competitive countries thus fails to take place.

> The more competitive countries tend to see the world as a Friedman world.
> The less competitive countries tend to see the world as a Keynes world.

10.4 The Natural Rate of Interest, the Friedman World and the Keynes World

We can define *a transitional zone for the risk-free real interest rate on the capital market*. This zone consists of the range of real, risk-free interest rate levels at which a transition from the Friedman world to the Keynes world or a transition from the Keynes world to the Friedman world is to be regarded as a real possibility, such that people's thinking and actions adapt to the imminent danger or opportunity that such a transition represents. In this transitional zone, there will normally also be disagreement about whether we are currently in a Friedman world or a Keynes world.

Figure 10.1 provides a graphic representation of this idea. The red line represents the relationship between the global level of public debt D (plotted on the horizontal axis) and the equilibrium interest rate at (hypothetical) full employment. The latter is plotted on the vertical axis. As discussed in Chap. 2 on capital-theoretical foundations, we understand D as the independent variable and r as the dependent variable here. The natural rate ρ ("rho" in the graph) is located

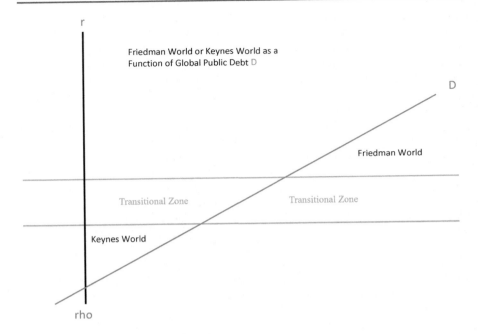

Fig. 10.1 Friedman world or Keynes world as a function of global public debt. *Source* Authors' own presentation

where $D = 0$. At a high level of global public debt D, there is no doubt that we are in a Friedman world. At a very low level of public debt D, there is no doubt that we are in a Keynes world, since, due to the liquidity trap, central banks cannot lower the interest rate to the level required for full employment under conditions of price stability. As we have drawn the graph, ρ is in the range of the Keynes world: Full employment with stable prices is only possible, if global public debt is positive. Further up, there is the transitional zone, in which the transition from a Keynes world to a Friedman world or, vice-versa, from a Friedman world to a Keynes world is not unlikely. In this transitional zone, there is also no consensus about whether we are currently in a Friedman world or in a Keynes world.

Now, it is obvious that the position of the natural rate ρ is of great significance for the international coordination of economic and, especially, fiscal policy: The natural rate of interest is the point of intersection between the red D-r curve and the vertical axis on which the full-employment rate is plotted. At a constant slope of the D-r curve, the lower the natural rate is, the larger is the range of the Keynes world and the smaller is the range of the Friedman world. If, as we have argued in this book, there is *a secular tendency for the natural rate of interest to fall*, then there is also a secular tendency for the range of the Keynes world to grow and the range of the Friedman world to shrink. The need for international coordination of fiscal policy is thus growing.

10.5 Unilateral Action and the Rules of Free Trade

It has always been the case that the rules of free trade are not respected in their pure form. Tariff and non-tariff import barriers and conscious intervention in foreign exchange markets are of particular relevance here. Within the framework first of the GATT and then of the WTO, there were and are procedures whose purpose is to keep tariff and non-tariff barriers to trade in check and, if possible, to reduce them. We do not want to go into the details here. We should, however, recall the following point on which experts are agreed: The stronger the global economy, the easier it is to contain and to dismantle barriers to trade.

A second field of unilateral action is targeted intervention in currency markets by central banks, in order to alter the competitiveness of their country's economy. As a rule, a country intervening to devalue its currency provokes greater consternation among other countries than intervention in the opposite direction. In the short and medium terms, devaluing the currency increases a country's competitiveness, but, at the same time, it increases inflationary pressures on the domestic market and undermines international trust in the currency in question.

As shown above, the following can be observed: If real interest rates are high internationally, then this is a price signal for capital scarcity. If the employment situation is good, then net capital imports are welcome from a country's perspective —and hence so too are the current account deficits that go with them. If real interest rates are low internationally, then a full-employment equilibrium is precarious. The danger of slipping into a recession or even a depression then shapes the general perception of the situation and the discussion in the media. In this case, the global economy is either in a Keynes world or not far from it.

We can again use the image of the "split personality" in comparing high and low full-employment real interest rates. If citizens are always both (potential or actual) producers and consumers, the focus is on their role of consumers when there is full employment with high real interest rates, since the risk of long-term unemployment is low. If full employment is not assured and the real rate is low, then citizens are interested, above all, in their role as producers. In this case, their thinking and action is determined especially by job concerns.

In light of the finding of the previous section, we can draw the following conclusion:

> When the natural rate of interest falls, the weight of the producer in the voter's split personality rises at the expense of the weight of the consumer. The political economic situation is thus a function of the level of the natural rate of interest.

The WTO is an institution that has only limited possibilities for imposing sanctions on member states that violate its rules. Among other things, WTO proceedings are long and drawn-out. As we could see in the recent past, moreover, a member state like the USA can effectively paralyze the WTO dispute settlement apparatus. Hence, the rules of free trade can only be upheld, if the most important WTO members really want to uphold them.

But the ability to act of the governments of WTO member countries depends on there not being massive opposition among the majority of voters. Otherwise, sooner or later, the moment comes when the member in question resorts to unilateral measures that are not in accordance with the rules of free trade, but that—rightly or wrongly—are regarded as beneficial to voters' job security.

10.6   The New Protectionism

The election of Donald Trump and the trade policy that he has pursued as president are symptomatic of the fact that forces in the global economy have shifted in the direction of protectionism. Trump's election—which hardly anyone expected a year earlier—was not, in our view, an inexplicable "accident." It points to a change in the electorate, which is less and less impressed by the achievements of globalization and is assigning more and more weight to its costs in the form of job losses.

Modern protectionism can thus be understood as a contemporary version of anti-machinery "Luddite" movements. The fear of losing one's job that is provoked by advances in digitalization are a modern form of the fears that the invention of the spinning machine and the mechanical loom provoked in their time. Trump's 2016 election as president of the USA is thus a symptom of a natural rate of interest that is becoming increasingly negative.

There is no doubt that the USA is one of the main "winners" in the process of globalization. We have only to think of the sensational global changes coming from Silicon Valley and other American hubs of digital innovation. If there were no grateful global market for the products of the American IT industry, its profits would be far lower. The model of producing software in the USA, but the hardware in China led to the earlier incredible success of these companies on the stock exchange. As of the end of December 2020, the five most valuable companies in the world are currently American digital pioneers.

Globalized finance has also contributed to increased prosperity in the USA. The global investment market does not only create substantial income streams for financial professionals in its capital New York, but also for their American customers. Many middle-class Americans derive a considerable part of the income on their savings from the dividends of American and non-American multinational companies. A large part of the shares of the major Germany companies included in the DAX-30 index are held by American funds. The influx of foreign capital into the USA also promotes American prosperity. The return on these investments is far lower than the return on American capital invested abroad as shareholdings. By far the greater part of the foreign capital in the USA is invested in fixed-rate assets: to a large extent, in American treasury bonds. This means that American investors can borrow at far lower interest rates than they could without these capital imports.

This phenomenon has, after all, been described by Bernanke as a "saving glut" (Bernanke 2005).

Nevertheless, the discussion among American voters is increasingly focused on the relocation of jobs abroad within the framework of globalized value chains. (There is a growing literature on this subject. Cf., for example, Rodrick 2018 and Komlos and Schubert 2019, which includes extensive bibliographical references.)

Trump used his executive powers to impose a protectionist line. This included employing measures that are usually not regarded as part of trade policy at all: like, for example, the sanctions against Iran. As is well known, the latter also affect German firms, which Trump has threatened to exclude from the American market unless they stop their deliveries to Iran. The protectionist line of American trade policy is now also part of President Biden's agenda. If he wants to maintain and increase voters' support in the mid-term elections, he needs to be protectionist— unless, as we propose below, free trade rules are complemented by obligations of WTO members to aim at nearly zero disparity between exports and imports.

Recent US trade policy highlights a strength that the USA has always had. *The USA represents the largest domestic market in the world.* For many exporters, especially from Asia, it is an even more important sales market than the European Common Market. If we take, for example, the current conflict between the USA and China, the USA holds the better cards, because American imports from China are far greater than Chinese imports from the USA. (Cf. also Felbermayr 2019, as well as Fetzer and Schwarz 2019. The latter analyze the political economy of the new trade policy using simulations.)

In times in which the full-employment level of the interest rate is either in the range of the Keynes world or in the transitional zone, *access to the domestic market is the strongest card that a country or a common market comprising several countries can play in trade diplomacy.* This is the strength that Trump was exploiting in his international trade policy (cf. also Simon 2019). Politically, Biden cannot afford not to play this card. He may do this with greater diplomatic skill than his predecessor, but he will remain protectionist.

This strength is further increased by the USA's high *current account deficit.* If tariff barriers are set up everywhere, the job losses appear to be greater for voters in the USA's supplier countries than for voters in the USA itself. In other words: One can suggest to American voters that high tariff barriers that are the same level for American imports and exports amount to a "re-importing" of American jobs. (The trained specialist in macroeconomics knows that things are more complicated in the context of a general equilibrium and cannot be reduced to such a "re-import" optic.)

In an interview with the *Financial Times* (July 20, 2018), Henry Kissinger let it be known that: "I think Trump may be one of those figures in history who appears from time to time to mark the end of an era and to force it to give up its old pretenses" (Kissinger 2018). Kissinger may be right. In matters of trade policy, Trump may have been not so much the cause of the new protectionism as its beneficiary. American trade negotiators can be expected to continue playing the card of the USA's strength even after the end of the Trump era—under pressure from an electorate for whom jobs have become more important than low prices.

Even before Trump, the USA occasionally exerted political pressure to make exports to the USA more difficult. In East Asia, Japan depends on the US military for protection. With the growing military power of China, this dependency is becoming greater. Moreover, Japan has long relied on being able to export to the USA without major trade barriers. Thus, decades ago already, the USA "forbade" Japanese authorities from devaluing the yen, so that private Japanese savings, which exceed full-employment investment, could be diverted abroad. As consequence, Japan had to offset these excess private savings by high fiscal deficits, in order to maintain full employment with only a slight export surplus. We presume that the Japanese population would have preferred a different economic policy solution.

10.7   A Multilateral Balanced Account Agreement

From our finding that the natural interest rate level is already negative today and will tend to slide even further into the minuses in the future, we conclude that there will likely be no going back to the de facto rules of the pre-Trump era. If free trade is preserved and if most other currencies remain convertible into US dollars, the interest rate in dollars will no longer rise to levels corresponding to an undeniable return to the Friedman world. Under these conditions, the net inflow of large amounts of capital into the USA will ensure that real interest rates in dollars remain low. In political–economic terms, however, such a hypothetical situation is not sustainable. Due to high current account deficits, American voters will compel any congressional majority to play the card of the USA's large domestic market, just as has happened vis-à-vis Japan for decades already and as Trump has done in generalizing the earlier Japan policy.

Our proposal for modifying the international trade regime is intended to safeguard free trade in political-economic terms. We thus propose:

> **A multilateral balanced account agreement**
> The OECD plus China region undertakes to uphold the rules of free trade. At the same time, however, each currency area in this region undertakes to bring its current account balance close to zero by using appropriate fiscal measures.

We will say something about the implementation below. For the moment, let us just note the following: If the current accounts of the currency areas are more or less balanced, then it will always be possible to respond to the advocates of protectionist measures that foreign retaliatory measures will cost about as many jobs as the original measures "gain." Protectionists in countries with current account deficits are thus deprived of a popular argument.

As we have shown, the resurgence of protectionism is tied to low real interest rates, which can be attributed, in turn, to the already negative and still falling natural rate. If, however, real interest rates are below the steady state growth rate of a country, then additional public debt does not represent any additional burden on future generations. If, furthermore, the additional debt is used to promote public and private investment, then it even increases prosperity as compared to investing the excess savings abroad at low interest rates. At low interest rates, the additional public debt for the purpose of eliminating a current account surplus is thus a better way of providing for the future, even when we leave aside the free trade that it "purchases" (cf. also Blanchard 2019).

Although risk-free real interest rates will remain low in our opinion, the proposed balanced account agreement should also be enacted if the level of the real rate is high at full employment. In this case, the countries with current account surpluses should not be required to increase their public debt. It is up rather to the countries with current account deficits to diminish the latter by slowing down the growth in their public debt.

A kind of symmetry thus comes into being. The agreement has the effect of shifting the interest rate in the direction of the economy's growth rate. At an interest rate level below the growth rate, the countries with current account surpluses increase their public debt, as a consequence of which global interest rates rise. At an interest rate level above the growth rate, the countries with current account deficits reduce their public debt, as a consequence of which global interest rates fall. These corrections based on the balanced account agreement increase overall prosperity in the OECD plus China region, because the Golden Rule of Accumulation applies (cf. Chap. 2 on capital-theoretical foundations). But they also increase prosperity in the countries that are required to undertake the corrective measures: For even apart from the balanced account agreement, when interest rates are low, it makes sense for a country to increase its public debt, in order to finance more public investment and/or reduce taxes that have distorting allocational effects. And even apart from the balanced account agreement, when interest rates are high, it makes sense for a country to roll back public debt, in order not to have a heavy debt service burden in the future.

References

Bernanke, Ben. 2005. *The global saving glut and the U.S. current account deficit*. Speech 77. Washington (D.C.): Board of Governors of the Federal Reserve System.

Blanchard, Olivier. 2019. Public Debt and Low Interest Rates, AEA Presidential Lecture 2019. *American Economic Review* 109 (4): 1197–1229.

Felbermayr, Gabriel. 2019. „Es geht um die Weltherrschaft" (Interview). *Handelsblatt*. 6 May 2019.

Fetzer Thiemo and Carlo Schwarz. 2019. *Tariffs and Politics: Evidence From Trump's Trade Wars*. CES-Ifo Working Paper 7553. Munich: Ifo-Institut.

Friedman, Milton. 1953. The Case for Flexible Exchange Rates, in: *Essays in Positive Economics*, ed. Milton Friedman, 157–203. Chicago (IL): University of Chicago Press.

Keynes, John Maynard. 1931. Economic Notes on Free Trade II. *New Statesman and Nation.* 7 April 1931.

Keynes, John Maynard. 1936. *The General Theory of Employment, Interest and Money.* London: Macmillan.

Kissinger, Henry. 2018. Henry Kissinger: "We are in a very, very grave period" (Interview). *Financial Times.* 20 July 2018.

Komlos, John and Hermann Schubert. 2019. Die Entwicklung sozialer Ungleichheit und ihre politischen Implikationen in den USA. *Wirtschaftsdienst* 99 (3): 216–223.

Krämer, Hagen M. 2011. Keynes, Globalisierung und Strukturwandel. In *Keynes 2.0 – Perspektiven einer modernen keynesianischen Wirtschaftstheorie und Wirtschaftspolitik.* Jahrbuch Ökonomie und Gesellschaft 23, eds. Harald Hagemann and Hagen Krämer, 183–215. Marburg: Metropolis-Verlag.

Krugman, Paul. 1979. Increasing Returns to Scale, Monopolistic Competition, and International Trade. *Journal of International Economics* 9: 469–479.

List, Friedrich. 1841. *Das nationale System der politischen Ökonomie.* Stuttgart: Cotta.

Olson, Mancur. 1982. *The Rise and Decline of Nations: Economic Growth, Stagflation and Social Rigidities.* New Haven (CT): Yale University Press.

Rodrick, Dani. 2018. Populism and the economics of globalization. *Journal of International Business Policy* 1(1–2): 12–33.

Rosling, Hans, Ola Rosling and Anna Rosling Rönnlund. 2018. *Factfulness.* New York (NY): Flatiron Books.

Simon, Hermann. 2019. Die Macht der Mächte. *Frankfurter Allgemeine Zeitung,* 6 June 2019.

Smith, Adam. 1776. *An Inquiry into the Nature and Causes of the Wealth of Nations.* London: W. Strahan and T. Cadell.

Stolper, Wolfgang and Paul A. Samuelson. 1941. Protection and Real Wages. *Review of Economic Studies* 9 (1): 58–73.

Europe, the Euro and German Demographic Renewal

11

Abstract

Access to the domestic market is nowadays the trump card of trade diplomacy. The larger the domestic market, the more effective it is. The euro is thus the decisive pillar of the European single market. The German debt brake is incompatible with the long-term stability of the euro. For as long as it applies, full employment can never be achieved in the eurozone as a whole. Under current fiscal policy, full employment would require unrealistically high export surpluses. A euro doomed to underemployment will collapse. Hence, the international fiscal order must also be applied among the nation states in the euro area. Germany's resulting obligations offer an opportunity for a German demographic renewal by aggressively encouraging the immigration of skilled workers.

11.1 The Single Market

When the process of European unification began after the Second World War with the European Coal and Steel Union and then the European Economic Community, the goal of these steps was to ensure peace in Europe. At the same time, economic recovery was closely linked to the East–West conflict and, in particular, the Cold War between the two world powers, the USA and the Soviet Union. For a long time, members of the common or "single" market were only countries that were also close allies of the USA by way of membership in NATO. It was only starting in the 1990s, after the fall of the Berlin Wall and the dissolution of the Soviet Union, that countries that were not part of NATO also joined the single market: in particular, Austria, Sweden and Finland. The political and military climate had changed. Apart from economic criteria, a "community of values" was now decisive for membership in the European Union—not participation in a military alliance

© The Author(s) 2021
C. C. von Weizsäcker and H. M. Krämer, *Saving and Investment in the Twenty-First Century*, https://doi.org/10.1007/978-3-030-75031-2_11

anymore. But membership in a common market also requires that certain basic preconditions of a market-based economic order are fulfilled.

Among citizens, however, there is still no consensus today on which matters should be subject to a common and uniform approach in the EU. The Brexit vote in the summer of 2016 showed that certain EU regulations are so unpopular that a majority of voters may support their country withdrawing from the common market. Many people are of the opinion that the decisions taken in Brussels, Strasbourg and Luxembourg reflect a lack of understanding of the principle of *subsidiarity*.

If we compare the history of the process of European unification up to now and the formation and consolidation of the USA, we find that, in addition to the much greater linguistic diversity in Europe, there is also an important difference in the constitution of the two federal structures. In Europe, member states have the right to withdraw from the union. The individual states comprising the USA do not have such a right. Twice in the nineteenth century, under Jackson and later under Lincoln, the USA fought civil wars triggered by member states' wanting to secede. Twice, a federal army under the command of the president of the USA had to defeat a separatist army to avert secession. The right to withdraw from the European Union is, of course, closely connected to the fact that it would be unthinkable in the twenty-first century to prevent the secession of a member state by military means.

What are the conditions for the persistence of a union of states in which each member state has the right to secede? We want to examine this question from the point of view of economic policy in particular, using ideas that we have developed in the prior chapters of this book.

11.2 Europe's Global Political Environment: International Demand Power

Picking up on our analysis of free trade in the last chapter, we want here to point to the enormous dynamism of the global economy and of global society. It is not only the Chinese economic miracle that has marked world politics in recent decades. As Hans Rosling and his co-authors have convincingly demonstrated in their book *Factfulness*, many observers from rich countries have blinders on that prevent them from being sufficiently aware of the great progress that has been made in the developing countries and especially in the so-called emerging economies (cf. Rosling et al. 2018). We have already touched upon the rapidly increasing average life expectancy of the global population in Chap. 3 (on desired wealth). According to the 2017 UN population forecast, based on the trend in birth rates, the global population can be expected to peak in about 100 years and to decline again from then on (United Nations 2017). It is fairly certain that some of the countries that are still considered today as "emerging economies"—such as India, Brazil, Indonesia, Iran and others—will join the club of rich countries in the course of the twenty-first century. In the last 12–15 years, for instance, per capita real income in India has doubled. At the same time, the Indian birth rate has fallen sharply.

We can thus assume that the relative importance of Europe in the global economy will decrease. The share of European GDP in global GDP will continue to fall. The rest of the world will become less and less dependent on European high-tech products. Whatever European technology can do, the technology of China, Japan, South Korea, Israel, Singapore, India or Brazil can increasingly do as well. The USA has long been Europe's equal in technical terms, even if there are differences from one sector to another, sometimes in favor of the USA, sometimes in favor of Europe.

No matter the form of government, public authorities are always interested in offering citizens as many employment opportunities as possible. Economic growth has thus to keep pace with population growth and increased labor productivity. As discussed in the last chapter, in light of the proximity of the Keynes world, the size of the domestic market is the most important card that any country can play in international trade diplomacy.

A world of potential *international demand power* is increasingly coming into being. The concept of demand-side market power comes from competition policy and antitrust law. It refers to the phenomenon of large retailers being able to obtain more favorable purchasing conditions in negotiations with manufacturers than smaller buyers are able to obtain. This has led, for example, to a strong process of concentration in the retail food sector. (Cf. various opinions of Germany's Monopoly Commission on the food retail trade, as well as Chap. V of its 2012 main report [Monopolkommission 2012].) If free trade cannot be relied upon as the institutional regime of the global economy, then it is also advisable for a continent like Europe to adapt to the phenomenon of international demand power.

Concretely, this means that—other things being equal—larger states or larger currency areas can expect to enjoy better conditions in international trade than smaller states or smaller currency areas. Of course, certain smaller countries—like, for instance, Switzerland or Israel or Singapore—can achieve or obtain advantages through superior flexibility, which may compensate for their lack of size. But here it is always a matter of specific, historically evolved advantages that are not available to every small state.

Today, better conditions of international trade mean, in particular, better export opportunities to other countries or currency areas.

We have already mentioned a striking example of international market power in the previous chapter: the effective threat by the US administration to prohibit German firms from exporting to the USA, if they violate US sanctions against Iran. Germany's exports to Iran are "peanuts" in comparison to German exports to the USA and already existing German direct investment in the USA.

11.3   The Euro and the Single Market

In the debate that preceded the introduction of the euro, the proponents of a common currency saw it as a vehicle for accelerating the process of integration. The opponents argued that the member states were not yet ready for a common currency, given entirely different national "economic styles" (Müller-Armack; cf. Dietzfelbinger 1998). The time since its introduction has not led to a clear victory of the one side or the other. Friedman's (1997) prophecy that the euro would fail has not come true, but neither has it brought about the progress in European integration for which its proponents had hoped. The global economy has, however, adjusted to the fact that the euro will remain the currency of a large economic area.

The soaring value of the euro against the dollar before the 2007–2008 financial crisis is a thing of the past. The Greek crisis and the fragility of the southern euro countries forced the European Central Bank to adopt a policy of maintaining the lowest possible interest rates. Simultaneously, confidence in the stability of the eurozone waned on the international capital markets. As a result, the exchange rate of the euro against the dollar was significantly lower than it had been. This did not only help the competitiveness of the southern euro countries, but also the competitiveness of the considerably stronger northern euro countries. It is in no small measure thanks to this "weak" euro that Germany, before COVID-19, enjoyed its high export surpluses and thus too full employment and "healthy" public finances.

It should not be forgotten, however, that the resolutely expansionary fiscal policy pursued by the USA under President Obama made a major contribution to the overcoming of the 2007–2009 global financial crisis. Helped also by an expansionary monetary policy on the part of the Federal Reserve, the USA again became the engine of the global economy, which stabilized global demand for goods and services by running a substantial current account deficit.

The following analysis of the euro and its problems builds on previous analyses by various economists. Three books, in particular, should be mentioned here: Brunnermeier et al. (2016), Sinn (2014) and Stiglitz (2016).

Today, the euro area has an export surplus, which is important for the fact that the employment situation has improved and that, with the exception of Greece, no deflationary crisis has arisen in the southern euro countries. But the employment situation remains unsatisfactory in the southern euro countries. Many observers in Germany and other northern euro countries put the blame for this still unsatisfactory situation on the domestic policies of the southern countries, which, in their view, have not had the courage to undertake deregulatory measures. Both critics and supporters of current eurozone economic policy agree that the relative prices between the different eurozone countries are distorted. There is disagreement on whether correcting them should occur by way of further deflation in southern Europe or higher inflation in the northern part of the euro area. We do not want, however, to provide extensive analysis of this topical issue here.

There is also the idea of splitting the eurozone into a northern eurozone with a strong euro-1 and a southern eurozone with a weak euro-2. From the point of view of the southern countries, there is something to be said for this. For today's relatively "weak" euro is still stronger than a euro-2 only comprising the southern countries would be. The current euro may be gratifyingly weak for German industry; nevertheless, it is precisely because of German industry that it is stronger than the southern euro countries could possibly want it at the moment.

The arguments of some commentators in favor of a strong northern euro or euro-1 are not very convincing. This euro-1 would have a significantly higher exchange rate against the dollar than the present euro. It would thus exert deflationary pressure on the northern euro countries, leading to an economic slowdown. With given fiscal policy, the latter would probably have to resort to intervening on the foreign exchange market, like Switzerland does, in order to prevent the euro-1 from having too high a dollar value. This is possible for the Swiss National Bank: Even a Trump administration had little against a deliberate weakening of the Swiss franc, since this is primarily achieved by the Swiss National Bank purchasing euros and thus strengthening the euro. But the weakening of the euro-1 by its central bank would have to be achieved by massively buying up dollars. This would, in turn, bring into action any US administration, which would attack such behavior as a violation of the rules of the system of free trade. In the interest of preserving free trade and also for the benefit precisely of the people in the euro-1 area, a northern euro or euro-1 would have to refrain from massive manipulations of the exchange rate against the dollar. In order not to be pushed into a recession or even depression and a deflationary trap by a high euro-1 exchange rate, the member states might have to make extensive use of fiscal policy to boost demand. At the same time, the monetary policy of the euro-1 central bank would have to be aimed at maintaining the lowest possible interest rates. Debt brakes on the German model would thus be incompatible with membership in the northern euro area.

These observations on a hypothetical northern euro are based, of course, on our analysis that the OECD plus China region is in a Keynes world, or at least in the transitional zone between a Keynes world and a Friedman world, and can be expected to remain so for a long time. The details can be found in the previous chapter (Chap. 10) on the struggle between free trade and protectionism.

A "strong" northern euro is thus not even advisable for the potential members of the northern euro area themselves. Nonetheless, the thought experiment involved in imagining this sort of northern euro is of interest, because it makes clear the other side of this coin: namely, that the potential northern euro countries benefit from the fact that the euro is so weak due to the membership of the economically weaker southern euro states. As long as international economic policy tolerates this state of affairs, Germany can afford its debt brake, precisely because it uses the same currency as countries that are far removed from any debt brake.

In Germany, the current situation is often depicted as follows: Germany, with its high export surpluses, is the economic engine of the eurozone, inasmuch as these export surpluses and the resulting high employment in Germany also lead to higher

German demand for goods from France, Italy, Spain, Portugal and Greece. This observation is correct to the extent that it holds other things being equal, i.e., at a given exchange rate of the euro against the dollar as reference currency and against other currencies. But it is misleading to the extent that Germany is in such a good position on the global market precisely because it is part of a monetary union with the countries whose economic engine it allegedly represents. For then it becomes clear that France, Italy, etc., suffer precisely from the fact that the euro area also includes Germany and the other more competitive member states. The euro is "too strong" for France, Italy, etc. and forces these countries into deflation. Once we see this connection between the euro exchange rate and German current account surpluses, nothing is left of the idea that Germany is the economic engine of the eurozone.

11.4   The Euro as Pillar of the Single Market

If our analysis in the previous chapter is correct, viz. to the effect that it is strategically advantageous for a region to be part of a large internal market, then Europe's single market represents an advantage for the people of Europe that goes beyond the advantages that are usually mentioned in international trade theory. What is at issue then is that an individual European nation like Italy, for example, not become the target of trade policy manipulations on the part of other big "markets" like the USA, China and India. The single market means precisely that trade policy issues are decided upon by its members collectively, thus preventing an imbalance in the strength of the negotiating positions of one of the global giants and any individual European country. The coordination of trade policy within Europe is thus important for ensuring that the community of values of the European nations can be sustained.

The problems arising for Great Britain after Brexit are also connected to the fact that it is far more interesting for any of the world's countries to have access to the European single market than to the British market. The European Union can certainly adopt a friendly "good neighbor" policy toward Great Britain—and thus reduce the separation pains that the latter will experience. And we have to hope that the remaining 27 EU members are wise enough to adopt such a policy toward the renegade ex-member. It is by no means certain that they will, however—especially since not all 27 member states are in as good a position economically as Germany, for example. But, in any case, the backing that Great Britain enjoys in negotiations with non-European powers has been diminished by Brexit.

The current problems with Italy show that further withdrawals from the single market cannot be ruled out, even if such secession is not beneficial for the country in question. The stabilization of the single market is not automatic. It also cannot be ruled out that member states will formally remain in the European Union, but, nonetheless, adopt national measures that undermine the internal market rules. The problems that the European Union is currently having in terms of the rule of law with member states like Poland, Hungary or Romania demonstrate the extent of the potential centrifugal forces that the European Union has to resist.

A stable euro is an important, perhaps indeed decisive, pillar for holding the European Union together. Stable in two senses: firstly, as regards its purchasing power. In Chap. 9 on monetary stability and the stability of the open society, we discussed the relationship between a stable value of the currency and the stability of a free, democratic social order. But the stability of the euro also entails that citizens can rely on its continued existence.

If the euro were to fail and national currencies were to take its place again, this would be a sign of weakness for the European single market. Whatever the reason for the collapse of the common currency, in the new era of international economic policy, it will be seen by big non-European countries (the USA, China, India, Russia and Brazil, for example) as a signal that the European countries can be played off against each other: That the big countries can now bring the demand power created by their size to bear against the much smaller European countries, because the common defense of interests no longer seems to work in Europe. This can give rise to a diplomatic and political dynamic that then actually does lead to the de facto collapse of the rules of a common market.

Thus, for example, each of the individual national currencies could be linked to different potential candidates for the role of the future global reference currency. China's global "New Silk Road" strategy could thus be supplemented by a currency component. If, for example, the neo-D-mark is pegged to the yuan to counter the US accusation of currency manipulation for the purpose of devaluation, whereas the more inflation-prone national currencies like the neo-lira are pegged to the dollar, then, as a matter of course, Europe's national markets will also begin to grow apart.

Among other things, a common currency like the euro also serves to ensure that in the Keynes world, the lack of a Nash equilibrium for intra-European free trade cannot lead to new national protectionist strategies using exchange rate policy. For there is no national exchange rate policy to be abused anymore. The common currency thus directs the focus of national policy toward the rules that have to be followed if a country wants to remain part of the monetary union. One cannot draw the bow of discipling national policy via the common currency too tautly, however —otherwise it breaks. We will turn now to this last point in greater detail.

11.5 The Problem of National Current Account Balances

Germany exhibits a high export surplus and hence also a high current account surplus. And this is not only sporadically the case, but is practically a "structural" feature. To this export surplus, there also corresponds a substantial excess of aggregate savings as compared to aggregate investment. Ante COVID-19, households, the corporate sector and the state were are all running surpluses in Germany. This is unusual for the OECD countries. In most of them, both the corporate sector and the state run structural deficits.

If each member state of the European Union had its own national currency, we would be able directly to apply the considerations that we presented in the chapter on free trade in the new era of international economic policy. The essence of our proposal was that in a Keynes world with low real interest rates, countries with current account surpluses should eliminate them by increasing their fiscal deficit. Germany would accordingly have to abandon its debt brake to fulfill its obligations under the balanced account agreement that we have proposed. In perfectly symmetrical fashion, in a Friedman world, countries with current account deficits would be obligated to reduce their fiscal deficit to contribute to lowering real interest rates. At present, however, we are clearly in the Keynes world of low real interest rates.

But this balanced account agreement remains attractive even if a group of countries has a common currency. This is the case for the euro. Thus, the balanced account agreement between the different currency areas should also apply for the euro area. Trump had accused Germany of engaging in a form of covert currency manipulation at the expense of American jobs by virtue of its membership in a monetary union with far weaker partners. If, in the Keynes world of the new era of international economic policy, the national priority is the creation or preservation of as many jobs as possible and no longer facilitating the most inexpensive possible imports, then the accusation is not entirely off-base. We do not share this view as far as German intentions are concerned. But the result is the same as it would be if Germany had deliberately joined a monetary union with weaker partners, in order to benefit from a weak currency for the purpose of creating jobs.

The anger of the other eurozone countries that Germany incurs as a result of its current account surpluses is a serious problem for the cohesion of the European Union and the political stability of the euro. We already showed above that the notion that Germany is the economic engine of the eurozone thanks to its immense export surpluses is misleading. The resultant strengthening of the euro against other world currencies, and, in particular, against the dollar, makes it more difficult for the weaker euro countries to achieve full employment. It is already the case today, when there is insufficient employment in the southern euro countries, that the euro area runs current account surpluses. With given fiscal policy and with full employment in the euro area as a whole, the current account surplus of the euro countries as a percentage of gross domestic product would be comparable to the surplus that Germany runs now. But, if dollar interest rates are no longer rising significantly, the exchange rate of the euro would then be far higher than it is today. But this means that *such eurozone current account surpluses cannot occur.*

In other words, if Germany and the other comparable northern euro countries retain their present fiscal policies, then the southern euro countries cannot reach the goal of high employment. If they tried to do so by way of additional public debt, the capital market would punish them with high risk premiums. It would not even be necessary for the European Commission to take any disciplinary action.

This would be a potentially explosive situation for the euro. At best, an extremely expansionary US fiscal policy with consequent high dollar interest rates could bring about a transition onto the terrain of the Friedman world. In political-economic terms, it is, however, likelier that under any USA presidency non-market interventions will take place in the USA of a sort that will take the world even further away from the virtues of free markets and free trade. As an example, we need only think of the price controls that were decreed by President Nixon at the height of the Vietnam crisis.

If there is no such extremely expansionary US fiscal policy, the impossibility of achieving full employment in the euro area with current northern European fiscal policy may deprive the euro of its integrative function. A revolt of the southern euro countries, such as has already been foreshadowed in various elections and protest movements, will then indeed lead to a partition of the euro zone, if not to an outright return to national currencies.

11.6 Investment Promotion as the Solution?

One often hears that governments should do more to encourage investment. The hope is that a higher rate of investment will lead to higher growth and a more dynamic economy. And it is also hoped that the gap between private saving and private investment will be reduced. Overregulation is frequently identified as an important obstacle to investment.

It is not our intention to examine the issue of investment conditions in detail in this book. We believe that our analysis of the private savings surplus is valid, regardless of whether the thesis that governments can and should create more favorable investment conditions is right or wrong. In dealing with the subject of excess saving, it is important to think not only in flow variables like "saving" and "investment," but also in stock variables like "desired wealth" and "real capital stock." *Time variables* are also helpful. Look at the ratio between "desired wealth" and "consumption per year" (the variable Z from Chaps. 2 and 3 on the natural rate of interest and on desired wealth). Then compare it with the ratio between "real capital" and "consumption per year" (the variable T, i.e., the period of production, from Chaps. 2 and 4 on the natural rate of interest and on real capital).

There is no doubt that a government policy that promotes current investment can lead to an increase in the share of gross investment in gross domestic product. If, however, we ask whether such measures also increase the *capital tied up in the production process* relative to current consumption, we cannot avoid considering the specific nature of the investment promotion. The latter should, after all, be economically productive: We do not want, to use the Keynes example, to promote the construction of economically unproductive "pyramids," but rather the construction of such plant and equipment as increases productive capacities. Ultimately, investment promotion is supposed to help to raise peoples' standard of living. This observation is practically identical to the following one: Ultimately, promotion of private investment is supposed to improve consumption possibilities. But this alone does not tell us whether public promotion of investment increases or decreases the ratio between the capital tied up in the private system of production and total consumption.

A more precise analysis reveals the following: At a real interest rate r that is a correct intertemporal price signal, investment promotion that does nothing other than increase the capital intensity of the production process with the same technology only makes sense if this interest rate is greater than the steady state growth rate g. This is the Golden Rule of Accumulation, which we derived in generalized form in Chap. 2. If we are in the Keynes world, however, then $r < g$ holds (cf. also Blanchard 2019). Hence, for the Keynes world, public promotion of a pure increase in capital intensity with the same technology is out of the question, because it leads to *sustained* lower consumption.

Investment promotion whose purpose is to change technology is a particular form of promoting economic growth. Whether—other things being equal—this form of promoting technical progress is likely to increase the capital tied up in the private production process has to be studied more closely. If we think of the buzzword of digitalization, which is so popular nowadays, skepticism is in order. When Germany's governing coalition launches a program for promoting artificial intelligence, it has, above all, the competitiveness of German industry in the global economy in mind. The point is to create jobs in Germany and to protect existing jobs by giving employees additional training. But whether this *German* promotion of growth increases or decreases the capital tied up in the *global* production process cannot be determined a priori from the fact that it ensures that there are more jobs in Germany. It could be that jobs are thus created in Germany, but using machines that eliminate existing jobs in the global economy or at least reduce the average roundaboutness of production in the global economy.

In the theoretical literature, there is a simple model that gives an answer to the question posed here on the amount of capital tied up in production (Solow et al. 1966). In this model, technical progress is "embodied." Each individual technical advance is only introduced into the production process by building equipment (machines) that translates this advance into practice. When, for example, a particular step in the production process gets automated, the old equipment is scrapped and replaced by new equipment.

In this model, we can now ask how the ratio of the capital tied up in production to current consumption changes, if, at a given steady-state real interest rate, the rate of technical progress is increased. Solow et al. (1966) model is analyzed in Weizsäcker (2021, Chap. 5, Sect. 1), where there is a clear answer to this question: At a given real interest rate, the relative amount of capital tied up in the production process (i.e., this capital divided by current consumption) is *less*, the greater the rate of technical progress.

To the extent that this outcome of the model is representative for the real world, we arrive at the following conclusion: In a Keynes world—namely, in a world with low real interest rates—an economically sensible form of investment promotion does nothing to increase the ratio between capital tied up in production and current consumption. The opposite is rather the case.

The intuition corresponding to this outcome is as follows: The greater the rate of technical progress, the faster the real capital stock "turns over" or, in other words, the faster it is renewed. A greater rate of technical progress leads to the share of gross investment in gross domestic product also being greater. But the machines lose value faster. Their useful life is shorter, if technical progress is greater. But a shorter lifespan of plant and equipment leads to less capital being tied up in relation to the output produced annually by this capital together with the other factors of production, labor and land. Every economist knows that the capital tied up in the provision of housing as compared to annual value output is much greater than the capital tied up in the production of industrial goods. And every informed observer of economic life is aware that the lifespan of residential buildings is far longer than the economically useful life of production facilities in manufacturing. The economically useful life of fixed assets is the most important variable for determining the relative amount of capital tied up in production processes. Faster technical progress reduces the economically useful life of plant and equipment.

As already noted at the outset of our book, we can sum up our main thesis in the following sentence: *The lifespan of people is rising, the lifespan of machines is falling.*

Public promotion of private investment may or may not make sense for other reasons, depending on the specific situation. But it contributes nothing to solving the problem of excess private savings.

Of course, a deviation from the steady state can generate a temporary fireworks display of publicly induced increased private investment and thus boost the economy. Inasmuch as the problem is not the structural excess of private savings, but a temporary deficiency in the "animal spirits" of potential investors, a classical Keynesian strategy of encouraging investment through tax breaks or public subsidies may well be helpful. In this sort of situation, these stimulus measures also increase the value of existing plant and equipment, which are thus more fully utilized. The side effect of investment promotion on the value to existing plant and equipment is in this case the opposite of the effect when growth is promoted by encouraging technical progress.

11.7 A European Balanced Account Agreement, but "No Bailouts"

German authorities made the bitter pill of separation from the D-mark sweeter for German voters by promising them a euro that is subject to monetary rules under which German taxpayers would never have to pay for the public debt of other member states no matter what. This promise was not kept: Greece was supposedly "too big to fail."

But the Greek crisis also fits the general empirical finding that the insolvency of a state is always accompanied by a current account deficit of the country in question. No one fears Japanese fiscal insolvency, even though, relative to domestic product, Japan's debt is greater than that of Greece was at the start of its crisis.

This finding can be used to argue for the following arrangement for the eurozone countries:

> The balanced account agreement that we proposed in the last chapter should
> not only be applied to the current account of the euro area as a whole, but also
> to the current accounts of the individual members of the eurozone. In addi-
> tion, however, the no-bailout principle should be reaffirmed: Every member
> state is responsible for its own solvency. No country may expect other
> eurozone countries to relieve it of the burden of its public debt.

A balanced account agreement on the level of the individual euro area countries
is necessary, if only because otherwise the euro area as a whole will not be able to
fulfill its obligations under the worldwide balanced account agreement. This
especially applies for the part of the balanced account agreement relating to the
Keynes world, in which interest rates on the global capital market are low. Due to
European demographics, the euro area tends to have a particularly high private
savings surplus. If the eurozone or the European Union assumes the obligation to
maintain a balanced current account, then, in light of decentralized responsibility
for fiscal policy, it can only meet this obligation if the member states, in turn,
assume analogous obligations. This means that if we are in a Keynes world, the
countries with current account surpluses must quickly increase their fiscal deficits.
This is all the more urgent inasmuch as the weaker eurozone members are on their
own as far as the security of their public debt is concerned. They have, therefore, to
pursue a very cautious fiscal policy; and hence, they cannot make any contribution
to reducing the current account surplus of the euro area by undertaking a more
expansionary fiscal policy.

The instruments to be used in implementing this sort of intra-European balanced
account agreement will not be discussed in detail here. But we will touch upon a
few points regarding the German case in the next section.

11.8   The Result for Germany: Demographic Renewal

The upshot of our analysis is this: We can expect to be in a Keynes world for a long
time, since the tendency of the natural rate of interest is to become increasingly
negative. Hence, there must also be an intra-European balanced account agreement.
The fiscal policies of the eurozone member states have to be put at the service of
such a balanced account agreement. Within the eurozone, complete national
autonomy in fiscal policy is no longer compatible with the integrative function of
the euro in maintaining a truly functional common market in Europe. And in the
new era of international economic policy, Europe needs the latter. Political economy thus teaches us that *the German debt brake is incompatible with upholding the
commercial interests of the European and hence also the German population.*

A German fiscal strategy compatible with the proposed balanced account agreement could consist of increasing public investment far beyond the level presently envisaged in medium-term fiscal planning. Publicly financed infrastructure is normally *complementary to private real capital*. Better transport routes, a better supply of well-educated, highly skilled workers, and better publicly funded research institutions all increase the profitability of private real capital.

Hence, at low interest rates and with a current account surplus, an increase in public deficits does not crowd out private investment, so long as this increase serves to finance public investment.

Such a program of deficit-financed increased public investment also serves to promote the immigration of skilled workers from abroad and especially the faster integration of refugees into the labor market and into German society. It thus also represents a contribution to improving the age distribution of the population living in Germany.

As concerns this last point, let us recall what a contrast there is between the UN world population forecasts and the Federal Statistical Office's projections of how Germany's population will evolve. Figures 11.1 and 11.2 show this contrast.

Since the completion of the 13th Coordinated Population Projection in 2015, there has been a major influx of refugees into Germany. Hence, in 2017, the Federal Statistical Office supplemented variant 2 of the population forecast by a variant 2A. Variant 2A temporarily increases net immigration relative to variant 2 and then, like in variant 2, anticipates net immigration of 200,000 persons per year starting in

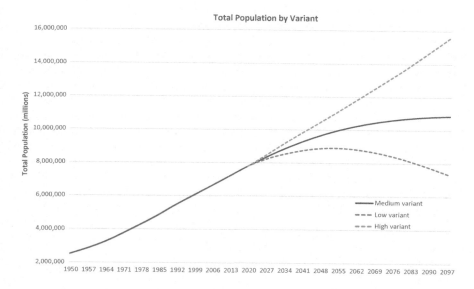

Fig. 11.1 UN world population prospects. *Source* United Nations (2017)

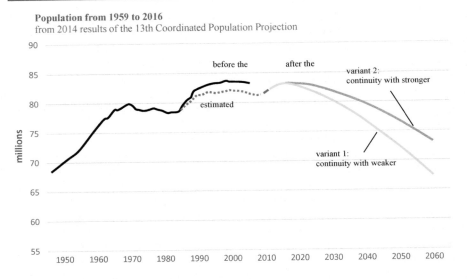

Population from 1959 to 2016
from 2014 results of the 13th Coordinated Population Projection

Fig. 11.2 Population development in Germany, 1950–2060. *Source* Authors' presentation based on data from Federal Statistical Office Germany (Statistisches Bundesamt 2015)

2021. Moreover, the birth rate has been raised from 1.4 to 1.5 children per woman. This results in a population of 76.5 million people in 2060.

Based on the Federal Statistical Office's Coordinated Population Projection, we can see by comparing variant 1 (net immigration of 100,000 people per year) and variant 2 (net immigration of 200,000 people per year) that a difference of 100,000 people per year in net immigration leads to a difference of around five million people in the population in 2060. Hence, assuming variant 2A, we can calculate that net immigration of approximately 350,000 people per year would be sufficient to stabilize Germany's population in the long term.

We advocate using the outlined setup of a global balanced account agreement, in order to manage Germany's obligations under the agreement so that they give rise to *German demographic renewal*. Here, some further remarks on this.

It is absurd that in a world where there is still high population growth, the population of one of the best governed countries in the world, viz. Germany, should fall. We believe that this absurdity will not become reality. Either Germany will continue to prosper: In this case, the pressure of immigration and the pull for immigration (the latter because of the great need for skilled workers) will be so strong that the population in Germany will not decline. Or: Germany will do so poorly that young skilled workers will emigrate, thus making it no longer possible to finance the welfare state, thus accelerating the loss of population, and thus making conditions even worse—so that, in the end, it is no longer possible to say that Germany is one of the best governed countries in the world.

Hence, demographic renewal should be strived for in any case. If public investment is tailored to this goal, the resulting boost in domestic demand would lead anyway to a fall in Germany's current account surpluses. *German demographic renewal would thus represent an important contribution to realizing a global balanced account agreement.*

11.9   A "Just" Distribution of Employment Opportunities

A program for German demographic renewal like the one that we have proposed here can also be understood as the better way of developing German prosperity. Thanks to the elimination of current account surpluses that goes with it, it also helps the other eurozone countries. It thus serves to stabilize the euro and the European single market. In the context of the new era of international economic policy, these favorable effects of such a policy for other countries are also good for Germany. It is thus not a policy that is implemented at the expense of some other group, whether domestically or abroad. The benefit that other countries derive from the German policy shift does not conflict with the benefit that Germany itself derives from the policy. It is a "win-win" situation.

But, in addition, it is worth pointing out that the return on Germany's net exports of savings leaves much to be desired. By far the greater part of German capital exports are invested in loans with "fixed" interest rates. We put the modifier in quotation marks, because such investments have already proven to be the source of major losses on several occasions. We need only think of the German regional banks [*Landesbanken*] that failed due to misguided investments abroad, thus costing taxpayers a great deal of money. The returns achieved on nominally fixed-rate foreign investments are minimal in today's Keynes world. On our assessment, the overall economic benefit of the public investment proposed here is far greater. If this investment is viewed as part of the process of demographic renewal that we have called for, then the gain in prosperity can be seen not only in a given population enjoying better public infrastructure, but also in the fact that the influx of industrious immigrants that it triggers serves to improve the age distribution of the population, reducing the relative share of retirees. People already living in Germany today and their descendants benefit from the arrival of the newcomers thanks to the better age structure.

Instead of the "*décadence*" of a shrinking population on German soil, Germany will become a country of new beginnings: a magnet for young, industrious people from all over the world. The USA, the traditional global magnet for immigration with its entrepreneurial dynamism, can serve as model, if it is combined with the specifically European irenicism of the German welfare state: a welfare state that is big enough to fulfill its specific functions, but not so sprawling as to interfere with economic incentives—a welfare state that provides support, but also makes demands.

Moreover, we should not forget the implicit public debt that arises under current fiscal policy due to the "wobbliness" of the euro. The Damocles sword of a possible Italian insolvency and withdrawal of Italy from the euro has to be kept in mind. If such a scenario appears imminent, there is a danger that Germany, at the head of the strong euro states, would provide financial assistance to avert Italy's insolvency, keep it in the euro, and thus avoid greater damage. The implicit "quasi-guarantee" that Germany provides for Italian public debt is obviously not written down anywhere. But no private guarantor of such liabilities would undertake this sort of guarantee without requiring the borrower to pay a substantial fee every year. As Milton Friedman said, "There is no such thing as a free lunch." The advantages that German exporters derive from the weakness of the euro come with an implicit price: The capital market assumes that Germany is providing an implicit guarantee of the sort discussed, precisely *because* it is aware of the advantages of euro weakness for German prosperity. The turbulence that disappointing this expectation would provoke on the capital market would already be reason enough for German authorities to take the path of least resistance and "pay up."

In other words, the German guarantee of the euro with its current membership can only be implicit and not explicit, so that the capital market has to live with the risk that someday Germany might not "pay up" after all. For this is the only way that the euro remains in its currently weak state that offers German exporters this competitive advantage.

The implicit debt that we have discussed here can be massively reduced, if Germany submits to a balanced account agreement of the sort that we have described—and attaches a declaration to it to the effect that, after massively reducing its current account surplus, it no longer considers itself obliged to prop up financially another eurozone country that is starting to founder under its public debt burden.

The basic idea of the balanced account agreement can also be expressed as follows. Nation states still retain the monopoly on the use of violence. Hence, only nation states can bring about a negative net wealth of their respective public sectors, so that citizens can enjoy net wealth greater than their real assets. Due to the negative natural rate of interest, it makes sense for nation states to make ample use of this possibility deriving from their monopoly on the use of violence. At an interest rate level below the growth rate of the economy, the collective public debt ratio D can be maintained without burdening the future. (Cf. also the AEA Presidential Lecture by Olivier Blanchard of 4 January 2019: Blanchard 2019.) If raising a national public debt ratio D when interest rates are low does not harm one's own country, does not burden future generations, and in fact benefits other countries, then ideas of global justice will also change. It will then be regarded as just for countries that can afford higher public debt without affecting their credit rating to make use of this possibility, so that countries that have a problematic credit rating can improve it by reducing their public debt with the collective public debt ratio D remaining constant.

Germany should not pay off Italy's public debt, but it is in Germany's own interest to increase its own debt, because, among other reasons, it will then be easier for Italy itself to reduce its level of indebtedness.

References

Blanchard, Olivier. 2019. Public Debt and Low Interest Rates, AEA Presidential Lecture 2019. *American Economic Review* 109 (4): 1197–1229.

Brunnermeier, Markus K., Harold James and Jean Pierre Landau 2016. *The Euro and the Battle of Ideas*. Princeton (NJ): Princeton University Press.

Dietzfelbinger, Daniel. 1998. *Soziale Marktwirtschaft als Wirtschaftsstil – Alfred Müller-Armacks Lebenswerk*. Gütersloh: Kaiser.

Friedman, Milton. 1997. Why Europe Can't Afford the Euro. *The Times*. 19 November 1997.

Monopolkommission. 2012. *Neunzehntes Hauptgutachten der Monopolkommission 2010/2011*. Bundestagsdrucksache 17/10565. Bonn: Monopolkommission.

Rosling, Hans, Ola Rosling and Anna Rosling Rönnlund. 2018. *Factfulness*. New York (NY): Flatiron Books.

Sinn, Hans-Werner. 2014. *The Euro Trap*. Oxford: Oxford University Press.

Solow, Robert M., James Tobin, Carl Christian von Weizsäcker and Menahem Yaari. 1966. Neoclassical Growth with Fixed Factor Proportions. *Review of Economic Studies* XXXIII 2: 79–115.

Statistisches Bundesamt. 2015. *13. Koordinierte Bevölkerungsvorausberechnung*. Wiesbaden: Statistisches Bundesamt.

Stiglitz, Joseph. 2016. *The Euro: How a Common Currency Threatens the Future of Europe*. New York (NY): Norton.

United Nations. 2017. *United Nations, Department of Economic and Social Affairs, Population Division, World Population Prospects: The 2017 Revision, Key Findings and Advanced Tables*. ESA/P/WP/248. New York (NY): United Nations.

Weizsäcker, Carl Christian von. 2021. *Capital Theory of the Steady State – Or: T+L=Z-T*. https://www.coll.mpg.de/Weizsaecker/CapitalTheory2021 and https://www.springer.com/9783658273620.

The Global Economy After the End of Capital Scarcity: A Utopian Proposal

12

Abstract

Extrapolating from List (*Das nationale System der politischen Ökonomie*. Cotta, Stuttgart, 1841), we explain the paradox of China: A poor country can experience tumultuous growth precisely by exporting more capital on balance than it imports. More growth can be created in developing countries by their running current account surpluses vis-à-vis the OECD plus China region. Public debt in the OECD plus China region would have then to be managed in such a way that full employment is preserved despite the current account deficit. Such a strategy would be beneficial for both groups of countries. For the time being, this is a utopian proposal. Realizing it would mean yet another restructuring, in addition to that associated with digitalization. The opposition of those who could lose their jobs as a result will ensure that this sort of reorientation of global trade policy will remain politically unfeasible for a long time still.

12.1 From Fairy Tale to Political Economy in Ten Years

Written in 1836:
> *They tell a tale in old Cologne*
> *of little elves in days long gone,*
> *when weary workers, should they please,*
> *could laze about and take their ease.*
> *And then by night –*
> *oh, what a sight!*
> *The little elves came chattering,*
> *hustling, bustling, clattering.*

C. C. von Weizsäcker and H. M. Krämer, *Saving and Investment in the Twenty-First Century*, https://doi.org/10.1007/978-3-030-75031-2_12

They rubbed and they scrubbed,
they swept, washed and scurried,
they cleaned and they hurried
to finish the work,
and before you knew it,
whatever there was to be done,
they'd do it!

First stanza of *The Elves of Cologne.*
Poem by August Kopisch (translation by Anthea Bell)

Written in 1841:
Friedrich List's book *The National System of Political Economy.*

Written in 1846:

For as soon as the distribution of labour comes into being, each man has a
particular, exclusive sphere of activity, which is forced upon him and from
which he cannot escape. He is a hunter, a fisherman, a herdsman, or a
critical critic, and must remain so if he does not want to lose his means of
livelihood; while in communist society, where nobody has one exclusive
sphere of activity but each can become accomplished in any branch he
wishes, society regulates the general production and thus makes it possible
for me to do one thing today and another tomorrow, to hunt in the morning,
fish in the afternoon, rear cattle in the evening, criticise after dinner, just as I
have a mind, without ever becoming hunter, fisherman, herdsman or critic.
Karl Marx and Friedrich Engels, *The German Ideology.*

It was in 1836 that the German poet August Kopisch (1998 [1836]) composed
his lyrical apotheosis of the magical elves of Cologne *from olden days*. A mere ten
years later, Karl Marx and Friedrich Engels penned their famous passage expressing
similar sentiments, but now in the guise of political economy and a vision of the
future. Friedrich List's work on the economic *present*, *The National System of
Political Economy*, came into being exactly halfway along this path from the past
into the future. In it, the author placed Germany, as well as other countries like
France and the USA, on the middle level of three levels of economic development.
According to List, Great Britain, the most advanced economy of the time, was on
the third and highest level of development. On his account, other more backward
countries, like Russia, for example, were on the first level.

For List, the free trade program advocated by the British classical school was
suitable for the lowest and highest levels, but not for the second level in between
them. In a way, List's levels correspond to the division into "developing countries,"

"emerging economies," and "rich countries" that is customary today. In 1841, politically fragmented Germany and the USA were what we now call "emerging economies." For the emerging economies of his time, List recommended placing protective tariffs on goods produced by the manufacturing industry of the third stage countries.

List justifies this different treatment of the different levels by his theory of what he called the "productive powers" of a national economy. These productive powers of agricultural production or manufacturing are influenced by the institutional conditions of each country. Now, List sees a crucial difference between the productive powers of agriculture and those of manufacturing. An important part of the idea of "productive powers" was later taken over by mainstream neoclassical theory in the concept of *positive externalities*. In List's view, these positive externalities are, above all, to be observed in manufacturing and less so in agriculture.

Among other things, the development of the "productive powers" in an emerging economy also involves learning from the rich countries: at the time, then, learning from Great Britain. In the case of Germany industry, part of this learning from British industry later took place by way of activities that could be classified as "industrial espionage."

According to List, without import barriers, it is hard for the nascent manufacturing sector of an industrializing country to compete with the mature manufacturing sector of a rich country. As a result, the economic potential of positive externalities in the industrializing country does not get developed or at least not sufficiently developed. By using import tariffs to make manufactured goods from the rich countries more expensive, an industrializing country can make it easier for domestic manufacturing to develop and thus take advantage of the positive externalities and economies of scale of the manufacturing sector.

Following List, mainstream economics refers to this as the process of a country's "industrial education." The argument for "educational" tariffs of this sort is recognized in trade theory—under the name of the "infant industry argument." Defenders of free trade warn against putting too much weight on them, however. They rightly point out that import tariffs can also be misused to protect inefficient domestic production from international competition—and to do so precisely at the expense of overall economic development and the restructuring that goes with it. The ossification of existing structures as a result of import tariffs has to be weighed against their function as stimulant for emerging industries with positive externalities.

Historical experience with such a policy of protective tariffs is mixed. There is reason to think that it ultimately harmed development in Latin America, but benefited development in East Asia. Apart from one exception, it is not our intention to discuss these different experiences here. We want rather to continue to tease out the connections between trade policy and our thesis of the negative natural rate of interest. With this goal in mind, we make use of the—chronological—embedding of Friedrich List's theory among the backward- and forward-looking utopias of a world without the toil and drudgery of production. By way of our theory of the negative natural rate, we want to transform this embedding from a purely chronological embedding into a causal one. We are aware that, in political–economic terms, we will thus be moving on utopian terrain.

However, this sort of thought experiment—this sort of experiment in utopian thinking—can also help us to understand the phenomenon of the negative natural rate somewhat better.

12.2   The End of Capital Scarcity is Not the End of Time Scarcity

Many people moan about the lack of time, and they also moan about the lack of interest income. At first sight, this seems paradoxical: As we have shown, low interest rates are, after all, a consequence of the fact that we live in an age in which capital—from the perspective of the global economy—is no longer scarce. But if in the Böhm-Bawerkian approach that we have adopted here, capital is basically time, then how can capital be abundant, but time extremely scarce?

The answer lies in the existence of a monetary economy with a system of credit. In such an economy, saving and investment diverge. Inasmuch as they lend, individual economic actors can save without investing. And, inasmuch as they borrow, they can invest without saving. Expressed in terms of stock variables, the individual economic actor's real assets are not equivalent to his or her net wealth. The latter can be greater or smaller than the former. Thus, when we speak of the end of capital scarcity, what we mean is that in terms of the global economy (or, in our analysis, the OECD plus China region), privately desired wealth is greater than productively usable real assets even at a real interest rate of zero. A still greater time gap between the original inputs of labor and land, on the one hand, and the outputs in the form of consumer goods, on the other, does not lead to any greater productivity of the production process.

But scarcity of time is something like an anthropological constant. People do a great deal to increase their life expectancy: to prolong their lives. This is one of the forms taken by the fundamental scarcity of time. And, together with progress in medicine and hygiene, it is in no small measure due to peoples' desire to have more time that life expectancy has increased all over the world and in all likelihood will continue to increase. But not even an increased lifespan, and not even the time that has been gained thanks to it, has led to a diminution in the subjective perception of time scarcity. The perception of time scarcity is perhaps even greater today than in earlier times (this is to say, than in earlier times of peace). Diogenes has moved further and further away from us. This may in no small part be due to the fact that the possibilities for communication transcending spatial distances have increased so much today. The potential for contact with other people and groups of people is thus far greater than it was before. The scarce factor in making use of this potential is just one's own time. This applies for private and professional activities alike.

And it is precisely this urge to have more time, this desire to live longer, that is one of the reasons why capital is no longer scarce, as we have shown in detail in Chaps. 1 and 3 on wealth and desired wealth.

But the divergence between privately desired wealth and economically productive real assets offers an opportunity to accommodate the desire for more time to an even greater extent than has been understood up to now. According to our analysis, under conditions of full employment, this divergence is bridged over by the state, as the only legitimate "Ponzi" scheme operator, having negative net wealth. It thus allows private net wealth to be greater than economically productive real assets. But public debt (as a stock) on which only minimal interest is paid creates the possibility that people will increasingly not want to and not have to work as much for money, that they will thus have more leisure time and hence their private time budget will be greater, and that hence the scarcity of their own time will diminish.

In the following, we will connect this idea to List's idea of the positive externalities of production in emerging economies. We will thus get closer to the utopia of the elves of Cologne. Is the fairy tale a model for the world of the future?

12.3   The Chinese Economic Miracle

The discovery of the "saving glut" by Bernanke (2005) and others occurred as a reaction to the hardly orthodox phenomenon of massive capital exports on the part of a then developing country: China. And these capital exports were part of a historical process that can be called the "Chinese economic miracle." In 1980, three-quarters of China's population still lived in absolute poverty. Today, just forty years later, China's per capita income measured on the basis of purchasing power parity is more than a third of that of Germany. In light of its considerably larger population, China is thus a country whose national product is roughly equal to that of the USA. In military and diplomatic terms, China is already regarded as a world power.

These two facts, Chinese capital exports and the tumultuous growth of its national product, are causally linked. It is precisely *because of its successful export industries* that Chinese productivity was able to increase so rapidly. What China has been striving for since 1980 with its economic reforms is to learn from the West. The (partial) introduction of a market economy served this purpose. And by exporting, Chinese firms learned the business practices that had come to prevail in the rich countries by being successful within the framework of a stable legal and property order.

Anyone who wants to sell successfully in a Western market economy must provide his or her customers, firstly, with goods of satisfactory quality at, secondly, competitive prices and, thirdly, must be able to deliver the goods on time. In the West, sales normally do not happen by bribing the customer's buyer. In traditional societies, the "virtues" of the market economy that we have mentioned here are for the most part only to be found occasionally and often only as rare exceptions. The individualism of modern market societies is scorned. What counts is solidarity in the family: in the clan to which you belong and into which you were born. The duty of loyalty toward the group makes it difficult to break from tradition like a Schumpeterian entrepreneur. Margins are high and price competition is to an overwhelming extent unwanted. Small, inefficient firms are not the exception, but the rule.

China had already been "modernized" by Communist rule after 1948. Medical care improved greatly. The "one child policy" created a good demographic basis for per capita economic growth. But the "Great Leap Forward" and the ensuing Cultural Revolution led the country into a dead end, resulting in millions of people dying of starvation. But Mao Zedong could not destroy the industriousness of the Chinese people, despite all his efforts. This industriousness went "underground" during the Cultural Revolution. When niches of private economic activity were introduced on the agricultural collectives at the start of the reforms pursued under the leadership of Deng Xiaoping, agricultural yields soared. The possibility to study at schools and universities again and to obtain professional qualifications was eagerly used and quickly bore fruit. The initial success encouraged the political leadership to go further with market reforms. The know-how of the Chinese minorities in the neighboring capitalist countries and of Taiwan's predominantly Chinese population was also extensively used.

"Learn from your customer" is a promising business motto in all countries. But it is especially apt when the society of which your customer forms part is far more prosperous and far more productive than your own. And this was the situation in which Chinese firms found themselves after 1980. For China, it was a stroke of luck that free international trade was the prevailing ideal in the Western world. As a result, borders were relatively open for Chinese goods. And thus China was able to learn from its customers in a big way.

We do not want here to sing the praises of China or of Western China policy. There are also, needless to say, dark sides to this cohabitation between democrat countries and a large country with a one-party state. China's rise left not only winners in its wake in the West, but also, of course, losers. The 2016 election of Donald Trump as president in the USA and the referendum vote for Brexit in the UK can be attributed, among other things, to the votes of such losers in the process of globalization. And China's rise increased their number. For it accelerated restructuring in the Western economies. And there is no such thing as growth without losers.

Overall, however, the Western economies have benefited from China's success. Labor productivity in the West increased as low-skilled jobs were eliminated and migrated to China, while, at the same time, being replaced by more demanding, better paid jobs at home. There is no doubt that Germany has been one of the biggest winners in this process of restructuring. It should not be forgotten, moreover, that capital exports from China have lowered interest rates on the global market—and that they have done so with constant employment and rising average wages in the West.

12.4 Friedrich List and the Chinese Economic Miracle

Friedrich List fought for German protective tariffs on British industrial goods, so that German industry could undergo a learning process and develop positive externalities. Germany's manufacturing industry took advantage of these opportunities during the nineteenth century and by the end of the century was the equal of Great Britain's. Learning from Great Britain was the order of the day on the Continent at the time. Kaiser Franz Joseph's wife Elisabeth of Austria (better known as "Sissi") had Carl Menger appointed as the tutor of Crown Prince Rudolf. The latter traveled around Great Britain with Menger to familiarize himself with the world's leading economic power and to learn from it (Hamann 1978). After the Meiji Revolution and the associated opening toward the West, Japan also experienced an economic upswing based on learning from the more advanced countries. Friedrich List's ideas also provided inspiration for the Japanese economic policy of the time.

There are thus parallels in economic history to the Chinese economic miracle of the recent past.

If we consider the overall process of all the historical experiments à la List, there is no doubt that they have contributed to accelerating global economic growth while, at the same time, distributing global wealth more evenly. If, as a result of this overall process, East Asia, including China, has caught up with Europe and North America today, then this has both increased global prosperityand distributed it more evenly.

And, on balance, the West, i.e., Europe and North America, have benefited from this process. East Asia supplies the West with goods that are of the same quality, but cheaper. The material standard of living in the Western world has risen thanks to the fact that global trade has mobilized a large number of workers from East Asia to produce consumer and capital goods for the West. And the latter have been paid for with the products of workers in the West, whose capacities would otherwise have been tied up producing less valuable products for the domestic market.

Considering the mutual benefit that both the Western world and the up-and-coming East Asian countries have derived from globalization, we cannot help but ask whether this lesson of economic history should be used so that the rest of the world can also benefit from Listian policies of the same sort. This is the question to which we will turn now.

12.5 A Two-Country Thought Experiment

In trade theory, issues of a certain complexity are often first thought through using a two-country model. This is the method that we will use here. We thus divide the world into two regions: the "North" and the "South." The North consists of the economic area that is the special focus of our book: the OECD countries plus China. The South comprises the rest of the world. We now treat these two regions as two countries, each with its own single currency. We call the North's currency the "dollar" and the South's currency the "rupee."

Let X be the South's trade surplus, expressed as a percentage of domestic consumption. If $X = 0$, then the current accounts of both countries are balanced. If $X > 0$, then the South exports more than it imports; if $X < 0$, then the South imports more than it exports. In the spirit of the theory of Friedrich List, we now stipulate that there is a positive correlation between the growth rate g of the South's national product and the South's trade surplus X. Let X be the independent variable here and g the dependent variable: The growth-promoting "learning" of the Southern "student" from the Northern "teacher" is all the more successful, the more the South focuses on exporting to the North. This is precisely the lesson of the economic history of East Asia since the Second World War and especially of China since Deng Xiaoping's pragmatic turn. Figure 12.1 depicts this relationship. For reasons that will become clear below, we turn the dependent variable g upside down: A higher g is below a lower g.

We now add a second functional relationship to this first one: viz. that between the dollar/rupee exchange rate w and the South's trade surplus X. The weaker the rupee is in real terms relative to the dollar, the more competitive the South is and the greater is its trade surplus. This causal relationship is represented in Fig. 12.2.

Note that in Fig. 12.2, the independent variable w is plotted on the vertical axis and the dependent variable X on the horizontal axis.

The third causal relationship concerns the North. It consists of the exchange rate w and the public debt ratio D that is required to achieve full employment in the North. The higher the value of the dollar in real terms against the rupee, i.e., the higher w is, the more competitive is the South and the less competitive is the North. The North's public debt must then be all the higher to allow for full employment. In other words: If the real interest rate is close to zero with stable prices and hence cannot fall any further, then the more capital from the South there is on the Northern capital market, i.e., the stronger the effect of Bernanke's "saving glut," the

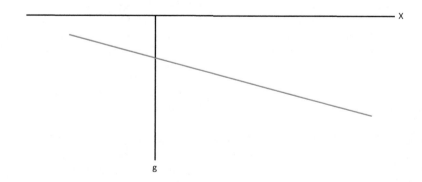

Fig. 12.1 Growth as a function of trade surplus. *Source* Authors' own presentation

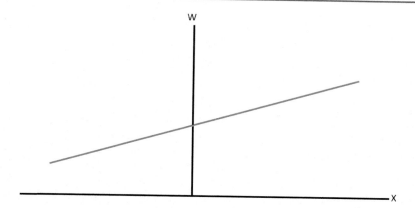

Fig. 12.2 Trade surplus as a function of the exchange rate. *Source* Authors' own presentation

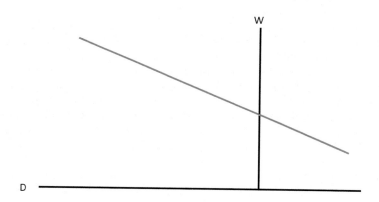

Fig. 12.3 Northern public debt as a function of the exchange rate. *Source* Authors' own presentation

more public debt must take over the role of satisfying the level of desired wealth. Figure 12.3 shows this relationship.

Note that public debt D is plotted from right to left: the further left, the greater the public debt. As already noted, the public debt in question is that required for full employment in the North.

We thus have three causal relationships, which we can also express as the functions f, g and h. After each formula, we indicate the theoretical source of the causal relationship it encapsulates.

$g = g(X)$: "Learning from customers" (F. List).
$X = f(w)$: Neoclassical theory.
$D = h(w)$: The theory of the present book.

These three equations contain four variables. Economic policy can now set the value of one of the four variables, in order to generate the values of the other three. We assume that it uses central bank interventions to determine the real exchange rate w. We will discuss how this is done a few sentences further on. If the exchange rate w is given, then market processes will give rise to a trade surplus X and this, in turn, will result in a Southern growth rate g. Furthermore, the North adjusts its public debt D to the exchange rate, so that there is full employment in the North.

Figure 12.4 provides a graphical representation of this reasoning. We choose two exchange rates to compare their effects. The low exchange rate corresponds to the green line connecting the other three variables. The high exchange rate corresponds to the blue line connecting the other three variables.

The graph in Fig. 12.4 is nothing other than a composite image of the three previous graphs. The four variables are depicted on the four lines starting from point zero. The exchange rate w is plotted on the "northern line" that goes upward, the South's trade surplus X on the "eastern line," the South's growth rate g on the "southern line," and North's full-employment public debt D on the "western line."

We have drawn the graph so that it reflects our theory of the negative natural rate of interest. In Chaps. 2–8 of the present book, we show that the North has a negative natural rate. The model of a closed economy that we have used for the

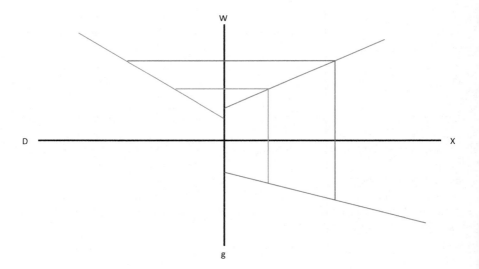

Fig. 12.4 Two alternatives: blue: high w; green: lower w. *Source* Authors' own presentation

North corresponds to a Southern trade surplus of zero. We can see from the graph that at an exchange rate that generates a Southern trade surplus of zero, the North's full employment public debt is positive. This reflects our thesis that with stable prices the interest rate cannot fall to the level of the negative natural rate.

We will now briefly discuss the technique for setting the exchange rate. The two central banks have to agree on the exchange rate. They can then steer the exchange rate toward the target value by each of them buying or selling the other currency. Moreover, by announcing the target exchange rate, they can also get other market actors to steer toward this target rate by way of their portfolio decisions. What is crucial is the credibility of the announcement that the two central banks are in agreement about the rate. If the announcement is credible, then the "forward guidance" on the part of the two banks should work. Assuming that the full-employment equilibrium interest rate in the North is approximately zero, monetary and fiscal policy have to be coordinated for the goals of price stability and high employment to be achieved simultaneously. "High employment" or "full employment" is a level of employment that leads to neither inflationary nor deflationary wage pressures. Friedman (1968) coined the term "natural rate of unemployment" for the unemployment that remains.

The thought experiment developed here is not a "model" that can be tested econometrically. Such a model would have to depict a dynamic, i.e., development over time, in order then to be tested using available macroeconomic time series. Our thought experiment belongs rather to the tradition of equilibrium analysis, as it has been practiced for centuries in economic theory. This tradition includes the works of Francois Quesnay, Adam Smith, David Ricardo, Alfred Marshall, Léon Walras, and John Maynard Keynes—and, of course, Paul Samuelson's neoclassical synthesis.

John Hicks's interpretation of Keynes's *General Theory* using a model with six variables (Hicks 1937) is a similar attempt to represent an economic idea by means of an equilibrium model that is as simple as possible. Like the thought experiment developed here, Hicks's model contained three behavioral equations: the consumption function, the investment function and the demand function for liquidity. The price level and its changes are not explicitly modeled in either the Hicks model of the Keynesian theory or the thought experiment developed here. The Hicks model has to be understood as a model of underemployment, whereby, however, the possibility of a deflationary process is not taken into consideration. Thus, the best way of reading the Hicks model is that it presupposes a stable price level. Price stability is likewise assumed in the thought experiment presented here.

This experiment only makes sense, if, as we showed earlier, the natural interest rate is negative. As long as we are in the "Friedman world," about which we have spoken in the previous two chapters, it is the sole responsibility of the central bank to ensure that there is simultaneously price stability and high employment. The function $D = h(w)$ that we have stipulated here makes no sense in the Friedman world. For as long as the full-employment real interest rate remains positive, it is up to the nation state to decide how high it wants its public debt to be. The domestic interest rate level corresponding to full employment will, however, be influenced by external factors: for example, by the exchange rate.

As one of its key findings, our thought experiment shows that a higher exchange rate of the dollar (= a lower exchange rate of the rupee) is advantageous for both countries: the North and the South. This will be immediately obvious for the South. Inasmuch as the South can make better use of the learning potential of exports when the exchange rate of its own currency is lower, a lower exchange rate also corresponds to higher growth. At the same time, more jobs will be created in the South, so that the incentives for migration to the North will be lower. But the North also benefits. Full employment will be brought about through the required level of public debt. At a higher exchange rate of the dollar, the terms of trade improve for the North. Hence, there is also a positive effect on Northern prosperity. In addition, at a real interest rate of zero and a real growth rate that is to be set as positive, public expenditure can be financed with lower tax rates. For at a growth rate g that is to be taken as given, the steady-state primary deficit that is consistent with stability is higher, the higher the public debt ratio D. At an interest rate of zero, the household income $\hat{w} = w(1 - (r - g)D)$[1], which was defined in the chapter on the natural rate of interest, is, after all, given by $\hat{w} = w(1 + gD)$. The primary deficit per labor year that is consistent with stability is precisely wgD. Since taxes have a distorting effect that increases disproportionately with increasing tax rates, the prosperity gained per worker is even greater than wgD. The decline in the incentive to immigrate to the North that is associated with the higher Southern growth is also good for the North. The last few years have shown the vehemence with which a majority in the North bridles at immigration from the South.

If we consider the two economies as a whole, both thus benefit from raising the exchange rate. As long as we ignore the distributive effects within the two countries, the latter thus brings about a "Pareto improvement." It is to these distributive effects that we turn now.

12.6   The Utopia of a Demand-Oriented Growth Strategy for Developing Countries

In the previous section, we went through a thought experiment that we could call a *demand-oriented growth strategy for developing countries*. According to our analysis, it benefits not only the South, but also the North. It is, nonetheless, utopian. Northern thinking runs along different lines. The Northern public associates helping the South with "development aid." This has long consisted primarily of financial assistance. As concerns cash flows, the latter is, however, exactly the opposite of the demand-oriented growth strategy for poorer countries that we have presented here. The goals of financial assistance to poorer countries have been internationally agreed upon, but never achieved. Were they to be achieved, then this

---

[1] Here and in the following few lines ω is the "wage rate" and not the rate of exchange

assistance would bring about a reduction of around three-quarters of a percent of Northern GDP in the Southern current account. In keeping with the thought experiment of the preceding section, this means that the growth of developing countries is *diminished* by this financial assistance. But numerous well-intended charitable campaigns on behalf of poor countries are also counterproductive. A prime example of this are donations of old clothes, which, in reality, make it more difficult for the recipient countries to develop their own garment industry.

Of course, there are also numerous well-organized investment projects, such as those of the World Bank, which contribute to the prosperityof the recipient countries. But this project funding predominantly consists of repayable loans. Moreover, it demands a certain discipline from the recipient country, in the sense of rational, economically efficient use of scarce monetary resources. Its utility consists less in funds being temporarily made available as in the recipient countries learning how businesses can be economically efficient and how to select suitable investment projects that are worth financing.

By contrast, development aid—which is, above all, also a form of aid for the donor country's exports—is problematic from the point of view of the recipient country's growth. Politically, however, it is much easier to get support for it in the donor country. *The political economy of development aid is a kind of subform of the political economy of protectionism.* One "does good" in a poor, foreign country and thereby creates sales outlets for one's own industry (Easterly 2006). China's Silk Road project is a gigantic example.

Even if the demand-oriented growth strategy for the South that we have sketched out would increase prosperityin the North, it would also be associated with massive restructuring. In a transitional period, of course, numerous jobs would be destroyed in the North: especially in export-oriented industries and industries that are exposed to competition from imports. On the other hand, more jobs would come into being in other industries. In a "Keynes world," however, the jobs argument is paramount for voters. There would be strong opposition to shifting to such a strategy. For the jobs being lost are concrete—they are visible in the present—whereas the jobs that will replace them are abstract and for the moment intangible. Moreover, the champions of the status quo would be eager to seize on the argument that these new jobs are to be created through increased public debt: that it is a matter of replacing already existing jobs by "jobs purchased on credit."

In a sense, it is because its high current account deficit is practically a structural feature that the USA has up to now pursued a policy of promoting other countries' growth. Since, moreover, it is the country that controls the global reference currency, it has never experienced balance of payments problems. The world has been happy to provide the means for financing the current account deficit by exporting capital to the USA. At the same time, these current account deficits also contributed to the fact that China could successfully launch and pursue its export-oriented growth strategy. But the election of Donald Trump as president in 2016 is a signal that such a demand-oriented promotion of other countries' growth no longer reflects the will of the American electorate. And, as discussed already in Chap. 10, this "new protectionism" will also be pursued by his successor Joe Biden.

Our analysis of the political economy of international economic policy in Chap. 10 attributes the worldwide resurgence of protectionism precisely to the phenomenon of the negative natural rate of interest, which, as shown in the present chapter using a two-country model, offers the opportunity to pursue a strategy of demand-oriented growth promotion.

There is no way of resolving this paradox in the short to medium term. Now and for the foreseeable future, there is neither the awareness nor the political will required for a restructuring that would take us in the direction of a demand-oriented growth strategy for the developing countries.

But it is worth at least fighting for the principle of free trade—also for the benefit of the poor countries. For there are numerous barriers to exports from the poor countries to the rich ones.

12.7 A Utopian Look into the Future

The digitalization of all human life, along with the rise of artificial intelligence, is perceived as an opportunity, but also as a threat. Many people fear that work is "disappearing." But precisely from the perspective of international competition, the promotion of restructuring toward more digitalization, and, in particular, also artificial intelligence, is being called for. If it really were the case that these technical developments take work away from global society, then we would have to regard promoting them in the interest of national competitiveness as a "beggar thy neighbor" policy like imposing import tariffs. We thus believe that it is important to be able to show conclusively that work in the North is not disappearing.

Our theory of the negative natural rate of interest rate and the reinterpretation of public debt based on it can help us here. In Sect. 12.2, we pointed out that the end of capital scarcity, i.e., the negative natural rate of interest, should not be confused with an end to the scarcity of time. The latter remains. Thanks to modern means of communication, the potential for beneficial interaction is so great that one's own time is, more than ever, the limiting factor. Hence, a reduction in the share of the labor time devoted to wage-earning in a lifetime cannot be regarded as any catastrophe, so long as, despite this reduction, the monetary means are still available to satisfy the individual's consumption wants.

Taken to an—unrealistic—extreme, the productivity gains from digitalization could be exclusively used to reduce wage-oriented labor in the North, so that there would no longer be any real growth of the economy. This would then be in the spirit of the picture that Marx and Engels paint of communist society, in which: "... society regulates the general production and thus makes it possible for me to do one thing today and another tomorrow, to hunt in the morning, fish in the afternoon, rear cattle in the evening, criticise after dinner, just as I have a mind, without ever becoming hunter, fisherman, herdsman or critic" (Marx and Engels 1970, 1846], p. 53). But then there is also no longer any need for detailed regulation of production by the state, since people, whether for money or because they simply want to be helpful to others, do work voluntarily within the framework of the division of labor.

We do not have to ponder today what exactly such a society would look like or how large the role of exchange via money would still be in it. As a medium of exchange that balances supply and demand amidst a great variety of goods, it will always be superior to detailed state planning. Nonetheless, the share of goods that are altruistically produced (as opposed to being produced for profit) may, of course, be higher than it is today. Today, there are still an enormous amount of activities for which there is demand, but whose performance is associated with "onerous" labor. These activities are carried out in exchange for monetary compensation and are thus relatively expensive—to a not insignificant extent, also because the state is essentially financed by taxation of the market-mediated division of labor. This is why, in the spirit of the notion of "induced technical change," the potential of digitalization and of artificial intelligence will be directed, above all, at rationalizing these sorts of activities: so that the technical change in question will be such as to lower the disutility of labor.

If this hypothesis is correct, then another side of technical progress through digitalization will be that it tends to rationalize, in particular, low-skilled jobs out of existence. For there is a tight negative correlation between the level of qualifications that is required for an activity and the "onerousness" that is associated with it. Thus, technical change that rationalizes onerous labor out of existence would appear to be a generator of unemployment among the unskilled.

This makes the goal of full employment all the more important. The elimination of low-skilled jobs in favor of the creation of skilled jobs should be carried out in such a way that persons with limited qualifications do not fall into the abyss of unemployment. But this requires a flexible fiscal policy, which, in further developing macromanagement of a Keynesian inspiration, does not shy away from taking on public debt at what we can expect to be persistently low interest rates.

12.8 The Gist of the Argument

In this chapter, we have connected the elfin utopia of a world without onerous labor and a further development of Friedrich List's theory. Instead of using the latter to justify a policy of "educational" tariffs, we have reshaped it, in light of the experience of East Asia and especially China, into an argument for free trade—and especially for promoting exports from poor countries to rich ones. By way of List's idea of learning from technically and organizationally superior customers, this should in turn promote economic growth in the developing countries. In order for this strategy to be compatible with full employment in the rich countries, we have to find a different attitude toward public debt than that which has prevailed up to now. For in this context, public debt increases the prosperity of the rich countries. In a sense, onerous labor is "outsourced" to the South and replaced by less onerous labor in the North. We thus come a step closer to Marx and Engel's idyllic conception of a communist society without onerous work.

But, for the moment, this is all just a utopia.

References

Bernanke, Ben. 2005. *The global saving glut and the U.S. current account deficit.* Speech 77. Washington (D.C.): Board of Governors of the Federal Reserve System.
Easterly, William Russell. 2006. *The White Man's Burden: Why the West's Efforts to Aid the Rest Have done so Much Ill, and so Little Good.* London: Penguin Press.
Friedman, Milton. 1968. The Role of Monetary Policy. *American Economic Review* 58 (1): 1–17.
Hamann, Brigitte. 1978. *Rudolf – Kronprinz und Rebell.* Wien: Amalthea.
Hicks, John R. 1937. Mr. Keynes and the Classics – A Suggested Interpretation. *Econometrica* 5 (2): 147–159.
Kopisch, August. 1998 [1836]. *The Elves of Cologne*, trans. Anthea Bell. New York: North-South Books.
List, Friedrich. 1841. *Das nationale System der politischen Ökonomie.* Stuttgart: Cotta.
Marx, Karl and Friedrich Engels. 1970 [1846]. *The German Ideology*, ed. C. J. Arthur. New York: International.

Concluding Remarks on Economic Policy

13

Abstract

The German debt brake is not compatible with the long-term stability of the euro. "New thinking" requires that public debt and price stability are no longer opponents, but rather allies in the Keynes world of persistently low interest rates. The proposed balanced account agreement is made more concrete here: An appropriate target (real) interest rate on the global capital market is between one and 1.5% per year lower than the growth rate of the OECD plus China region. If the actual interest rate is below the target rate, the countries with current account surpluses undertake to increase their public debt period D gradually according to a definite formula. In symmetrical fashion, if the real interest rate is "too high," countries with current account deficits have the duty to reduce their public debt period. The rules of the balanced account agreement replace the debt brake. They are the instruments of sound fiscal policy.

13.1 Summary Part 1: Economic Policy in Germany, Europe and the World

In the second part of our book, we have examined some questions on international economic policy that derive from the fact of the Great Divergence. The economic policy of democratic countries is conducted under the conditions of political economy: i.e., under the conditions for having electoral success among citizens. In Chap. 10, we put forward the following basic thesis: The level of the natural rate of interest has a decisive influence on the relative weight of voters' interests as producers and their interests as consumers. With a falling natural rate, the weight of their interests as producers rises. This analysis explains the "Trump phenomenon" and especially the new wave of protectionism. Today, the strongest card that a nation can play in the international game of trade relations is the access of other

© The Author(s) 2021
C. C. von Weizsäcker and H. M. Krämer, *Saving and Investment in the Twenty-First Century*, https://doi.org/10.1007/978-3-030-75031-2_13

nations to its own internal market. And this card is all the stronger, the bigger that internal market is—and the American internal market is very big. Thus, in a "Keynes world," we arrive at new international rules: at a "New Trade Policy."

This led us in Chap. 10 to propose a *balanced account agreement*: The rules of global free trade (the WTO and related multilateral negotiations on cutting tariffs) should be supplemented and thus politically reinforced by an international obligation for countries to use their fiscal policies to bring about balanced current accounts. In a "Friedman world" with high real interest rates, it is the duty of countries with current account deficits to bring their current accounts into balance by reducing their public debt. In a "Keynes world" with low real interest rates, it is the duty of countries with current account surpluses to bring their current accounts into balance by way of increased public debt. In the "Keynes world," the citizens of all countries will thus be able to understand that international trade and globalization "distribute jobs fairly" around the world. And an electoral majority in each country will thus become convinced that the benefits of globalization and the free movement of goods are greater than the costs.

Such a balanced account agreement merely obliges countries to adopt a fiscal policy that is in their own interest in any case. At low real interest rates, additional public debt is not a burden for the future and future generations in countries that are presently running current account surpluses. This is the charm of the "dynamic inefficiency" that goes along with these low interest rates: More consumption today does not have to be purchased with less consumption in future. And more public investment today is even an additional bonus for future generations. And vice versa: At the high real interest rates of a "Friedman world," the obligation for countries with current account deficits to reduce their public debt is in their own interest in any case.

Chapter 11 was, above all, about Europe. One of the effects of the euro is to eliminate countries' temptation to obtain (temporary) competitive advantages for their own industry by devaluing the national currency. In the Keynes world, it is thus also an obstacle to concluding bilateral "deals" with non-European powers at the expense of the other EU member states. In this way, the euro is also a pillar of the European single market. But this is particularly significant in the age of the "New Trade Policy," because, given the size of the European single market, access to it is a particularly strong card in international trade negotiations.

To stabilize the euro politically, the balanced account agreement has also to be applied to the individual current accounts of the countries in the eurozone. Populists in the Mediterranean eurozone countries see the euro as a German tool for selling German goods as cheaply as possible at the expense of jobs in the South of Europe. As crude as the economics of this view may be, one has to acknowledge that it is right on one point, which is also emphasized by the US government: The weakness of the southern euro countries makes the exchange rate of the euro far lower than, for example, that of a euro limited to the northern members would be. And this helps German exports.

Moreover, the following has also to be taken into account. Let us assume that nothing changes in the basic outlines of the present fiscal policy of the eurozone countries. What then would a euro area in which there is pervasive full employment look like? Given its demography, it would undoubtedly be characterized by a massive excess of private saving (in the conventional sense, i.e., not including contributions to social security programs) over private investment, which would thus be reflected in high trade surpluses. But this precisely will not come to pass, because such a strong currency would appreciate massively. And this would make precisely these trade surpluses impossible. And in the age of the "New Trade Policy," holding the exchange rate of the euro low by way of massive dollar purchases by the ECB is out of the question. The USA (and soon probably China as well) could "veto" such a move, threatening otherwise to impose tariffs in retaliation.

In light of the success of politicians like Matteo Salvini, we cannot expect a country like Italy to remain in the euro, if this impossibility of full employment in the euro area becomes widely known. *But this means that Germany's debt brake is not compatible with the stability of the euro.* Only a significantly more expansionary fiscal policy in the "strong" euro countries can save the euro in a world that can be expected to remain a "Keynes world" for the foreseeable future. The "strong" euro countries, led by Germany, would thus have to increase their deficits, in order to allow the "weak" euro countries to reduce their debt levels without excessive "austerity" and, moreover, to find remaining in the euro area "enjoyable." It is, in a sense, "by accident" and not thanks to wise planning that Covid-19-induced public deficits are leading to a higher German debt period D.

In the context of a changed fiscal policy in the spirit of the proposed "balanced account agreement," Germany can, of course, insist that it will not intervene on behalf of the public debt of other eurozone countries. This would (finally!) fulfill a promise that Germany's Christian Democrats and other German parties made in the late 1990s, when pleading with German voters not to get into a funk because of the departure of the D-mark.

At low interest rates, a more expansionary fiscal policy could be used for public investment that is primarily aimed at bringing about German demographic renewal. We refer here to Sect. 11.8. For us, it is a paradox that when the United Nations is forecasting considerable growth in the global population for the entire twenty-first century, the official German outlook, based on the population projections of the Federal Statistical Office, is that of a secular decline in population. It seems to us that greater demographic realism is required here. A comparatively well-functioning country with a competitive economy cannot avoid being involved in the migratory movements that are increasingly occurring around the world. The German state (including federal, regional and local authorities) should not put its head in the sand, but rather actively shape net immigration—also for the benefit of the native population—and it should invest massively in doing so. It is well known that Germany has a great need for skilled workers at the moment. And for demographic reasons, it is even more evident that in future, Germany will only be able to obtain a sufficient number of skilled workers via immigration from other countries.

If Germany decides to join such a balanced account agreement, then there will be a public debate about how the required deficit spending should be used. Depending on the political orientation of the government, it could be used for increased efforts to improve education, increased expansion of rail and road networks, increased efforts to improve the health care system, increased efforts to give the Bundeswehr a genuine operational capability, increased efforts to promote the transition to renewable energies or, as proposed here, increased efforts to foster demographic renewal. Considering the relative merits of these various goals would require a different book than this one.

13.2 Summary Part 2: Stability and Utopia

The Great Divergence described in the first part of our book gets expressed in the Fundamental Equation of Steady-State Capital Theory:

$$L + T = Z - D$$

The period of production T, i.e., relative real capital requirements, remains constant over time; the waiting period Z, i.e., relative desired wealth, increases over time—and it does so worldwide. The growing divergence between the relative wealth desired by private persons and constant relative capital requirements has to be bridged over by a growing public debt period D, if the goal of price stability at full employment, i.e., of a non-negative real interest rate, is to be maintained.

If our analysis is theoretically and empirically correct, then it requires "*new thinking*" about the long-term economic and social conditions for an "open," democratically constituted society. In Chaps. 9 and 12, we try to make a start in such "new thinking." On the basis of historical and also very recent experience, Chap. 9 examines some (but by no means all) functional conditions of the democratically constituted Open Society. The structure of the welfare state is key here. Reduced to a simple formula, the welfare state is a condition for the coexistence between a democratic social order and the only known form of economic life that really works and constantly brings about material progress: the market economy.

On the other hand, the welfare state should not be overextended, if we do not want to destroy the system of incentives proper to a market economy. But to prevent the danger of an overgrown welfare state from becoming reality, it has to be possible for people to make provision for their own future. They have to be able to believe in the principle of subsidiarity. They have really to want to take responsibility for their futures. Monetary stability is key for this. It makes *abstract saving* possible for the individual in the form of purchasing power that can be mobilized in future. This is the real purpose of price stability. Price stability is not some neoliberal fad of a few economics professors. It is the basis on which citizens are able to grasp their duty to provide for their own futures and it is a constant reminder of this duty. For while it is true that "*ultra posse nemo obligatur*"—no one can be obligated beyond what is possible—it is price stability that ensures that the *"posse"* is satisfied: citizens *can* provide for their own futures.

Now, you may ask: What is the "new thinking" on price stability here? The answer is that it is the relationship between the objective of price stability and the incurring of public debt that has to be rethought. For proponents of free markets, the defense of price stability usually goes together with a critical attitude toward public debt. This is in no small measure due to the historical experience that governments have again and again used inflation to shift the burden of public debt from the state to its creditors. Price stability and public debt are here opposed to one another: There is "either price stability or public debt."

But the Great Divergence calls for increasing public debt to stabilize full employment, and this postulate makes public debt and price stability into allies. They are no longer opposed to one another, but rather complementarity to one another. It is logically conceivable that full employment could be brought about without increasing relative public debt: namely, by striving for negative real interest rates. This would go together with inflation, in order to get around the zero lower bound of nominal interest rates. De facto, savers are thus deprived of the possibility of investing their money in risk-free financial instruments of stable real value. This provokes a "flight to tangible assets," which is connected to greater overall investment. But taking refuge in tangible assets is only an apparent solution to the problems. Firstly, such investment is economically unproductive; secondly, it is extremely dangerous for the stability of the economic and social order when people are denied the possibility of making provision for their future by means of investment instruments of stable value. The call for government intervention will then become too strong to ignore. And such intervention will overwhelm the state's capacities. Democratic elections will then lead to a rejection of the market economy: ultimately, with extremely high costs in terms of both material standard of living and personal freedom.

This is what makes public debt into an ally of price stability. *The epitome of price stability is a non-negative, risk-free real rate of interest.* But the latter is only compatible with full employment if the desired wealth of private citizens (represented by the waiting period Z) is made compatible with the lower capital requirements of the system of production (represented by the period of production T) by sufficiently high net public debt. This is what was shown in Chap. 9.

In Chap. 12, we undertook an exercise in the "new thinking" in considering the *developing countries*. For conventional thinking, developing countries immediately bring to mind "development aid" in the form of financial assistance. We use the example of China as developing country, in order to turn this association completely around. The rapid rise of China in recent decades has, as it were, been connected to financial assistance for the rich countries. China's current account balance has long been positive, and it is at times very substantially so. The Chinese central bank is by far the largest creditor of the US Treasury. These high net capital exports of the Chinese economy go together with China's extremely successful exporting of goods. China has used the opportunity of free trade to raise its standard of living and create domestic jobs. By exporting, China has familiarized itself with the commercial practices of the rich countries: "Learning from customers" has been the Chinese recipe for success in recent decades.

In our admittedly "utopian" Chap. 12, we apply the Chinese model to all the developing countries. Our position is that the best development aid that the rich countries can provide to the poorer countries is *a massive increase in imports* from them. Two main instruments can facilitate this. (1) The elimination of many import barriers to goods and services from developing countries. (2) Maintaining an exchange rate between the currencies of the rich countries (the "dollar") and the currencies of the poor countries (the "rupee") that makes it easier for developing countries to export to the rich countries and to replace imports from the rich countries with their own products.

It is thanks precisely to the Great Divergence that this sort of promotion of growth in the developing countries is possible, in principle, without sacrificing full employment in the rich countries. At persistently low interest rates, public debt in the rich countries can be further increased, in order to make room for goods and services from the developing countries without the rich countries having, *on balance*, to suffer job losses.

This is, however, utopian. For it is only on balance that unemployment is avoided in the rich countries. Numerous jobs in the rich countries would fall victim to such a strategy. The new jobs that come into being to replace them would be overwhelmingly found in other sectors. And the jobs being lost are *concrete*, whereas the new jobs to come cannot be identified in advance. Hence, they are *abstract*. The interest group connected to the concrete, existing jobs will oppose such a policy, and there is not any interest group for the future, but today still abstract jobs.

Nonetheless, as an exercise in "new thinking," this sort of utopian scenario is useful.

13.3 Fiscal Policy as Steering Instrument: The Appropriate Real Interest Rate

In the Friedman world, the central bank steers the economy by way of its monetary policy, which is today primarily interest rate policy. In doing so, it is helped by the "automatic stabilizers" in the government budget: The deficit is bigger or smaller depending on the economic situation. Hence, disposable income and (after tax) corporate profits fluctuate less than national product. We will not go into the structural, microeconomic details of the functioning of this automatic stabilizer here. The keyword is "market asymmetry." The prices of goods are predominantly higher than the short-term marginal costs. Sellers are structurally hungry for transactions, whereas buyers are, for the moment, satiated after the transaction has been completed. Thus, in macroeconomic terms, national product and aggregate demand dance in tandem. As Hayek (1945) teaches, prices are signals of scarcity with whose help productive cooperation between people can succeed despite knowledge being dispersed in society. But knowledge about prices is also dispersed and therefore imperfect. Adapting to this imperfection leads to the abovementioned market asymmetry. It makes possible the synthesis of Hayek and Keynes (Weizsäcker 2005). And it makes possible neo-Keynesian macroeconomics (Woodford 2003).

Cyclical fluctuations that are too strong to be offset by interest rate policy alone can already occur in the Friedman world of a positive natural rate of interest. In other words, the problems cannot be solved just by "Taylor rules" (Taylor 1993). Hence, policymakers have long used fiscal policy as an additional steering instrument. At other times, it was, however, precisely fiscal policy itself that contributed to destabilizing the economy.

In Chap. 10, we showed that in the Friedman world, fiscal policy can, in principle, be an autonomous national competence. We also showed that this is not the case in the Keynes world. In the Keynes world, citizens' politically articulated interests as producers outweigh their politically articulated interests as consumers. This is why there is the potential here for politically virulent controversy about the "international distribution of jobs." The aim of our proposal for a balanced account agreement is to save free international trade despite this conflict potential. If all countries' current accounts are balanced, then we can speak, at least as an approximation, of a "fair international distribution of jobs."

We want now to discuss some basic ideas for the architecture of the international balanced account agreement.

The first step is to set a common international target interest rate for government bonds with a high (or the highest) credit rating. This should be expressed as real interest rate, since it has to be possible to compare it to the growth rate of the OECD plus China region. The advancing of the Keynes world at the expense of the Friedman world is based on the Great Divergence. The significance of net public debt for citizens is increasing over time. This has been explained in detail in the present book. Therefore, the significance of the interest rate at which the government can borrow is also increasing. In the interest of the stability of the economy as a whole, this rate should not be too high.

We regard the overall growth rate of the economy as a critical point of reference for the real interest rate. In our analysis, this overall growth rate is, more precisely, the steady-state growth rate of the OECD plus China region. It can be estimated to be between 2.5 and 3% per year. If the government has to pay an interest rate that is higher than the steady-state growth rate, then the budget has to have a primary surplus in the steady state. For reasons of stability, this strikes us as problematic. A non-positive or even negative primary balance should be strived for.

An interest rate equal to the growth rate maximizes the steady-state wealth of the representative citizen—provided that the interest rate at which the government can borrow is the correct price signal for the marginal productivity of capital in the production sector and for the intertemporal substitution of consumption and labor supply in the consumption sector. Hence, there is some reason to steer toward the economy's growth rate as equilibrium interest rate. But besides maximizing steady-state prosperity, the stability of the overall system is also at issue. Hence, we propose that the targeted annual real interest rate should be one to one-and-a-half percentage points (1–1.5%) lower than the growth rate of the area in question. According to current estimates, this would imply a real interest rate of 1.5% per year for the OECD plus China region.

What we mean is, of course, the interest rate after taxes. For allocation decisions are determined by after-tax interest rates in both the system of production and the system of consumption. If the average tax on interest income in the area as a whole is 25%, then the real pre-tax interest rate to be strived for would be two percent per year.

According to our approximation formula

$$\Omega = \frac{1}{2}(r - g)^2 \left\{ \psi T^2 + \gamma Z^2 \right\}$$

at a targeted international real interest rate of $r = 1.5\%$ per year on the highest-rated public debt and a growth rate $g = 2.5\%$ per year, the loss in prosperity relative to the "optimal" interest rate $r = g$ amounts to less than one percent, if we use the values $\psi = 1$, $\gamma = 1.5$, $T = 4$ and $Z = 10$ and $g - r = 1\%$ per year, which correspond to our empirical estimates. At $g = 3\%$ per year and hence $g - r = 1.5\%$ per year, we would obtain a loss in prosperity of just under two percent. This sacrifice of steady-state prosperity is worth it to us, if the stability of the system of public debt can thus be better secured. We derived the values for the variables used here in Chap. 8.

If further research comes to the conclusion that the risk-free real interest rate r for public debt is lower than the marginal productivity of capital, then the steady-state loss in prosperity that results from maintaining a safety margin of 1–1.5% lower than the growth rate would be even less than is calculated using the formula for Ω. For, in this case, the prosperity-maximizing steady-state interest rate is itself lower than the growth rate (cf. Sect. 2.10).

13.4 Fiscal Policy as Steering Instrument: The National Level

In keeping with the "philosophy" of the proposed balanced account agreement, it is the duty of countries with current account surpluses to act when real interest rates are low. Conversely, at high real interest rates, it is the duty of countries with current account deficits to act. The boundary between low and high interest rates is the internationally agreed target level of the real interest rate. We have proposed an after-tax interest rate of 1.5% per year as target. In what follows, we call this targeted real interest rate level r^*. National interest rate levels may, of course, differ from the international real interest rate level. In particular, the national nominal, and perhaps also real, interest rate level may deviate from the international real interest rate level due to the fact that the country in question has a lower credit rating and hence has to pay higher interest than countries with the best credit rating. The following rule should principally apply for countries with the highest credit rating.

Let X represent a country's current account balance as a percentage of domestic consumption. X is thus a dimensionless variable, since it is a coefficient of two variables that have the same dimension: namely, €/year. Recall that in a closed economy, such as the OECD plus China region in our treatment, the equilibrium real interest rate r is an increasing function of the debt period D in the steady state. Hence, if, at low interest rates $r < r^*$, the countries with a current account surplus increase their public debt period and the countries with a current account deficit hold their public debt period constant, then the average public debt period of the area rises. We can thus expect a rising real interest rate r. Conversely, if, at high interest rates $r > r^*$, the countries with a current account deficit reduce their public debt period, whereas the countries with a current account surplus maintain their existing public debt period, then average relative public debt falls and, as consequence, so too does the interest rate level. The effect of the balanced account agreement is thus to bring the interest rate level closer to its target value.

The rule that we propose has the following general form. The steering variable that we are considering is the time derivative of the debt period D. We designate it as $\dot{D}$. Now, we propose that:

1. If $X > 0$ and $r^* > r$, then $\dot{D} = m(r^* - r)^2 X^2$, $m > 0$ should apply.
2. If $X < 0$ and $r > r^*$, then $\dot{D} = -m(r - r^*)^2 X^2$, $m > 0$ should apply.

It is a good idea to make the standard deviations $r^* - r$ and X quadratic in the provisions, so that the provisions have a disproportionately strong effect for large deviations as compared to small deviations.

The question of the appropriate size of the proportionality parameter m would need be studied more closely. Using simulation models would probably be the best way to do so.

As already noted above, such an agreement does not represent too painful a restriction of countries' freedom of action, since a debt policy of the sort prescribed by it is in any case in the interest of each of the countries concerned. But such an internationally agreed rule does, of course, restrict their freedom of action. This is, however, a feature of all binding international agreements. Despite this fact, such agreements are frequently concluded, because every party expects advantages from the obligations placed upon the others. This will normally be the case here too: If Germany, by accepting the obligation to use fiscal policy to make its current account more balanced, obtains the agreement of other countries to show greater fiscal responsibility and, furthermore, to do nothing against global free trade, then the advantages of this agreement for Germany far outweigh any possible disadvantages associated with it.

Such a balanced account agreement would undoubtedly bring about anticipation effects. If countries with current account deficits know that Germany will soon be rolling back its export surpluses by way of a more expansionary fiscal policy, then the other countries—whether other European countries or countries in North

America or East Asia—will act differently in anticipation of this fact. If Italian or Greek voters know that Germany will soon be rolling back its export surpluses, then the populist slogan that the euro is a ploy to "steal" jobs from Mediterranean countries will evaporate.

Let us dispose of one theoretical objection to our proposal for an international balanced account agreement right away. Anyone who persists in believing in "Ricardian equivalence" à la Barro (1974) will object that a current account surplus cannot be reduced by more public debt nor a current account deficit by less public debt, because, in anticipation of additional taxes to repay the increased debt, citizens will save more, so that aggregate domestic demand does not rise at all. Of course, every good economist knows that the derivation of the Barro-Ricardo effect requires an interest rate greater than the growth rate of the economy. But the Great Divergence, which is the key to our whole approach, is incompatible with the assumption of a long-term, risk-free interest rate that is greater than the rate of growth.

13.5 A Replacement for the Debt Brake

In a single country without foreign relations, it is conceivable that, despite the Great Divergence, the constitution might require the use of a debt brake of the sort found in the German constitution or "Basic Law." For this debt brake only relates, after all, to the "tip of the iceberg" of all public debt. We have demonstrated this both theoretically and empirically in the first part of our book: The implicit public debt entailed by the present form of the welfare state is far greater than explicit public debt. Hence, if a country wants to make the ratio of explicit public debt to annual national product tend toward zero by using a "debt brake" and wants this, nonetheless, to be compatible with the secular increase in relative desired wealth and the constant capital coefficient, then there is no other option than gradually expanding implicit public debt even more. Entitlements to retirement benefits are the main component of the latter. One would thus make the value of these entitlements rise in parallel to the rise in citizens' relative desired wealth. It is not our intention to discuss how such a policy could be practically implemented in legislation. Whether, however, it represents the apex of wisdom can be doubted. It may well be a feasible public debt policy, but far from an optimal one.

In any case, this model of a single, isolated country has nothing to do with the political–economic reality of a globalized world economy. Referring to Chap. 11, we showed above that in the age of the Keynes world and the "New Trade Policy," the debt brake is structurally incompatible with a stable euro. This is because it is incompatible with full employment in the euro area.

Our proposed balanced account agreement is to be understood as a replacement for the debt brake. It creates other obligations for German fiscal policy. But the obligation to pursue a stability-oriented fiscal policy remains. Countries should still not overdo it with their public debt. But now there is not only a cyclical signal for fiscal policy, as is already the case today, but also an equally important "price signal" for fiscal policy. This price signal is the interest rate.

And, unlike the debt brake, the balanced account agreement takes the new conditions of the Keynes world into account. As a result of the continuing rise in relative desired wealth, the latter has superseded the Friedman world. With sound fiscal policy, a return to the Friedman world of high real interest rates is not to be expected. Nonetheless, voters' interests as producers are paramount in the Keynes world. And they are thus decisive for international trade relations. The balanced account agreement takes this into account. The debt brake has no adequate response to it. The balanced account agreement can do justice to the slogan of a "fair international distribution of jobs," but the debt brake cannot.

13.6   Conclusion: $L + T = Z - D$ Requires New Thinking

Steady-state capital theory, with its fundamental equation $L + T = Z - D$, is the *theoretical* entryway to the *Great Divergence* between the period of production T, which is constant over time, and relative desired wealth Z, which increases over time in parallel to growing prosperity. This Great Divergence is also *empirically supported*. As long as we understand that explicit public debt is only the tip of the iceberg of all public debt, we can recognize that the volume of the latter, as represented by the public debt period D, has already grown to a half-dozen years of total consumption today. Relative desired wealth has already raced this much ahead of the relative private real assets that can be productively used. And Z will continue to grow —and it makes sense for D to grow with it. For technical progress (digitization, artificial intelligence, progress in medicine, 3-D printing, etc.) appears to be accelerating rather than slowing down, and it seems that this technical progress tends to reduce the relative amount of capital tied up in the production process—i.e., T—rather than increase it. Just looking at gross investment is misleading. Depreciation is rising even faster.

This is why new thinking is needed. Price stability and public debt are no longer opponents; they are now friends, and they will continue to be in future. The question of the stability of public finances needs a different answer than the debt brake today.

In this book, we have taken some first steps on the terrain of the required new thinking. But there is still a great deal more to be done by economics as a discipline.

References

Barro, Robert J. 1974. Are Government Bonds Net Wealth? *Journal of Political Economy* 82 (6): 1095–1117.

Hayek, Friedrich A. von. 1945. The Use of Knowledge in Society. *American Economic Review* 35 (4): 519–530.

Taylor, John B. 1993. Discretion Versus Policy Rules in Practice. *Carnegie-Rochester Conference Series on Public Policy* 39: 1–214.

Weizsäcker, Carl Christian von. 2005. Hayek und Keynes: Eine Synthese. *Ordo* 56: 95–111.

Weizsäcker, Carl Christian von. 2021. Capital Theory of the Steady State – Or: T+L = Z–D. https://www.coll.mpg.de/Weizsaecker/CapitalTheory2021 and https://www.springer. com/97836 58273620.

Woodford, Michael. 2003. *Interest and Prices: Foundations of a Theory of Monetary Policy.* Princeton (NJ): Princeton University Press.

Appendix: Two Faces of Public Debt

14

14.1 The Two Faces of Public Debt[1]

Public debt is at the same time private wealth. Both sides of the phenomenon have to be kept in mind when considering the optimal budget. When there are low real interest rates and high trade surpluses, reducing public debt is the wrong policy.

(Blurb by the FAZ editors—author's note.)

Firstly, Germany has a highly developed welfare state. Secondly, the free exchange of goods, all across Europe and indeed all around the world, is a key element of the German economic system. Thirdly, to the acclaim of voters, German policy is committed to the goal of price stability. Is the debt brake compatible with these three guiding principles of German economic policy? I doubt it. In the German discussion, public debt is only seen in a negative light—wrongly, as I will show.

Explicit and implicit public debt in Germany comes to around 10 trillion euros. This corresponds to private assets of citizens of exactly the same amount. The citizens are the state's creditors: partly, in the form of explicit claims on the state equivalent to the explicit public debt; and, to a greater extent, in the form of implicit assets in the form of retirement benefit and pension claims for which they have paid in the past by way of contributions and deductions from their salaries (in the case of

---

[1]Originally published in the *Frankfurter Allgemeine Zeitung* (FAZ) of June 4, 2010, p. 12.

C. C. von Weizsäcker and H. M. Krämer, *Saving and Investment in the Twenty-First Century*, https://doi.org/10.1007/978-3-030-75031-2_14

civil servants). Implicit claims on the healthcare system and to assistance in the case of need (welfare and unemployment benefits) are also implicit wealth for citizens and implicit public debt of exactly the same amount for the state. The wealth of citizens corresponding to the public debt of around 10 trillion euros is equivalent to approximately five times annual private and public consumption.

The total private net wealth of citizens is, of course, even greater. In addition to the net claims on the state just mentioned, there are also real assets in the form of real capital invested in Germany. This consists of real estate, plant and equipment, and inventories. Furthermore, Germans have net foreign claims. The sum of the assets consisting of real capital invested in Germany and net foreign claims is approximately equal to the net claims on the state. The total private net wealth of Germany's residents thus comes to around 20 trillion euros or around ten times annual private and public consumption. It is thus the equivalent of ten years of consumption in Germany. I refer to the ratio of private wealth to annual private and public consumption as the "saving period." The German saving period is thus around 10 years. It is equivalent to per capita wealth of around 250,000 euros.

This saving period of ten years can be attributed to German demographics and to the welfare state that Germany has built up over the last 120 years. Life expectancy has risen substantially during this time. It comes today to around 80 years and is continuing to rise. The increase in life expectancy has been connected to a steady increase in the average retirement period. Over the course of the last 40 years, the average amount of time during which retirees receive benefits from the social security system has increased from 10 to 17 years, thanks to more effective health care, decreasing health risks from environmental pollution, citizens' changed lifestyles and consumption habits, and changed and hence "healthier" working conditions.

We are considering explicit and implicit wealth in the form of the claims amassed by an active worker or a retiree enrolled in the social security system. There is a rule of thumb, which I cannot elaborate upon here: This wealth is, on the average for all age cohorts, equivalent to a saving period that is exactly half of the average retirement period, i.e., a saving period of eight-and-a-half years. This saving period includes the retirement benefit claims deriving from paid contributions (including those of employers). It also includes wealth in the form of claims on the healthcare system: Health insurance premiums in the public health insurance system bring about substantial implicit "savings" for old age, since they are not, after all, a function of age for people who are still economically active, even though healthcare costs are highly dependent on age. Public nursing care insurance premiums are also, to a large extent, claims amassed by beneficiaries. Finally, the welfare system is also, in part, a sort of implicit saving for the risk of poverty in old age. In addition, there are also the private savings of this population group.

In other words, if both our social security system and our welfare system worked like the funded schemes that are customary in private insurance, then they would have a capital fund to cover their future obligations to beneficiaries and, together with beneficiaries' private savings, this fund would amount to around eight-and-a-half times the beneficiaries' annual consumption.

We can use the same rule of thumb to calculate the wealth amassed for retirement purposes among the parts of the population that are not covered by the social security system. These consist of entrepreneurs, freelancers, senior management and civil servants. The latter, in particular, have considerable pension claims. In addition to saving for one's old age (and that of one's spouse or partner), wealth is also left as an inheritance. Inheritance plays a major role in Germany. To a very large extent, business assets, for example, are left to children as an inheritance or transferred to foundations. Civil servants and senior management often leave unencumbered residential property to their children and also financial assets. Hence, on my estimate, the wealth of this stratum of the population is equivalent to around twelve times the annual private and public consumption attributable to it. The saving period is thus around 12 years here.

This brings us to an overall average for explicit and implicit private wealth for retirement and inheritance purposes equivalent to a saving period of ten years. What is important about this explanation of private wealth is that this ten-year saving period is a kind of structural parameter, which cannot be changed without massively altering the welfare state or the country's social structure. In order substantially to reduce this ten-year saving period, it would be necessary either to undertake deep cuts in public retirement benefits or to make private retirement planning and inheritance impossible for better-off strata, whether through taxation or by other means. Both steps would ultimately be tantamount to destabilizing our market-based democratic social order.

Could the private capital supply be placed domestically, if the state did not have any demand for capital? Today, such private real assets come to approximately four times annual consumption. This is the result of investment activity in a period of predominantly low real interest rates that has persisted for a long time. Investment always involves risk. Firms only invest if they expect a return that is considerably greater than zero. Under conditions of price stability, there is little scope for further interest rate cuts that could possibly result from a reduction in public debt. For nominal interest rates cannot fall below zero. Hence, I do not see any significant potential to absorb the existing high capital supply in the production of goods.

In other words, the theory according to which private investment is crowded out by public debt is no longer valid for Germany today. It would be valid if we had high real interest rates, which served to make it more difficult for the private sector to have access to the capital supply, in order thus to facilitate the sale of public debt instruments. With a large enough clientele and enough equity, entrepreneurs do not have any difficulty in financing investments via loans in our banking system. In light of the provision for retirement and inheritance discussed above, an insufficient supply of savings is never the reason for the failure of domestic investment plans. Reducing public debt thus does not lead to more real capital in Germany.

The contrary is to be feared. An extremely thrifty fiscal policy will lead to cuts in public investment in infrastructure. Transport routes will be neglected; school buildings will remain in their current poor condition given the desolate state of municipal finances. The bottlenecks in the normal course of economic and social life for which the public authorities are responsible will become more and more painful—among other things, at the expense of future economic growth and future tax revenue.

A reduction of public debt leads to increased capital exports. The shortfall in domestic demand corresponding to the smaller budget deficits will stimulate exports and restrict imports. Thus, more foreign assets can be accumulated through domestic saving. But this recipe for increasing economic wealth has an Achilles' heel, which has been revealed by the Greek crisis. How secure are foreign assets? The only possible target countries for rational investment of private wealth are the rich countries or China. The demographics of all these countries are similar to those of Germany. Life expectancy is similarly high—even in China. The retirement period is similarly long. Desire to leave an inheritance to one's children is no less or only slightly less than in Germany. Ultimately, these countries thus also have a similar saving period as Germany and hence an excess of private wealth.

Although a developing country, China exports, on balance, more capital than it imports. This is because, given the absence of a social safety net, private savings are so high that even the frenetic domestic investment activity is not enough to absorb all the savings. The International Monetary Fund is hoping that the global economy will be stabilized thanks to the introduction of a public retirement plan in China, which would lead to a decline in saving and an increase in consumer demand. The IMF is thus hoping for a stroke of the pen from the Chinese government that will lead to a drastic rise in implicit public debt.

But can it be right for global prosperity that China massively increases its public debt, while Germany is reducing its public debt? Both countries are significant net exporters of capital. If China reduces its trade surpluses by introducing a social security system, should this be offset by increased German trade surpluses? What then of the trade deficits of the USA, Portugal, Ireland, Greece, Spain (the PIGS), Hungary, the Baltic States and many others, which are the necessary correlate of the trade surpluses of Germany, China and a few other countries. For there are no trade surpluses without trade deficits. Are not countries with trade deficits everywhere being encouraged to return to the path of virtue, to tighten their belts, to reduce their budget deficits and hence also their trade deficits? How is this compatible with a German policy that increases Germany's trade surpluses?

In light of the persistently low real interest rates and the structural excess of private capital supply over private real capital demand in the relevant countries, the goal cannot be a collective lowering of public debt. There is no crowding out of private investment by public deficits in the global economy consisting of the rich countries and China. There is only a problem of excessive public debt in individual countries with high current account deficits, such as Greece, for example, or the USA. As long as creditors' confidence in these deficit countries (mistakenly) remained intact, their high demand contributed to a global economic bubble, from which, among others, German exports also greatly benefited. The fact that Germany ran no deficit in its 2007 budget was thanks to this bubble. We owe this to Greece, the USA and the other countries with trade deficits. At the time, all the savings of German households went into capital exports, since both the state and the corporate sector were self-financing. In particular, the longstanding US trade deficit and the euphoria triggered by the euro in the Southern and Eastern European countries have covered up the excess of private capital supply as compared to private capital demand.

But today the capital markets no longer have confidence in the deficit countries. Most of these countries have to consolidate their finances radically. Even the United States is undergoing an awakening and adapting to the reality. Americans are beginning to save again and are thus in the process of joining the countries with a structural excess of private capital supply. The USA will no longer be the "engine" of the global economy or at least it will not regain the same force that it had previously. If the IMF has its way, American deficits will be replaced as "engine of the global economy" by the implicit Chinese budgetary deficit that the introduction of a public retirement plan will suddenly bring about. There appears to be no solution without public deficits.

Public debt has two faces. On the one hand, it potentially competes with private borrowers who are seeking loans to form real capital (potential crowding-out). On the other hand, it corresponds to private wealth of exactly the same amount, which gets added to the real assets of the global economy, thus allowing for a level of retirement savings that goes beyond the capital uptake capacity of the productive sector. Which of the two faces is the decisive one for economic policy can be read off from the real interest rate level. If the latter is high, then public and private demand for credit are in competition with each other: Less public debt lowers interest rates and creates more room for real capital formation. If, when prices are stable, the real interest rate level, and hence the nominal interest rate level, is low, then it cannot fall any further from reducing public debt, since nominal interest rates cannot become negative. Reducing public debt does not have any effect of stimulating investment in this situation. To the contrary, since aggregate demand also falls along with this reduction, investment will tend to decline.

We need to find a common approach to the right amount of public debt on a global scale. The duty of a country to consolidate its finances and to reduce its public debt is all the more paramount, the higher its current account deficit. Conversely, however, countries with current account surpluses can also have a duty to increase budget deficits. For a generalized reduction in public deficits may simply lead to a crisis, since, precisely because of the low interest rates, private investment will not replace the public demand that is lost.

Greece, Portugal and Spain can only succeed in consolidating their finances if the economy in Europe is good, and this might require countries like Germany to expand, rather than limit, their structural, i.e., non-cyclical, budget deficits. For climate policy, it may make sense for individual countries to lead by example in reducing CO_2. But in the case of public debt, this kind of "eager beaver" approach can be precisely the wrong one. The best contribution Germany can make to overcome the European sovereign debt crisis may be a significant lowering of German taxes.

Things would be completely different if real interest rates were high, so that a joint consolidation of public finances would lead to lower interest rates and a corresponding increase in private investment. The lesson that has to be drawn from this is that the right public debt policy is heavily dependent on the level of real interest rates. A rigid debt brake, such as the one now planned for Germany, cannot be the right way. With the required consolidation of finances in many other European countries, it can even lead to a depression.

As history teaches us, a depression will destroy free international trade and reinforce the disintegrative tendencies in the European Community—to the great detriment of the German export industry. It would be a fatal error, if a false, because purely negative, understanding of public debt would destroy the integrated global economy and hence, ultimately, strike the free market economy at its very core.

But how can the confidence of the capital markets be restored, if we want to avoid a race among countries to reduce their public debt that will result in a depression? At least to a large extent, the form taken by public debt should be a different one. There is a fear that high public debt could lead countries to abandon price stability. Inflation-indexed bonds are one possible response. These are gradually becoming more common. But we can also go one step further: I propose government bonds whose coupon is indexed to the growth rate of a country's (nominal) national product. In this case, the state's interest payments would always move in parallel to its tax revenue, which rises and falls with national product. Government bonds of this sort can also be an attractive form of investment for the country's citizens. Investors are, so to say, in the same boat as their co-citizens, with whom they tend to compare themselves. At a given public debt ratio, the country can improve its credit rating by issuing such bonds instead of conventional ones. This enlarges the scope for raising the level of public debt, thus allowing the population's desire for amassing retirement savings to be better accommodated.

Public debt is at the same time private wealth. Both sides of the phenomenon have to be kept in mind when considering the optimal budget. When there are low real interest rates and high trade surpluses, reducing public debt is the wrong policy.

Bibliography

Abel, Andrew B., N. Gregory Mankiw, Lawrence Summers and Richard Zeckhauser. 1989. Assessing Dynamic Efficiency: Theory and Evidence. *Review of Economic Studies* 56 (1): 1-19.

Aghion, Philippe, Antonin Bergeaud, Timo Boppart, Peter J. Klenow and Huiyu Li. 2019. Missing Growth from Creative Destruction. *American Economic Review* 109 (8): 2795-2822.

Alvaredo, Facundo, Anthony B. Atkinson, Lucas Chancel, Thomas Piketty, Emmanuel Saez and Gabriel Zucman. 2017. *Distributional National Accounts (DINA) Guidelines: Concepts and Methods Used in the World Wealth and Income Database*. Version June 9th, 2017. WID.world Working Paper Series No. 2016/1. http://wid.world/document/dinaguidelines-v1/.

Anselmann, Christina. 2020. *Secular Stagnation Theories. A Historical and Contemporary Analysis with a Focus on the Distribution of Income*. Cham: Springer.

Arnott, Richard J. and Joseph E. Stiglitz. 1979. Aggregate Land Rents, Expenditure on Public Goods, and Optimal City Size. *Quarterly Journal of Economics* 93 (4): 471-500.

Arrow, Kenneth J., Hollis B. Chenery, Bagicha S. Minhas and Robert M. Solow. 1961. Capital-Labor Substitution and Economic Efficiency. *Review of Economics and Statistics* 43 (3): 225-250.

Backhouse, Roger E. 2019. Alvin Harvey Hansen. In *The Elgar Companion to John Maynard Keynes*, eds. Robert W. Dimand and Harald Hagemann, 451-455. Cheltenham: Edward Elgar.

Backhouse, Roger E. and Mauro Boianovsky. 2016. Secular stagnation: The history of a macroeconomic heresy. *European Journal of the History of Economic Thought* 23 (6): 946-970.

Baldenius, Till, Sebastian Kohl and Moritz Schularick. 2019. *Die neue Wohnungsfrage: Gewinner und Verlierer des deutschen Immobilienbooms*. Bonn: Macrofinance Lab.

Barro, Robert J. 1974. Are Government Bonds Net Wealth? *Journal of Political Economy* 82 (6): 1095-1117.

Bauluz, Luis E. 2017. *Revised and extended national wealth series: Australia, Canada, France, Germany, Italy, Japan, the UK and the USA*. WID.world Working Paper Series No. 2017/23. https://wid.world/document/revised-extended-national-wealth-series-aust-ralia-canada-france-germany-italy-japan-uk-usa-wid-world-technical-note-2017-23/.

Bernanke, Ben. 2005. *The global saving glut and the U.S. current account deficit*. Speech 77. Washington (D.C.): Board of Governors of the Federal Reserve System.

Billig, Assia. 2016. *Compiling the actuarial balance sheet for the Canada Pension Plan – methodological overview. Presentation to the Eurostat/ILO/IMF/OECD Workshop on Pensions. Paris, 9.3.2016*. http://www.osfi-bsif.gc.ca/Eng/Docs/OCA-Assia-Billig-03092016-Slides.pdf.

Blanchard, Olivier. 2019. Public Debt and Low Interest Rates, AEA Presidential Lecture 2019. *American Economic Review* 109 (4): 1197-1229.

Blanchard, Olivier and Philippe Weil. 2001. Dynamic Efficiency, the Riskless Rate, and Debt Ponzi Games Under Uncertainty. *Advances in Macroeconomics* 1 (2): 1-23.

Blanco, M. Artola, Luis E. Bauluz, Clara Martínez-Toledano. 2018. *Wealth in Spain, 1900-2014: A Country of Two Lands.* WID.world Working Paper Series No. 2018/5. https://wid.world/document/wealth-spain-1900-2014-country-two-lands-wid-world-wor-king-paper-2018-5/.

Blaug, Mark. 1962. *Economic Theory in Retrospect.* Homewood (IL): Richard D. Irwin.

Board of Governors of the Federal Reserve System. 2020a. *Enhanced Financial Accounts, State Pensions, State and Local Pension Funding Status and Ratios by State, 2002-2018.* https://www.federalreserve.gov/releases/z1/dataviz/pension/comparative_view/table/.

Board of Governors of the Federal Reserve System. 2020b. *Z1-Financial Accounts, L.119.b Federal Government Employee Retirement Funds: Defined Benefit Plans.* https://www.federalreserve.gov/apps/fof/DisplayTable.aspx?t=l.119.b/.

Board of Governors of the Federal Reserve System. 2020c. *Financial Accounts of the United States – Z.1, Flow of Funds, Balance Sheets, and Integrated Macroeconomic Accounts,* 3rd Quarter 2020. Washington (D.C.). https://www.federalreserve.gov/releases/z1/20201210/z1.pdf.

Board of Trustees OASDI. 2016. *The 2016 Annual Report of the Board of Trustees of the Federal Old-Age and Survivors Insurance and Federal Disability Insurance Trust Funds.* Washington (D.C.): U.S. Government Publishing Office.

Board of Trustees OASDI. 2020. *The 2020 Annual Report of the Board of Trustees of the Federal Old-Age and Survivors Insurance and Federal Disability Insurance Trust Funds.* Washington (D.C.): U.S. Government Publishing Office.

Boettke, Peter J. 2018, *F.A. Hayek – Economics, Political Economy and Social Philosophy.* London: Palgrave-Macmillan.

Bofinger, Peter and Mathias Ries. 2017. Excess saving and low interest rates: Theory and Empirical Evidence. CEPR Discussion Paper 12111. London: Centre for Economic Policy Research. https://cepr.org/active/publications/discussion_papers/dp.php?dpno=12111.

Böhm-Bawerk, Eugen Ritter von. 1891 [1889]. *The Positive Theory of Capital,* trans. William Smart. London and New York: Macmillan.

Böhm-Bawerk, Eugen Ritter von. 1913. Eine „dynamische" Theorie des Kapitalzinses. *Zeitschrift für Volkswirtschaft, Socialpolitik und Verwaltung* 22: 520-585 and 640-57.

Bönke, Tim, Markus M. Grabka, Carsten Schröder and Edward N. Wolff. 2019. A Head-to-Head Comparison of Augmented Wealth in Germany and the United States. *The Scandinavian Journal of Economics.* Online: 28 March 2019. https://doi.org/10.1111/sjoe.12364.

Braakmann, Albert, Jens Grütz and Thorsten Haug. 2007. Das Renten- und Pensionsvermögen in den volkswirtschaftlichen Gesamtrechnungen. Methodik und erste Ergebnisse. *Wirtschaft und Statistik* 12: 1167-1179.

Brunnermeier, Markus K., Harold James and Jean Pierre Landau 2016. *The Euro and the Battle of Ideas.* Princeton (NJ): Princeton University Press.

Bundesministerium für Gesundheit. 2018. *Daten des Gesundheitswesens 2018.* Berlin: Bundesministerium für Gesundheit.

Bundesministerium für Gesundheit. 2019. *Finanzierungsgrundlagen der gesetzlichen Krankenversicherung.* Berlin: Bundesministerium für Gesundheit. https://www.bundesgesundheitsministerium.de/finanzierung-gkv.html.

Bundesverfassungsgericht, BVerfGE 53, 257.

Bundesversicherungsamt. 2017. *Leitfaden zur Altersrückstellungsverordnung für die gesetzlichen Krankenkassen und ihre Verbände, Version: 8 December 2017.* https://www.bundesversicherungsamt.de/fileadmin/redaktion/Krankenversicherung/Altersversorgungsverpflichtungen/Leitfaden_KK-AltRueckV_Stand_8._12.2017.pdf.

Coase, Ronald H. 1937. The Nature of the Firm. *Economica* 4 (16): 386-405.

Coase, Ronald H. 1960. The Problem of Social Cost. *Journal of Law and Economics* 3: 1-44.

Deaton, Angus. 2013. *The Great Escape: Health, Wealth, and the Origins of Inequality*. Princeton (NJ): Princeton University Press.

Debreu, Gérard. 1959. *Theory of Value. An Axiomatic Analysis of Economic Equilibrium*. New Haven: Yale University Press.

DeLong, J. Bradford. 2017. *Three, Four... Many Secular Stagnations!* https://www.brad-ford-delong.com/2017/01/three-four-many-secular-stagnations.html.

Deutsche Bundesbank. 2008. Integrated sectoral and overall balance sheets for Germany. In: *Monthly Report* January 2008, 31-45.

Deutsche Bundesbank. 2019. Vermögen und Finanzen privater Haushalte in Deutschland: Ergebnisse der Vermögensbefragung 2017. *Monatsberichte der Deutschen Bundesbank* April 2019: 13-44.

Deutsche Bundesbank and Statistisches Bundesamt (Federal Statistical Office). 2015. *Balance sheets for institutional sectors and the total economy 1999-2014*. Deutsche Bundesbank: Frankfurt am Main and Statistisches Bundesamt: Wiesbaden.

Deutsche Bundesbank and Statistisches Bundesamt (Federal Statistical Office). 2018. *Balance sheets for institutional sectors and the total economy 1999-2017*, Deutsche Bundesbank: Frankfurt am Main and Statistisches Bundesamt (Federal Statistical Office): Wiesbaden.

Deutsche Bundesbank and Statistisches Bundesamt (Federal Statistical Office). 2020. *Balance sheets for institutional sectors and the total economy 1999-2019*. Deutsche Bundesbank: Frankfurt am Main and Statistisches Bundesamt: Wies-baden.

Diamond, Peter A. 1965. National Debt in a Neoclassical Growth Model. *American Economic Review* 55 (5): 1126-1150.

Dietzfelbinger, Daniel. 1998. *Soziale Marktwirtschaft als Wirtschaftsstil – Alfred Müller-Armacks Lebenswerk*. Gütersloh: Kaiser.

Easterly, William Russell. 2006. *The White Man's Burden: Why the West's Efforts to Aid the Rest Have done so Much Ill, and so Little Good*. London: Penguin Press.

Economist. 2019. Public Pensions - State of Denial. 16 November 2019: p. 65-66.

Eggertsson, Gauti B., Neil R. Mehrotra und Jacob A. Robbins. 2019. A Model of Secular Stagnation: Theory and Quantitative Evaluation. *American Economic Journal: Macroeconomics* 11 (1): 1-48.

Epstein, Larry G. and Stanley E. Zin. 1989. Substitution, Risk Aversion and the Temporal Behavior of Consumption and Asset Returns: A Theoretical Framework. *Econometrica* 57 (4): 937-960.

Eucken, Walter. 1952. *Grundsätze der Wirtschaftspolitik*. Tübingen: Mohr-Siebeck.

European Commission, IMF, OECD, UN and World Bank. 2009. *System of National Accounts 2008*. https://unstats.un.org/unsd/nationalaccount/docs/SNA2008.pdf

European Union and OECD. 2015. *Eurostat-OECD compilation guide on land estimation*. Luxembourg: European Union and OECD.

Eurostat. 2013. *European System of Accounts: ESA 2010*. Luxembourg: Publications Offce of the European Union.

Eurostat. 2019. *Balance sheets for non-financial assets (Dataset)*. http://ec.europa.eu/eurostat/web/products-datasets/-/nama_10_nfa_bs.

Eurostat. 2020. *Pensions in National Accounts (nasa_10_pens)*. https://ec.europa.eu/eurostat/web/pensions/data/database.

Fernandes, Nuno, Miguel A. Ferreira, Pedro Matos and Kevin J. Murphy. 2013. Are U.S. CEOs Paid More? New International Evidence. *Review of Financial Studies* 26(2): 323-367.

Felbermayr, Gabriel. 2019. „Es geht um die Weltherrschaft" (Interview). *Handelsblatt*. 6 May 2019.

Fetzer Thiemo and Carlo Schwarz. 2019. *Tariffs and Politics: Evidence From Trump's Trade Wars*. CES-Ifo Working Paper 7553. Munich: Ifo-Institut.

Fisher, Irving. 1906. *The Nature of Capital and Income*. New York (NY): Macmillan.

Fisher, Irving. 1907. *The Rate of Interest*. New York (NY): Macmillan.

Freudenberg, Christoph. 2017. Alterssicherungssysteme in der Finanzierungsrechnung. In *Die gesamtwirtschaftliche Finanzierungsrechnung. Revision und Anwendung in ökonomischen Analysen*, Berliner Beiträge zu den Volkswirtschaftlichen Gesamtrechnungen, vol. 1, eds. Reimund Mink and Klaus Voy, 323-347. Marburg: Metropolis-Verlag.

Friedman, Milton. 1968. The Role of Monetary Policy. *American Economic Review* 58 (1): 1-17.

Friedman, Milton. 1953. The Case for Flexible Exchange Rates, in: *Essays in Positive Economics*, ed. Milton Friedman, 157-203. Chicago (IL): University of Chicago Press.

Friedman, Milton. 1997. Why Europe Can't Afford the Euro. *The Times*. 19 November 1997.

Gaudette, Étienne, Bryan Tysinger, Alwyn Cassil and Dana P. Goldman. 2015. Health and Health Care of Medicare Beneficiaries in 2030. *Forum for health economics & policy* 18 (2): 75-96.

Geerolf, Francois. 2018. *Reassessing Dynamic Efficiency*. Manuscript UCLA.

Goldsmith, Raymond W. 1985. *Comparative National Balance Sheets, A Study of Twenty Countries, 1688-1978*. Chicago (IL): The University of Chicago Press.

Gordon, Robert J. 1990. *The Measurement of Durable Goods Prices*. Cambridge (MA): National Bureau of Economic Research.

Gordon, Robert J. 2016. *The Rise and Fall of American Growth. The U.S. Standard of Living since the Civil War*. Princeton (NJ): Princeton University Press.

Hamann, Brigitte. 1978. *Rudolf – Kronprinz und Rebell*. Wien: Amalthea.

Hansen, Alvin H. 1936. Mr. Keynes on Underemployment Equilibrium. *Journal of Political Economy* 4 (5): 667-686.

Hansen, Alvin H. 1939. Economic Progress and Declining Population Growth. *American Economic Review* 29 (1): 1-15.

Hansen, Alvin H. 1941. *Fiscal Policy and Business Cycles*. London: Allen and Unwin.

Hansen, Alvin H. 1953. *A Guide to Keynes*. London: McGraw Hill.

Hansen, Alvin H. 1966. Stagnation and Under-Employment Equilibrium. *Rostra Economica Amstelodamensia*. 15 November 1966: 7-9.

Harberger, Arnold C. 1998. A Vision of the Growth Process. *American Economic Review* 88 (1): 1-32.

Haug, Thorsten. 2018. Berechnung der Pensions- und Rentenanwartschaften in den volkswirtschaftlichen Gesamtrechnungen. Berechnungsmethodik und Ergebnisse. *Wirtschaft und Statistik* 2: 77-90.

Hautle, Willy. 2016. *Integrierte makroökonomische Konten und Stock-Flow konsistente Modelle: mit Anwendungen zur Grossen Rezession*. Norderstedt: BoD – Books on Demand.

Hayek, Friedrich A. von. 1937. Economics and Knowledge. *Economica* 4 (13): 33-54.

Hayek, Friedrich A. von. 1945. The Use of Knowledge in Society. *American Economic Review* 35 (4): 519-530.

Hayek, Friedrich A. von 1967. Rechtsordnung und Handelnsordnung. In *Zur Einheit der Rechts- und Staatswissenschaften*, ed. Erich Streißler, 195-230. Karlsruhe: C.F. Müller.

Hein, Eckhard. 2016. Secular stagnation or stagnation policy? Steindl after Summers. *PSL Quarterly Review* 69 (276): 3-47.

Hellwig, Christian and Guido Lorenzoni. 2009. Bubbles and Self-Enforcing Debt. *Econometrica* 77 (4): 1137-1164.

Hellwig, Martin. 2019. Target-Falle oder Empörungsfalle – Zur deutschen Diskussion um die Europäische Währungsunion. *Perspektiven der Wirtschaftspolitik* 19 (4): 345-382.

Hellwig, Martin F. 2020a. *Dynamic Inefficiency and Fiscal Interventions in an Economy with Land and Transaction Costs*, Discussion Paper 2020/07, Max Planck Institute for Research on Collective Goods, Bonn.

Hellwig, Martin F. 2020b. Martin F., Property taxes and dynamic inefficiency: A correction of a "correction", *Economics Letters*, 197 (109603).

Hicks, John R. 1932. *The Theory of Wages*. London: Macmillan.

Hicks, John R. 1937. Mr. Keynes and the Classics – A Suggested Interpretation. *Econometrica* 5 (2): 147-159.

Hicks, John R. 1939. *Value and Capital*. Oxford: Clarendon Press.

Hobbes, Thomas. 1651. *Leviathan, or, The Matter, Forme and Power of a Common-wealth Ecclesiasticall and Civil*. London: Printed for Andrew Crooke.

Holzmann, Robert. 1998. *Financing the Transition to Multi-Pillar*. Social Protection Discussion Paper No. 9809. Washington (D.C.): World Bank.

Holzmann, Robert, Robert Palacios and Asta Zviniene. 2004. *Implicit pension debt: Issues, measurement and scope in international perspective*. Social Protection Discussion Paper No. 0403. Washington (D.C.): World Bank.

Homburg, Stefan. 1991. Interest and Growth in an Economy with Land. *Canadian Journal of Economics* 24 (2): 450-459.

Homburg, Stefan. 2015. Overaccumulation, Public Debt and the Importance of Land. *German Economic Review* 15(4): 411-435.

Horvat, Branko. 1958. The Optimum Rate of Investment. *Economic Journal* 68 (272): 747-767.

IMF (International Monetary Fund). 2013. *Public sector debt statistics: guide for compilers and users*. 2nd ed.. Washington (D.C.): International Monetary Fund.

IMF (International Monetary Fund). 2016. *Implementing Accrual Accounting in the Public Sector*. Technical Notes and Manuals. Prepared by Joe Cavanagh, Suzanne Flynn, and Delphine Moretti. Washington (D.C.): International Monetary Fund.

IMF (International Monetary Fund). 2018a. *Fiscal Monitor. Capitalizing on Good Times*. April 2018. Washington (D.C.): International Monetary Fund.

IMF (International Monetary Fund). 2018b. *Fiscal Monitor. Managing Public Wealth*. October 2018. Washington (D.C.): International Monetary Fund.

IMF (International Monetary Funds). 2018c. *Global Debt Database*. https://www.imf.org/~/media/Files/Publications/fiscal-monitor/2018/April/data/gdd121318.ashx?la=en.

Jastrow, Joseph. 1899. The Mind's Eye. *Popular Science Monthly* 54: 299-312.

Jordà, Òscar, Katharina Knoll, Dmitry Kuvshinov, Moritz Schularick and Alan M. Taylor. 2019. The Rate of Return on Everything, 1870-2015. *Quarterly Journal of Economics* 134 (3): 1225-1298.

Kaier, Klaus and Christoph Müller. 2015. New figures on unfunded public pension entitlements across Europe: concept, results and applications. *Empirica* 42 (4): 865-895.

Kaldor, Nicholas. 1961. Capital Accumulation and Economic Growth. In *The Theory of Capital*, ed. F.A. Lutz and D. C. Hague, 177-222. London: St. Martin's Press.

Keynes, John Maynard. 1919 [1971]. The Economic Consequences of the Peace. In *The Collected Writings of John Maynard Keynes*, Bd. 2: The Economic Consequences of the Peace, eds. Elizabeth Johnson and Donald Moggridge. London and Basingstoke: Macmillan.

Keynes, John Maynard. 1930 [1972]. Economic Possibilities for Our Grandchildren. In *The Collected Writings of John Maynard Keynes*, vol. 9: Essays in Persuasion, eds. Elizabeth Johnson and Donald Moggridge, 321-332. London and Basingstoke: Macmillan.

Keynes, John Maynard. 1931. Economic Notes on Free Trade II. *New Statesman and Nation*. 7 April 1931.

Keynes, John Maynard. 1936. *The General Theory of Employment, Interest and Money*. London: Macmillan.

Keynes, John Maynard. 1937. Some economic consequences of a declining population. *The Eugenics Review* 29 (1): 13-17. Reprinted 1973. In *The Collected Writings of John Maynard Keynes*, vol. 14: The General Theory and After (Part II: Defence and Development), eds. Elizabeth Johnson and Donald Moggridge, 124-133. London and Basingstoke: Macmillan.

Keynes, John Maynard. 1943 [1980]. The Long-Term Problem of Full Employment. In *The Collected Writings of John Maynard Keynes*, Volume XXVII: Activities 1940–1946. Shaping the Post-War World: Employment and Commodities, eds. Elizabeth Johnson and Donald Moggridge, 320-325. London and Basingstoke: Macmillan.

Kissinger, Henry. 2018. Henry Kissinger: "We are in a very, very grave period" (Interview). *Financial Times*. 20 July 2018.

Kopisch, August. 1998 [1836]. *The Elves of Cologne*, trans. Anthea Bell. New York: North-South Books.

Komlos, John and Hermann Schubert. 2019. Die Entwicklung sozialer Ungleichheit und ihre politischen Implikationen in den USA. *Wirtschaftsdienst* 99 (3): 216-223.

Kotlikoff, Laurence. 1992. *Generational Accounting: Knowing Who Pays and Knowing When for What We Spend*. New York (NY): The Free Press.

Krämer, Hagen M. 2011. Keynes, Globalisierung und Strukturwandel. In *Keynes 2.0 – Perspektiven einer modernen keynesianischen Wirtschaftstheorie und Wirtschaftspolitik*. Jahrbuch Ökonomie und Gesellschaft 23, eds. Harald Hagemann and Hagen Krämer, 183-215. Marburg: Metropolis-Verlag.

Krämer, Hagen M. 2020. Verteilungspolitische Interventionen. *List Forum für Wirtschafts- und Sozialpolitik* 46 (2): 117–155.

Krämer, Hagen M. 2021. *Einkommens- und Vermögensverteilung in Deutschland. Entwicklungen, Ursachen, Maßnahmen*. Wiso Diskurs, Analysen und Konzepte zur Wirtschafts- und Sozialpolitik. Bonn: Friedrich-Ebert-Stiftung.

Kurz, Heinz D. 2017. *Economic Thought: A Brief History*. New York: Columbia University Press.

Kurz, Heinz D. 2021. The Spectre of Secular Stagnation Then and Now. In *Stagnations- und Deflationstheorien*. Schriften des Vereins für Socialpolitik, vol. 115/XXXVIII, Studien zur Entwicklung der ökonomischen Theorie Volker Caspari, 10–53. Berlin: Duncker & Humblot.

Krugman, Paul. 1979. Increasing Returns to Scale, Monopolistic Competition, and International Trade. *Journal of International Economics* 9: 469-479.

Larson, William 2015. *New Estimates of Value of Land of the United States*. April 3, 2015. Washington (D.C.): Bureau of Economic Analysis. https://www.bea.gov/system/files/papers/WP2015-3.pdf.

Lenze, David G. 2013. *State and Local Government Defined Benefit Pension Plans: Estimates of Liabilities and Employer Normal Costs by State, 2000-2011*. Working paper. Washington (D. C.): Bureau of Economic Analysis.

Lequiller, François and Derek Blades. 2014. *Understanding National Accounts*. 2nd ed. Paris: OECD Publishing.

Lewis, W. Arthur. 1954. Economic Development with Unlimited Supplies of Labour. *The Manchester School* 22 (2): 139-191.

Li, Yang and Xiaojing Zhang. 2017. *China's National Balance Sheet: Theories, Methods and Risk Assessment*. Singapur: Springer. http://www.springer.com/cda/content/document/cda_download document/9789811043840-c2.pdf?SGWID=0-0-45-1608746-p180735840.

List, Friedrich. 1841. *Das nationale System der politischen Ökonomie*. Stuttgart: Cotta.

Lutz, Friedrich. 1967. *Zinstheorie*. 2nd ed. Tübingen: Mohr-Siebeck.

Luxemburg, Rosa. 1951 [1913]. *The Accumulation of Capital*. trans. Agnes Schwarzschild. London: Routledge and Kegan Paul.

Marx, Karl and Friedrich Engels. 1967 [1848]. *The Communist Manifesto*, trans. Samuel Moore. London: Penguin.

Marx, Karl and Friedrich Engels. 1970 [1846]. *The German Ideology*, ed. C. J. Arthur. New York: International.

Marx, Karl. 1976 [1867]. *Capital: A Critique of Political Economy*, vol. 1, trans. Ben Fowkes. London: Penguin/New Left Books.

Marx, Karl. 1981 [1894]. *Capital: A Critique of Political Economy*, vol. 3. trans. David Fernbach, London: Penguin/New Left Books.

Meade, James. 1975. The Keynesian Revolution. In *Essays on John Maynard Keynes*, ed. Milo Keynes, 82-88. New York (NY): Cambridge University Press.

Meadows, Dennis L., Donella H. Meadows, Jørgen Randers, William W. Behrens III. 1972. *The Limits to Growth. A Report for the Club of Rome's Project on the Predicament of Mankind*. New York (NY): Universe Books.

Mehrling, Perry G. 1997. *The Money Interest and the Public Interest: American Monetary Thought, 1920–1970*. Cambridge (MA): Harvard University Press.

Menger, Carl. 1871. *Grundsätze der Volkswirtschaftslehre*. Wien: Braumüller.

Mink, Raimund and Marta Rodríguez Vives (eds.). 2010. European Central Bank and Eurostat Workshop on Pensions, 29-30 April 2009. Frankfurt am Main: European Central Bank.

Monopolkommission. 2012. *Neunzehntes Hauptgutachten der Monopolkommission 2010/2011.* Bundestagsdrucksache 17/10565. Bonn: Monopolkommission.

Müller, Christoph, Bernd Raffelhüschen and Olaf Weddige. 2009. *Pension obligations of government employer pension schemes and social security pension schemes established in EU countries.* Studie im Auftrag der Europäischen Zentralbank. Freiburg: Forschungszentrums Generationenverträge, Universität Freiburg.

Müller-Armack, Alfred. 1950. Soziale Irenik. *Weltwirtschaftliches Archiv* 64: 181-203.

Munnell, Alicia H., Jean-Pierre Aubry and Mark Cafarelli. 2013. *The Funding Of State And Local Pensions: 2013-2017.* Boston (MA): Center for Retirement Research at Boston College.

Novy-Marx, Robert and Joshua D. Rauh. 2011. Public Pension Liabilities: How Big Are They and What Are They Worth? *Journal of Finance* 66 (4): 1207-1246.

OECD. 2017a. *Pensions at a Glance 2017: OECD and G20 Indicators.* Paris: OECD Publishing.

OECD. 2017b. *Health at a Glance 2017: OECD Indicators.* Paris: OECD Publishing.

OECD. 2018. *National Accounts, Annual National Accounts, Detailed Tables and Simplified 9B. Balance sheets for non-financial assets, N1: Produced Assets; NS1: Total economy less NS13: General Government.* OECD, Paris. https://stats.oecd.org/Index.aspx?DataSetCode=SNA_TABLE9B.

OECD. 2019a. *Detailed National Accounts, SNA 2008 (or SNA 1993): Balance sheets for nonfinancial assets, OECD National Accounts Statistics (database).* https://doi.org/10.1787/data-00368-en.

OECD. 2019b. *Households' financial and non-financial assets and liabilities – Annual and Quarterly – archived.* http://stats.oecd.org/OECDStat_Metadata/ShowMetadata.ashx?Dataset=7HA_A_Q&ShowOnWeb=true&Lang=en.

OECD. 2019c. *National Accounts, Annual National Accounts, Detailed Tables and Simplified Accounts. 9B. Balance sheets for non-financial assets.* https://doi.org/10.1787/data-00368-en.

OECD. 2019d. *The OECD Collection of Annual Estimates of Pension Entitlements in Social Insurance: First Main Findings,* Working Party on Financial Statistics, COM/SDD/DAF(2019) 4. Paris: OECD. http://www.oecd.org/officialdocuments/publicdisplaydocumentpdf/?cote=COM/SDD/DAF(2019)4&docLanguage=En. Accessed: 1 January 2021.

OECD. 2020a. *Guidelines for the OECD Table on Social Insurance Pension Schemes (Table 2900).* https://www.oecd.org/statistics/data-collection/Guidelines%20on%20the%20OECD%20table%20on%20social%20insurance%20pension%20schemes.pdf. Accessed: 1 January 2021.

OECD. 2020b. Notes to OECD Pension Metadata Sheet. OECD: Paris. https://www.oecd.org/sdd/na/OECD-Social-Pension-Scheme-Metadata-United-States.pdf Accessed: 3 January 2021.

Olson, Mancur. 1982. *The Rise and Decline of Nations: Economic Growth, Stagflation and Social Rigidities.* New Haven (CT): Yale University Press.

Osterhammel, Jürgen. 2010. *Die Verwandlung der Welt – Eine Geschichte des 19. Jahrhunderts.* Munich: C.H. Beck-Verlag.

Palley, Thomas I. 2016. Why Negative Interest Rate Policy (NIRP) Is Ineffective And Dangerous. *Real-World Economics Review* 76. http://www.paecon.net/PAEReview/issue76/Palley76.pdf.

Palley, Thomas I. 2019. The fallacy of the natural rate of interest and zero lower bound economics: why negative interest rates may not remedy Keynesian unemployment. *Review of Keynesian Economics* 7 (2): 151-170.

Phelps, Edmund S. 1961. The Golden Rule of Capital Accumulation. *American Economic Review* 51 (4): 638-643.

Piketty, Thomas. 2014. *Capital in the Twenty-First Century,* Cambridge (MA): Harvard University Press.

Piketty, Thomas and Gabriel Zucman. 2013. *Capital is Back: Wealth-Income Ratios in Rich Countries, 1700-2010. Data Appendix.* http://piketty.pse.ens.fr/files/PikettyZucman2013Appendix.pdf.

Piketty, Thomas and Gabriel Zucman. 2014. Capital Is Back: Wealth-Income Ratios in Rich Countries, 1700–2010. *Quarterly Journal of Economics* 129 (3): 1255–310.

Piketty, Thomas, Emmanual Saez and Gabriel Zucman. 2018. Distributional national accounts: Methods and estimates for the United States. *Quarterly Journal of Economics*. 133(2): 553-609.

Piketty, Thomas, Li Yang and Gabriel Zucman. 2017. *Capital Accumulation, Private Property and Rising Inequality in China: 1978–2015*. WID.world Working Paper Series No. 2017/6. http:// wid.world/document/t-piketty-l-yang-and-g-zucmancapital-accu-mulation-private-property-andinequality-in-china-1978-2015-2016/.

PKV (Verband der Privaten Krankenversicherung). (various years) *Zahlenbericht der Privaten Krankenversicherung*. Cologne: Verband der Privaten Krankenversicherung e.V.

Polanyi, Karl. 1944. *The Great Transformation*. New York (NY): Farrar and Rinehart.

Polanyi, Michael. 1958. *Personal Knowledge, Towards a post-critical philosophy*. Chicago (IL): Chicago University Press.

Popper, Karl. 1945. *The Open Society and its Enemies*. London: Routledge.

Quesnay, Francois. 1758. *Tableau Economique, et Maximes Générale du Gouvernement Economique*. Versailles.

Rachel, Lukasz und Lawrence H. Summers. 2019. On Falling Neutral Real Rates, Fiscal Policy, and the Risk of Secular Stagnation. *Brookings Papers on Economic Activity* March 4: 1-66.

Raffelhüschen, Bernd. 1999. Generational Accounting in Europe. *American Economic Review: Papers and Proceedings* 89 (2): 167-170.

Reinhart, Carmen M. and Kenneth S. Rogoff. 2009. *This Time is Different: Eight Centuries of Financial Folly*. Princeton (NJ): Princeton University Press.

Reinsdorf, Marshall, David Lenze and Dylan Rassier. 2014. *Bringing Actuarial Measures of Defined Benefit Pensions into the U.S. National Accounts*. Paper prepared for the IARIW 33rd General Conference, Rotterdam, the Netherlands. August 2014. http://www.iariw.org/papers/2014/ReinsdorfPaper.pdf.

Rodrick, Dani. 2018. Populism and the economics of globalization. *Journal of International Business Policy* 1(1-2): 12-33.

Rosling, Hans, Ola Rosling and Anna Rosling Rönnlund. 2018. *Factfulness*. New York (NY): Flatiron Books.

Ryan-Collins, Josh, Toby Lloyd and Laurie Macfarlane. 2017. *Rethinking the Economics of Land and Housing*. London: Zed Books.

Safranski, Rüdiger. 2014. *Romanticism: A German Affair*, trans. Robert E. Goodwin. Evanston, Illinois: Northwestern University Press

Sahlins, Marshall. 1968. Notes on the Original Affluent Society. In *Man the Hunter*, ed. R.B. Lee and I. Devore, 85-89. New York (NY): Aldine.

Samuelson, Paul A. 1958. An Exact Consumption-Loan Model of Interest with or without the Social Contrivance of Money. *Journal of Political Economy* 66 (6): 467-482.

Samuelson, Paul A. 1959a. A Modern Treatment of the Ricardian Economy I: The Pricing of Goods and of Labor and Land Services. *Quarterly Journal of Economics* 73 (1): 1-35.

Samuelson, Paul A. 1959b. A Modern Treatment of the Ricardian Economy II: Capital and Interest Aspects of the Pricing Process. *Quarterly Journal of Economics* 73 (2): 217-231.

Samuelson, Paul A. 1976. Alvin Hansen as a Creative Economic Theorist. *Quarterly Journal of Economics* 90 (1): 24-31.

Schmalwasser, Oda and Aloysius Müller. 2009. Gesamtwirtschaftliche und sektorale nichtfinanzielle Vermögensbilanzen. *Wirtschaft und Statistik* (2): 137-147.

Schmalwasser, Oda and Nadine Weber. 2012. Revision der Anlagevermögensrechnung für den Zeitraum 1991 bis 2011. *Wirtschaft und Statistik* 11: 933–947.

Schmalwasser, Oda and Sascha Brede. 2015. Grund und Boden als Bestandteil der volkswirtschaftlichen Vermögensbilanzen. *Wirtschaft und Statistik* (6): 43-57.

Schnabl, Gunther. 2019. Central Banking and Crisis Management from the Perspective of Austrian Business Cycle Theory. In *The Oxford Handbook of the Economics of Central Banking 2019*, eds. David G. Mayes, Pierre L. Siklos and Jan-Egbert Sturm, 551-584. Oxford: Oxford University Press.

Schumpeter, Joseph. A. 1934 [1911]. *The Theory of Economic Development*. trans. Opie. Cambridge, MA: Harvard University Press.

Schumpeter, Joseph A. 1954. *History of Economic Analysis*. New York (NY): Oxford University Press.

Shiller, Robert J. 2017. Narrative Economics. *American Economic Review* 107 (4): 967-1004.

Shiller, Robert J. and Mark J. Kamstra. 2010. Trills Instead of T-Bills: It's Time to Replace Part of Government Debt with Shares in GDP. *The Economists' Voice* 7 (3): Article 5.

Simmel, Georg. 1978 [1900]. *The Philosophy of Money*, trans. Tom Bottomore and David Frisby. London: Routledge and Keegan Paul.

Simon, Herbert. 1962. The Architecture of Complexity. *Proceedings of the American Philosophical Society* 106 (6): 467-482.

Simon, Herrmann. 2012. *Hidden Champions – Aufbruch nach Globalia*. Frankfurt am Main: Campus.

Sinn, Hans-Werner. 2014. *The Euro Trap*. Oxford: Oxford University Press.

Simon, Hermann. 2019. Die Macht der Mächte. *Frankfurter Allgemeine Zeitung*, 6. June 2019.

Smith, Adam. 1776. *An Inquiry into the Nature and Causes of the Wealth of Nations*. London: W. Strahan and T. Cadell.

Solow, Robert M. 1956. A Contribution to the Theory of Economic Growth. *Quarterly Journal of Economics* 70 (1): 65-94.

Solow, Robert M. 1957. Technical Change and the Aggregate Production Function. *Review of Economics and Statistics* 39 (3): 312-320.

Solow, Robert M. 1963. *Capital Theory and the Rate of Return*. De Vries Lectures. Amsterdam: North-Holland.

Solow, Robert M., James Tobin, Carl Christian von Weizsäcker und Menahem Yaari. 1966. Neoclassical Growth with Fixed Factor Proportions. *Review of Economic Studies* XXXIII (2): 79-115.

Spahn, Heinz-Peter. 1986. *Stagnation in der Geldwirtschaft. Dogmengeschichte, Theorie und Politik aus keynesianischer Sicht*. Frankfurt am Main and New York (NY): Campus.

Statistisches Bundesamt. 2015. *13. Koordinierte Bevölkerungsvorausberechnung*. Wiesbaden: Statistisches Bundesamt.

Statistisches Bundesamt. 2020. *Fachserie 3: Land- und Forstwirtschaft, Fischerei, Reihe 5.1 Bodenfläche nach Art der tatsächlichen Nutzung 2019*. Statistisches Bundesamt: Wiesbaden.

Stefanescu, Irina and Ivan Vidangos. 2014. *Introducing Actuarial Liabilities and Funding Status of Defined-Benefit Pensions in the U.S. Financial Accounts*. Finance and Economics Discussion Series Note. 2014-10-31. Washington (D.C.): Board of Governors of the Federal Reserve System.

Stiglitz, Joseph. 2016. *The Euro: How a Common Currency Threatens the Future of Europe*. New York (NY): Norton.

Stolper, Wolfgang and Paul A. Samuelson. 1941. Protection and Real Wages. *Review of Economic Studies* 9 (1): 58-73.

Summers, Lawrence H. 2013. *Speech at IMF Fourteenth Annual Research Conference in Honor of Stanley Fischer*. 8 November 2013. Washington (D.C.): International Monetary Fund.

Summers, Lawrence H. 2014. US Economic Prospects: Secular Stagnation, Hysteresis, and the Zero Lower Bound. *Business Economics* 49: 65-73.

Summers, Lawrence H. 2015. Demand Side Secular Stagnation. *American Economic Review: Papers and Proceedings* 105 (5): 60-65.

SVR (German Council of Economic Experts). 2011. *Herausforderungen des demografischen Wandels – Expertise im Auftrag der Bundesregierung*. Occasional Report. Wiesbaden: Statistisches Bundesamt.

Taylor, John B. 1993. Discretion Versus Policy Rules in Practice. *Carnegie-Rochester Conference Series on Public Policy* 39: 195-214.

Teulings, Coen and Richard Baldwin (eds.). 2014. *Secular Stagnation: Facts, Causes and Cures*. London: CEPR Press. http://www.voxeu.org/sites/default/files/Vox_secular_stagnation.pdf.

Tichy, Gunther. 2016. Vom Kapitalmangel zum Savings Glut: Ein Phänomen der Wohlstands-gesellschaft. In *Keynes, Schumpeter und die Zukunft der entwickelten kapitalistischen Volkswirtschaften*, eds. Harald Hagemann and Jürgen Kromphardt, Schriften der Keynes Gesellschaft, Bd. 9, 33-68. Marburg: Metropolis-Verlag.

Tobin, James and William C. Brainard. 1977. Asset Markets and the Cost of Capital. In *Economic Progress, Private Values and Public Policy: Essays in Honor of William Fellner*, ed. Bela Balassa and Richard Nelson, 235-262. Amsterdam: North Holland.

Tobin, James. 1969. A general equilibrium approach to monetary theory. *Journal of Money, Credit and Banking* 1: 15-29.

Uhlig, Harald and Mathias Trabandt. 2011. The Laffer Curve Revisited. *Journal of Monetary Economics* 58 (4): 305-327.

United Nations. 2017. *United Nations, Department of Economic and Social Affairs, Population Division, World Population Prospects: The 2017 Revision, Key Findings and Advanced Tables.* ESA/P/WP/248. New York (NY): United Nations.

van de Ven, Peter. 2017. A full accounting for wealth. Including non-financial assets. In *Financial Accounts*, eds. Peter van de Ven and Daniele Fano, 279-302. Paris: OECD Publishing.

van de Ven, Peter and Daniele Fano (eds.). 2017. *Understanding Financial Accounts.* Paris: OECD Publishing.

Waldenström, Daniel. 2017. Wealth-Income Ratios in a Small, Developing Economy: Sweden, 1810–2014. *Journal of Economic History* 77(1): 285-313.

Weizsäcker, Carl Christian von. 1961. *Wachstum, Zins und optimale Investitionsquote.* Dissertation, Universität Basel. Published as: Weizsäcker, Carl Christian von. 1962. *Wachstum, Zins und optimale Investitionsquote.* Tübingen: Mohr-Siebeck.

Weizsäcker, Carl Christian von. 1971. *Steady State Capital Theory.* Heidelberg: Springer.

Weizsäcker, Carl Christian von. 1974. Substitution Along the Time Axis. *Kyklos* XXVII (4): 732-756.

Weizsäcker, Carl Christian von. 1977. Organic Composition of Capital and Average Period of Production. *Revue d'Economie Politique* 87 (2): 198-231.

Weizsäcker, Carl Christian von. 2005. Hayek und Keynes: Eine Synthese. *Ordo* 56: 95-111.

Weizsäcker, Carl Christian von. 2010. Das Janusgesicht der Staatsschulden. *Frankfurter Allgemeine Zeitung.* 4 June 2010: 12 (published in the appendix to this book as "The Two Faces of Public Debt").

Weizsäcker, Carl Christian von. 2011. *Public Debt Requirements in a Regime of Price Stability.* Preprint 2011/20. Max Planck Institute for Research on Collective Goods. Bonn: 1-59.

Weizsäcker, Carl Christian von. 2014a. Die normative Ko-Evolution von Marktwirtschaft und Demokratie. *Ordo* 65: 13-43.

Weizsäcker, Carl Christian von. 2014b. Public Debt and Price Stability. *German Economic Review* 15 (1): 42-61.

Weizsäcker, Carl Christian von. 2016. Keynes und das Ende der Kapitalknappheit. In *Keynes, Schumpeter und die Zukunft der entwickelten kapitalistischen Volkswirtschaften*, eds. Harald Hagemann and Jürgen Kromphardt, Schriften der Keynes Gesellschaft, Bd. 9, 21-31. Marburg: Metropolis-Verlag.

Weizsäcker, Carl Christian von. 2018. Verteilungswirkungen von Staatsschulden. *List Forum für Wirtschafts- und Sozialpolitik* 44 (2): 143-152.

Weizsäcker, Carl Christian von. 2021. *Capital Theory of the Steady State – Or: T+L = Z – D.* https://www.coll.mpg.de/Weizsaecker/CapitalTheory2019 and https://www.springer.com/9783 658273620.

Werding, Martin. 2011. *Demographie und öffentliche Haushalte – Simulationen zur langfristigen Tragfähigkeit der gesamtstaatlichen Finanzpolitik in Deutschland*, Arbeitspapier 03/2011 des Sachverständigenrats zur Begutachtung der gesamtwirtschaftlichen Entwicklung, Wiesbaden: Statistisches Bundesamt.

Wicksell, Knut. 1936 [1898]. *Interest and Prices: A Study of the Causes Regulating the Value of Money*, trans. R. F. Kahn. London: Macmillan.

WID.world (World Inequality Database), ed. von Facundo Alvaredo, Anthony B. Atkinson, Lucas Chancel, Thomas Piketty, Emmanuel Saez and Gabriel Zucman. https://wid.world/.

Woodford, Michael. 2003. *Interest and Prices: Foundations of a Theory of Monetary Policy.* Princeton (NJ): Princeton University Press.

World Bank. 2019. *DataBank – World Development Indicators.*https://databank.world-bank.org/data/home.aspx.

World Bank. 2020. *World Bank Open Data.*https://data.worldbank.org/.

Wright, Stephen. 2004. Measures of Stock Market Value and Returns of the US Nonfinancial Corporate Sector, 1900-2002. *Review of Income and Wealth* 50(4): 561-584.

Yared, Pierre. 2019. Rising Government Debt: Causes and Solutions for a Decades Old Trend. *Journal of Economic Perspectives* 33 (2): 115-140.

Zwijnenburg, Jorrit. 2017. *Unequal Distributions? A study on differences between the compilation of household distributional results according to DINA and EGDNA methodology.* Paris: OECD. wid.world/wp-content/uploads/2017/11/054-DNA_OECD.pdf.

Author Index

A
Arrow, Kenneth J., 18, 72, 109, 252

B
Barro, Robert J., 108, 318
Bernanke, Ben, 218, 271, 297, 300
Bernholz, Peter, 250
Biden, Joseph, 271, 305
Blanchard, Olivier, 10, 109, 217, 238, 273,
    284, 290
Böhm-Bawerk, Eugen Ritter von, 6, 8, 18, 23,
    29, 30, 40, 63, 66, 69–74, 79, 80, 82,
    83, 226, 231
Boulding, Kenneth E., 70
Buchanan, James, 250

C
Chenery, Hollis B., 72
Coase, Ronald H., 8, 82

D
Debreu, Gérard, 18, 109, 226
DeLong, J. Bradford., 218
Deng Xiaoping, 298, 300
Diamond, Peter A., 40

E
Engels, Friedrich, 10, 53, 67, 250, 294, 306
Eucken, Walter, 70, 256

F
Fisher, Irving, 70, 71
Frey, Bruno, 250
Friedman, Milton, 278, 290, 303

G
Gaitskell, Hugh, 70
George, Henry, 113
Goethe, Johann Wolfgang von, 1

Gordon, Robert J., 90, 217
Gossen, Hermann Heinrich, 250

H
Hansen, Alvin H., 10, 207, 211–218
Harrod, Roy, 70, 231, 233, 240
Hayek, Friedrich A. von, 70, 251, 314, 315
Heidegger, Martin, 250, 252
Hellwig, Christian, 110
Hellwig, Martin, 109, 156
Hicks, John R., 29, 40, 70, 72, 74, 233, 240,
    303
Hobbes, Thomas, 105, 106, 109, 139

J
Jordà, Òscar, 66, 225, 237, 238, 240, 241

K
Kaldor, Nicholas, 6, 65, 70, 72
Keynes, John Maynard, 34, 70, 202, 205–210,
    216, 217, 262, 263, 265, 303, 315
Kirchgässner, Gebhard, 250
Knight, Frank, 70
Kopisch, August, 294
Kotlikoff, Laurence, 109, 138
Krämer, Hagen M., 127, 229, 263
Krugman, Paul, 262
Kurz, Heinz D., 209, 238

L
Lange, Oskar, 70
Lewis, W. Arthur, 112
List, Friedrich, 3, 262, 293–295, 297, 299, 300,
    302, 307
Lutz, Friedrich, 70
Luxemburg, Rosa, 67

M
Machlup, Fritz, 70

© The Editor(s) (if applicable) and The Author(s) 2021
C. C. von Weizsäcker and H. M. Krämer, *Saving and Investment
in the Twenty-First Century*, https://doi.org/10.1007/978-3-030-75031-2

Subject Index

Printed in Great Britain
by Amazon